T&T CLARK LIBRARY OF NEW TESTAMENT GREEK

1

Series Editor
Stanley E. Porter
McMaster Divinity College, Canada

Series Editorial Board
David L. Mathewson, Jermo van Nes, Francis G. H. Pang, Yoon Man Park,
Margaret G. Sim, Xiaxia E. Xue

LINGUISTIC DESCRIPTIONS OF THE GREEK NEW TESTAMENT

NEW STUDIES IN SYSTEMIC FUNCTIONAL LINGUISTICS

Stanley E. Porter

t&tclark
LONDON • NEW YORK • OXFORD • NEW DELHI • SYDNEY

T&T CLARK
Bloomsbury Publishing Plc
50 Bedford Square, London, WC1B 3DP, UK
1385 Broadway, New York, NY 10018, USA
29 Earlsfort Terrace, Dublin 2, Ireland

BLOOMSBURY, T&T CLARK and the T&T Clark logo are
trademarks of Bloomsbury Publishing Plc

First published in Great Britain 2023
Paperback edition published in 2025

Copyright © Stanley E. Porter, 2023

Stanley E. Porter has asserted his right under the Copyright,
Designs and Patents Act, 1988, to be identified as Author of this work.

All rights reserved. No part of this publication may be reproduced or transmitted
in any form or by any means, electronic or mechanical, including photocopying, recording, or any
information storage or retrieval system, without prior permission in writing from the publishers.

Bloomsbury Publishing Plc does not have any control over, or responsibility for, any third-party
websites referred to or in this book. All internet addresses given in this book were correct at the
time of going to press. The author and publisher regret any inconvenience caused if addresses have
changed or sites have ceased to exist, but can accept no responsibility for any such changes.

A catalogue record for this book is available from the British Library.

A catalog record for this book is available from the Library of Congress.

ISBN: HB: 978-0-5677-1001-7
PB: 978-0-5677-1005-5
ePDF: 978-0-5677-1002-4
eBook: 978-0-5677-1004-8

Series: Library of New Testament Greek, volume 1

Typeset by Integra Software Services Pvt. Ltd.

To find out more about our authors and books visit www.bloomsbury.com
and sign up for our newsletters.

CONTENTS

LIST OF FIGURES AND TABLES	vi
PREFACE	vii
ABBREVIATIONS	x
Introduction to This Volume on Linguistic Descriptions	1

Part I Linguistics and New Testament Study

1 Linguistic Theory and New Testament Greek Study I: Linguistic Schools and Traditional Grammar ... 9

2 Linguistic Theory and New Testament Greek Study II: Modern Linguistics and Its Schools of Thought ... 36

Part II Systemic Functional Linguistics and New Testament Study

3 Metaphor in the New Testament: Expressing the Inexpressible through Language within a Systemic Functional Linguistics Perspective ... 81

4 Rhetoric and Persuasion in the New Testament from a Systemic Functional Linguistics Perspective ... 110

5 Defining Cognition through Systemic Functional Linguistics System Networks and the Greek of the New Testament ... 137

6 Orality and Textuality and Implications for Description of the Greek New Testament from a Systemic Functional Linguistics Perspective ... 157

Conclusion	179
BIBLIOGRAPHY	182
MODERN AUTHORS INDEX	213
ANCIENT SOURCES INDEX	220

LIST OF FIGURES AND TABLES

FIGURES

4.1	Systemic network of attitude including potential realizations of speech functions	122
5.1	Systemic network of attitude including potential realizations of speech functions	143

TABLES

4.1	Major Greek speech functions	122
5.1	Major Greek speech functions	144
6.1	Lexical density (Mt. 5–7)	171
6.2	Total lexical density (Mt. 5–7)	171
6.3	Grammatical intricacy (Mt. 5–7)	171
6.4	Total grammatical intricacy (Mt. 5–7)	171
6.5	Lexical density (Acts 12 and Acts 18)	172
6.6	Total lexical density (Acts 12 and Acts 18)	172
6.7	Grammatical intricacy (Acts 12 and Acts 18)	172
6.8	Total grammatical intricacy (Acts 12 and Acts 18)	173
6.9	Lexical density (Rom. 2 and 1 Cor. 4)	173
6.10	Total lexical density (Rom. 2 and 1 Cor. 4)	174
6.11	Grammatical intricacy (Rom. 2 and 1 Cor. 4)	174
6.12	Total grammatical intricacy (Rom. 2 and 1 Cor. 4)	174
6.13	Lexical density comparison	175
6.14	Grammatical intricacy comparison	175

PREFACE

The essays in this volume provide descriptions of various important topics in Greek linguistics from a Systemic Functional Linguistics (SFL) perspective. I do not elucidate at this point what I mean by SFL, because, first, I have described Greek using this linguistic theory from the advent of my academic career and have offered numerous definitions and expositions to guide readers, and, second, I offer further definitions both formally and implicitly throughout the rest of this volume, sufficient for those who wish to explore the topics treated in this volume. In fact, each chapter provides further elucidation of what I understand SFL to be based upon how I position it in relation to other linguistic theories or how I utilize it—or at least a small part of its elaborate architecture—to describe a topic within Greek and New Testament studies.

The origins of this volume extend over the last several years, when I have had occasion to address topics that I believe are important in Greek linguistics. As a result, I have been asked to offer papers or have volunteered myself to present papers on topics that I believe require further exploration, especially from a Systemic Functional Linguistics perspective. I have readily taken the opportunity to do so, and I now share the expanded and, I trust, refined treatments of those topics in the following essays.

The first two chapters originated in several papers that I have previously delivered. These include: "The Limitations and Opportunities of Linguistic Theory in New Testament Greek Language Study," delivered at the conference "Putting the Pieces Together: Formalizing Units and Relations in the Biblical Languages," as part of the Bingham Colloquium, McMaster Divinity College, June 15, 2018; selective portions from "Lecture 1: The Origins of New Testament Theology and Greek Linguistics" and "Lecture 2: The Present State of New Testament Theology and Greek Linguistics," both from the series of three lectures "Can Greek Linguistics Inform New Testament Theology?" delivered as the Lindsey and Lois Ellis Lectures in New Testament Theology at Southwestern Baptist Theological Seminary, Fort Worth, TX, February 28 to March 1, 2019; "Linguistic Schools," delivered at the conference "Linguistics and New Testament Greek: Key Issues in the Current Debate" at Southeastern Baptist Theological Seminary, April 26–27, 2019; and "Where Have All the Greek Grammarians Gone? And Why Should Anyone Care?" delivered as the Presidential Address for the Canadian Society of Biblical Studies at its annual meeting, Vancouver, BC, June 1–3, 2019.

I wish to thank my McMaster Divinity College colleagues Christopher Land and Francis Pang for their comments on the earlier draft of the Bingham Colloquium paper, which has been greatly expanded and reshaped from the original and is scheduled to appear in its revised and greatly expanded form as "Linguistic Theory in Greek and Hebrew Language Study," in *Putting the Pieces Together: Formalizing Units and Relations in the Biblical Languages*, edited by Stanley E. Porter, Christopher D. Land, and Francis G. H. Pang, McMaster New Testament Studies (Eugene, OR: Pickwick, in press). I wish to thank my friends Terry Wilder and Jeffrey Bingham, as well as the rest of the New Testament department, for their inviting and sponsoring my lectures at Southwestern Baptist Theological Seminary. Chapters One and Two are reconfigured especially from parts of chapters one and three in Stanley E. Porter, *New Testament Theology and the Greek Language: A Linguistic Reconceptualization* (Cambridge: Cambridge University Press, 2022), copyright © 2022 Reprinted with permission. I wish to thank Ben Merkle and Robert Plummer for inviting me to participate in the conference at Southeastern Baptist Theological Seminary. An abbreviated form of the original paper, with the larger original form being edited and used for this volume, has appeared as Stanley E. Porter, "Linguistic Schools," in *Linguistics and New Testament Greek: Key Issues in the Current Debate*, ed. David Alan Black and Benjamin L. Merkle (Grand Rapids: Baker, 2020), 11–36. Excerpt from *Linguistics and New Testament Greek* by David Alan Black and Benjamin L. Merkle, copyright © 2020 Used by permission of Baker Academic, a division of Baker Publishing Group. Finally, I wish to thank the Canadian Society of Biblical Studies for the honor of having been elected to serve as president and having been given the opportunity to deliver my presidential address. I was also pleased by the enthusiastic response that I received afterwards from many members. This paper, a shorter and more focused version, has been published as Stanley E. Porter "Where Have All the Greek Grammarians Gone? And Why Should Anyone Care," *BAGL* 9 (2020): 5–37.

The third to fifth chapters were originally presented as three papers at the invitation of Dr. Aldred Genade in my role as a plenary speaker for the "First International Conference on the New Testament Text, Meaning and Cognition," for the Faculty of Theology, North-West University, Potchefstroom Campus, South Africa, March 4–6, 2015. The first of these papers, "The Use of Metaphor in the New Testament from a Modified Systemic Functional Perspective," was further refined and presented as a public lecture, "Metaphor in the New Testament: Expressing the Inexpressible through Language," at the University of Otago, Dunedin, New Zealand, June 21, 2018, and at Laidlaw College, Auckland, New Zealand, June 25, 2018. All these chapters have been expanded from their original form to include further discussion and examples. I appreciate the fact that Aldred also included Dr. Bonnie Howe, a cognitive linguist and New Testament scholar, as the second plenary speaker at the conference, so that we were able to engage in fruitful discussion of our differing perspectives and linguistic theories and their applications. I also wish to thank Allan Bell, Paul Trebilco, Tim Meadowcroft, and Mark Keown for their hospitality while in New Zealand. I also must thank Allan and Tim for inviting me to participate in the "Sociolinguistics Symposium Twenty Two: Crossing Borders: South, North, East, West," at the University of Auckland, New Zealand, June 27–30, 2018, and present a paper on the complex multilingualism of Paul the Apostle, published elsewhere.

The sixth chapter of this volume was originally presented as "Orality and Textuality and Implications for the New Testament," in the "New Testament Canon, Textual Criticism, and Apocryphal Literature: Orality and Textuality in Early Christianity" section of the Evangelical Theological Society 2017 Annual Meeting, Providence, RI, November 15–17, 2017, and has been modified and expanded further in light of discussion with my colleagues in the McMaster Divinity College Origins of the Gospels project, especially with my doctoral student, Ji Hoe Kim, who has himself now published an outstanding article on this topic.

I also wish to thank several of my doctoral and former doctoral students at McMaster Divinity College who have responded to various ideas in the chapters in this volume. The pleasure of working with exceptional students is one that has incredible rewards, as various ideas are explored and discussed simply for the sake of understanding. I will always value the times I have had to critically and constructively discuss our research together. I single out for mention Ji Hoe Kim, John Lee, Vinh Nguyen, and Dr David Yoon and especially Dr Zachary Dawson for their ideas and comments, as well as Zach's excellent editing to prepare the manuscript for publication.

ABBREVIATIONS

AA	*American Anthropologist*
AYB	Anchor Yale Bible Commentary
BAGL	*Biblical and Ancient Greek Linguistics*
BBET	Beiträge zur biblischen Exegese und Theologie
BECNT	Baker Exegetical Commentary on the New Testament
BINS	Biblical Interpretation Series
BTB	*Biblical Theology Bulletin*
BZNW	Beihefte für Zeitschrift für neutestamentliche Wissenschaft
CBR	*Currents in Biblical Research*
CGTC	Cambridge Greek Testament Commentary
CQ	*Classical Quarterly*
CSL	Cambridge Studies in Linguistics
CTL	Cambridge Textbooks in Linguistics
CWMH	Collected Works of M. A. K. Halliday
ECHC	Early Christianity in Its Historical Context
FN	*Filología Neotestamentaria*
GBS	Guides to Biblical Scholarship
HNT	Handbuch zum Neuen Testament
ICC	International Critical Commentary
IFG1	M. A. K. Halliday. *An Introduction to Functional Grammar*. 1st ed. London: Arnold, 1985.
IFG4	M. A. K. Halliday. *Halliday's Introduction to Functional Grammar*. Revised by Christian M. I. M. Matthiessen. 4th ed. London: Routledge, 2014.
JL	*Journal of Linguistics*
JLSMi	Janua Linguarum, Series minor
JP	*Journal de Psychologie*
JSNTSup	Journal for the Study of the New Testament Supplements

JSOTSup	Journal for the Study of the Old Testament Supplements
LBS	Linguistic Biblical Studies
LENT	Linguistic Exegesis of the New Testament
LLC	*Literary and Linguistic Computing*
LN	Johannes P. Louw and Eugene A. Nida. *Greek–English Lexicon of the New Testament Based on Semantic Domains*. 2 vols. New York: United Bible Societies, 1988.
LNTS	Library of New Testament Studies
MBSS	McMaster Biblical Studies Series
MDU	*Monatshefte für deutschen Unterricht*
MnS	Mnemosyne Studies
MNTS	McMaster New Testament Studies
NIGTC	New International Greek Testament Commentary
NovT	*Novum Testamentum*
NTM	New Testament Monographs
SBG	Studies in Biblical Greek
SBLDS	SBL Dissertation Series
SemeiaSt	Semeia Studies
SNTG	Studies in New Testament Greek
SNTSMS	Society for New Testament Studies Monograph Series
SP	Sacra Pagina
SWPLL	*Sheffield Working Papers in Language and Linguistics*
TCLP	*Travaux Cercle Linguistique de Prague*
TJ	*Trinity Journal*
TNTC	Tyndale New Testament Commentaries
WBC	Word Biblical Commentary
WTJ	*Westminster Theological Journal*
WUNT	Wissenschaftliche Untersuchungen zum Neuen Testament

Introduction to This Volume on Linguistic Descriptions

There are many conceptions, and possibly even more preconceptions, about linguistics and interpretation of the New Testament. There are some who conceive of linguistics in a very narrow sense, with the tendency to equate it with the traditional categories of language. In that sense, linguistics is just a fancy word for study of language, something that has been undertaken in various ways for at least the last several centuries. In one sense, as I hope to show in this volume, this is correct. Language has been studied for several centuries and in that regard linguistics is nothing new. Others think of linguistics as a highly arcane and technical "science," in which there are complex formulas that describe rules of language that have only limited application outside of technical linguistic treatments. For those with this conception, linguistics is a field of limited value, because it is very hypothetical and does not address questions of how real language is used. In one sense, this response is also correct, at least insofar as linguistics is a technical discipline with its own language and vocabulary (although I will not be using any symbolic logic in my linguistic descriptions). There are other more moderate voices who understand linguistics as a shorthand for a variety of approaches to language that have been developed within the last one-hundred or so years. This development took place for a variety of reasons and in several major intellectual centers and resulted in the rise of what has sometimes been called structuralism, one of the most important intellectual movements of the twentieth century. Linguistics according to this definition is a recognized area of academic endeavor, with its own vocabulary and jargon, mostly applied to spoken language, with great diversity of opinion that sometimes makes one wonder whether linguists can agree on anything. In one sense, this conception is certainly correct as well. The rise of modern linguistics fits comfortably within the development of a variety of so-called social sciences at the beginning of the twentieth century, even though it did not emerge as a discipline in its own right until around the 1950s, in part because of the translation of Ferdinand de Saussure's *Course in General Linguistics* into English in 1959.[1] Perhaps because of its relatively recent advent, or perhaps because of other reasons, such as its perceived lack of direct connection to other academic areas, linguistics has not made as significant inroads into some areas of intellectual endeavor as it has into others. Biblical studies is one of those areas, with New Testament studies included within this observation. But biblical studies is not alone in not embracing the insights of modern linguistics, even though it is strikingly odd that biblical studies appears to have a voracious appetite for consuming

---

[1] Ferdinand de Saussure, *Course in General Linguistics*, ed. Charles Bally and Albert Sechehaye, with Albert Riedlinger, trans. Wade Baskin (New York: Philosophical Library, 1959 [1916]).

whole other academic fields. However, it has now been over sixty years since Saussure's major work was translated into English and this should be long enough to allow for others to assess the significance of linguistics for biblical study.

One might legitimately wonder why there has been so much hesitation regarding the use of linguistics. One argument that I often hear is that it is difficult to understand linguistics and even more difficult to see how it makes a difference in interpretation of the biblical text. I accept this criticism. Some of the contiguous fields that have most readily been adopted into and adapted for New Testament study do not have the technical apparatus or apparent difficulty as do many of the schools of modern linguistics. I am thinking here of such areas as so-called literary criticism or social-scientific criticism. These fields are, in fact, much more technically demanding and theoretically rigorous than is often represented in biblical studies, but the versions in which they are often imported into and then unloaded on biblical studies appear, at least to me, to be chastened and contained versions of the original. This does not answer the question, however, of why linguistics has not been incorporated into New Testament studies. Another argument that I have sometimes heard is that linguistics is a highly diverse field, and so it is difficult to know which type of linguistics one should use. Related to this reason is the idea that, because the field is so diverse, there is not just no single way to do linguistics (there is not, although one might argue that some linguistic theories are more useful than others), but there is therefore no assurance that using a linguistic method will arrive at the kinds of determinate meanings that some often seek in biblical studies. I also have some sympathy with these reasons as well. Linguistics is a difficult and complex field of intellectual inquiry, with many different theories on offer. I will survey some of these in this volume, and I warn my readers now that this may add to their sense of confusion rather than clarify their perceptions. However, linguistics is not alone in not being able to offer definitive meanings to the interpreter, any more than can any other interpretive approach, whether it is represented as grammatical-historical or higher-critical or historical-critical or one of the newer approaches. This does not mean that all linguistic theories are therefore the same or of equal value, or lack of value, for interpretation. To the contrary, I believe that we can learn from many different theories, even if we believe that some are more useful than others.

This volume is an attempt to open up the field of linguistics, and in particular one particular approach to linguistics, Systemic Functional Linguistics (SFL), so that readers can appreciate the possible contributions of linguistics to biblical studies. I have therefore structured the volume in two parts to aid in understanding the progression of thought.

The first part focuses upon the wider field of linguistics and New Testament Greek study. This first part is concerned with setting the stage for part two by discussing the wide variety of linguistic theories in contemporary language study and placing this within the context of the major periods of language study since the Enlightenment. In Chapter One, I begin by defining linguistic schools of thought as linguistic theories that have attracted concentrated efforts by others. There are many different linguistic theories that are vying for attention within the field of contemporary language study, but not all of these become schools of linguistics, because they do not form the necessary critical mass of scholarly attention. Having defined the relationship between linguistic theories and their resulting schools, I turn to the two major earlier periods of language discussion. I here offer a brief discussion of the major characteristics of the rationalist and comparative-historical periods, categorized under the label of traditional grammar. These periods are characterized by differing, even if overlapping, sets of features. One can readily see how the rationalist period led to the comparative-historical period. We are probably familiar with the work of such scholars as Georg Benedikt Winer, Friedrich Blass, Albert Debrunner, James Hope Moulton, and A. T. Robertson, all of whom I will say more about in the first chapter. Winer was a leading figure in the rationalist approach to New Testament Greek, while the others represented the comparative-historical approach. What may be more surprising to many students of the New Testament, however, is how these periods are still alive and seen to be enacted in many works of contemporary New Testament Greek studies. The major reference works used in New Testament Greek studies remain products of comparative-historicism. Even more noteworthy, perhaps, is the fact that some of the works of New Testament Greek scholarship that have more recently been written also follow the rationalist or comparative-historical approaches. This brings us back to the major issues raised at the beginning of this introduction. Why is it that modern linguistics has been resisted in New Testament Greek study, to the point that many if not most New Testament scholars are content to rely upon works that follow language theories that, while valuable and useful in their times, have now been superseded by the discoveries of modern linguistics?

The second chapter is concerned with the rise of modern linguistics. I offer a more variegated history of its development than is often found in short introductions of this type, especially in New Testament Greek studies. However, this is not meant to be an introduction either to linguistics or to its history, and so I must necessarily be summative. I look at three major influences upon the rise of modern linguistics—Ferdinand de Saussure in Geneva, the Prague Linguistic School, and the study of native languages in North America. These three important linguistic complexes had a huge impact upon the development of structural linguistics in its various forms. Much of this theoretical work was done in the first half of the twentieth century, and so some of it, in particular the Prague Linguistic Circle, was overshadowed by the events surrounding the Second World War. These events led to the demise of the Prague School and the restriction of research and even dissemination of information. As I already indicated, it was not until after the Second World War that Saussure's *Course* was translated into English and that serious modern linguistic study became widespread even within universities. I chart some of these developments.

More importantly for this volume, I also examine the major schools of linguistics that are currently relevant for study of the Greek New Testament. In some regards various theories have risen and fallen over the course of the last fifty or so years. However, I have identified three types of schools within which there are six schools of thought. By a school of linguistics, I mean an association of a number of scholars who are at least loosely collaborating to promote a particular linguistic theory. The first category is Formalist Schools, with emphasis upon the forms of language. The two theories in this category are transformational-generative grammar based on the significant work of Noam Chomsky and Construction Grammar represented by the voluminous work of Paul Danove. The second category is Cognitive Schools, with its emphasis upon human cognition and how language fits within the larger field of cognitive studies. The two theories in this category are Cognitive Linguistics, which has become one of the fastest-growing areas within linguistics, and Relevance Theory, with its emphasis upon non-code qualities of language. The third category is Functional Schools, where the emphasis is upon the functional capacity of language. The two theories in this category are cognitive-functionalism with its blend of cognitive and functionalist criteria and SFL based upon the semantic-based system networks of Michael Halliday. As one can readily appreciate from the categories and their labels, there is some overlap within these categories. However, they form a continuum so that the theories on the extremes represent significantly different theories of language and how we understand and describe it. I make no apology for arguing for a form of SFL. I lay a brief foundation for this linguistic theory in this summary but take up the challenge by way of exemplification in part two.

The second part of this volume provides studies in Greek linguistics that utilize SFL to illuminate texts and issues. However, this volume is not meant as an introduction to SFL but an introduction to how SFL might address some interesting linguistic issues that pertain to New Testament studies, including New Testament Greek studies. In other words, the four topics that I have chosen are not the typical kinds of subjects that are often associated with linguistics. If one were to ask how linguistics might inform New Testament Greek studies today, general answers might include such topics as verbal aspect (probably the single most discussed topic), voice (especially deponency and the middle voice, where there has been significant recent research), and a few other topics. This volume does not address such topics, or only addresses them tangentially to other linguistic topics that are more directly discussed. This volume focuses upon topics that are both much more within the mainstream of biblical studies and, at the same time, much more specialized and hence not as widely written upon, at least from a linguistic standpoint. There are four such topics in this volume.

Chapter Three addresses the question of metaphor. Metaphor, of course, is a topic that has been discussed both popularly and within the scholarly literature for a long time. Philosophers, literary scholars, cognitive scientists, and linguists, among many others, have all developed a variety of theories on what constitutes a metaphor and how metaphors work within language. It is hard to imagine that there can be anything new to say in the area of metaphor studies, but I believe that there are new avenues opened up by SFL. Most theories of metaphor are either lexical or cognitive in nature. In SFL, lexical metaphor is recognized as a mismatch between semantic domains, but SFL emphasizes a second and arguably more important form of metaphor in grammatical metaphor. Grammatical metaphor is a way of describing how different forms of language are used to express similar ideas. There has been some important recent work in grammatical metaphor in biblical studies, and I attempt to capture the significance of this work and expand its usefulness. In this chapter, I treat both lexical and grammatical metaphor from a SFL perspective and provide examples of how metaphor helps us to understand the use of language within the New Testament.

The next chapter, Chapter Four, addresses the topic of rhetoric and persuasion. Rhetorical studies have become a large topic within New Testament studies. Especially in the 1990s and into the early part of the twenty-first century, rhetorical studies were utilized on a broad range of New Testament literature with the anticipated outcome of resolving a number of interpretive issues. These theories never answered all of the questions that they raised, and since then there have been both a quelling of enthusiasm for rhetorical studies and an acceptance of them in limited contexts. In this chapter, I recognize that basic rhetorical questions are important for interpretation but attempt to use SFL to transpose them into linguistic questions, especially related to the concept of persuasion. As a result, I introduce the importance of the appraisal system within Greek linguistics as a way of linguistically capturing and describing questions of rhetoric within a linguistic theory that allows for more precise discussion. This is an exciting area of discussion within SFL and within New Testament Greek studies, in which it is recognized that the language that we use is not simply designed to provide an objective presentation but is itself evaluative.

Chapter Five returns to the question of cognition. Cognitive studies are a growing area of academic and intellectual endeavor, and within them Cognitive Linguistics is located. Cognitive Linguistics continues to grow more popular within contemporary linguistic studies. There are no doubt many insights that can be gained from Cognitive Linguistics, even by those of us who do not accept the basic premises or outworkings of the theory. One of the areas that Cognitive Linguistics has made its most significant contribution is in the area of cognitive metaphor theory and a variety of further developments. I address some of those in Chapter Three. In this chapter, I not only extend further my critique of Cognitive Linguistics but I examine SFL to see if within its systemic structure it provides a means of examining cognitive processes. I turn to the system networks that are integral to SFL. System networks are networks of systems that capture lexicogrammatical or semantic choices within the language. In that sense, they capture the potential of the language system but also provide a graphic representation of the process of decision-making in which language users engage. This provides a means of describing cognition in functional linguistic terms, without becoming preoccupied with human cognitive processing.

In Chapter Six, the last substantive chapter of the volume, I turn to the question of orality and textuality. Modern linguistics has traditionally focused upon examination of spoken language (or oral texts), while biblical studies only has written texts to consider. This too has perhaps contributed to skepticism that modern linguistics has much to offer the study of ancient written biblical documents. However, SFL has played an important role in discussing orality and textuality not as a disjunction but as a cline or continuum. In other words, rather than seeing these as opposed to each other, with inherent value judgments being made about either one or the other taking precedence, SFL has shown that there are describable linguistic characteristics of oral texts and of written texts. One is not better than the other—however this is described, such as in terms of lexical density or syntactical complexity or other stereotypes of language often associated more with social positions than linguistic findings—but they are simply different. In this chapter, I examine some of the characteristics of oral texts and some of those of written texts and use these as a means of examining some portions of the New Testament to determine whether we have written texts or oral texts or written texts that originated as oral texts. This opens up numerous possibilities for examination of the varieties of language within the Greek New Testament.

I then conclude the volume by incorporating the various strands of my argument into a cohesive final statement. I do not try to make any claims that are grander than they need to be, but I hope that the volume encourages the use of linguistics, and in particular SFL, in new ways in biblical interpretation. This volume provides a healthy and instructive mix of theoretical discussion and numerous examples to give a sufficient indication of how linguistics, especially SFL, can offer new insights into some problems not usually addressed by linguistic means in New Testament studies. The Greek of the New Testament is a set of documents that merits our best linguistic textual description.

PART ONE

Linguistics and New Testament Study

CHAPTER ONE

Linguistic Theory and New Testament Greek Study I

Linguistic Schools and Traditional Grammar

INTRODUCTION

For a discipline with as much ostensive diversity as is often perceived within it, New Testament Greek study offers far fewer linguistic theories than are to be found in the general field of linguistics. Despite these limitations, there are, nevertheless, several significant theories that are utilized and warrant examination. This first part attempts to place contemporary language research on the Greek New Testament into its proper context. These first two chapters introduce the linguistic theory that is more fully expounded in subsequent chapters of this volume.[1] However, this part introduces this linguistic theory, Systemic Functional Linguistics (SFL), in relation to the major schools of linguistics and their use within New Testament Greek studies. In order to place these two chapters in their proper place within linguistic description of the Greek New Testament, one must attend to how various theories of language have influenced or been reflected in the study of the Greek language found in the New Testament.

The importance of discussion of these various linguistic theories and the schools that have developed around them is evident in a variety of ways. As I shall make clear in the discussion that follows in this chapter, the history of the study of the Greek of the New Testament is part of the wider study of language and linguistics. Despite this, the field of New Testament Greek studies has not always been clear in its methodologies, whether in their use, their origins, or even their identification and definition. As a result, what might well be labeled a positivist view of language reflective of pre-linguistic eras of thought has come to be widely accepted by many New Testament Greek scholars. This positivist view treats language as if it provides unmediated access to established and irrefutable facts of language, realia, that contain within them their self-evident interpretation. The Greek language, thereby, is seen to be a static and invariable entity that is pre-descriptive in nature; that is, there is the assumption, whether explicit or

---

[1] There is a range of terminology that is often used in speaking of various intellectual constructs. These terms include: theory, model, approach, paradigm, school, among others. There is no doubt similarity in the way that they are used, but there may also be differences implied by them. I use all these terms, sometimes interchangeably and sometimes distinctly, but try to be relatively consistent in using "theory" to refer to various linguistic theories that have been developed over the years, especially during the modern linguistic period, and I use "school" to refer to groups of linguists who congregate around one or more of these theories. I have not always made such distinctions in other works, and so nothing of great significance should be read into the practice here. In all uses, I have attempted to be clear in what I am saying.

implicit, that there is an essentialist nature of the Greek language that we, as Greek grammarians and linguists, have progressively discovered over the years and have come to accept as providing unquestionable truths about the language and how to understand it. The further assumption is that this description is simply the way the Greek language is. The study of language takes on formulaic and even mathematical and logical properties in the hands of such scholars. At this stage of study, according to this position, we are no longer in the process of engaging in new descriptions of Greek, but we are fine-tuning our previous and agreed-upon understandings of the language. There are many problems with such a position, some of them factual and others conceptual, but the major ones to note at this point are that this positivist view is out of harmony with virtually every other academic and intellectual field of study in its retention of its connection to the past, it is out of keeping with other developments in the study of language that have progressed in various stages to what has come to be called modern linguistics, and, finally, it is inaccurate regarding the study of ancient Greek, including the Greek of the New Testament, where changing conceptions of various of its elements are still to be described, conceptions with significant new insights to offer interpreters.

A useful and now widely recognized instance to illustrate how descriptions of language change and insights are altered or refined—one with recognized significance for the study of New Testament Greek—is found in relatively recent linguistic memory.[2] This instance is the discussion of verbal aspect that has emerged over the last thirty or so years. Previous to this most recent period of study, the verbal system of Greek was first described as primarily temporal, relying upon a common set of time-based descriptors often also used of other Indo-European languages. The Greek verbal system was said to recognize *Zeitstufe* (temporal stages), rather than *Zeitart* (kind of time), to use the descriptive categories found in one of the early treatments of such matters in Greek.[3] Without entirely abandoning the temporal explanation, there later was recognition that this temporal descriptive framework was unsatisfactory and that the ancient Greek verbal edifice, on at least some occasions, is also concerned not just with *when* an action occurred but with *how* it occurred. Many will be familiar with this discussion over the semantics of the tense-forms of Greek and their relationship to what was traditionally called *Aktionsart* or "kind of action,"[4] now sometimes called lexical aspect.[5] Around thirty to forty years ago,

---

[2]There is a growing number of accounts of the history of discussion of the Greek verb in light of modern aspect studies. Within New Testament studies, see Stanley E. Porter, *Verbal Aspect in the Greek of the New Testament, with Reference to Tense and Mood*, SBG 1 (New York: Peter Lang, 1989), 17–65. For a recent treatment of many of the range of issues in aspect studies, see Robert I. Binnick, ed., *The Oxford Handbook of Tense and Aspect* (Oxford: Oxford University Press, 2012). One notices a variety of approaches to the issue, not all of them necessarily helpful to study of New Testament (or other ancient) Greek.

[3]See Georg Curtius, *Die Bildung der Tempora und Modi im Griechischen und Lateinischen sprachvergleichend dargestellt* (Berlin: Wilhelm Besser, 1846; ET *The Greek Verb: Its Structure and Development*, trans. A. S. Wilkins and E. B. England [London: John Murray, 1880]); and Curtius, *Erläuterungen zum meiner griechischen Schulgrammatik* (Prague: Tempsky, 1863; ET *Elucidations of the Student's Greek Grammar*, trans. E. Abbott, 2nd ed. [London: John Murray, 1875]).

[4]See Karl Brugmann, *Griechische Grammatik* (Munich: Beck, 1885; 4th ed., ed. Albert Thumb, 1913), 538–41.

[5]This is just one of several terms used, including not just lexical aspect but procedural aspect, situation aspect, among others. They do not necessarily mean the same things, as their modifiers reflect. See the valuable but underappreciated study by Francis Pang, *Revisiting Aspect and Aktionsart: A Corpus Approach to Koine Greek Event Typology*, LBS 14 (Leiden: Brill, 2016). These views are opposed to morphological or grammatical aspect, a category not as widely used in aspect studies as some of the categories of lexical aspect that seem to dominate study especially of non-morphologically rich languages (e.g., English, as opposed to Greek). Most discussions of aspect, even in such a work as Binnick's handbook, are discussions of lexical aspect, not morphological aspect. The failure to note this has bedeviled discussion of aspect, including (and especially) aspect studies of New Testament Greek.

however, the term "verbal aspect" was introduced into the discussion of verbal semantics as a better description of the Greek verbal system, even if the term "aspect" was variously defined from the start.[6] Some focused upon aspect as concerned with authorial viewpoint and others upon the internal or external (temporal) constituency of processes.[7] According to at least one prominent form of aspect theory, the Greek verbal system was classified as aspect prominent not tense prominent, so that the so-called Greek tense-forms were used to grammaticalize a subjective semantic choice of conception of processes by the language user, not the time at which the event occurred or as reflective of it as a temporal event.[8] There are variations upon this and similar definitions.

This third major reconception and redefinition of the semantics of the Greek verbal system introduced recent linguistic categories into the discussion of the Greek of the New Testament and resulted in a debate, sometimes relatively heated—at least by academic standards—of the semantics of the Greek verbal system, and whether it was aspect or tense prominent and what that means, not just for describing the Greek verbal system but for understanding the entire Greek language.[9] I have an opinion of which view is correct in this continuing debate but at this point that is not the focal issue. What is important to note is the importance of this language discussion in New Testament scholarship and how linguistics has played a role in the development of various ideas. The traditional view of Greek, the temporal view previously noted, sounds like a description of German—a

---

[6]The first modern study was the study in French by Jens Holt, *Études d'aspect*, Acta Jutlandica Aarskrift for Aarhus Universitet 15.2 (Copenhagen: Universitetsforlaget I Aarhus, 1943), influenced by the Danish structuralist Louis Hjelmslev (see Chapter Two); followed in ancient Greek studies in Spanish by M. Sanchez Ruipérez, *Estructura del Sistema de Aspectos y Tiempos del Verbo Griego Antiguo: Análysis Funcional Sincrónico*, Theses et Studia Philologica Salmanticensia 7 (Salamanca: Colegio Trilingue de la Universidad, 1954), influenced by Roman Jakobson and the Prague School of linguistics (see Chapter Two); the study by Juan Mateos, *El Aspecto Verbal en el Nuevo Testamento*, Estudios de Nuevo Testamento 1 (Madrid: Ediciones Cristiandad, 1977); with the first monograph in English on aspect by Bernard Comrie, *Aspect*, CTL (Cambridge: Cambridge University Press, 1976) and on ancient Greek in English published by Porter, *Verbal Aspect*, followed by Buist Fanning, *Verbal Aspect in New Testament Greek* (Oxford: Oxford University Press, 1990), with a number of works published since. Porter and Fanning illustrate from the start some of the major differences in definition, creating two paths generally followed by aspect studies to the present. On the Fanning/Porter debate, see Stanley E. Porter and D. A. Carson, eds., *Biblical Greek Language and Linguistics: Open Questions in Current Research*, JSNTSup 80 (Sheffield: Sheffield Academic, 1993), 18–82, with papers by Porter and Fanning, and responses by Daryl Dean Schmidt and Moisés Silva.
[7]Both viewpoint and internal/external constituency are heralded by Fanning, *Verbal Aspect*, 83–4, 85; and Constantine R. Campbell in *Verbal Aspect, the Indicative Mood, and Narrative: Soundings in the Greek of the New Testament*, SBG 13 (New York: Peter Lang, 2007), 8. Both characterizations of aspect seem to derive from Bernard Comrie, *Aspect*. These views retain either an objectivist or temporal view of aspect that I believe is not indicated by morphological aspect. Some have even argued for aspect as a temporal category, a proposal that ends up confusing a number of categories within the tense–aspect–mood trichotomy. See Christopher J. Thomson, "What Is Aspect? Contrasting Definitions in General Linguistics and New Testament Studies," in *The Greek Verb Revisited: A Fresh Approach for Biblical Exegesis*, ed. Steven E. Runge and Christopher J. Fresch (Bellingham, WA: Lexham, 2016), 13–80. One might well get the impression that aspect is a temporal category from some of the discussion in general linguistics, which, I believe, fails to distinguish morphological aspect from lexical aspect, and tends to impose categories from one's metalanguage upon other languages (e.g., ancient Greek).
[8]Porter, *Verbal Aspect*, 1, with modification of the definition in light of further issues raised in the discussion. The terminology of a language being "aspect prominent" is of more recent vintage, and is evidenced in D. N. S. Bhat, *The Prominence of Tense, Aspect and Mood* (Amsterdam: John Benjamins, 1999).
[9]Some of that debate is seen in the various essays in Steven E. Runge and Christopher J. Fresch, eds., *The Greek Verb Revisited: A Fresh Approach for Biblical Exegesis* (Bellingham, WA: Lexham, 2016), responded to by Stanley E. Porter, "Revisiting the Greek Verb: An Extended Critique," *FN* 31 (2018): 3–16; and in Buist Fanning, Constantine R. Campbell, and Stanley E. Porter, *The Perfect Storm: Critical Discussion of the Semantics of the Greek Perfect Tense under Aspect Theory*, ed. D. A. Carson, SBG 21 (New York: Peter Lang, 2021).

heavily tensed language—or, perhaps even more importantly, of English—also a tensed language but one that also has categories for kinds of action and is more toward the middle of a temporal–aspectual cline, even if slightly more toward the temporal side. At least it seems more like a description of one of these (or other possible languages) than it does a description of Greek that is based upon Greek verbal structure without concern for typological or metalanguage considerations. One of the major tendencies of linguistic descriptions is for the descriptions of languages other than one's own to end up looking a lot more like descriptions of one's own language than they do of languages that may have resemblances or historical relations to one's own, and even sometimes of languages very different from one's own. I suspect that the interpreters' understandings of English and German were, for at least many of those involved in the discussion of ancient Greek over the years, far more important in their examinations of Greek than attempting to offer a description of Greek without drawing upon these well-established categories, especially as they represented the first language of the involved analyst. This situation no doubt occurs because of the need for a metalanguage to describe language.

My point here is that I believe that much of the resistance to an aspectual view of Greek is not based upon a comprehensive attempt to describe the Greek language, something I and a few others perhaps besides those already mentioned have attempted to do. It is based instead upon one's prior belief that the question of the semantics of the Greek verbal system had already been resolved—if not by the ancient Greeks themselves then by the Latin grammarians or by the rationalists or surely by the comparative philologians or by language typologists who wish to find typological characteristics of a variety of languages or even by an innate understanding of one's own language. This is especially the case when one considers that, at least by one scholarly accounting, there are as many tenseless languages as tensed languages among the world's languages,[10] so conceiving of tenseless languages should not be foreign to one attempting to describe another language, even if one is working from an Indo-European standpoint. There are still many linguistic features of ancient Greek, including the Greek of the New Testament, that require further modeling and remodeling in light of further linguistic research. Much of what is labeled as linguistic description is simply one projecting one's prior understanding of language, usually in terms of one's first language or traditional grammatical categories, upon another language. That situation is one major reason why linguistic theories are so important. Linguistic theories—and the linguistic schools of thought that grow up around them—are attempts to find conceptual theories that enable us to examine language while minimizing simply either accepting what we have been told or what we have accepted about language or even about a particular language without further reflection or avoiding merely imposing our own language upon another. We must instead provide a linguistic framework that acknowledges its presuppositions and helps us to think about language in new ways by using the framework of a particular linguistic theory.

In this chapter, I wish to discuss the notion of what constitutes a school of linguistics, before examining two earlier periods of language study that have continued to have influence upon New Testament Greek study, often characterized as reflecting traditional

---

[10] See Jo-Wang Lin, "Tenselessness," in *The Oxford Handbook of Tense and Aspect*, ed. Robert I. Binnick (Oxford: Oxford University Press, 2012), 668–95, esp. 669. By citing this article, I am not necessarily making any stronger claim than that when examining ancient Greek, including the Greek of the New Testament, we must be open to classifying the language in terms other than simply as a tensed language, that is, a language that primarily encodes temporal reference.

grammar. I do this as a prelude to discussing the rise and development of modern linguistics and the major schools of linguistics within New Testament Greek studies in the second chapter. Both chapters together serve as a prelude to the more focused studies of individual linguistic phenomena in the four substantive chapters that follow. I will make further mention of some of these schools of thought in these subsequent chapters, but always in the context of utilizing SFL—to be explicated further in Chapter Two—to describe the linguistic data.

In regard to various linguistic schools of thought, biblical studies is a problematic discipline, because unlike other disciplines, where there is much more methodological exclusivism, biblical studies often demands that a scholar attempt to be expert in a variety of methods that are usually eclectically blended together without differentiation in ways that do not always occur in other disciplines. There are few biblical scholars who are not at least competent in the historical-critical method, as well as knowing something about other post-historical-critical methods, such as social-scientific criticism, literary criticism, and the like (or at least knowing enough about them not to like them). Linguistics, however, is simply not like that. The theoretical boundaries are much more strongly and exclusively drawn, to the point that some may be aware of what are sometimes called "linguistic wars" that have broken out among those who have called into question the theories of others.[11] This does not mean that there are no instances of the practice of eclectic borrowing, but such eclectic theoretical blending occurs less frequently or perhaps less overtly in linguistics. Being a master and practitioner of several different linguistic theories is not just unpracticed but is often overtly discouraged, because it not only implies a crossing of inappropriate boundaries but puts inappropriate demands upon the specialist knowledge of the linguist and upon the theory itself. Therefore, I cannot claim to be expert in all the linguistic theories and schools that I will be discussing in this chapter and the next (I am not, nor do I wish to be), but I will attempt to do the best that I can in presenting each one and offering some representative examples of work within each school of thought. I will also offer some evaluative comments as an aid in understanding each school, before proposing some general summative statements regarding New Testament Greek language study.

DEFINING LINGUISTIC SCHOOLS OF THOUGHT

Before I divide the New Testament linguistic world into its various schools of thought in Chapter Two, one must ask the question of what constitutes a linguistic school, and how one decides what constitutes a linguistic school within New Testament Greek studies. On the one hand, making such distinctions seems at first glance to be relatively straightforward, until one investigates the wider field of language and linguistic study and how this has developed in relationship to the study of New Testament Greek.

In 1980, the linguist Geoffrey Sampson published his volume *Schools of Linguistics*, an excellent introduction to linguistic schools of thought up to the time of writing and

---

[11] The linguistic wars refer, in particular, to disputes that occurred within the ranks of Chomskyan linguists (see Chapter Two). However, the range of differences among various linguistic schools has prompted even linguists to ask the question of what linguists who subscribe to various theories have in common. On the issues on which linguists agree, see Richard Hudson, "Some Issues on Which Linguists Can Agree," *JL* 17 (1981): 333–43; cf. Stanley E. Porter, "Studying Ancient Languages from a Modern Linguistic Perspective: Essential Terms and Terminology," *FN* 2 (1989): 147–72.

publication. He defines a linguistic school in a way that is consistent with my previous comments: "Often one individual or a small group of original minds has founded a tradition which has continued to mould approaches to language in the university or the nation in which that tradition began; between adherents of different traditions there has usually been relatively limited contact."[12] When I turn to defining such schools in New Testament studies in Chapter Two, I will use this definition to define schools of linguistics. I will identify the significant figures within each school, with the stipulation that a minimum publication requirement is mandated of two major monographs or equivalent in the field of linguistics or linguistic theory and at least two major monographs in the field of New Testament Greek studies, and that some tangible sign of continuing work by the school as an acknowledged school is required. I realize that by imposing this publication requirement I run the risk of excluding some approaches to linguistics that some working within New Testament Greek studies might follow and find useful. However, the notion of school, as Sampson indicates, implies the founding of a tradition that continues to shape scholarship, rather than consisting simply of an individual who holds to a particular theory (although I will admittedly make a singular but significant exception to this rule, as will be seen in the discussion in Chapter Two). Sampson also notes several other factors that are worth observing in considering linguistic schools.

I can only offer a rough outline of the schools of thought in New Testament Greek studies based upon major figures and as reflected by those who follow within the tradition as practitioners; I recognize that individual scholars will have their own variations upon the major concepts endorsed by the school. This internal variation is to be expected. I am sure that I will miss some schools of thought that may be of significance in other countries, especially as I am concentrating upon, though not exclusively referring to, those working in English-language Greek New Testament scholarship. I am also concentrating upon what Sampson calls "core" linguistic fields, not what he terms "peripheral branches," so I am not going to discuss sociolinguistics, multilingualism, and the like, although I will touch lightly upon that very broad and encompassing subject called discourse analysis.[13] I also am not going to deal in detail with various areas of applied linguistics, such as second language teaching (the teaching of elementary or intermediate Greek), translation studies, or phonological theories regarding Greek—as interesting as these areas may be (I have written on all of them, so I agree that they are valuable, just not in this volume).

As a result of his investigation, Sampson lists the following schools of linguistics. He treats the nineteenth century as a prelude (I will discuss this period later in this chapter due to its continuing relevance for New Testament study), and then deals with the following areas: Ferdinand de Saussure and language as social fact, the Descriptivists (including Franz Boas, Leonard Bloomfield, Charles Hockett, and Kenneth Pike and the work of the early stages of the Summer Institute of Linguistics), the Sapir-Whorf hypothesis, the functional linguistics of the Prague School, Noam Chomsky and generative grammar, the relational grammar of Louis Hjelmslev, Sydney Lamb, and Peter Reich, Generative

---

[12]Geoffrey Sampson, *Schools of Linguistics* (Stanford, CA: Stanford University Press, 1980), 9.
[13]I have treated this elsewhere. See, for example, Stanley E. Porter and Andrew W. Pitts, "New Testament Greek Language and Linguistics in Recent Research," *CBR* 6.2 (2008): 214–55, esp. 235–41, where we identify five schools of discourse analysis within New Testament studies: Summer Institute of Linguistics (inspired by Tagmemics), SFL (see elsewhere in this volume), Continental European, South African (colon analysis), and a fifth school we label "eclectic." These categories are developed further in Stanley E. Porter and Matthew Brook O'Donnell, *Discourse Analysis and the Greek New Testament: Text-Generating Resources*, T&T Clark Library of New Testament Greek 2 (London: T&T Clark, 2023).

phonology, and, finally, the London School of J. R. Firth and Michael A. K. Halliday. Those who are acquainted with these scholars will recognize that Sampson takes a generally diachronic view of these schools of linguistics, and in the process encompasses most of the schools of thought that one might well expect to encounter in such a study up to 1980—acknowledging that there might well be other schools that have developed since then, such as the Cognitive School, a topic on which Sampson expresses a strong opinion in his later writing.[14] There is much of value in this approach to the topic and I will draw upon it in my discussion. However, Sampson does not discuss the full range of linguistic theories, because some of them do not qualify as "schools" in his analysis.

The only similar study that I know regarding biblical studies—besides my own previous study of linguistic schools in New Testament studies (see discussion in Chapter Two)—is by Jeremy Thompson and Wendy Widder. In an article entitled "Major Approaches to Linguistics," they list and briefly treat the following approaches: comparative philology, structural linguistics, functionalism (including functionalism, Systemic Functional Grammar, and Role and Reference Grammar), generative grammar, discourse analysis, and Cognitive Linguistics. Besides including discourse analysis, which stands out in this survey as not being like the others, Thompson and Widder present a roughly diachronic study, even if this is somewhat problematic in treating the three functionalists before generative grammar. One of the major shortcomings of their survey is that they fail to give suitable recognition to the most productive school of New Testament Greek study or its major proponents, SFL (even though they mention Systemic Functional Grammar).[15] This is an unfortunate and unexplainable oversight that limits the reliability of their survey.

There have been other ways suggested for differentiating linguistic theories and schools, to be sure. The American linguists Robert Van Valin and Randy LaPolla discuss a wide variety of syntactical theories. They differentiate between what they call the "syntactocentric perspective" and the "communication-and-cognition perspective," or, in other words, basically Chomsky as syntactocentered and everyone else.[16] The syntactocentric perspective is attributed to Chomsky and his many followers, and is characterized—whether in its earliest phrase-structure grammar or transformational grammar or later Government and Binding Theory/Principles and Parameters or minimalist program (with recursion as the minimal feature of language)[17]—by its

---

[14]Geoffrey Sampson, *The Linguistics Delusion* (Sheffield: Equinox, 2017), 77–87. Sampson has written a number of other books in linguistics, with one common theme being his criticism of Chomskyan formalism. See further discussion in Chapter Two.

[15]Jeremy Thompson and Wendy Widder, "Major Approaches to Linguistics," in *Linguistics and Biblical Exegesis*, ed. Douglas Mangum and Josh Westbury (Bellingham, WA: Lexham, 2017), 87–134. Other shortcomings are the limited and unrepresentative bibliographies provided. It appears that both authors are Old Testament rather than New Testament scholars. For other topical surveys, see Stanley E. Porter, "Greek Grammar and Syntax," in *The Face of New Testament Studies: A Survey of Recent Research*, ed. Scot McKnight and Grant R. Osborne (Grand Rapids: Baker, 2004), 76–103; Porter and Pitts, "New Testament Greek"; Constantine R. Campbell, *Advances in the Study of Greek: New Insights for Reading the New Testament* (Grand Rapids: Zondervan, 2015); and Dana M. Harris, "The Study of the Greek Language," in *The State of New Testament Studies: A Survey of Recent Research*, ed. Scot McKnight and Nijay K. Gupta (Grand Rapids: Baker, 2019), 120–36.

[16]Robert D. Van Valin Jr. and Randy J. LaPolla, *Syntax: Structure, Meaning and Function*, CTL (Cambridge: Cambridge University Press, 1997), 8–15. Cf. Leonard Talmy, *Toward a Cognitive Semantics*, 2 vols. (Cambridge, MA: MIT Press, 2000), 1:1–4, who basically defines linguistics as Chomsky and Cognitive Linguistics, leaving out any functional theories.

[17]Noam Chomsky, *Syntactic Structures*, JLSMi 4 (The Hague: Mouton, 1957); Chomsky, *Aspects of the Theory of Syntax* (Cambridge, MA: MIT Press, 1965); Chomsky, *Lectures on Government and Binding* (Dordrecht: Foris, 1981); and Chomsky, *The Minimalist Program* (Cambridge: MA: MIT Press, 1995), among many other works.

including an "autonomous cognitive faculty"[18] (Universal Grammar) that results in human internal grammar that follows linguistic universals. Such linguistics does not investigate language use (performance) but focuses upon the speaker's competence, and especially the psychological dimensions of language such as its acquisition, even if one is not concerned with psychological processes themselves. In other words, in the terms of Saussure (see Chapter Two), the emphasis is on *langue*, or language system, not *parole*, or speech. According to Van Valin and LaPolla's summary, this syntactocentric perspective on linguistics provides an analysis of grammar but not of language, if language is defined as what humans actually produce (*parole*).[19] Such an approach to language has spawned a number of further theories, according to Van Valin and LaPolla, such as Generalized Phrase Structure Grammar, Relational Grammar, and Categorial Grammar. One of the characteristics of such language study, however, based in part upon the work of the American descriptivist linguist Leonard Bloomfield, is the minimization of meaning and the emphasis upon form, hence these theories are often called formal grammars.

The communication-and-cognition perspective, according to Van Valin and LaPolla, essentially includes everything else in linguistic theory. This large group of theories is unified around the view that linguistics focuses upon use of language either for communicative purposes or as a reflection of cognitive processing in relation to other cognitive systems, with grammar or syntax as relatively less significant to these greater concerns and meaning or function being more important. As Van Valin and LaPolla admit, the linguistic theories that this perspective subsumes are numerous and diverse. They include Functional Grammar or grammars in their various types (including Continental, St. Petersburg, and West Coast or Oregon forms), Role and Reference Grammar, Systemic Functional Grammar (SFG), Tagmemics, Lexical-Functional Grammar, Head-Driven Phrase Structure Grammar, Construction Grammar, Autolexical Syntax, Word Grammar, Meaning-text theory, Cognitive Grammar, Prague School Dependency Grammar, and French functionalism, to list only what must be an incomplete list (and it is, as one can also think of Stratificational Grammar or Columbia School Linguistics, both functional models), along with a number of what they call independent linguists (who would presumably not qualify as being part of a school, according to Sampson's definition).[20]

Whereas Chomsky dominates the first group, the syntactocentric, there is no single dominant linguist in the second group, communication-and-cognition, apart from a relatively unified yet widespread rejection of the syntactocentric perspective. However, Van Valin and LaPolla also admit that there is a continuum from communicative on the one end and cognitive theories on the other of the continuum of communication-and-cognition perspectives. On the communicative side is Michael Halliday's SFG, which they characterize as "perhaps the most radical discourse-pragmatic view, a 'top-down' analytic model which starts with discourse and works 'down' to lower levels

---

[18]William Croft and D. Alan Cruse, *Cognitive Linguistics*, CTL (Cambridge: Cambridge University Press, 2004), 1.
[19]Van Valin and LaPolla, *Syntax*, 9.
[20]Van Valin and LaPolla, *Syntax*, 12, list as independent linguists Michael Silverstein, Ray Jackendoff, Ellen Prince, Talmy Givón, Susumu Kuno, Leonard Talmy, Sandra Thompson, and Anna Wierzbicka. Not all might fit as conveniently as others, and one might also think of others to place in this category. I would have thought that most of these were classifiable, some of them even in the syntactocentric and others in the communication-and-cognition perspective.

of grammatical structure."[21] On the cognitive side is Ronald Langacker's Cognitive Grammar, which is reducible to three major components, semantics, phonology, and symbolic representation.[22] Van Valin and LaPolla place the other theories in the middle of the continuum, singling out Role and Reference Grammar (Van Valin and LaPolla's own theory) and Simon Dik's (Continental) Functional Grammar for exemplary reference within this medial position.[23]

This categorization may, however, require further refinement or refinements. For example, if we utilize Van Valin and LaPolla's division, Construction Grammar, with its descriptive and non-transformational properties, is closer to Langacker's Cognitive Grammar than it is to the theories listed as standing in the middle with some of their functional tendencies. Furthermore, Tagmemics has some features in common with Role and Reference Grammar, such as a rank scale or levels of representation, but it has arguably more in common with SFG, with not only a rank scale but what SFG would call levels or strata (in essence this is a non-formal rank scale), a top-down approach, and a comprehensive and encompassing theory of context as well as structures. Whereas this differentiation by Van Valin and La Polla has the advantage of preserving structuralist binarism—perhaps unnecessarily so—it has the disadvantage of lumping everyone who is not a Chomskyan together. However, I do not believe that it is accurate to necessarily disconnect the cognitive linguists from the Chomskyans and to link them with the functionalists, especially as many of the founding figures in Cognitive Linguistics were originally Chomskyan formalists who were either departing from Chomsky or at least redefining their past. Being even more aggressively critical, one might question entirely the divide along the lines of Chomsky and his Universal Grammar against all the rest, and instead place Chomsky and his major developers, whether positively or negatively, so long as they pursue a psychological or cognitive dimension, on the one side, with the other perspectives lumped together on the other. The result here would be that Chomsky is joined by (from the choices of Van Valin and LaPolla) Lexical-Functional Grammar, Head-Driven Phrase Structure Grammar, Construction Grammar, probably Autolexical Syntax, and, most noteworthily perhaps, Cognitive Grammar. These together form a group that might be characterized as syntacto-cognitive-centric. This would leave, on the other pole of the resulting cline, Role and Reference Grammar on the one extreme (closest to the syntacto-cognitive-centric models) with movement toward Word Grammar, various dependency grammars (Mel'cuk and Prague), Functional Grammars (Continental, Russian, United States, and French), Tagmemics, and then SFG on the other, forming a relatively smaller and more focused yet still diverse group of functional theories.[24]

---

[21] Van Valin and LaPolla, *Syntax*, 12; cf. M. A. K. Halliday, *Halliday's Introduction to Functional Grammar*, rev. Christian M. I. M. Matthiessen, 4th ed. (London: Routledge, 2014). Much more will be said about Halliday and various theories he has propounded in the following chapters.

[22] Van Valin and LaPolla, *Syntax*, 13; cf. Ronald N. Langacker, *Cognitive Grammar: A Basic Introduction* (Oxford: Oxford University Press, 2008), 5.

[23] Van Valin and LaPolla, *Syntax*, 13; cf. Simon C. Dik, *The Theory of Functional Grammar*, ed. Kees Hengeveld, 2 vols. (Berlin: Mouton de Gruyter, 1997).

[24] I have been helped in my re-categorizations by Flip G. Droste and John E. Joseph, eds., *Linguistic Theory and Grammatical Description* (Amsterdam: John Benjamins, 1991); and Pius ten Hacken, *Chomskyan Linguistics and Its Competitors* (Sheffield: Equinox, 2007); see also Edith A. Moravcsik and Jessica R. Wirth, eds., *Syntax and Semantics: Current Approaches to Syntax* (New York: Academic Press, 1980). See also John E. Joseph and Talbot J. Taylor, eds., *Ideologies of Language* (London: Routledge, 1990), in response to those who argue for an objectivist perspective of at least some views of language (often connected with transformational-generative grammar and its Universal Grammar). Such is not the case for any theory or school.

The German linguist John Bateman has proposed the more nuanced categorization of approaches to the study of language as focusing upon whether language is seen as being in contexts, in texts, in heads, or in groups, four different places to locate language. Chomskyans would locate language in texts, cognitivists in heads, and functionalists in contexts or groups.[25] This differentiation makes clear that various linguistic schools place their primary focus upon different centers of linguistic attention or even centers of authority. This is a useful distinction that helps to orient one to various linguistic theories. Even though Bateman suggests four such foci, in effect there are three.

This results in what more reasonably seems to be three major groupings of linguistic schools of thought along this continuum: formal (Chomsky and his linguistic descendants), cognitive (in the middle because of their origins in Chomskyanism but their departure on several major fronts, not least Universal Grammar or nativism), and functional (from Role and Reference Grammar to SFG) models. This conforms to an arguably more straightforward schema suggested by the French linguist David Banks, who distinguishes among formal, cognitive, and functional theories of language.[26] This distinction recognizes the complexity of differing models of linguistic thought but categorizes them into broad categories that also appreciate common and different features, arranged along an appropriate continuum as previously discussed. This is the distinction that I will use in describing the major linguistic schools in New Testament Greek language study in Chapter Two. If one were to explore these categorizations in more detail, one would no doubt wish to refine significantly this segmented continuum as one places various theories along the several clines. However, before we turn in the next chapter to these various schools, I wish to place their development within a useful historical context.

TRADITIONAL GRAMMAR

Before I turn in the next chapter to the formalists, cognitivists, and functionalists within New Testament Greek studies, however, I should include a section on traditional grammar, as represented in the rationalist and comparative-historical schools of language study, as they have had the largest influence as schools—if they can be considered such—in New Testament Greek study to date, and continue to have an almost unaccountable influence, as I will further show.[27] I include traditional grammar as a category as a useful means of conjoining and talking about two major periods in language study before the rise of modern linguistics, for the simple reason that there are many who are engaged in New Testament Greek study who still follow the principles laid out in these schools of thought, even though these schools of thought have been superseded and replaced by various theories and schools of modern linguistic study. Their abiding legacy is

---

[25] John A. Bateman, "The Place of Systemic Functional Linguistics as a Linguistic Theory in the Twenty-First Century," in *The Routledge Handbook of Systemic Functional Linguistics*, ed. Tom Bartlett and Gerard O'Grady (London: Routledge, 2017), 11–26, here 11–12. One may well question whether these locations are correct, and whether Chomskyan generativists would locate language in heads. I wish to thank my colleague, Dr. Christopher Land, for raising questions about Bateman's scheme.

[26] David Banks, *A Systemic Functional Grammar of English: A Simple Introduction* (London: Routledge, 2019), 1; cf. Banks, *The Birth of the Academic Article: Le Journal des Sçavans and the Philosophical Transactions 1665–1700* (Sheffield: Equinox, 2017), 7.

[27] These two periods in language study are discussed in expanded form in Stanley E. Porter, *New Testament Theology and the Greek Language: A Linguistic Reconceptualization* (Cambridge: Cambridge University Press, 2022), ch. 1, which I draw freely upon in my discussion here.

part of the syndrome that I previously defined, in which there is a continuation of an approach to language based upon belief that it is in some way essentially correct, even if further thought has moved beyond such categories. The product is left intact even if the underlying supporting structure has been vacated. To a large extent, that is what has happened in New Testament Greek language study: the foundations have eroded with the building left precariously standing.

I use the term "traditional grammar" to refer to an approach to language that is what might be called pre-linguistic, that is, not before the study of language but before such study has come to be associated with the principles and approaches of modern linguistics. In a useful introductory volume, the linguist David Crystal defines the major features of traditional grammar as follows: the failure to recognize the difference between spoken and written language, emphasis upon restricted forms of written language (such as literary texts or exemplary texts by particular authors), a failure to recognize various forms of language and how they are used (whether dialects or registers), the tendency to describe language in terms of another language, often Latin (as already noted), the appeal to logic as a means of describing and even assessing language, and the tendency to evaluate language as more or less logical or complex or primitive or beautiful or the like.[28] These kinds of traditional criteria grew out of a long history of discussion of language that dates back to the ancients and continued until the advent of modern linguistics, and they have even continued to be used in some areas of language study. They were found in the two major periods of post-Enlightenment language study before the rise of modern linguistics, the rationalist, and comparative-historical periods.[29] They have had an important influence upon the development of linguistics and an abiding legacy in some New Testament Greek language study.

Rationalist Language Study

Rationalism as a philosophical movement grew out of the Enlightenment, that seventeenth- and eighteenth-century intellectual movement that marked the beginning of modernism.[30] The Enlightenment was not only an important watershed in most Western thought but also influenced and was a product of the study of language. It was characterized by several features now associated with modernism: rationalism, a shift from dogmatic to empiricist epistemology, an emphasis upon naturalism (as opposed to supernaturalism), and dissolution of the divide between the secular and the sacred. This desacralization focused upon the Bible. The movement is perhaps captured best in the

---

[28]David Crystal, *What Is Linguistics?*, 3rd ed. (London: Edward Arnold, 1974), 9–17. See also Porter, "Studying Ancient Languages," 163–6.
[29]See R. H. Robins, *A Short History of Linguistics*, 3rd ed. (London: Longman, 1990), esp. 148–217, for the basic facts recounted here. Other useful histories of linguistics for this period—although not all equally helpful regarding various individuals or schools of thought—include Milka Ivić, *Trends in Linguistics*, trans. Muriel Heppell, JLSMi 42 (The Hague: Mouton, 1965), 37–66; Maurice Leroy, *The Main Trends in Modern Linguistics*, trans. Glanville Price (Oxford: Blackwell, 1967), 11–47; Sampson, *Schools of Linguistics*, 13–33; Julia Kristeva, *Language—The Unknown: An Initiation into Linguistics*, trans. Anne M. Menke (New York: Columbia University Press, 1989), 172–216; Pieter A. M. Seuren, *Western Linguistics: An Historical Introduction* (Oxford: Blackwell, 1998), 49–139; P. H. Matthews, *Grammatical Theory in the United States from Bloomfield to Chomsky*, CSL 67 (Cambridge: Cambridge University Press, 1993); and Keith Allan, *The Western Classical Tradition in Linguistics*, 2nd ed. (London: Equinox, 2010).
[30]On the Enlightenment, see Norman Hampson, *The Enlightenment* (Harmondsworth: Penguin, 1968); and Dorinda Outram, *The Enlightenment* (Cambridge: Cambridge University Press, 1995), esp. 31–46. More detailed discussion of some German debates is found in Avi Lifschitz, *Language and Enlightenment: The Berlin Debates of the Eighteenth Century*, Oxford Historical Monographs (Oxford: Oxford University Press, 2012).

work of the Dutch philosopher Baruch Spinoza (1632–77). Although Spinoza was not an empiricist, he certainly was a rationalist, who believed in deduction from common knowledge to arrive at generalizations or universals and then moved to the particular.[31] Spinoza believed in God, but his equation of God with knowledge (he has been accused of being a pantheist who equated God with the material universe) led directly to the rise of Deism, in which God is removed from the world. Spinoza's philosophical approach also led him to skepticism regarding the Bible, because he subjected it to an uncompromising rationalism that demanded explanation and did not allow for inconsistency (and he found plenty of inconsistency throughout).[32]

The rationalist period of language study went hand in hand with the Enlightenment. This period extends from roughly the middle of the seventeenth to the turn of the nineteenth centuries (1650–1800), with the rise of Romanticism (more precisely some would say in 1798, with the publication of *Lyrical Ballads* by William Wordsworth and Samuel Taylor Coleridge).[33] Language study during the rationalist period was dominated by philosophers and linguists who approached language from a rationalist perspective and demanded that language follow rationalist principles of consistency and balance. Even though historical concerns were discussed from the start in language study, these historical concerns were framed within the rationalist perspective as an attempt to account for the origins and development of language, with the fundamental assumption being that accounting for origins was tantamount to explaining function and meaning. Several of the language advances in philosophy of this period are worth noting. The French philosopher Étienne Bonnot de Condillac (1714–80), who established John Locke's empirical deductive thought in French circles, believed that "abstract vocabulary and grammatical complexity developed from an earlier individual concrete vocabulary with very few grammatical distinctions or constraints."[34] This viewpoint reflects his epistemology of sensation. Jean-Jacques Rousseau (1712–78), the fellow French philosopher, believed similarly,[35] although his Romantic tendencies—that helped to usher in Romanticism—resulted in more passionate views of the earlier stages, rather than Condillac's more objective characterization. The German philosopher Johann Gottfried Herder (1744–1803), who held to early evolutionary views, developed Condillac's thought further and "asserted the inseparability of language and thought; language is the tool, the content, and the form of human thinking,"[36] in which they develop together in parallel ways.[37]

---

[31] See H. G. Hubbeling, *Spinoza's Methodology* (Assen: Van Gorcum, 1967).
[32] See Baruch Spinoza, *Theological-Political Treatise*, trans. Samuel Shirley, 2nd ed. (Indianapolis: Hackett, 2001). Spinoza was not alone, but part of a wider Enlightenment trend. See Jeffrey L. Morrow, *Three Skeptics and the Bible: La Peyrère, Hobbes, Spinoza, and the Reception of Modern Biblical Criticism* (Eugene, OR: Pickwick, 2016).
[33] See William Wordsworth and Samuel Taylor Coleridge, *Lyrical Ballads*, ed. R. L. Brett and A. R. Jones, 2nd ed. (1798; repr., London: Routledge, 1991). Wordsworth's "Preface" was first published in the 1800 edition.
[34] Robins, *Short History*, 165. See Étienne Bonnot de Condillac, *Essai sur l'origine des connaissances humaines*, Oeuvres de Condillac, ed. Georges Le Roy, 3 vols. (Paris: Presses Universitaires de France, 1947), 1:1–118.
[35] See Jean-Jacques Rousseau, *Essay on the Origin of Languages*, in *On the Origin of Language*, trans. John H. Moran and Alexander Gode (Chicago: University of Chicago Press, 1966), 5–74.
[36] Robins, *Short History*, 166; cf. Kristeva, *Language*, 193–4, who places Herder, a transitional figure, at the beginning of the historicist period of linguistics (see later in this chapter). See Johann Gottfried Herder, *Essay on the Origin of Language,* in *On the Origin of Language*, trans. John H. Moran and Alexander Gode (Chicago: University of Chicago Press, 1966), 87–166.
[37] Herder's thought also led to development of German historicism, with its emphasis upon cultural relativism and historical destiny that eventually led, through Wilhelm von Humboldt (see later in this chapter), to the German socialist, or Nazi, movement. See D. W. Bebbington, *Patterns in History: A Christian View* (Downers Grove, IL: InterVarsity, 1979), 92–116.

The effects of such rationalist thought are also found in discussion of language during this period. Language discoveries of the rationalist period include those of William Jones (1746–94)—a British judge in India who was expert or competent in twenty-eight languages—who posited that Sanskrit, Latin, Greek, and the Germanic languages had historical relations. He summarizes his view of Sanskrit in relation to other languages in this way: "The *Sanscrit* [sic] language, whatever be its antiquity, is of a wonderful structure; more perfect than the *Greek*, more copious than the *Latin*, and more exquisitely refined than either, yet bearing to both of them a stronger affinity, both in the roots of verbs and in the forms of grammar, than could possibly have been produced by accident."[38] This kind of statement typifies rationalism, in which judgments are made on the basis of conformity to a perceived ideal organization and rational structure. The Cambridge Platonist James Harris (1758–1835), now not very much remembered, began "by deducing grammar from ontology, since the verb, to him, denotes nothing less than existence itself."[39] Besides illustrating the rationalist tendency to unhelpfully equate philosophy with language, Harris's view of the verb, however, further includes the idea that "the character of human existence" is "one that is radically temporal, marked by the pervasive presence of time in the ever mutable existence as its constant 'Concomitant.'"[40] The tense-forms "'define with more precision, what kind of Past, Present, or Future' (98) is represented by a given tense."[41] A final example among others that might be cited was Harris's nemesis, John Horne Tooke (1736–1812). Following in the line of Condillac regarding language development, Tooke believed there were two parts of speech, the noun and the verb, from which all other classes were derived, a view based upon philosophical presuppositions. He extended his theory of derivation to word development, using an agglutinating paradigm (words are like building blocks that attach parts to each other at the ends),[42] a theory that is limited at best as many languages are not constructed along such rationalistically consistent lines.

The rationalist period of language study was characterized by a philosophical orientation that logically deduced the nature of language from prior philosophical understandings and beliefs, usually grounded in beliefs about reality or metaphysics. As a result, there was the notion of better and worse formed languages, thought and language were inseparable and linked in a direct relationship, tense-forms indicated reality grounded in time, and more complex forms were developed from simpler ones to the point of language beginning with a minimal number of elements. Even if the historical paradigm had some heuristic value, the basis of language study in philosophy and belief about reality proved to be too much to sustain in later even historical thought.

We now turn to New Testament Greek grammatical discussion that reflects the rationalism of this period. Georg Benedikt Winer's (1789–1858) *Grammatik des neutestamentlichen Sprachidioms*, although not the first New Testament Greek grammar,

---

[38]William Jones, *Discourses: Delivered at the Asiatick Society 1785–1792* (repr., London: Routledge/Thoemmes, 1993), 34. Cf. Robins, *Short History*, 149–50.
[39]Hye-Joon Yoon, *The Rhetoric of Tenses in Adam Smith's The Wealth of Nations* (Leiden: Brill, 2018), 47.
[40]Yoon, *Rhetoric of Tenses*, 48.
[41]Yoon, *Rhetoric of Tenses*, 49, referring to p. 98 in James Harris's *Hermes, or, a Philosophical Inquiry Concerning Universal Grammar* (London, 1765).
[42]John Horne Tooke, ΕΠΕΑ ΠΤΕΡΟΕΝΤΑ, *or the Diversions of Purley*, ed. Richard Taylor, 2 vols. (London: Thomas Tegg, 1829; repr., London: Routledge/Thoemmes, 1993).

was the most important and fully represented the rationalist period. The first was that of Georg Pasor (1570–1637) in 1655.[43] Even though there had been a couple earlier ones, Winer's was the most important and exemplified the rationalist principles. It has certainly been the most enduring, even to the present. Winer was a major figure in nineteenth-century German intellectual life. Although not as widely known today as he once was and as he deserves to be, Winer's influence upon New Testament scholarship was immense, even if most of it lately being indirect. Educated at the University of Leipzig, Winer was head of the Leipzig University library, then a professor in Erlangen, before returning to Leipzig in 1832 as professor of theology. Winer wrote on a range of subjects, including various theological and biblical topics, but he is best known for his work in languages. This includes writing an introduction to Aramaic and his major grammar of New Testament Greek.[44]

Winer was also on the forefront of a new phase of Greek language study, even if, as we shall see, he was not up to date with wider language study, as he wrote in the rationalist mode even though the rationalist period, as previously discussed, had already passed. Prior to Winer, study of Greek was dominated by the categories of Latin grammar being used for both labeling and description, along with a basic descriptivism sometimes verging on prescriptivism. The rise of rationalist thought in the eighteenth century led to a rethinking of how to study ancient languages. Winer was the first to apply systematically the rationalist framework to understanding New Testament Greek, in which Greek was seen as a logically based set of categories. The first edition of Winer's *Grammatik* appeared in 1822, and it went through a succession of editions during Winer's lifetime in 1828, 1830, 1836, 1844, and the sixth edition in 1855. After his death, there was a seventh and then an incomplete eighth edition.[45] There were also several English translations, the most well-known one by W. Fiddian Moulton (father of the well-known English Greek grammarian James Hope Moulton; see later in this chapter) in 1870, with two further editions (1877, 1882).[46]

All of Winer's grammar is worth reading, but the introduction provides especially instructive reading, because it establishes Winer's presuppositions regarding language. These presuppositions are arguably well represented in the subtitle to the English translation in which Greek is said to be a "sure basis" for exegesis, thus grounding exegesis in language and hence in a view of reality. These presuppositions include Winer's attempt to see New Testament Greek reflecting the fact that Jewish writers wrote in contemporary

---

[43] Georg Pasor, *Grammatica graeca sacra Novi Testamenti Domini nostri Jesu Christi* (1655). He also published the first New Testament Greek(-Latin) lexicon.

[44] Winer is often remembered as the teacher of Constantine Tischendorf. He inspired in Tischendorf a love for exegesis of the Greek New Testament through his development of the seminar style of teaching, rather than simply using lectures. See Stanley E. Porter, *Constantine Tischendorf: The Life and Work of a 19th Century Bible Hunter* (London: Bloomsbury, 2015), 11–76.

[45] Georg Benedikt Winer, *Grammatik des neutestamentlichen Sprachidioms* (Leipzig: Vogel, 1822; 2nd ed., 1828; 3rd ed., 1830; 4th ed., 1836; 5th ed., 1844; 6th ed., 1855), all during Winer's lifetime. The seventh edition was prepared by Gottlieb Lünemann (Leipzig: Vogel, 1868), and an eighth edition was begun by Paul Schmiedel, but never finished (Göttingen: Vandenhoeck & Ruprecht, 1894–8). Winer uses Tischendorf's second edition of the Greek New Testament in his sixth edition.

[46] G. B. Winer, *A Treatise on the Grammar of New Testament Greek, Regarded as a Sure Basis for New Testament Exegesis*, trans. W. F. Moulton, 3rd ed. (Edinburgh: T&T Clark, 1882). For an introduction to this translation, including information on both Winer and William Fiddian Moulton his translator, see Stanley E. Porter, "William Fiddian Moulton and Greek Grammar: An Introduction to Moulton's Translation of Winer's Grammar," in Winer, *A Treatise on the Grammar of New Testament Greek, Regarded as a Sure Basis for New Testament Exegesis*, trans. William Fiddian Moulton, 3rd ed. (Edinburgh: T&T Clark, 1882; repr., London: Bloomsbury, 2019), xi–xl. Other translators of Winer into English were Moses Stuart and Edward Robinson in 1825, J. H. Agnew and O. G. Ebbeke in 1839, Edward Masson in 1859, and J. Henry Thayer (of Lünemann's edition) in 1869.

Greek. The resulting mix of their Greek and Semitic languages formed a unified type of grammar, what he calls a "single syntax."[47] Winer specifically speaks of the "rational method" of Greek language study, which he equates with an empirical approach.[48] Winer's recognition of his place within the history of Greek grammar is important in understanding his approach to his subsequent discussion. He follows rationalist principles throughout, including rationalist principles of consistency and regularity based upon empirical evidence (or at least the perception of empirical evidence) being applied as a conscious effort to counter the perceived subjectivity of pre-modern thought.

As a result, the study of language was early on an extension of empirical and rationalist approaches to philosophy, often with undue influence of Latin. This approach is specifically seen in Winer's grammar when he confines the meanings of the Greek tense-forms to temporal categories, no doubt based upon the use of his metalanguage German and perhaps because of some of the prevailing thought regarding tense-forms and reality (as well as views of the temporal meanings of Latin verb forms). As a result, Winer states that "Strictly and properly speaking no one of these tenses [of Greek] can ever stand for another"; for example the present tense-form is "used for the future in appearance only,"[49] because the label indicates that, logically and rationalistically speaking, it must only be a present tense-form.

> [W]here such an interchange seems to exist, either it exists in appearance only, there being in point of fact some assignable reason (especially of a rhetorical kind) why this tense is used and no other; or else it must be ascribed to a certain inexactness belonging to the popular language, through which the relation of time was not conceived and expressed with perfect precision.[50]

Winer cites not only the present tense-form "used for the future in appearance only ..."[51] but also the present tense-form "used for the aorist, as an historical tense ..."[52]

In all of these instances, Winer indicates that tense-substitution may occur but is apparent only because the label indicates that, logically and rationalistically speaking, it must only be a present tense-form. The strong equation of time and tense-form is clear in Winer and has come to be a legacy in Greek language study, at least up until being questioned in more recent times. Winer approaches the article similarly. Although he does not refer to a definite article, only the article, he states that "before a noun as a true article, it indicates that the object is conceived as definite, either from its nature, or from the context, or by reference to a circle of ideas which is assumed to be familiar to the reader's mind."[53] In other words, in rationalist fashion, the "true" article indicates

---

[47] Winer, *Grammar*, 3.
[48] Winer, *Grammar*, 7.
[49] Winer, *Grammar*, 331.
[50] Winer, *Grammar*, 331.
[51] Winer, *Grammar*, 331. Winer states further: "when an action still future is to be represented as being as good as already present, either because it is already firmly resolved on, or because it must ensue in virtue of some unalterable law (exactly as in Latin, German, etc.)." This statement is consistent with Winer's rationalist approach, as well as the influence of Latin and German on his conception of Greek.
[52] Winer, *Grammar*, 333. Winer continues: "only when the narrator wishes to bring a past event vividly before us, as if it were taking place at the present moment ..." This statement also is consistent with Winer's rationalist approach to the tense-forms, with absolute temporal reference governing tense conceptualization.
[53] Winer, *Grammar*, 131. Winer's appreciation of context or what might be called a presupposition pool in more recent linguistic thought is noteworthy, even if he forces this into the definiteness of the article.

definiteness, and by implication the lack of an article does not. Greek however has no definite article, simply an article, as there is no meaningful contrast within the article, but the terminology of "definiteness" seems to be based upon a principle of rationalist inclusiveness. More important, however, is Winer's reliance upon his rationalist and empirical approach to the study of Greek, an approach that reflects the rationalist age.

Winer's grammar would otherwise be simply a curiosity of linguistic history were it not for the fact that the rationalist approach was followed by others[54] and in fact is still widely found in New Testament Greek language study. The rationalist approach is in evidence in the approach found in numerous beginning Greek grammars, where tense-forms and temporality are equated as if there is an inherent logic in their meanings and names, reference is often made to the "definite" article (Greek has no definite article), and other similar comments are made. I have surveyed numerous such elementary grammars, and the vast majority fall within this category, from that of William Rainey Harper (and Revere Franklin Weidner) (1893) through J. Gesham Machen (1923) to William Mounce (1993; 4th ed. 2019) to probably Daniel Zacharias (2018), and many others besides.[55]

Even more disturbing, I believe, is the fact that several widely used intermediate-level grammars continue to reflect the rationalist approach as well. There are far fewer intermediate grammars that have been written in the last hundred years, but the most obvious examples of the rationalist approach are found in Daniel Wallace's *Greek Grammar beyond the Basics* and the more recent Andreas Köstenberger, Benjamin Merkle, and Robert Plummer's *Going Deeper with New Testament Greek*.[56] These grammars may not at first appear to be rationalist grammars, because they discuss topics within modern linguistics, but they nevertheless seem to be written from this standpoint. The authors were probably unaware of such issues when they wrote their grammars, because they probably believed that they were simply following the tradition of how New Testament Greek grammars are written. Wallace, to his credit, accepts such ostensibly linguistic notions as "semantics and semantic situation," "synchronic priority," and "structural priority."[57] However, his few modern linguistics categories are found side by side with some nonlinguistic judgments. For example, he states that his volume contains a "multitude of syntactical categories, some of which have never been in print before," "no discussion of discourse analysis," "minimal material on lexico-syntactic categories," defaulting to the lexicons, the concept of "undisputed examples," a resurgence of

---

[54] E.g., Thomas Sheldon Green, *A Treatise on the Grammar of the New Testament Dialect; Embracing Observations on the Literal Interpretation of Numerous Passages* (London: Bagster, 1842); Alexander Buttmann, *A Grammar of the New Testament Greek*, trans. J. H. Thayer (Andover: Warren F. Draper, 1880).

[55] I have classified the following, roughly in chronological order of their first edition: William Rainey Harper and Revere Franklin Weidner (1893), J. Gresham Machen (1923), Ray Summers (1950), Eric Jay (1958), Samuel Cartledge (1959), D. F. Hudson (1960), John Wenham (1965), Ernest Cadman Colwell with Ernest Tune (1965), Molly Whittaker (1969), Edward W. Goodrick (1976; rev. 1980), Cullen Story and Lyle Story (1979; rev. 2018, but with some modifications), R. A. Martin (1980), James Found (1983), James Hewett (1986; rev. 2009), John Dobson (1988; rev. 1992), James Efird (1990), James Swetnam (1992), Frank Beetham (1992), William Mounce (1993), William Countryman (1993), David Alan Black (1993), Clayton Croy (1999), A. K. M. Adam (1999), Reto Schoch (2000), Peter Kevern and Paula Gooder (2004), Gavin Betts (2004), B. H. McLean (2011), and probably H. Daniel Zacharias (2018). There are no doubt others.

[56] Daniel B. Wallace, *Greek Grammar beyond the Basics: An Exegetical Syntax of the New Testament* (Grand Rapids: Zondervan, 1995); Andreas J. Köstenberger, Benjamin L. Merkle, and Robert L. Plummer, *Going Deeper with New Testament Greek: An Intermediate Study of the Grammar and Syntax of the New Testament* (Nashville: B&H, 2016); cf. Merkle and Plummer, *Greek for Life: Strategies for Learning, Retaining, and Reviving New Testament Greek* (Grand Rapids: Baker, 2017).

[57] Wallace, *Greek Grammar*, xi, xvi, 4–6.

diachrony, a compromised notion of structure that does not include system, and his very odd (and unlinguistic) belief in the "cryptic nature of language."[58] These claims distance Wallace's work from a modern linguistic approach and indicate in many instances a rationalist approach.

Köstenberger, Merkle, and Plummer, however, do not even include as much linguistic information as does Wallace. Nevertheless, although both these grammars admittedly refer to more recent linguistic notions, in particular study of verbal aspect when they treat the verb (although I do not think that their understanding on the matter is correct; but that is another issue), both also retain constant reminders of the rationalist approach to language that often culminates in a taxonomic logical structure for description of various elements of the language. The Greek language is not seen as a coordinated system, but as a logically prescribed set of options to be consistently filled. Wallace therefore uses the English translation "of" as a means of characterizing many of the uses of the genitive case. The use of translation in this way is characteristic of traditional grammar of the rationalist (and comparative-historical) period. However, the use of English "of" is so highly problematic that it cannot provide a guide to Greek usage. Wallace then attempts to provide a complete taxonomy of the case by enumerating thirty-three different uses of the genitive.[59] He provides an extended defense of temporality by equating tense-form and time, which we earlier saw distinguished the rationalist philosophers, and by appealing to similar arguments as the rationalists utilized, including comparisons to other languages and philosophical principles (such as Occam's razor).

Köstenberger, Merkle, and Plummer, while perhaps in some ways an improvement by bringing up to date some of the recent discussions of topics, attempt to define the meanings of the tense-forms in rationalist terms (such as when they define stative aspect as a "combinatory aspect" merging perfective and imperfective, which notions go back at least as far as Friedrich Blass),[60] utilize a traditional lexical-incremental form of morphology (each morpheme adds what amounts to lexical information),[61] and attempt to find a place within their conspectus for all of the previous suggestions, such as coordinating the five and eight-case systems.[62] Köstenberger, Merkle, and Plummer definitely seem to reflect the Enlightenment quest for certainty when they speak of applying a particular grammatical tendency to save "the reader from drawing the wrong conclusion."[63] Despite

---

[58] Wallace, *Greek Grammar*, xii–xvii, 2, 4–9. For more detail on Wallace's grammar, see Stanley E. Porter, "So What Have We Learned in the Last Thirty Years of Greek Linguistic Study?" in *Getting into the Text: New Testament Essays in Honor of David Alan Black*, ed. David L. Aiken and Thomas W. Hudgins (Eugene, OR: Pickwick, 2017), 9–38, esp. 13–14.
[59] Wallace, *Greek Grammar*, 72–5.
[60] Köstenberger, Merkle, and Plummer, *Going Deeper*, 231; cf. Friedrich Blass, *Grammatik des Neutestamentlichen Griechisch* (Göttingen: Vandenhoeck & Ruprecht, 1896), 194, and others since.
[61] Köstenberger, Merkle, and Plummer, *Going Deeper*, 190. The category is from Gregory Stump, *Inflectional Morphology: A Theory of Paradigm Structure* (Cambridge: Cambridge University Press, 2001), passim. The lexical-incremental view is also found in William Mounce, *Morphology of Biblical Greek* (Grand Rapids: Zondervan, 1994).
[62] Köstenberger, Merkle, and Plummer, *Going Deeper*, 51–2.
[63] Köstenberger, Merkle, and Plummer, *Going Deeper*, 50.

any agreement (or disagreement) I may have with both Wallace and Köstenberger et al., my point here is that their approach reflects the rationalist approach to language.

The rationalist school of language thought has now been superseded, although some of its contributions have been incorporated into subsequent thought about language. However, in study of the Greek New Testament there are still significant works—especially beginning grammars, but also several intermediate grammars—that continue to be written within this school of language thought and continue to have influence upon the learning and knowledge of the Greek language.

Comparative-Historical Language Study

Comparative-historical language study emerged in the nineteenth century from the rationalist approach to language of the previous period. There was not a hard line that divided the two, as they shared some major assumptions. The rationalist period already had a historical and even comparative component to it, but comparative-historical language study drew upon more philosophically limited empirical speculation. This comparative study occurred as more languages came to be known and then to be studied in relation to each other and under the influence of the developmental hypothesis of knowledge that came to dominate the period and eventually ended with the rise of modern linguistics (1800–1916). The rise of modern linguistics is usually dated to the publication in 1916 of Ferdinand de Saussure's (1857–1913) *Course in General Linguistics*,[64] but I will challenge that assumption in Chapter Two. In any case, this provides a terminal date for this period in the first quarter of the twentieth century.

There are several major intellectual influences upon the development of the comparative-historical period of language study. The two most important are probably the developmental hypothesis and the rise of Romanticism. The developmental hypothesis, already adumbrated in previous philosophical thought, came to full expression in the writings of the philosopher and sociologist/anthropologist Herbert Spencer (1820–1903). Spencer took an expansive view of the notion of evolution (writing relatively independently of Charles Darwin, and in fact slightly before him) and applied it in a teleological and positivist way to phenomena outside of the natural world, and hence to society as well.[65] Spencer's views had a huge impact upon the nineteenth century and specifically the developmental hypothesis that came to drive language study, as well as having more widespread influence upon numerous other fields. The comparative-historical approach was also influenced by the philosophical movement called Romanticism (itself heavily influenced by German idealism), with its emphasis upon the self, subjectivity, and experience,[66] and in particular by the writings of the Romantic poet and philosopher Friedrich Schlegel (1772–1829). Schlegel helped to turn the emphasis of linguistics from the rationalist philosophical approach that looked to external relations to the human in order to situate reality to an orientation that attended to the internal structure of the language, in particular its morphology or the small

---

[64] See Robins, *Short History*, 180–217.
[65] Stanislav Andreski, ed., *Herbert Spencer: Structure, Function and Evolution* (London: Michael Joseph, 1971). Cf. Frederick Copleston, *A History of Philosophy*, vol. 8 part 1 (Garden City, NY: Image, 1966), 142–68.
[66] On Romanticism, see Hugh Honour, *Romanticism* (Harmondsworth: Penguin, 1979); and Roy Porter and Mikuláš Teich, eds., *Romanticism in National Context* (Cambridge: Cambridge University Press, 1988). Paul Johnson, *The Birth of the Modern: World Society 1815–1830* (New York: HarperCollins, 1991), links Romanticism to the rise of modernism.

identifiable structures of meaning. Schlegel himself apparently formulated the term "comparative philology" (*vergleichende Grammatik*) (1808) to describe the comparisons of both derivational and inflectional morphology that he thought were important to establish the structural relationships among languages.[67]

The comparative-historical approach to language attracted the efforts of some of the most productive thinkers of any period.[68] It is often said to have been initiated by two early, seminal writers. The first was the Danish linguist Rasmus Rask (1787–1832), who was more of a typologist than a historicist or geneticist,[69] and the second was the German linguist Jacob Grimm (1785–1863). Rask wrote grammars for several languages, such as Old Norse (1811) and Old English (1817), and based upon his comparative studies formulated a number of laws regarding sound changes across languages and showing their relationships. Grimm, along with his brother, was responsible for documenting the German fairy-tale tradition among their major accomplishments (they were early form critics). Jacob wrote the first Germanic grammar (1819–37), in which he developed terminology still used in linguistics (and probably known to students of Greek), such as references to strong and weak verbs, ablaut or vowel gradation (e.g., the vowel change in λείπω and ἔλιπον), and umlaut to describe conditioned vowel change. By so doing, Grimm founded the discipline of *Germanistik* or the study of Germanic languages.[70] Grimm's sound-change law (or Grimm's generalization, as he realized) accounts for consonant changes among some indo-Germanic languages (later supplemented by Verner's law on accent), but also recognizes the individual character of languages and hence nations (following Herder). This is considered one of the major breakthroughs of comparative philology, even if it has subsequently been subject to serious modification and refinement.[71]

The importance of the comparative-historical movement was fully developed in the work of the German linguist Franz Bopp (1791–1867), who wrote several major works in comparative grammar in the mid-nineteenth century. His first major work compared the conjugation system of Sanskrit with Greek, Latin, Persian, and German (1816), in an attempt to reconstruct the grammar of their common original language that had given rise to what came to be called the Indo-European family of languages.[72] He later wrote an important comparative grammar (1857).[73] In doing so, Bopp developed what came

---

[67]Robins, *Short History*, 187. See Friedrich Schlegel, *Ueber die Sprache und Weisheit der Indier: Ein Beitrag zur Begründung der Alterthumstunde* (Heidelberg: Mohr und Zimmer, 1808; repr., London: Routledge/Thoemmes, 1995), 84. On his (and his brother, A. W. Schlegel's) contribution to Romanticism, see J. G. Robertson, *A History of German Literature*, ed. Dorothy Reich, 6th ed. (Edinburgh: William Blackwood, 1970), 372–6.
[68]Representative essays by many of the leading figures of the comparative-historical approach are found in Winfred P. Lehmann, ed., *Reader in Nineteenth-Century Historical Indo-European Linguistics* (Bloomington: Indiana University Press, 1967), including essays by Rasmus Rask, Franz Bopp, Jacob Grimm, Wilhelm von Humboldt, August Schleicher, Karl Brugmann, Eduard Sievers, and Ferdinand de Saussure.
[69]Kristeva, *Language*, 198–9, but who notes Rask's rejection of Romanticism, even though he wrote comparative Indo-European works.
[70]Jacob Grimm, *Deutsche Grammatik* (Göttingen: Dieterichschen Buchhandlung, 1819–37).
[71]See N. E. Collinge, *The Laws of Indo-European* (Amsterdam: John Benjamins, 1985), 63–76, where he also includes discussion of Rask; cf. 203–16 on Verner's law, named after Karl Verner (1846–96), a Danish language scholar.
[72]Franz Bopp, *Über das Conjugationssystem der Sanskritsprache in Vergleichung mit jenem der griechischen, lateinischen, persischen und germanischen Sprache*, ed. R. J. Windischmann (Frankfurt am Main: Andreäischen, 1816; repr., London: Routledge/Thoemmes, 1995).
[73]Franz Bopp, *A Comparative Grammar of the Sanscrit, Zend, Greek, Latin, Lithuanian, Gothic, German, and Sclavonic Languages*, ed. H. H. Wilson, trans. Lieutenant Eastwick, 3 parts in 2 vols. (London: James Madden, 1845–50; repr., Hildesheim: Georg Olms, 1985).

to be recognized as the principles and practices of comparative philology, including how one describes their historical and genetic relationships as the means of describing and understanding them. The German philosopher and linguist Wilhelm von Humboldt (1767–1835), who, along with his brother, founded the Humboldt University in Berlin, was a highly creative and original thinker. He saw language as having its own energy, originating from an inner language form (1836).[74] Humboldt's emphasis upon the dynamic "energy" that exists between the speaker and the hearer has been variously interpreted as an incipient functionalism and a creative capacity that anticipated the Universal Grammar of Noam Chomsky.[75] In his work, Humboldt followed those who defined the types of language as agglutinative, isolating, and flexional, categories that are still often used to describe languages typologically. As previously mentioned, Humboldt also saw language as particular to individual nations or groups of speakers and as undergoing development at varying rates and in varying ways, a view that fed into the rise of German historicism. The German linguist August Schleicher (1821–68) made a major advance in comparative philology with his tree diagram of the relations among the languages, which had the effect of establishing both relational and historical (synchronic and diachronic) interdependencies among languages (1862),[76] even if diachrony took precedence over synchrony during the comparative-historical period. This interrelationship also had the effect of demoting Sanskrit, which was forced to occupy its rightful place in the hierarchy and not be seen as the near-perfect language that took pre-eminence above others, and of reinforcing a linguistic relativism among languages, again ripe for German historicism.

This comparative-historical period arguably reached its tumultuous culmination in the thought of the New Grammarians (German *Junggrammatiker*).[77] These New Grammarians included the German linguist Karl Brugmann (1849–1919) and his fellow scholar Berthold Delbrück (1842–1922), who together wrote one of the most important works outlining the field of comparative philology (1886–1900).[78] The New or Young Grammarians were an informal group of younger generation German (and sometimes other) linguists who took a scientistic approach to language and teased out the implications of their predecessors regarding various rules of language, often alienating the older generation of scholars who were more biologically oriented. As a result, the New Grammarians believed that all sound changes, regardless of the languages involved (and they were being compared), followed exceptionless rules. In order to formulate such rules of change, the New Grammarians in effect developed the idea of dialectology and principles of language conservatism, as means of explaining exceptions, and this led to development of language geography. In 1885, as previously noted, Brugmann published the first edition of his Greek grammar, reflecting comparative-historical

---

[74] Wilhelm von Humboldt, *Über die Verschiedenheit des menschlichen Sprachbaues und ihren Einfluss auf die geistige Entwickelung des Menschengeschlechts* (Berlin: Königlichen Akademie der Wissenschaften, 1836; ET *On Language: On the Diversity of Human Language Construction and Its Influence on the Mental Development of the Human Species*, ed. Michael Losonsky, trans. Peter Heath [Cambridge: Cambridge University Press, 1999]). Humboldt's so-called "Kawi Introduction" was the first of three volumes of exposition of the Kawi language found in Java. Humboldt finished the manuscript around the time of his death, and it was published posthumously.
[75] See Robins, *Short Grammar*, 192–3. The notion of the creative use of language associated with Chomsky's view of language has been strongly attacked.
[76] August Schleicher, *Compendium der vergleichenden Grammatik der indogermanischen Sprachen; kurzer Abriss einer Laut- und Formenlehre der indogermanischen Ursprache* (Weimar: Hermann Böhlau, 1861; 4th ed., 1876).
[77] Kurt R. Jankowsky, *The Neogrammarians*, JLSMi 116 (The Hague: Mouton, 1972).
[78] Karl Brugmann and Berthold Delbrück, *Grundriss der vergleichenden Grammatik der Indogermanischen Sprachen*, 5 vols. (Strassburg: Trübner, 1886–1900). See also Brugmann, *Kurze Vergleichende Grammatik der Indogermanische Sprachen*, 3 vols. (Strassburg: Trübner, 1903).

principles and introducing the term *Aktionsart* to the field of Greek grammar (even if similar concepts were already found in such authors as Georg Curtius [1820–85]).⁷⁹ Saussure, a student of Brugmann, was himself a member of this group that marked the transition from emphasis upon diachronic to synchronic study of language and the advent of what has come to be called modern linguistics. I will say more on this transition in Chapter Two.

One can see that comparative historicism has several similarities with the earlier rationalist period, including further development of the historical and comparative dimensions. However, comparative historicism also made its own contribution to language study. In fact, it is still one of the most productive periods of language study, as new questions of language were addressed especially with German scholarly rigor. These comparative-historical features included the predominance of the developmental theory that focused upon explanations of language origins, diachrony taking precedence over synchrony (a clear distinction between the two occurred later), description of intricate and complex relations among languages, and detailed descriptions of individual elements of these languages.

Three major grammars of New Testament Greek that reflect the comparative-historical linguistic perspective were written during this time and continue to influence its study. They continue to be the most widely used reference grammars in English-language New Testament scholarship, as they are virtually the only ones having been written. The first major comparative-historical New Testament Greek grammar was published by Friedrich Blass in 1896, followed soon afterwards by James Hope Moulton's *Prolegomena*, published in 1906, and A. T. Robertson's massive grammar in 1914.

Friedrich Blass (1843–1907), who was a professor first in Kiel and then Halle, was a renowned German classical philologist whose areas of established competence included producing critical editions of ancient authors (his major area of expertise was textual criticism), addressing topics in New Testament studies, and writing several different works on language.⁸⁰ His New Testament Greek grammar,⁸¹ which first appeared in 1896, was a transitional comparative-historical treatment of the Greek of the New Testament. In his preface to the first edition—dedicated to the German philologist Professor August Fick (1833–1916), who was professor of comparative philology at Göttingen University and then Breslau—Blass thanks Fick for his teaching him Sanskrit, and now, even though he did not follow in the same path of comparative language study but of Greek philology, he is offering this book on Greek to him. He notes his research interests in the earliest forms of language and its later developments, and hence the relationship of New Testament Greek to Attic, reflective of the concerns of both classical and comparative philology. Blass sees the Greek of the New Testament as not as rich as Attic, but constituting its own language system.⁸² In other words, Blass, although not a comparative philologian, places

---

⁷⁹Brugmann, *Griechische Grammatik*. Cf. the work of Curtius previously mentioned, including also Georg Curtius, *Griechische Schulgrammatik* (Prague: F. Tempsky, 1852).
⁸⁰See Ryder A. Wishart, "Friedrich Blass and A. T. Robertson: Comprehensive and Comparative Greek Grammars from the Modern Vantage Point," in *Pillars in the History of Biblical Interpretation, Volume 3: Further Essays on Prevailing Methods*, ed. Stanley E. Porter and Zachary K. Dawson, MBSS 6 (Eugene, OR: Pickwick, 2021), 89–109.
⁸¹Blass, *Grammatik*, with all subsequent editions published by the same publisher, Vandenhoeck & Ruprecht (see the next page for the dates of publication). See Stanley E. Porter and Jeffrey T. Reed, "Greek Grammar since BDF: A Retrospective and Prospective Analysis," *FN* 4 (1991): 143–64, esp. 143–9, where not only is the grammar's contrasting perspective with that of modern linguistics noted, but criticism of several specific features is made, including its comparison of New Testament with classical Greek, its lack of a systematic approach to language structure, its lack of a rigorous and explicit semantic terminology, and its tendency to understand Greek through translation into German or English.
⁸²Blass, *Grammatik*, iii–viii, his preface.

his Greek grammar within the wider field of comparative study, a program he continues throughout the book by bringing into play comparisons with contemporary Hellenistic Greek, some later ecclesial Greek, and certainly earlier, especially Attic, Greek.

Blass's grammar has had an interesting and continuing history. The first edition was translated by the British Septuagint scholar Henry St. John Thackeray into English in 1898. The German went through subsequent reprintings and editions in 1902, 1911, and then in a fourth edition by the Swiss comparative philologian Albert Debrunner (1884–1958) in 1913 (which introduced the differentiation between main and subordinate text by type size), then 1921, 1931, a more substantial revision in 1943, 1949, 1954, 1959, 1961, 1965 with a supplementary volume by David Tabachowitz, 1970 with a similar supplement, 1976 and subsequently edited by Friedrich Rehkopf, 1979, 1984, 1990, and 2001. The well-known English edition by the American scholar and iconoclast Robert Funk was a translation (1961) of the ninth and tenth German editions of 1954 and 1959.[83] The most important feature to note about this grammar, however, is that, no matter how many editions (in many cases being mostly reprintings) it has undergone, the grammar is in its essentials the same, with its comparative-historical dimension gaining in explicitness especially through the work of Debrunner. The comparative element was enhanced by the work of Debrunner beginning with the fourth edition (e.g., placing Semitic discussion before Latin), and retained in later editions and the translation by Funk. The number of paragraphs has been expanded, and some of the wording has been changed, but an examination of the actual content reveals much of the same grammar.

James Hope Moulton (1863–1917), who was a devout Methodist who became Greenwood Professor of Hellenistic Greek and Indo-European Philology in Manchester University, was educated as a comparative philologian at Cambridge, studying with some of the best-known comparative philologists of his day. He acknowledges that he writes from a comparative standpoint in the "Preface" to the second edition of his *Prolegomena*, the first of what was then projected as a three-volume grammar of the Greek of the New Testament.[84] When the German scholar G. Adolf Deissmann (1866–1937) recognized that the Greek of the New Testament was similar in both lexis and syntax to the documentary papyri being discovered in Egypt near the end of the nineteenth century,[85] Moulton took up the challenge to describe how the syntax of the Greek of the New Testament was similar to that of these papyri. Moulton published his *Prolegomena* in 1906 and it went through two quick subsequent editions in 1906 and 1908, with Moulton adding two appendixes. Moulton then undertook work on the second volume, on accidence and word-formation. He had written about two-thirds of this volume when the First World War erupted. Moulton went on a teaching and missionary tour to India from 1916 to 1917, as he was a recognized expert in Indian religion, in particular Zoroastrianism,

---

[83] Friedrich Blass and Albert Debrunner, *A Greek Grammar of the New Testament and Other Early Christian Literature*, trans. Robert W. Funk (Chicago: University of Chicago Press, 1961).

[84] James Hope Moulton, *Prolegomena*, vol. 1 of *A Grammar of New Testament Greek* by James Hope Moulton (Edinburgh: T&T Clark, 1906; 2nd ed., 1906; 3rd ed., 1908), vii–xv. See Stanley E. Porter, "James Hope Moulton and Koine Greek: An Introduction to Moulton's *Prolegomena*," in Moulton, *Prolegomena*, vol. 1 of *A Grammar of New Testament Greek*, 3rd ed. (Edinburgh: T&T Clark, 1908; repr., London: Bloomsbury, 2019), vii–xlv.

[85] G. Adolf Deissmann, *Bible Studies*, trans. Alexander Grieve, 2nd ed. (Edinburgh: T&T Clark, 1903); Deissmann, *Light from the Ancient East*, trans. L. R. M. Strachan (London: Hodder and Stoughton, 1910). Deissmann and Moulton were joined as a triumvirate in arguing for the koine Greek of the New Testament by Albert Thumb (1865–1915), *Die griechische Sprache im Zeitalter des Hellenismus: Beiträge zur Geschichte und Beurteilung der κοινή* (Strassburg: Trübner, 1901).

while the theological colleges in Britain were closed during the war. On his return trip from India, having met his friend J. Rendel Harris (1852–1941) in Egypt, Moulton was crossing the Mediterranean when his ship was sunk by a German U-boat. Moulton died in a life raft from exposure in April 1917, leaving his grammar unfinished.

Moulton's second volume on accidence and word-formation was finished by his student Wilbert Francis Howard (1880–1952), who completed the last section of the book, the introduction, and an appendix that Moulton himself had planned to write on Semitisms in the New Testament, and published the entire volume in three fascicles over ten years.[86] The major controversy regarding this volume is whether Moulton himself would have modified his views regarding Semitic influence on the Greek of the New Testament, as Howard contended and to some extent reflected in the appendix. The third and an additional fourth volume in the series, on *Syntax* and *Style*, were written by Nigel Turner (1916–70), but he does not follow the same language theory and reverts to a style of thought that precedes the rationalist period in his belief in a special, almost Holy Ghost, Greek.[87] The comparative philological approach of Moulton is seen in how he situates the Greek of the Hellenistic era in relation to the development of Greek, one of the major frameworks of the comparative-historical method. This is explicitly seen in his first chapter, where he offers his general description of the Greek of the New Testament in relation to the common or koine Greek and distinguishes it from other views of the evidence, in light of the discoveries of Deissmann and others.

The culmination of the comparative-historical method in the study of the Greek of the New Testament is seen in the massive grammar of the American Southern Baptist scholar A. T. Robertson (1863–1934).[88] This grammar, which was published in its first edition in 1914, first began, as Robertson tells us in the Preface to the first edition, as an attempt to revise Winer's grammar. He soon realized, however, that such a plan would not work out, because "[s]o much progress had been made in comparative philology and historical grammar since Winer wrote his great book."[89] Robertson recognized that Moulton was engaged in a common endeavor, but he pressed on, and the result was a grammar of nearly 1,400 pages (including indexes) and addenda that took it to over 1,450 pages, with the addenda having their own indexes! Robertson provides a 24-page list of works most often cited, including two additional pages for the third edition, and the list is full of comparative philologians as well as others.[90] These include: Blass

---

[86] James Hope Moulton and Wilbert Francis Howard, *Accidence and Word-Formation*, vol. 2 of *A Grammar of New Testament Greek* by James Hope Moulton (Edinburgh: T&T Clark, 1919–29). Cf. Stanley E. Porter, "James Hope Moulton and Wilbert Francis Howard and Greek Phonology and Morphology: An Introduction to Moulton and Howard's *Accidence and Word-Formation*," in Moulton and Howard, *Accidence and Word-Formation*, vol. 2 of *A Grammar of New Testament Greek* by James Hope Moulton (Edinburgh: T&T Clark, 1919–29; repr., London: Bloomsbury, 2019), ix–lxxii.

[87] Nigel Turner, *Syntax*, vol. 3 of *A Grammar of New Testament Greek* by James Hope Moulton (Edinburgh: T&T Clark, 1963). Cf. Stanley E. Porter, "Nigel Turner and Greek Syntax: An Introduction to Moulton's Third Volume, *Syntax*," in Turner, *Syntax*, vol. 3 of *A Grammar of New Testament Greek* by James Hope Moulton (Edinburgh: T&T Clark, 1963; repr., London: Bloomsbury, 2019), ix–l. Nigel Turner, *Style*, vol. 4 of *A Grammar of New Testament Greek* by James Hope Moulton (Edinburgh: T&T Clark, 1976). Cf. Stanley E. Porter, "Nigel Turner and Greek Style: An Introduction to Moulton's Fourth Volume, *Style*," in Turner, *Style*, vol. 4 of *A Grammar of New Testament Greek* by James Hope Moulton (Edinburgh: T&T Clark, 1976; repr., London: Bloomsbury, 2019), vii–xliv.

[88] A. T. Robertson, *A Grammar of the Greek New Testament in the Light of Historical Research* (Nashville: Broadman, 1914; 4th ed., 1934). On Robertson, see Wishart, "Blass," 89–109.

[89] Robertson, *Grammar*, vii–xv, quotation vii (in the edition of 1934).

[90] Robertson, *Grammar*, lxiii–lxxvi (in the edition of 1934).

(although note that he saw himself more as a classical philologist, even though he had studied comparative philology) and with him Debrunner, Bopp, Brugmann, Curtius, Delbrück, Peter Giles a contemporary of Moulton at Cambridge who wrote one of the best general introductions to comparative philology, Otto Hoffmann who wrote a historical account of the Greek dialects, A. N. Jannaris who wrote a historical Greek grammar (see later in this chapter), Paul Kretschmer, Karl Krumbacher, Antoine Meillet a transitional figure to modern linguistics, Moulton, Max Müller, Hermann Paul a New Grammarian, Eduard Schwyzer (or Schweizer), E. H. Sturtevant, Thumb, Jacob Wackernagel, W. D. Whitney the American Sanskrit scholar, and Joseph Wright.[91]

Robertson devotes his first chapter to positioning his grammar in relation to both his predecessors and the current thought on language. He notes the pre-Winer and then Winer periods, before referring to the, for him, "modern period." And for him, this was the modern or contemporary period. The modern period focuses upon Deissmann and Moulton, with Robertson wisely noting that many other contemporary contributors writing during the modern period still maintain the "old standpoint" (e.g., Edwin Hatch, William Henry Simcox, Philip Schaff, Joseph Viteau, E. A. Abbott, and Ernest De Witt Burton, some of whom specifically wrote on grammatical topics).[92] The new tools available for study by Robertson are headed by comparative philology, which Robertson calls a linguistic revolution, aided by Jones's discovery of Sanskrit and its relationship to Greek. Robertson concludes with a quick survey of scholarship from Bopp to Brugmann, with references to major scholars whose works he uses listed in his bibliography. Robertson then describes advances in Greek grammar and on particular authors, the texts now available, and the role of later Greek and other languages such as Hebrew and Aramaic. In other words, Robertson clearly positions his grammar as a comparative philological grammar informed by the most important comparative philologians, a view seen throughout his grammar with his attention to language development, comparisons with other languages (especially Sanskrit), and even the importance of viewing the language as a whole. The same perspective of comparative philology is reflected in Robertson's earlier beginning grammar, in which he acknowledges his debt to the well-known Baptist scholar and preacher John Broadus (1827–95) (and Robertson's father-in-law) for his introduction to comparative philology.[93]

---

[91]For those scholars whose works are not cited elsewhere, see Peter Giles, *A Short Manual of Comparative Philology*, 2nd ed. (London: Macmillan, 1901); Otto Hoffmann, *Die Griechischen Dialekte in ihrem historischen Zusammenhange*, 3 vols. (Göttingen: Vandenhoeck & Ruprecht, 1891-8); A. N. Jannaris, *A Historical Greek Grammar Chiefly of the Attic Dialect* (London: Macmillan 1897); Paul Kretschmer, *Einleitung in die Geschichte der Griechischen Sprache* (Göttingen: Vandenhoeck & Ruprecht, 1896); Karl Krumbacher, *Das Problem des neugriechischen Schriftsprache* (Munich: G. Frank'schen, 1902); Antoine Meillet, *Introduction à l'étude comparative des langues indo-européennes* (Paris: Hachette, 1903); Max Müller, *Three Lectures on the Science of Language* (Chicago: Open Court, 1891); Hermann Paul, *Principles of the History of Language*, trans. H. A. Strong (London: Longmans, Green, 1888); Eduard Schweizer, *Grammatik der Pergamenischen Inschriften* (Berlin: Weidmannsche, 1898); E. H. Sturtevant, *Studies in Greek Noun Formation*, 4 vols. (Chicago: University of Chicago Press, 1910-13); Jacob Wackernagel, *Lectures on Syntax*, ed. David Langslow (Oxford: Oxford University Press, 2009); William Dwight Whitney, *The Life and Growth of Language* (London: Kegan Paul, Trench, Trübner, 1875; repr., London: Routledge/Thoemmes, 1994); Joseph Wright, *Comparative Grammar of the Greek Language* (London: Oxford University Press, 1912).

[92]Robertson, *Grammar*, 5–7.

[93]A. T. Robertson, *A Short Grammar of the Greek New Testament* (New York: Hodder and Stoughton, 1908), x-xi. This same perspective was continued in subsequent editions, up to the final tenth edition published in 1933, with W. Hersey Davis, with no acknowledgment that anything had changed in linguistics. Robertson notes that Broadus was a student of Gessner Harrison (1807–62) at the University of Virginia, who lectured on the perspective of Bopp, the major figure in comparative philology. See also William Hersey Davis, *Beginner's Grammar of the Greek New Testament* (New York: Doran, 1923), where in the introduction Robertson notes Davis's reliance upon comparative historicists, such as Brugmann, Delbrück, Thumb, and Moulton.

The comparative-historical perspective has continued in New Testament Greek grammatical study in several ways, in large part because of reliance upon these reference grammars. These grammars still loom large in New Testament Greek studies and are readily and often cited, probably without much thought about the linguistic theory that lies behind them. Whereas there are very few contemporary elementary New Testament Greek grammars, at least that I have seen, that overtly reflect comparative philology, there are some more sustained grammatical treatments.[94] The first set of works is intermediate-level grammars that follow the comparative philological tradition. The long-time Vienna professor Ludwig Radermacher (1867–1952) wrote *Neutestamentliche Grammatik* (which has never been translated into English) in 1911,[95] a grammar clearly within the German grammatical tradition but with greater emphasis upon the Greek of the New Testament as the koine. H. E. Dana and Julius R. Mantey in their long-used grammar provide in many respects simply an intermediate-level summary of the major categories of Robertson's grammar.[96] William Chamberlain (1890–1958) published an exegetical grammar that he says falls within the "historical grammar" tradition.[97] He cites such scholars as Whitney on Sanskrit, Robertson, Moulton, and Deissmann as of particular importance. The grammar by Maximilian Zerwick (1901–75) from the outset notes that it follows in the tradition of Blass and Debrunner's grammar.[98] The Cambridge professor C. F. D. Moule's (1908–2007) idiom book, though not an overt work of comparative philology, is fashioned after that manner as well.[99] Moule discusses *Aktionsart*, what he calls "kind of action," but perhaps better action types or lexical aspect. Curtis Vaughan and Virtus Gideon in their workbook on intermediate grammar base their work on that of Dana and Mantey.[100] They are followed in a similar pattern by James Brooks and Carlton Winbery in their syntax of New Testament Greek that also utilizes the eight-case system with antecedents in Indo-European philology.[101] A final grammar to mention, but one that is also highly problematic to characterize, is by Heinrich von Siebenthal.[102] Although in some ways he is aware and wishes to discuss modern linguistic issues (such as verbal

---

[94] A few exceptions are William Sanford LaSor, *Handbook of New Testament Greek: An Inductive Approach Based on the Greek Text of Acts*, 2 vols. (Grand Rapids: Eerdmans, 1973), who patterns his work mostly after comparative historicists, although he also has many elements of the rationalist grammar; and Thomas A. Robinson, *Mastering New Testament Greek: Essential Tools for Students* (Peabody, MA: Hendrickson, 2007), who emphasizes cognate vocabulary across languages, and even includes an appendix on Grimm's law.
[95] Ludwig Radermacher, *Neutestamentliche Grammatik*, HNT 1 (Tübingen: Mohr Siebeck, 1911; 2nd ed., 1925).
[96] H. E. Dana and Julius R. Mantey, *A Manual Grammar of the Greek New Testament* (New York: Macmillan, 1927).
[97] William Douglas Chamberlain, *An Exegetical Grammar of the Greek New Testament* (New York: Macmillan, 1941; repr., Grand Rapids: Baker, 1994), vii–viii.
[98] Maximilian Zerwick, *Biblical Greek Illustrated by Examples*, trans. Joseph Smith (Rome: Pontifical Biblical Institute, 1963 [1944]).
[99] C. F. D. Moule, *An Idiom Book of New Testament Greek* (Cambridge: Cambridge University Press, 1953; 2nd ed., 1959).
[100] Curtis Vaughan and Virtus E. Gideon, *A Greek Grammar of the New Testament: A Workbook Approach to Intermediate Grammar* (Nashville: Broadman, 1979).
[101] James A. Brooks and Carlton L. Winbery, *Syntax of New Testament Greek* (Washington, DC: University Press of America, 1979; repub., 1988).
[102] Heinrich von Siebenthal, *Ancient Greek Grammar for the Study of the New Testament* (Oxford: Peter Lang, 2019), a translation of Siebenthal, *Griechische Grammatik zum Neuen Testament* (Giessen: Brunnen; Basel: Immanuel-Verlag, 2011). The German edition makes clear that the later version is a revision of the earlier Ernst G. Hoffmann and Heinrich von Siebenthal, *Griechische Grammatik zum Neuen Testament* (Basel: Immanuel-Verlag, 1985). This last work is a Greek grammar written according to comparative-historical principles.

aspect and discourse analysis; see Chapter Two for further discussion), there are still many comparative-historical features retained in this work, such as the use of the same categories as in Blass and Debrunner for discussion of some of the cases.[103]

The second set of examples that utilize the comparative-historical method emphasizes its diachronic dimension. The most obvious example of comparative-historical philology, perhaps, is the movement to trace the diachronic development of Greek to the point of using its modern variety to inform understanding of the Greek of the New Testament. This approach is found, for example, in the work of Chrys Caragounis and of David Hasselbrook. Caragounis's *The Development of Greek and the New Testament* (an admittedly odd title) in the Preface notes that the book in its draft form carried the title "A Diachronic and Acoustic Approach to the New Testament," by which he means that it follows two strands, diachrony and an emphasis upon the sounds of the language.[104] The diachronic strand is concerned with "the historical development of the language morphologically and especially syntactically."[105] As a result, he argues for radical diachronic continuity of the Greek language over the span of its history. Caragounis also dismisses many if not most of the categories of modern linguistics. He instead draws heavily upon the work of such comparative and historical language scholars as A. N. Jannaris (1852–1909) and Georgios Hatzidakis (1843–1941).[106] Hasselbrook, in his study of New Testament lexicography, uses the subtitle "Advancing toward a Full Diachronic Approach with the Greek Language" (again an admittedly odd but descriptive title).[107] The first section of the book is on "The Necessity of Moving toward a Full Diachronic Approach," by which he means that we must not only look retrospectively to the history of the language but also look forward to its developments to understand the language adequately. A less explicit, but nonetheless no less comparative, approach is also taken by Murray Harris in his work on prepositions and theology. In this work, he claims not to be offering a thorough treatment of the prepositions, for which one (he says) should consult Blass-Debrunner-Funk or Robertson or similar (comparative historical) works, but an assessment of their theological significance.[108]

We need to note two important factors regarding both the rationalist and comparative-historical language schools. The first is that, no matter what developments may have occurred within linguistic thought (and some of those who persist in their rationalism and

---

[103] See the critique of the description of the dative case in Stanley E. Porter, "The Dative Case in Some Examples of Greek Grammatical Discussion," *FN* 34 (2021): 17–37.

[104] Chrys C. Caragounis, *The Development of Greek and the New Testament: Morphology, Syntax, Phonology, and Textual Transmission*, WUNT 167 (Tübingen: Mohr Siebeck, 2004).

[105] Caragounis, *Development*, vii.

[106] Jannaris, *Historical Greek Grammar*; cf. Chrys C. Caragounis, ed., *Greek: A Language in Evolution. Essays in Honour of Antonios N. Jannaris* (Hildesheim: Georg Olms, 2010), with the most insightful essay being Georgios K. Giannakis, "Can a Historical Greek Grammar Be Written?—An Appraisal of A. N. Jannaris' Work," 296–313 (despite the ill-advised intrusions of the editor). See also G. N. Hatzidakis, *Einleitung in die Neugriechische Grammatik* (Leipzig: Breitkopf & Härtel, 1892; repr. Hildesheim: Georg Olms, 1977). Caragounis's view also resembles the historical position of Thumb, who also was interested in modern Greek. See Albert Thumb, "On the Value of Modern Greek for the Study of Ancient Greek," *CQ* 8 (1914): 181–205.

[107] David S. Hasselbrook, *Studies in New Testament Lexicography: Advancing toward a Full Diachronic Approach with the Greek Language*, WUNT 2/303 (Tübingen: Mohr Siebeck, 2011). Hasselbrook, along with a number of others who have written on lexis in New Testament Greek, is reviewed in Stanley E. Porter, "Lexical Semantics and New Testament Greek: A Review Article of Some Major Works," *FN* 32 (2019): 113–55, esp. 125–6.

[108] Murray J. Harris, *Prepositions and Theology in the Greek New Testament* (Grand Rapids: Zondervan, 2012), 13.

comparative historicism are aware of such developments), there continue to be those that model these traditional forms of grammar in their work. The second is that these theories of language, which arguably have been superseded in subsequent linguistic thought (or else why these newer linguistic schools?), remain foundational within New Testament Greek studies, providing most examples of beginning New Testament Greek grammars, several of the intermediate Greek grammars, virtually all of the advanced reference grammars, and the support for numerous monographs that continue to be produced. The fact that this situation exists should be an item of major consternation among those who are concerned with the field of New Testament Greek studies and its being linguistically responsible.

CONCLUSION

This chapter has had two major purposes. The first purpose is to introduce the variety of theoretical models within the field of modern linguistics. For those who are unaware of the range of linguistic theories or their related schools of thought that have developed over the course of the twentieth century, this survey should help to establish the major ways in which contemporary linguists think about language. However, there has been a previous discussion of language before the emergence of this variety of linguistic theories. My second purpose has been to place this linguistic discussion within the wider field of previous study of language. Discussion of language did not begin with modern linguistics, nor in fact did it begin with those that I have labeled traditional grammarians. Nevertheless, for the sake of discussion, I have taken up the story of the development of western thought regarding language beginning with the Enlightenment and traced the two major approaches within the seventeenth to the early twentieth centuries.

These two major approaches, the rationalist and comparative historicist, represent developing thought regarding language. The rationalist period assumed Enlightenment presuppositions regarding such features as rationalism, empiricism, and naturalism, although still within a context of historical concerns. The comparative-historical period, influenced by Romanticism, shifted its philosophical orientation and focused much more upon historical and comparative concerns within the ascendant developmental hypothesis. More importantly perhaps for this monograph, however, is the continuing and abiding importance of these schools of thought for New Testament Greek language study. Most of the beginning Greek grammars follow the rationalist approach, while most (but certainly not all) of the established intermediate level and virtually all the reference grammars follow the comparative-historical approach. The next chapter will note some exceptions to this generality, but they remain relatively insignificant when compared to how the traditional grammatical models continue to dominate Greek language study. The next chapter will trace the development of modern linguistics and the emerging schools of linguistic thought within New Testament Greek language study.

CHAPTER TWO

Linguistic Theory and New Testament Greek Study II

Modern Linguistics and Its Schools of Thought

INTRODUCTION

In the previous chapter, I discussed the concept of linguistic theory and their associated schools of linguistic thought. I noted that there is a wide variety of linguistic theories within contemporary linguistics, even though there are fewer schools of linguistics. Scholars have proposed various ways to organize these schools of linguistics so as to make clear their similarities and differences. In order to put these schools of thought in an appropriate historical context, I discussed the two major periods in post-Enlightenment thought on language, before the emergence of modern linguistics. These two periods are the rationalistic and comparative-historical periods, both lumped together under the category of traditional grammar as a means of distinguishing them from modern linguistics. In this chapter, I will discuss the schools of modern linguistics within New Testament Greek study. Before I do that, however, this chapter turns to the foundations and development of modern linguistics that led to the emergence of the major schools of thought in New Testament Greek study. This brief history of modern linguistics must remain incomplete, as the twentieth century was full of a variety of schools of linguistic thought, some of them having passed out of use and others emerging along the way. Nevertheless, most of the schools of thought that continue to provide guidance for their practitioners and are used in New Testament studies in the twenty-first century have their origins in many of the principles that began to emerge in the previous periods and then emerged more fully with the rise of modern linguistics within the twentieth century.

The emergence of modern linguistics is a complex story, intertwined with previous language study and the emergence of several interwoven strands of thought regarding language. In many ways, the paradigm shift from traditional grammar to modern linguistics, or, perhaps better, the rationalist period to the comparative-historical period and then the comparative-historical period to the modern linguistic period, resembles the kind of movement that the philosopher of science Thomas Kuhn (1922–96) envisions in his *The Structure of Scientific Revolutions*.[1] In that important book, he notes how normal science—in this case, comparative-historical linguistics (which itself had paradigmatically displaced rationalist linguistics)—despite its ascendancy must address anomalies observed

---

[1] Thomas S. Kuhn, *The Structure of Scientific Revolutions* (Chicago: University of Chicago Press, 1962).

by other scholars. The number of anomalies increases, until the point where the anomalies are too many to ignore and can no longer be viewed simply as anomalies. At this point, a paradigm shift is precipitated, in which the governing paradigm is displaced by a new hypothesis that does not have the same readily apparent explanatory difficulties but opens new interpretive possibilities. The same is the case with the comparative-historical method. As it progressed, its categories of explanation became further hardened, especially in the thought of the New Grammarians. The New Grammarians not only observed sound changes but formulated ineluctable laws regarding such changes, even if they had to invent new categories to account for these persistent problems, such as dialectology. However, despite their efforts, there were always exceptions to their diachronically based phonological rules, to the point where the exceptions grew significantly in number. The environment was ripe for a new theory to displace the old and not just concretize what was known but suggest new avenues of knowledge.

THE FOUNDATIONS AND DEVELOPMENT OF MODERN LINGUISTICS

The new perspective on language represented by modern linguistics emerged in several different ways at different places and, when the dust had settled—and it took some time for the dust to settle—we had entered what could retrospectively be recognized as the modern linguistic period. There were many cultural, social, and philosophical, besides linguistic, influences that led to the emergence of what we now call modern linguistics. The major philosophical influence upon the rise of structural linguistics was probably the emergence of phenomenology as a philosophy, led by the thought of Edmund Husserl (1859–1938), whose *Logical Investigations* first appeared in 1900–1 and emphasized the metaphysical properties not of other phenomena but of the sign, of which language was an expression of it.[2] A little later in Britain and North America (e.g., 1920s on), logical positivism derived from the Vienna Circle of analytic philosophy, with its emphasis upon the verification principle and empiricism also had a significant influence upon seeing linguistics as a science after the model of the hard sciences.[3] There was also a general cultural malaise in late nineteenth-century Europe, focused upon Vienna, sometimes referred to as fin de siècle, that came to question the value of language and believed that

---

[2]Edmund Husserl, *Logische Untersuchungen* (Halle: M. Niemeyer, 1900–1; 2nd ed., 1913; ET *Logical Investigations*, trans. John N. Findlay [New York: Humanities, 1970]). See Julia Kristeva, *Language—The Unknown: An Initiation into Linguistics*, trans. Anne M. Menke (New York: Columbia University Press, 1989), 221–3; Stanley E. Porter and Jason C. Robinson, *Hermeneutics; an Introduction to Interpretive Theory* (Grand Rapids: Eerdmans, 2011), 49–57. On phenomenology, see W. T. Jones, *The Twentieth Century to Wittgenstein and Sartre*, vol. 5 of *A History of Western Philosophy*, 2nd ed. (New York: Harcourt, Brace, Jovanovich, 1975), 250–84.
[3]For selections, see A. J. Ayer, ed., *Logical Positivism* (New York: Free Press, 1959). On logical positivism, see Jones, *Twentieth Century*, 218–49. Ayer's major work popularizing logical positivism highlights its emphases in its title: Alfred Jules Ayer, *Language, Truth and Logic*, 2nd ed. (repr., New York: Dover, 1952 [1936]). On the Vienna Circle, see Siobhan Chapman, *Language and Empiricism: After the Vienna Circle* (Basingstoke: Palgrave Macmillan, 2008); and on defining analytic philosophy, see Karl-Otto Apel, *Analytic Philosophy of Language and the Geisteswissenschaften*, Foundations of Language Supplementary Series 4 (Dordrecht: Reidel, 1967), 1: analytic philosophy "recognizes as 'scientific' only the methods of the natural science in the wider sense of the word, insofar as they objectively explain the phenomena in question by reference to causal laws. This philosophy sees as its main goal the justification of this 'objective knowledge' and its separation from any kind of subjective 'Weltanschauung', i.e., theology, metaphysics or some other 'normative science.'"

language should attempt to mediate reality, even if signifier and signified were not joined. A writer such as Hugo von Hofmannsthal (1874–1929) in his 1902 short story "A Letter" (also known as "The Lord Chandos Letter") expresses the frustration with the limits of language in relation to reality.[4] Therefore, it is not surprising that linguistic thought emerged in several different contexts. There are at least three foci of the emergence of the New Linguistics.[5] These foci revolve around the research and writing of the Geneva language scholar Ferdinand de Saussure, the early and later developments of the Prague School of linguistics, and the studies in Native American language taking place in North America. Each of these three deserves some words of introduction.[6]

The ideas of Ferdinand de Saussure (1857–1913)[7] are by far the best known of these three strands lying behind the development of modern linguistics, and as a result he is often cited as *the* founder of modern linguistics. More to the point is that Saussure, having been a student of Karl Brugmann (1849–1919), was a member of the New Grammarians and so perfectly at home within the linguistics of his time. Saussure's doctorate completed at Leipzig in 1880 was appropriately entitled "Du génitif absolu sanscrit."[8] However, during this same time, he wrote an important book entitled *Mémoire on the Primitive System of Vowels in the Indo-European Languages*, published in 1879 when he was twenty-one years old (his only book published in his lifetime).[9] This book is concerned with the system of lengthening vowels in Indo-European languages. He also formulated a sound law regarding falling accent on final syllables in Lithuanian.[10] However, by the early years of the twentieth century, Saussure was lecturing on the topic of general linguistics along far different lines. From 1906 to 1911 on three different occasions, Saussure offered

---

[4]See Hugo von Hofmannsthal, *The Lord Chandos Letter and Other Writings*, trans. Joel Rotenberg (New York: New York Review Books, 2005), with "A Letter" (117–28) and an informative introduction by John Banville (vii–xii).

[5]R. H. Robins, *A Short History of Linguistics*, 3rd ed. (London: Longman, 1990), esp. 218–64, for the basic facts recounted here. Other useful histories of linguistics for this period include Milka Ivić, *Trends in Linguistics*, trans. Muriel Heppell, JLSMi 42 (The Hague: Mouton, 1965), 69–242; Maurice Leroy, *The Main Trends in Modern Linguistics*, trans. Glanville Price (Oxford: Blackwell, 1967), 49–140; Geoffrey Sampson, *Schools of Linguistics* (Stanford, CA: Stanford University Press, 1980), 34–235; Kristeva, *Language*, 217–61; Pieter A. M. Seuren, *Western Linguistics: An Historical Introduction* (Oxford: Blackwell, 1998), 140–296 and passim; P. H. Matthews, *Grammatical Theory in the United States from Bloomfield to Chomsky*, CSL 67 (Cambridge: Cambridge University Press, 1993); and Keith Allan, *The Western Classical Tradition in Linguistics*, 2nd ed. (London: Equinox, 2010).

[6]See Porter and Robinson, *Hermeneutics*, 155–63.

[7]On Saussure, see Jonathan Culler, *Saussure* (London: Fontana, 1976); and Robert de Beaugrande, *Linguistic Theory: The Discourse of Fundamental Works* (London: Longman, 1991), 6–33. For a view that calls Saussure's contribution into question and shows the importance of Sechahaye, see Pieter A. M. Seuren, *Saussure and Sechahaye: Myth and Genius. A Study in the History of Linguistics and the Foundations of Language* (Leiden: Brill, 2018); and a review of this work that offers some correction, see Marc Pierce, review of Seuren, *Saussure … Linguist List* 40–4335, November 14, 2019 (online).

[8]A copy of this dissertation is held at the Houghton Library of Harvard University. See Maria Pia Marchese, ed., *Ferdinand de Saussure, Phonétique: Il manoscritto di Harvard Houghton Library bMS Fr 266 (8)* (Florence: Unipress, 1995), viii.

[9]For an excerpt, see Ferdinand de Saussure, *Mémoire sur le système primitif des voyelles dans les langues indo-européennes* (Leipzig: Teubner, 1879; ET of excerpt from Paris: Vieweg, 1887 edition in "Mémoire on the Primitive System of Vowels in the Indo-European Languages," in *A Reader in Nineteenth-Century Historical Indo-European Linguistics*, ed. and trans. Winfred P. Lehmann [Bloomington: Indiana University Press, 1967], 217–24), where Saussure's notion of language as system is already present (218).

[10]See N. E. Collinge, *The Laws of Indo-European* (Amsterdam: John Benjamins, 1985), 149–52, citing Ferdinand de Saussure, "À propos de l'accentuation lituanienne," *MSL* 8 (1894): 425–46; Saussure, "Accentuation lituanienne," *Indogermanische Forschungen Anzeiger* 6 (1896): 157–66. See also Saussure, "Essai d'une distinction des différents a indo-européens," *MSL* 3 (1878): 359–70.

his general linguistics course at the University of Geneva. Saussure himself never lived to read the published form, as he died in 1913. It fell to two of his students who had heard his lectures, Charles Bally and Albert Sechehaye, to assemble a book from notes and other manuscripts (they in varying ways became his successors as well in the Geneva School). This volume appeared in 1916 in French and established the basis of what is sometimes referred to as general linguistics (although it was not translated into and published in English until 1959), with his emphasis upon *langue* (versus *parole*) or the language system.[11]

At the same time as Saussure was doing his speaking, there were other linguists who were shifting their perspective on the fundamental ways in which language is viewed. Some of those linguists later began to congregate around a core group of scholars in Prague.[12] In 1911, Vilém Mathesius (1882–1945), a young linguist from Prague, presented a paper entitled (in English translation) "On the Potentiality of the Phenomena of Language." He argued for the synchronic study of languages, or what he calls the "static oscillation of speech among the individuals inside the communities of language."[13] In 1926, Mathesius and a small but significant group of scholars held the first meeting of what would become the Prague Linguistic Circle. Some of the founding members included Jan Mukarovsky (1891–1975), who extended the school's work to the arts, especially literature;[14] Roman Jakobson (1896–1982), who had been a member of the Russian Formalists,[15] emphasized phonetics and phonology, and later would have a huge influence upon North American

---

[11] Ferdinand de Saussure, *Course in General Linguistics*, ed. Charles Bally and Albert Sechehaye, with Albert Riedlinger, trans. Wade Baskin (New York: Philosophical Library, 1959; ET of *Cours de linguistique générale*, ed. Charles Bally and Albert Sechehaye, with Albert Riedlinger [Paris: Payot et Rivages, 1995 (1916)]). See also Saussure, *Writings in General Linguistics* (Oxford: Oxford University Press, 2006), which offers potential insights into Saussure that have only recently been appreciated regarding his attention to the social dimension of language; and Edward McDonald, *Grammar West to East: The Investigation of Linguistic Meaning in European and Chinese Traditions* (Singapore: Springer Nature, 2020), 164–73 and 233–5. The Geneva School of linguistics formed around Saussure and his students. See Robert Godel, ed., *A Geneva School Reader in Linguistics* (Bloomington: Indiana University Press, 1969), including the introduction (1–25), where lines of connection between Geneva and elsewhere, such as Prague, are discussed. One line of connection to note is the Russian scholar Serge Karcevski (1884–1955), who studied in Geneva, returned to Moscow, and then returned to Europe, becoming one of the founders of the Prague Linguistic Circle. Bally, Saussure's successor in Geneva, was also held in high esteem by Russian scholars. See Martin J. Buss, *The Changing Shape of Form Criticism: A Relational Approach* (Sheffield: Sheffield Phoenix, 2010), 131 n. 39.

[12] On the Prague Linguistic Circle, see Josef Vachek, *The Linguistic School of Prague* (Bloomington: Indiana University Press, 1966), with helpful appendixes on its history and philosophical foundations; and F. W. Galen, *Historic Structures: The Prague School Project, 1928–1948* (Austin: University of Texas Press, 1985).

[13] Vilém Mathesius, "On the Potentiality of the Phenomena of Language," in *A Prague School Reader in Linguistics*, ed. Josef Vachek (Bloomington: Indiana University Press, 1964), 1–32, quotation 1. See René Wellek, "Vilém Mathesius (1882–1945): Founder of the Prague Linguistic Circle," in *Sound, Sign and Meaning: Quinquagenary of the Prague Linguistic Circle*, ed. Ladislav Matejka (Ann Arbor, MI: Department of Slavic Languages and Literature University of Michigan, 1976), 1–5.

[14] Jan Mukarovsky, *The Word and Verbal Art*, ed. and trans. John Burbank and Peter Steiner (New Haven: Yale University Press, 1977), with a helpful foreword by René Wellek on Mukarovsky's life (vii–xiii); see also Thomas G. Winner, "Jan Mukarovsky: The Beginnings of Structural and Semiotic Aesthetics," in *Sound, Sign and Meaning*, ed. Matejka, 433–55.

[15] See Lee T. Lemon and Marion J. Reis, eds. and trans., *Russian Formalist Criticism: Four Essays* (Lincoln: University of Nebraska Press, 1965) and S. Bann and J. E. Bowlt, eds., *Russian Formalism: A Collection of Articles and Texts in Translation* (Edinburgh: Scottish Academic Press, 1973).

linguistics, literary criticism, and the structuralist anthropologist Claude Lévi-Strauss (1908–2009);[16] and Nikolai Trubetzkoy (1890–1938), the Russian phonologist, who developed markedness theory.[17]

Rarely in the history of linguistics have so many major figures gathered together as a cohesive group and accomplished so much productive and potentially (although not necessarily fully realized or recognized) significant research on such areas as phonology, markedness theory, information structure (notions of topic and comment), and linguistic theories of literature and the arts. This group would last at least until 1948, when the rise to power of the communist government of Czechoslovakia would lead to the group's oppression and disbanding.[18] The basic beliefs and orientation of the Prague School were laid out in nine theses that they developed and presented in 1928 to the First Linguistics Congress in The Hague, the Netherlands.[19] A subsequent Manifesto of the Prague School was published in 1929 as a presentation at the First International Congress of Slavists, held in Prague.[20] Their published scholarship is today not nearly as well known as is other linguistic scholarship, because of both the linguistic difficulties (much of it was published in Czech) and the political obstacles (the movement and many of the people disappeared behind the Iron Curtain after the Second World War). Nevertheless, their clear focus upon the social use of language, including literature, distinguished them from the Saussureans as both structuralist and functionalist.[21]

The third group focused upon the study of American Indian languages in North America. The earlier research of Wilhelm von Humboldt (1767–1835) on the Kawi language,[22] a major

---

[16]Among many works, see Roman Jakobson, *On Language*, ed. Linda R. Waugh and Monique Monville-Burston (Cambridge, MA: Harvard University Press, 1990). On Jakobson's reaction to Saussure, see Ladislav Matejka, "Jakobson's Response to Saussure's Cours," *Cahiers de l'ILSL* 9 (1997): 169–76.

[17]Nikolai S. Trubetzkoy (spelling variable), *Introduction to the Principles of Phonological Descriptions*, trans. L. A. Murray, ed. H. Bluhme (The Hague: Martinus Nijhoff, 1968; ET of *Anleitung zu phonologischen Beschreibungen* [Brno: Cercle linguistique de Prague, 1935]); Trubetzkoy, *Principles of Phonology*, trans. Christiane A. M. Baltaxe (Berkeley: University of California Press, 1969; ET of *Grundzüge der Phonologie* [Prague: Travaux du Cercle linguistique de Prague, 1939]).

[18]There was somewhat of a revival of the Prague Circle after the war, but Mukarovsky renounced his previous structural linguistics and embraced Marxism. See René Wellek, "The Literary Theory and Aesthetics of the Prague School," in *Discriminations: Further Concepts of Criticism* (New Haven: Yale University Press, 1970), 275–303, esp. 292–3. As a result, the school never regained its importance, apart from in the area of the Functional Sentence Perspective. See Vachek, *Linguistic School*, 89–92, with Mathesius followed by Frantisek Daneš, Jan Firbas, and Vachek. See Firbas, *Functional Sentence Perspective in Written and Spoken Communication* (Cambridge: Cambridge University Press, 1992).

[19]See Marta K. Johnson, ed. and trans., *Recycling the Prague Linguistic Circle* (Ann Arbor, MI: Karoma, 1978), 1–31, the manifesto apparently having been drafted by Jakobson.

[20]See "Thèses présentées au Premier Congrès des philologues slaves," in *Prague School Reader in Linguistics*, ed. Vachek, 33–58.

[21]Vachek, *Linguistic School*, 6–7. See Vachek, ed., *Prague School Reader in Linguistics*; Paul L. Garvin, ed. and trans., *A Prague School Reader on Esthetics, Literary Structure, and Style* (Washington, DC: Georgetown University Press, 1964); and Peter Steiner, ed., *The Prague School: Selected Writings, 1929–1946* (Austin: University of Texas Press, 1982). On the influence of the Prague School on New Testament studies, see Jan H. Nylund, "The Prague School of Linguistics and Its Influence on New Testament Language Studies," in *The Language of the New Testament: Context, History, and Development*, ed. Stanley E. Porter and Andrew W. Pitts, ECHC 3, LBS 6 (Leiden: Brill, 2013), 155–221.

[22]See Wilhelm von Humboldt, *Über die Verschiedenheit des menschlichen Sprachbaues und ihren Einfluss auf die geistige Entwickelung des Menschengeschlechts* (Berlin: Königlichen Akademie der Wissenschaften, 1836; ET *On Language: On the Diversity of Human Language Construction and Its Influence on the Mental Development of the Human Species*, ed. Michael Losonsky, trans. Peter Heath [Cambridge: Cambridge University Press, 1999]).

intellectual study of a non-Indo-European language, had long-lasting effects and created a significant and enduring legacy in the development of modern linguistics. Several linguists who came to North America became fascinated with Native American languages. Franz Boas (1858–1942) was a German refugee who settled into North America (he had visited previously) because of its immense promise for the recording and classifying of a wide range of phenomena. Although educated in Germany as a physicist and geographer, Boas wrote on race and ethnicity, culture, and especially (for this chapter) and importantly language.[23] He noted that there were varieties of classification systems of language that could be used to describe its structures—including American Indian languages being analyzed along different lines than those traditionally used for European languages—and that there was a relationship between language and thought patterns, an idea extended to the notion that speakers might be forced to think according to the restrictions imposed by their linguistic categories.

Some of Boas's ideas were taken much further by Boas's student, Edward Sapir (1884–1939), who worked in both Canada and the United States, and whose student Benjamin Lee Whorf (1897–1941) was outspoken in his differentiation of language and behavior (Whorf never worked as a linguist but as an engineer).[24] Out of this work arose the so-called Sapir-Whorf hypothesis of language determinism. Language determinism has had a greater influence upon biblical studies than many scholars recognize and continues to be a topic of major research and debate within linguistics.[25] Expressions of this theory vary, but it essentially argues that one's conception of the world is determined (to some extent, ranging from soft to hard forms of the theory) by the structure of one's language, so that one's language in some way dictates how one conceives of the world, in such dimensions as time, color, relationship, and, perhaps even more importantly, the foundations of cultural conception.[26] Thus, Whorf argued that the Hopi Indians have a different conception of time than do Indo-Europeans because their language lacks a tense system, at least as the tense system is typically described in Indo-European languages, with extended implications for how different cultures construct their narratives of the world. This third strand of influence is important because of how it came to be related to

---

[23] Franz Boas, *Race, Language, and Culture* (Chicago: University of Chicago Press, 1940). His most famous writing on language is probably Boas, "Introduction," in *Handbook of American Indian Languages*, 3 vols. (Washington, DC: American Print Office, 1911–38), 1:1-83.
[24] Edward Sapir, *Language: An Introduction to the Study of Speech* (New York: Harcourt, Brace, 1921); Sapir, *Selected Writings in Language, Culture, and Personality*, ed. David G. Mandelbaum (Berkeley: University of California Press, 1949); and Benjamin Lee Whorf, *Language, Thought, and Reality: Selected Writings of Benjamin Lee Whorf*, ed. John B. Carroll, Stephen C. Levinson, and Penny Lee, 2nd ed. (Cambridge, MA: MIT Press, 2012). On Sapir, see Beaugrande, *Linguistic Theory*, 34–57.
[25] For a more detailed discussion, see Stanley E. Porter, *New Testament Theology and the Greek Language: A Linguistic Reconceptualization* (Cambridge: Cambridge University Press, 2022), esp. 128–29.
[26] See Charles Taylor, *The Language Animal: The Full Shape of the Human Language Capacity* (Cambridge, MA: Harvard University Press, 2016), 320–31, who takes a constitutive rather than designative view of language. See also Harry Hoijer, ed., *Language in Culture: Conference on the Interrelations of Language and Other Aspects of Culture* (Chicago: University of Chicago Press, 1954), an early volume in the discussion; and the more recent John A. Lucy, *Language Diversity and Thought: A Reformulation of the Linguistic Relativity Hypothesis* (Cambridge: Cambridge University Press, 1992); Lucy, *Grammatical Categories and Cognition: A Case Study of the Linguistic Relativity Hypothesis* (Cambridge: Cambridge University Press, 1992), who endorses a moderate form of the hypothesis; John J. Gumperz and Stephen C. Levinson, eds., *Rethinking Linguistic Relativity* (Cambridge: Cambridge University Press, 1996), who provide assessments of various dimensions of the discussion; and Penny Lee, *The Whorf Theory Complex: A Critical Reconstruction* (Amsterdam: John Benjamins, 1996). See also the chapter, "The Whorf Hypothesis," in Pieter A. M. Seuren, *From Whorf to Montague: Explorations in the Theory of Language* (Oxford: Oxford University Press, 2013), 29–84, who offers a critique of Whorf.

views of language and mentality in biblical studies, but also because it was important in the process of generalizing about language in modern linguistics.

Saussure's *Course in General Linguistics* appeared in French in 1916 but in English translation only in 1959 and so its influence was delayed in English-language circles. Although Saussure's ideas represented a significant change in linguistic perspective, even if already shared by others, the field of language study did not become recognizably generally linguistic until after the Second World War, with the spread of universal education.[27] In the meantime, Saussure and others, especially the Prague School, identified several major concepts that formed the basis of what came to be called structuralism, in particular, though not confined to, linguistic structuralism, which became much of the basis of modern linguistic thought. Structuralism became a dominant intellectual force in twentieth-century thought, especially in the field of linguistics, but also in the social sciences (e.g., sociology and anthropology), various humanities subjects (e.g., literary criticism), and even the hard sciences (e.g., mathematics).[28]

(1) The arbitrary nature of the sign: Saussure distinguished between the *signified* (thing signified) and the *significant* (signifier), with their relationship unmotivated, that is, without a necessary correlation. The sign is their point of unification, where sound and concept converge. Saussure probably got this notion of the arbitrary relationship of sound and concept from the New Grammarians, whose theory of regular sound change was only possible if the relationship between sign and concept is arbitrary.

(2) *Langue* versus *parole*: For Saussure, *langue* is the sign system held in common by users of a language, and *parole* is the user's personal and idiosyncratic use of that langue. Saussure distinguished the social from the individual, and the essential from the incidental, and gave priority to *langue* as the primary object of linguistic investigation. This distinction has been followed by many linguists, such as Noam Chomsky's emphasis upon competence over performance,[29] but not by all. The Prague School was varied in its opinion on the distinction.[30] Systemic Functional Linguistics (SFL) questions the entire distinction as one does not have one without the other.[31]

(3) Synchrony versus diachrony: Along with the first distinction, this is perhaps the most important distinction that Saussure made, even if he was not the first or only one to make it. Synchrony is concerned with the forms and sounds of a language at a given point, and diachrony with the changes that affect any language over time. The historical nature of language and the way it had been previously studied drove Saussure to this distinction in which analysis of a language occurs without influence from the historical (even though this idea was adumbrated by

---

[27]See Geoffrey Sampson, *The Linguistics Delusion* (Sheffield: Equinox, 2017), 1–3.
[28]See David Robey, ed., *Structuralism: An Introduction* (Oxford: Clarendon, 1973), for essays by structuralists representative of different disciplines. The following enumerated points synthesize what is found in Saussure, *Course*, passim, summarized with some modification in Porter and Robinson, *Hermeneutics*, 155–6, who are dependent upon Saussure and his interpreters, within a larger discussion of various types of structuralism. See Culler, *Saussure*, passim.
[29]Noam Chomsky, *Aspects of the Theory of Syntax* (Cambridge, MA: MIT Press, 1965), 4. Performance is now called I-language.
[30]Vachek, *Linguistic School*, 18–21.
[31]Peter H. Fries, "Systemic Functional Linguistics: A Close Relative of French Functional Linguistics?" *La Linguistique* 37.2 (2001): 89–100, esp. 92.

Humboldt), and was taken up by a number of significant linguists.[32] Some other linguistic schools, such as the Prague Circle and then SFL, see a closer relationship between the diachronic and synchronic dimensions, with the latter dependent upon the former.[33] Saussure's analogies of a chess game (the synchronic dimension is represented by the arrangement of the pieces on the board, regardless of their diachronic history) and the phloem system of the tree trunk (the rings of a synchronic slice are a condition of the diachronic filament system) have become well-known metaphors for this concept.[34]

(4) Language as difference: In language, there are only differences, and language and its meanings are based upon differences among its elements. If all elements are the same, they have no relative value within the system. This notion was later summarized as "*meaning* implies *choice*."[35] In other words, a meaningful distinction can only be made where a choice among different items is present.

(5) Language as system: The arbitrary nature of the sign is the basis for individual languages having their own sets of arbitrary relations. Each language divides up the world according to its own intertwined system, as opposed to being composed of a series of isolated and independent entities. SFL has emphasized the notion of language as system (and choice) and has developed networks of systems as a means of representing the language potential.

(6) Syntagmatic versus paradigmatic relations: This fundamental distinction between the horizontal and vertical relations has been differently emphasized by various linguistic theories. For Saussure, language functions in the single dimension of time in which individual elements exist in this one sphere (paradigmatically), even if they appear in a succession in relation to each other (syntagmatically). Other linguistic schools, such as Chomsky's phrase structure grammar, emphasize the syntagmatic over the paradigmatic,[36] and others still, such as SFL, attempt to balance the syntagmatic and the paradigmatic through its systems and structures.[37]

---

[32] Robins, *Short History*, 230, notes Otto Jespersen (1860–1943), *Language: Its Nature, Development, and Origin* (London: George Allen & Unwin, 1922); Alan Gardiner (1879–1963), *The Theory of Speech and Language* (Oxford: Clarendon, 1932; 2nd ed., 1951), who was influenced by Hermann Gunkel and had an influence upon Branisław Malinowski and hence upon the London School of linguistics (see later in this chapter) (Buss, *Changing Shape of Form Criticism*, 152–6, who also notes the possible influence of Gunkel upon Bally, who also influenced Firth, and the Russian Formalists, including Bakhtin); Karl Bühler (1879–1963), *Theory of Language: The Representational Function of Language*, trans. Donald Fraser Goodwin (Amsterdam: John Benjamins, 1990; ET of *Sprachtheorie: Die Darstellungfunktion der Sprache* [Jena: Gustav Fischer, 1934; repr., 1982]); and Louis Hjelmslev (1899–1965), *Principes de grammaire générale* (Copenhagen: Andr. Fred. Høst & Son, 1928) and *Le cátegorie des cas: Étude de grammaire générale*, 2 parts (Aarhus: Universitetsforlaget, 1935–7). He does not mention Mathesius, perhaps because he did not write a book on the topic.

[33] Matejka, "Jakobson's Response," 172–3, citing the 1929 Manifesto, which questions the distinction (Johnson, ed. and trans., *Recycling*, 1, found in the first principle).

[34] Robins, *Short History*, 180, also notes that some of the early works in linguistics still reflected diachronic or historical concerns, with reference to Jespersen's *Language*, 7, which still sees linguistics as a historical enterprise.

[35] This language is found in Charles E. Bazell, *Linguistic Form* (Istanbul: Istanbul Press, 1953), 81, and many linguists since. Two recent works on choice in language include: Gerard O'Grady, Tom Bartlett, and Lise Fontaine, eds., *Choice in Language: Applications in Text Analysis* (Sheffield: Equinox, 2013) and Fontaine, Bartlett, and O'Grady, eds., *Systemic Functional Linguistics: Exploring Choice* (Cambridge: Cambridge University Press, 2013), although neither volume (if indexes are to be believed) refers to Bazell.

[36] See Noam Chomsky, *Syntactic Structures*, JLSMi 4 (The Hague: Mouton, 1957).

[37] M. A. K. Halliday, "Introduction: On the 'Architecture' of Human Language," in Halliday, *On Language and Linguistics*, ed. Jonathan J. Webster, CWMH 3 (London: Continuum, 2003), 1–29, esp. 7–12 and 18–20.

(7) Language as social entity: Language exists as a social phenomenon (note *langue* previously discussed), in which the society establishes the norms for usage, and the use of language reflects a set of social conventions as a part of wider sets of semiological systems.

This general semiotic orientation became the basis of structuralism as a general phenomenon within the wide diversity of fields already mentioned. To these seven distinctly and clearly Saussurean categories, albeit with modifications and responses by other linguistic approaches, can be added several others from other early linguistic thought.

(8) Marked and unmarked members: Trubetzkoy differentiated phonology from phonetics, studied the sounds of languages, and identified them as either distinctive or non-distinctive. Beginning with minimal basic sound units (phonemes), Trubetzkoy identified their oppositions to each other on the basis of whether they were marked or unmarked for particular features, labeling the types of oppositions as privative (or oppositional), gradual (along a cline), or equipollent (all the others, thus relatively equal).[38] This is the beginning of markedness theory, developed and extended further (and beyond phonology) by Jakobson[39] and with it theories regarding grounding and prominence, all Prague Circle categories.[40]

(9) Form and function: Much early linguistics, following in the pattern of comparative-historical linguistics, was concerned with the individual forms of language, such as the case system or aspect system. Karl Bühler (1879–1963), the German psychologist and linguist, and a highly influential member of the Prague Circle, distinguished (besides other things) among functions of language: he identified three—representative, expressive, and appellative.[41] This notion

---

[38]See Nikolai S. Trubetzkoy, "Zur allgemeinen Theorie phonologischer Vokalsysteme," *TCLP* 1 (1929): 36–67; repr. in *Prague School Reader in Linguistics*, ed. Vachek, 108–42; Trubetzkoy, "A Theory of Phonological Oppositions," in *N. S. Trubetzkoy: Studies in General Linguistics and Language Structure*, ed. Anatoly Liberman, trans. Marvin Taylor and Anatoly Liberman (Durham, NC: Duke University Press, 2001), 14–21; ET of "Essai d'une théorie des oppositions phonologiques," *JP* 33 (1936): 5–18. See Vachek, *Linguistic School*, 54–64; cf. Tsutomu Akamatsu, *The Theory of Neutralization and the Archiphoneme in Functional Phonology* (Amsterdam: John Benjamins, 1988), 29–36, for an introduction to the terminology and discussion. See also Aleš Bičan, "Phoneme in Functional and Structural Phonology," *Linguistica Online* (2005): 1–14.

[39]See Roman Jakobson, "Signe zero," in *Mélanges de linguistique et de philology offerts à J. van Ginneken à l'occasion du soixantième anniversaire de sa naissance (21 avril 1937)* (Paris: Klincksieck, 1937), 143–52; repr. in Jakobson, *Selected Writings II: Word and Language* (The Hague: Mouton, 1971), 212–19. See Edwin L. Battistella, *Markedness: The Evaluative Superstructure of Language* (Albany: State University of New York Press, 1990), 5–10. I note that Jakobson eliminated equipollence and argued for markedness in terms of oppositional binarity. This has had a huge influence on subsequent markedness theory, sometimes called asymmetrical markedness (e.g., Edna Andrews, *Markedness Theory: The Union of Asymmetry and Semiosis in Language* [Durham, NC: Duke University Press, 1990]). However, it is highly debatable whether Jakobson's revision is satisfactory, as it overlooks symmetrical features. These are particularly important in Trubetzkoy's distinction between random and systemic, where oppositions begin as possible equals but are distinguished by systemic function (Trubetzkoy, *Principles of Phonology*, 31–45).

[40]Markedness theory later became a part of the set of language universals: see Joseph Greenberg, *Language Universals* (The Hague: Mouton, 1966). On grounding and foregrounding, see Bohuslav Havránek, "The Functional Differentiation of the Standard Language" and Jan Mukarovsky, "Standard Language and Poetic Language," both in *Prague School Reader on Esthetics*, ed. Garvin, 3–16 and 17–30.

[41]Bühler, *Theory of Language*; Bühler, *Schriften zur Sprachtheorie*, ed. Achim Eschbach (Tübingen: Mohr Siebeck, 2012), with all the essays but one having been written before *Sprachtheorie*. The last, "Das Strukturmodell der Sprache," was published in *TCLP* 6 (1936): 3–12 (220–8, in this reprint volume).

of the relationship between structure and function became foundational for the Prague School and was later developed by Michael A. K. Halliday (1925–2018) into the three metafunctions of language: ideational (or experiential and logical), interpersonal, and textual.[42]

(10) Syntax versus semantics: Related to form and function is the distinction between syntax and semantics. Early structuralist linguistics tended to concentrate upon the sound system and basic forms (morphology) of language. This was continued in American structuralism, and the basis of Chomsky's phrase structure grammar that excluded semantics.[43] The Prague Circle concentrated upon the sentence, and Mathesius developed the "Functional Sentence Perspective" (not his term, but a later term for it), in which the structural organization of the sentence conveyed a meaning.[44] The terms variously translated "theme/rheme" or (in Charles Hockett's translation) "topic/comment," closer in Czech to "basis/nucleus," came to identify the given and new parts of information in the sentence.[45]

The previous principles, possibly along with some others depending upon individual schools of linguistic thought, came to define modern linguistics and in particular structural linguistics. There are clearly points of correlation with earlier discussion of language, especially as such ideas were anticipated by seminal early thinkers (such as Humboldt). However, despite such lines of continuity, the major orientation of modern linguistics was significantly different from its predecessors in its emphasis upon system, structure, and synchrony, along with its recognition of the role of social function and the role of difference at various levels. Such shifts in orientation cannot be minimized and, in many ways, marked incommensurable differences from previous language study.

Structuralism, a movement that began to come to fruition from the 1930s onward,[46] came to dominate Western intellectual discourse in the first two-thirds of the twentieth century. Linguistic structuralism spread far and wide, with various forms of structuralism coming to be represented in various places, to the point that various distinct types of structuralism were developed. Some of the best known are: (1) the Copenhagen School of Hjelmslev and his Glossematics that emerged in the 1930s and 1940s;[47] (2) American structuralism represented most significantly by Leonard Bloomfield (1887–1949), who studied with Brugmann and whose 1933 book *Language* had a dominant influence upon American linguists,[48] such as Zellig Harris (1909–92), and even upon Chomsky

---

[42]M. A. K. Halliday, "Language Structure and Language Function," in *New Horizons in Linguistics*, ed. John Lyons (Harmondsworth: Penguin, 1970), 140–65, an early published reference to Bühler, with reference also to Prague (in particular Vachek, *Linguistic School*), in the context of the metafunctions. The metafunctions are developed further in a wide array of Halliday's writings.

[43]See Chomsky, *Syntactic Structures*; Chomsky, *Aspects*.

[44]See Vachek, *Linguistic School*, 89–92.

[45]Vachek, *Linguistic School*, 18 and note 3 (111). See Charles F. Hockett, *A Course in Modern Linguistics* (New York: Macmillan, 1958), 191 and 201.

[46]See Galen, *Historic Structures*, 27.

[47]Louis Hjelmslev, *Résumé of a Theory of Language*, ed. and trans. Francis J. Whitfield (Madison: University of Wisconsin Press, 1975 [manuscript 1943–4]); and Hjelmslev, *Prolegomena to a Theory of Language*, trans. Francis J. Whitfield, rev. ed. (Madison: University of Wisconsin Press, 1961 [1943]); and Hjelmslev, *Essais linguistiques* (Paris: Minuit, 1971 [1959]). On Hjelmslev, see Beaugrande, *Linguistic Theory*, 122–46.

[48]Leonard Bloomfield, *Language* (New York: Holt, Rinehart & Winston, 1933); and Charles F. Hockett, ed., *A Leonard Bloomfield Anthology* (Bloomington: Indiana University Press, 1970). On Bloomfield, see Beaugrande, *Linguistic Theory*, 58–87.

and his later phrase structure approach;[49] (3) British structuralism mediated through the anthropologist Bronisław Malinowski (1884–1942) to John R. Firth (1890–1960), the latter the first professor of general linguistics in the UK, and then to Halliday, from whence it spread to Australia and beyond;[50] and (4) French structuralism beginning with Saussure that absorbed both literary and philosophical influences from the Russian Formalists and eventually resulted in French narratology as found in A.-J. Greimas (1917–92).[51]

In most ways, modern linguistics as defined here survived the poststructural rebellion, often identified with Jacques Derrida and his initiating paper "Structure, Sign, and Play in the Discourse of the Human Sciences," delivered at the conference "The Languages of Criticism and the Sciences of Man" held in October, 1966, in Baltimore, Maryland.[52] Derrida questioned the notion of structure, attempted to sever the relationship of signifier and signified or at least to destabilize it, endorsed notions of play and freedom in sign systems, and deconstructed the structuralism and metaphysics of one of its major figures, the anthropologist Lévi-Strauss.[53] This is not to say that there were not effects

---

[49]See Chapter One regarding Chomsky in relation to other linguists and discussion in this chapter regarding his school of thought and New Testament studies.

[50]Bronisław Malinowski, "The Problem of Meaning in Primitive Languages," in C. K. Ogden and I. A. Richards, *The Meaning of Meaning: A Study of the Influence of Language upon Thought and of the Science of Symbolism*, 3rd ed. rev. (New York: Harcourt, Brace, 1930 [1923]), 296–336, as well as a number of anthropological studies; J. R. Firth, *Papers in Linguistics 1934–1951* (London: Oxford University Press, 1957); Firth, *Selected Papers of J. R. Firth 1952–59*, ed. F. R. Palmer (London: Longmans, 1968).

[51]E.g. André Martinet, *Elements of General Linguistics*, trans. Elisabeth Palmer (London: Faber and Faber, 1964; ET of *Elements de Linguistique Générale* [Paris: Armand Colin, 1960]); Martinet, *A Functional View of Language* (Oxford: Clarendon, 1962); A.-J. Greimas, *Structural Semantics: An Attempt at a Method*, trans. Daniel McDowell, Ronald Schleifer, and Alan Velie (Lincoln: University of Nebraska Press, 1983; ET of *Sémantique structural: Recherche de méthode* [Paris: Larousse, 1966]). Narratology is far too large a field to discuss at this point. For representative introductions, see Seymour Chatman, *Story and Discourse: Narrative Structure in Fiction and Film* (Ithaca, NY: Cornell University Press, 1978) and Mieke Bal, *Narratology: Introduction to the Theory of Narrative*, 3rd ed. (Toronto: University of Toronto Press, 2009), among many.

[52]Jacques Derrida, "Structure, Sign, and Play in the Discourse of the Human Sciences," in *The Structuralist Controversy: The Languages of Criticism and the Sciences of Man*, ed. Richard Macksey and Eugenio Donato (Baltimore: Johns Hopkins University Press, 1972), 247–65 (this essay was reprinted in *Writing and Difference*, trans. Alan Bass [Chicago: University of Chicago Press, 1978; ET of *L'écriture et la difference* (Paris: Seuil, 1967)], 278–93, which contains essays written from 1959 to 1967). For the tenets of deconstruction, as well as a critique, see David Lehman, *Signs of the Times: Deconstruction and the Fall of Paul de Man* (New York: Poseidon, 1992), esp. 93–113.

[53]Derrida specifically attacked Claude Lévi-Strauss, *The Raw and the Cooked*, trans. John and Doreen Weightman (New York: Harper and Row, 1969); Lévi-Strauss, *The Elementary Structures of Kinship*, trans. James Bell, John von Sturmer, and Rodney Needham (Boston: Beacon, 1969); Lévi-Strauss, *The Savage Mind* (Chicago: University of Chicago Press, 1966); Lévi-Strauss, *Race and History* (Paris: UNESCO Publications, 1958); and Lévi-Strauss, *Tristes tropiques*, trans. John Russell (London: Hutchinson, 1961). The metaphysical stream in structuralism went back to Husserl, as already noted, a figure that Derrida had critiqued as early as 1959 in a paper delivered at a French conference on "Genesis and Structure," published as "'Genèsse et structure' et la phénoménologie," in *Genèse et structure*, ed. Maurice de Gandillac, Lucien Goldmann, and Jean Piaget (The Hague: Mouton, 1964); ET in *Writing and Difference*, 154–68. Derrida also critiqued Husserl in his *Speech and Phenomena, and Other Essays on Husserl's Theory of Signs*, trans. David B. Allison (Evanston, IL: Northwestern University Press, 1973; ET of *La Voix et la phénomène: Introduction au problème du signe dans la phénoménologie de Husserl* [Paris: PUF, 1967]). Ian Hunter, "Scenes from the History of Poststructuralism: Davos, Freiburg, Baltimore, Leipzig," *New Literary History* 41.3 (2010): 491–516, sees Baltimore anticipated, at least as a dispute among the elite over metaphysics, in the debate between the two philosophers Ernst Cassirer (1874–1945), the Marburg neo-Kantian, and Martin Heidegger (1889–1976), the post-Kantian, at Davos in 1929 and then in Heidegger's inaugural comments as Rector of the University of Freiburg in 1933.

on the wider field of modern linguistics, as seen in the traditional notion of language as product becoming language as process (as in Julia Kristeva);[54] the recognition of language as intertextual; the move from univocal to dialogical and heteroglossic meaning (based upon the work of Mikhail Bakhtin [1895–1975]);[55] the move from linguistic systemic stability to fluidity and unboundedness (with Roland Barthes [1915–80], who dissolved the notion of the text as structural artifact and explored alternative textual goals, such as pleasure);[56] and recognition of structures of power being exercised through language (as in Michel Foucault [1926–84], who was a predecessor of Critical Discourse Analysis, which is concerned with language and power).[57] Most linguistics, however, has retained its fundamental structuralist orientation, even if it has been forced to recognize that language, rather than simply being a mirror or reflector of the world is at least a partial maker of its own world, a part of the social or individual construction or at least interpretation of reality. This destabilization may well be one of the reasons that linguistic study has not become more robust within biblical studies, an academic discipline that, despite its protestations otherwise, actively seeks definitive meanings, even if they are negative ones.[58]

Much more could profitably be said about the history and development of modern linguistic thought. I have only been able to touch on a few of the major figures and the high points in the history of a complex and convoluted—even if fascinating—intellectual journey. We may summarize this history by making several important observations. The first observation is that there are distinct lines of continuity between traditional grammar, especially as represented in comparative-historical language study, and modern linguistics. Saussure stood with a foot on both sides of the divide. Nevertheless, Saussure and others also saw that there were major problems with the comparative-historical language agenda and developed new approaches and thoughts regarding language. The second observation is that there were much similarity and difference even within the rising tide of modern linguistics. Saussure, the Prague linguists, and the American scholars all had a number of common orientations to language. However, they also had many significant differences

---

[54]See Julia Kristeva, Σημειωτική: Recherches pour une sémanalyse (Paris: Seuil, 1969), esp. 82–112; Kristeva, Revolution in Poetic Language, trans. M. Waller (New York: Columbia University Press, 1984). The notion of language as process and product has become part of SFL. See M. A. K. Halliday in Halliday and Ruqaiya Hasan, Language, Context, and Text: Aspects of Language in a Social-Semiotic Perspective, 2nd ed. (Oxford: Oxford University Press, 1989), 10–11.

[55]E.g., M. M. Bakhtin, The Dialogic Imagination: Four Essays, ed. Michael Holquist, trans. Caryl Emerson and Michael Holquist (Austin: University of Texas Press, 1981).

[56]Roland Barthes, The Pleasure of the Text, trans. Richard Miller (New York: Hill and Wang, 1975); Barthes, Image—Music—Text, trans. S. Heath (New York: Hill and Wang, 1977), along with many other works from his structuralist and poststructuralist periods.

[57]Michel Foucault, Language, Counter-Memory, Practice: Selected Essays and Interviews, ed. D. F. Bouchard, trans. D. F. Bouchard and S. Simon (Ithaca, NY: Cornell University Press, 1977); cf. Foucault, The Archaeology of Knowledge and the Discourse on Language, trans. A. M. Sheridan Smith (New York: Pantheon, 1972 [1969]). On CDA, among many works see Norman Fairclough, Critical Discourse Analysis: The Critical Study of Language, 2nd ed. (London: Longman, 2010); Fairclough, Discourse and Social Change (Cambridge: Polity, 1992); Fairclough, Analysing Discourse: Textual Analysis for Social Research (London: Routledge, 2003); Fairclough, Language and Power, 3rd ed. (Abingdon: Routledge, 2015). Many others have advocated for CDA as well.

[58]For a critique of especially poststructuralist appropriation of linguistics, but one that also offers a critique of the larger notion of structuralism, with emphasis of his criticism upon the formalist agenda (Bloomfield to Zellig Harris to Chomsky, and then in relation to the French structuralists), see Thomas G. Pavel, The Spell of Language: Poststructuralism and Speculation, trans. Linda Jordan and Thomas G. Pavel (Chicago: University of Chicago Press, 1989).

of opinion on several fundamental questions regarding what language is, how it works, and what is the proper focus of study. A third observation is that the development of modern linguistics has not followed a linear path but has taken a circuitous path. Along the way, there have been a variety of major figures, as well as many minor ones, who have made contributions to the discussion. Some of these have been enduring and others of them have been less so, even if they have been influential. The result is that there have been many linguistic theories proposed by a variety of linguists. The previous account, as detailed as it is, has not mentioned many such linguistic theories, including a good number that were mentioned in Chapter One. Nevertheless, we have observed certain lines being drawn around some of the concepts and people who continue to play a role in linguistic thought.

As one now looks back upon the major linguistic theories, they can be categorized in a variety of ways, as was suggested in our discussion of schools of linguistics in Chapter One. On the one hand, there are those schools of thought that are formalist; that is, they emphasize the forms and structures of language, with an emphasis upon syntax and not meaning. On the other hand, there are those schools of thought that are functionalist; that is, they do not emphasize the forms but the functions of language that are realized by or expressed by the forms of language. In the middle, there are those schools of thought that are cognitive; that is, they emphasize that the functions of language come about because of human cognitive processing. This last category is much more recent than the others and so has played a less significant role in the previous history, which has been concerned with the origins and early development of modern linguistics. I will say more about Cognitive Linguistics in the following discussion. I turn now to New Testament Greek language study to chart its developments and then to see how the major linguistic schools have expressed themselves in research and writing over the last forty or so years.

MODERN LINGUISTICS AND NEW TESTAMENT GREEK STUDY

The recognition of the importance of general, and in particular Saussurean, linguistics for biblical studies occurred in James Barr's (1924–2006) *The Semantics of Biblical Language* in 1961.[59] In this still important book, he uses linguistic criteria to criticize abuses of linguistic method in biblical studies, in particular the Biblical Theology movement. That it took over forty years for modern linguistics to penetrate biblical studies is not surprising. Geoffrey Sampson makes clear that the same kind of delay occurred in the field of linguistics itself.[60] Despite the work of Saussure (and others) in the early days of the

---

[59] James Barr, *The Semantics of Biblical Language* (Oxford: Oxford University Press, 1961). Barr relies heavily upon the linguist Stephen Ullmann (1914–76), *The Principles of Semantics*, 2nd ed. (Oxford: Blackwell, 1957), who is cited six times, more than any other linguist except the early transitional linguist Otto Jespersen, *Language and The Philosophy of Grammar* (London: George Allen & Unwin, 1924), cited a total of eight times. However, Barr also cites several other linguists or pre-linguists as well, such as (in alphabetical order) Bloomfield, Brugmann, Bühler, Berthold Delbrück (1842–1922), Firth, Joseph H. Greenberg (1915–2001), Gustave Guillaume (1883–1960), A. A. Hill (1902–92), Harry Hoijer (1904–76), Humboldt, Robert Longacre (1922–2014), Antoine Meillet (1866–1936), Eugene A. Nida (1914–2011), Sapir, Stanislav Segert (1921–2005), Leo Spitzer (1887–1960), Saussure, and Whorf.

[60] Sampson, *Linguistics Delusion*, 1–3.

century, it was not until the post-Second World War period that linguistics practitioners caught up with their own discipline's history. Barr's entering the affray in 1961, therefore, was at the outset of the discipline of biblical linguistics. He was followed relatively soon after by a few who attempted to continue and enhance his work. Some of those following in his steps were Johannes P. Louw (1932–2011), Moisés Silva, D. A. Carson, David Alan Black, and Peter Cotterell (1930–2021) and Max Turner, but there are others as well.[61]

Despite Barr's early adoption of the strong Saussurean perspective, it is nevertheless nearly sixty years since he published his book, and New Testament Greek language study reflecting a modern linguistic framework is still disappointingly infrequent, even if an initial positive response occurred relatively soon after Barr's pronouncements. In the area of beginning New Testament Greek grammars, there are arguably only a relatively small number that reflect the principles of modern linguistics. In fact, the number of linguistically informed beginning New Testament grammars is still woefully small, and their influence seems to be even smaller, as most of them are not widely used if much at all. The first to note is by Eugene Van Ness Goetchius, *The Language of the New Testament*.[62] This volume takes an explicit linguistic approach, being clearly indebted to the Bloomfieldian American structuralist approach of scholars such as Charles Hockett (1916–2000) (a fierce opponent of Chomsky; see below), Henry Gleason (1917–2007), Eugene Nida, and Charles Fries (1887–1967) (the so-called Descriptivists or post-Bloomfieldian structuralists).[63] These scholars are representatives of American structuralism's formal descriptive emphasis upon phonology and morphology, utilizing immediate constituent analysis and distribution.[64] The next example is by Robert Funk, whose beginning and intermediate grammar was also influenced by the American structuralists.[65] He was soon followed by B. Ward Powers, *Learn to Read the Greek New Testament*.[66] He too is dependent upon American structuralism, as well as more recent modern language teaching methods that emphasize meaning over translation. A fourth work is by Kendall Easley, who pays attention to the paragraph, is not time-bound in discussion of tense-forms, and has a sophisticated view of lexical meaning.[67] A further grammar by Stanley Porter, Jeffrey T. Reed, and Matthew Brook O'Donnell, *Fundamentals of New Testament Greek*, takes a SFL approach to Greek.[68]

---

[61] J. P. Louw, *Semantics of New Testament Greek* (Philadelphia: Fortress; Chico, CA: Scholars Press, 1982); Moisés Silva, *Biblical Words and Their Meaning: An Introduction to Lexical Semantics* (Grand Rapids: Zondervan, 1983); Silva, *God, Language, and Scripture: Reading the Bible in the Light of General Linguistics* (Grand Rapids: Zondervan, 1990); D. A. Carson, *Exegetical Fallacies* (Grand Rapids: Baker, 1984; 2nd ed., 1996); David Alan Black, *Linguistics for Students of New Testament Greek: A Survey of Basic Concepts and Applications* (Grand Rapids: Baker, 1988; 2nd ed., 2000); and Peter Cotterell and Max Turner, *Linguistics and Biblical Interpretation* (Downers Grove, IL: InterVarsity Press, 1989). These include the major introductory types of books that students often avail themselves of. More advanced works are cited elsewhere in Chapters One and below.

[62] Eugene Van Ness Goetchius, *The Language of the New Testament* (New York: Scribner, 1965).

[63] See Sampson, *Schools of Linguistics*, 57–80.

[64] See Robins, *Short History*, 232–6.

[65] Robert W. Funk, *A Beginning-Intermediate Grammar of Hellenistic Greek*, 3rd ed. (repr., Sonoma, CA: Polebridge, 2013 [1973]).

[66] B. Ward Powers, *Learn to Read the Greek New Testament: An Approach to New Testament Greek Based upon Linguistic Principles* (Adelaide: SPCK Australia, 1979; 5th ed., 1995), esp. Appendix B (192–212) and notes.

[67] Kendall H. Easley, *User-Friendly Greek: A Common Sense Approach to the Greek New Testament* (Nashville: B&H, 1994).

[68] Stanley E. Porter, Jeffrey T. Reed, and Matthew Brook O'Donnell, *Fundamentals of New Testament Greek* (Grand Rapids: Eerdmans, 2010).

Rodney J. Decker in *Reading Koine Greek: An Introduction and Integrated Workbook* acknowledges his linguistic approach, apparently influenced by Silva, Carson, Goetchius, and Porter, among others.[69] Frederick Long uses some principles of discourse based upon Porter (see later in this chapter) to shape his presentation of New Testament Greek and incorporates some recent work in linguistics, especially verbal aspect.[70] Chadwick Thornhill's *Greek for Everyone* takes a highly eclectic approach that at least provides a place for linguistics.[71] Finally, Richard Griffin and Constantine Campbell reflect some recent discussions of verbal aspect, pronunciation, and textual organization, even if many elements of their grammar—such as overall organization of their material—are traditional and not much different from that found in traditional grammars.[72] There may be others, but the field is not overwhelming.

Intermediate New Testament Greek grammars do not prove any more productive than do beginning grammars; in fact, there are probably even fewer of them. One must note the two volumes already mentioned by Funk and by Powers, whose beginning books also address or contain intermediate-level material. The next intermediate grammar is by Stanley Porter, *Idioms of the Greek New Testament*.[73] This volume was one of the first to make an explicit attempt to create an intermediate-level grammar that was based upon modern linguistic principles. It utilizes functional linguistics such as SFL (see the following discussion), as well as some elements from other functionalists, such as the slot and filler notion from Kenneth L. Pike's (1912–2000) Tagmemics.[74] Porter was followed fairly quickly by Richard Young, *Intermediate New Testament Greek: A Linguistic and Exegetical Approach*. He takes what he calls a "descriptive" approach with an emphasis upon "usage in context" as determining meaning,[75] while also offering thanks to John Callow of the Summer Institute of Linguistics. David Alan Black attempts to incorporate many of the relevant linguistic principles into an easy guide to intermediate Greek that is a companion for his introduction to linguistics.[76] Decker also includes some intermediate level material in his *Reading Koine Greek*. Finally, the most recent intermediate grammar that reflects principles of modern linguistics is David Mathewson and Elodie Ballantine

---

[69]Rodney J. Decker, *Reading Koine Greek: An Introduction and Integrated Workbook* (Grand Rapids: Baker, 2014). See also Christophe Rico, *Speaking Ancient Greek as a Living Language*, 2 vols. (Jerusalem: Polis Institute Press, 2015), for a linguistic approach to ancient Greek of the Hellenistic period, especially the first century.

[70]Frederick J. Long, Κοινὴ Γραμματική *Koine Greek Grammar: A Beginning-Intermediate Exegetical and Pragmatic Handbook* (Wilmore, KY: Glossa House, 2015). The eclectic nature of this work by a non-linguist makes some elements problematic.

[71]A. Chadwick Thornhill, *Greek for Everyone: Introductory Greek for Bible Study and Application* (Grand Rapids: Baker, 2016), although it also has elements of rationalism and comparative historicism.

[72]Richard J. Gibson and Constantine R. Campbell, *Reading Biblical Greek: A Grammar for Students* (Grand Rapids: Zondervan, 2017).

[73]Stanley E. Porter, *Idioms of the Greek New Testament* (Sheffield: Sheffield Academic, 1992; 2nd ed., 1994).

[74]See Kenneth L. Pike, *Language in Relation to a Unified Theory of the Structure of Human Behavior*, 2nd ed. (The Hague: Mouton, 1967), in which slots and fillers play a major role across classes of items. On Pike, see Beaugrande, *Linguistic Theory*, 88–121. See later in this chapter.

[75]Richard A. Young, *Intermediate New Testament Greek: A Linguistic and Exegetical Approach* (Nashville: Broadman and Holman, 1994), viii. Cf. the Introduction, where he makes further linguistic distinctions in the binary structuralist mode (e.g., communication act, implicit and explicit information, form and meaning, surface structure and deep structure, and semantics and pragmatics).

[76]David Alan Black, *It's Still Greek to Me: An Easy-to-Understand Guide to Intermediate Greek* (Grand Rapids: Baker, 1998).

Emig, *Intermediate Greek Grammar: Syntax for Students of the New Testament*, which follows, as it states, most closely the intermediate grammar by Porter.[77] There have been no major reference grammars of New Testament Greek produced from any modern linguistic perspective, although there have been numerous monographs—many of them to be mentioned later in this chapter—that approach various questions of Greek from linguistic perspectives.[78]

At this point, however, it is perhaps more instructive to turn from a chronological serialization of work within New Testament Greek grammatical study to consider the major schools of linguistic thought current in New Testament Greek study. I do not concentrate upon Greek grammars per se, but consider monographs and major studies that reflect these major schools of thought.

MAJOR LINGUISTIC SCHOOLS IN NEW TESTAMENT GREEK STUDY

I turn now to the three categories of modern linguistic schools of thought that I defined in Chapter One—that is, those developed after the Second World War in response to the work of Saussure, the Prague School, and American descriptivism in particular—in relationship to New Testament Greek language study. I treat them in the order of Formalist, then Cognitive, and finally Functional Schools, as indicated in Chapter One. A treatment of the broader field of linguistics would, as previously indicated, discuss many more schools of thought, but these seem to be the ones that have emerged as most recognizable in New Testament Greek language study over the last forty or so years and remain significant in contemporary Greek language study.

---

[77]David L. Mathewson and Elodie Ballantine Emig, *Intermediate Greek Grammar: Syntax for Students of the New Testament* (Grand Rapids: Baker, 2016), xv. The importance of what I am discussing is seen in a review of Mathewson and Emig's intermediate Greek grammar by Mark S. Giacobbe, review of David L. Mathewson and Elodie Ballantine Emig, *Intermediate Greek Grammar* ... *WTJ* 80.2 (2018): 376–9. The reviewer assesses Mathewson and Emig against Wallace's and Köstenberger et al.'s grammars (see Chapter One for discussion of them), and thinks Wallace is still the most useful. However, the reviewer does not recognize that he is comparing two different approaches to language, but he instead proceeds simply to compare them "point by point." So the reviewer, while noting that Mathewson and Emig include discourse analysis in their grammar, does not comment on the implications of the fact that Mathewson and Emig's approach has discourse considerations in mind, while Wallace, who is in fact antithetical to discourse analysis, does not and cannot. If one knows the language theory that a grammar follows, one then, to a large extent, can answer questions regarding how that grammar will describe various elements of language. On this basis alone, Wallace's volume should be consigned to second place in comparison with Mathewson and Emig's. More to the point is that the reviewer was not comparing like with like and probably should not have been making the comparison.

[78]A difficult grammar to place (as noted in Chapter One) is the revised intermediate grammar by Heinrich von Siebenthal. This work has enhanced its initial discussion in linguistics—such as expanded treatment of verbal aspect and inclusion of textlinguistics—from its earlier edition, although much of the rest of the grammar still follows the comparative-historical model of Blass and Debrunner. See Heinrich von Siebenthal, *Ancient Greek Grammar for the Study of the New Testament* (Oxford: Peter Lang, 2019), a translation of Siebenthal, *Griechische Grammatik zum Neuen Testament*, new ed. (Giessen: Brunnen; Basel: Immanuel-Verlag, 2011), expanding upon Ernst G. Hoffmann and Heinrich von Siebenthal, *Griechische Grammatik zum Neuen Testament* (Riehen: Immanuel, 1985). There are numerous places where the bibliography is inadequate, including on verbal aspect where major works are not cited, and there is over-dependence upon a general reference work (Duden's *Die Grammatik* [Mannheim: DudenVerlag, 2009]). See Stanley E. Porter, "The Dative Case in Some Examples of Greek Grammatical Discussion," *FN* 34 (2021): 17–37.

Formalist Schools

The Formalist Schools of New Testament Greek linguistics are so-named because of their emphasis upon the forms of language, as opposed to its meaning or function. For many people, when they think of linguistics they think of various formalist theories. These theories are often linked with such recognizable linguistic categories as phonology, morphology, and syntax, among others. In fact, for some scholars, it is as if the study of linguistics ends with the study of its forms, rather than including study of meaning, especially beyond the clause or sentence. As the linguist David Banks states concerning formalists, they "treat language as if it were no more than its form, a sort of linguistic algebra, with independent existence."[79] There are two major expressions of formalist linguistic schools within contemporary New Testament Greek study, Chomskyan formalism and Construction Grammar.

Chomskyan Formalism

The first linguistic school, and by far the most important so far as the wider field of linguistics is concerned, especially in North America, is the linguistic school that revolves around the research, writing, and influence of Noam Chomsky and those who have followed him.[80] Chomsky is just coming to the end of a productive career of sixty years as a linguist, with virtually all his scholarly career spent as a professor of linguistics at the Massachusetts Institute of Technology in Massachusetts, USA.[81] The formalist linguistics theory of Chomsky was developed first in the 1950s under the influence of two major figures, both of them his teachers, Jakobson at Harvard University and Harris at the University of Pennsylvania, where Chomsky was educated. Jakobson promoted a theory of phonemic universalism.[82] Harris approached language in terms of the "formal" distribution of elements, such as morphemes, apart from meaning, following in the Descriptivist tradition.[83] He also developed notions of generativity and transformations, which have been at the heart of Chomskyan linguistics.[84] As a result, Chomsky adopted what has sometimes been called a Cartesian (based on the belief in innate ideas of René Descartes [1596–1650]) perspective that results in the assumption that there is an "autonomous cognitive faculty,"[85] or a Universal Grammar, that results in human internal grammar that follows linguistic universals.[86] Such linguistics investigates not language use (performance) but the speaker's competence (Saussure's *langue* over *parole*), and especially the cognitive dimensions of language such as its acquisition.

---

[79]David Banks, *The Birth of the Academic Article: Le Journal des Sçavans and the Philosophical Transactions 1665–1700* (Sheffield: Equinox, 2017), 7.

[80]I refer to such linguistics as Chomskyan linguistics, rather than transformational-generative grammar, as a reminder of the influence of Chomsky on this school of linguistics, from which a variety of permutations have originated.

[81]On Chomsky, see Beaugrande, *Linguistic Theory*, 147–86.

[82]See Jakobson, *On Language*, passim (see the index for references).

[83]Zellig S. Harris, *String Analysis of Sentence Structure*, Papers on Formal Linguistics 1 (The Hague: Mouton, 1962).

[84]Sampson, *Schools of Linguistics*, 130–1, 134–5.

[85]Robert D. Van Valin Jr. and Randy J. LaPolla, *Syntax: Structure, Meaning and Function*, CTL (Cambridge: Cambridge University Press, 1997), 9.

[86]Noam Chomsky, *Language and Mind* (New York: Harcourt, Brace & World, 1968); expanded in *Language and Mind*, enlarged ed. (New York: Harcourt, Brace & World, 1972). Steven Pinker (*The Language Instinct: How the Mind Creates Language* [New York: William Morrow, 1994]) has become Chomsky's primary proponent of Universal Grammar.

Chomsky therefore provides an analysis of grammar but not of language, if language is defined as what humans actually produce (*parole*).[87] All this can be described apart from meaning. As the linguist P. H. Matthews states, "a systematic description of the 'internal structure' or 'expression' side of a language could, in principle, stand on its own,"[88] without appeal to meaning. Chomsky reflects this emphasis upon form over meaning in his phrase structure grammar, with its transformations, as found in his first two major works, *Syntactic Structures* (1957) and *Aspects of the Theory of Syntax* (1965). The theory presented here came to be known as his standard theory, later extended.[89] As Chomsky himself states, his theory "was completely formal and non-semantic," and "concerned with the syntactic component of a generative grammar, that is, with the rules that specify the well-formed strings of minimal syntactically functioning units (*formatives*) and assign structure information of various kinds both to these strings and to strings that deviate from well-formedness in certain respects."[90] The result is the well known and generally widely recognized Chomskyan phrase structure rewrite rules: S -> NP + VP (Sentence consists of a Noun Phrase and a Verb Phrase), etc., and tree diagrams. It was not until 1963 and later that semantics was explicitly introduced—not by Chomsky but by others who were within the orbit of Chomsky, such as George Lakoff—into transformational-generative grammar as generative semantics.[91] The result was inclusion of semantics in subsequent versions of Chomskyan linguistics, including Government and Binding and then Principles and Parameters or the minimalist program, the latest version of Chomsky's linguistic theory. Chomsky has also directly inspired several other linguistic theories and even schools, such as Generalized Phrase Structure Grammar, Relational Grammar, Categorial Grammar, and Head Driven Phrase Structure Grammar[92]—as well as Cognitive Linguistics, as I will note in my further comments—but, apart from Cognitive Linguistics, New Testament studies has not generally followed the Chomskyan line, at least not very much recently.

I have offered a lengthier description of Chomskyan theory—without doubt due to his significance in linguistics outside of New Testament studies[93]—than I normally would for such a school of thought where there are only a few Chomskyans to note within the sphere of New Testament Greek linguistics. These include Reinhard Wonneberger, Daryl D. Schmidt (1944–2006), Louw, Micheal Palmer, and, after a period of time, Richard Crellin. There may be a few others who have made incidental use of Chomsky, but these are the ones that I am aware of. Wonneberger probably did the most to generate interest in Chomskyan linguistics, although his lasting effect has been relatively minimal.

---

[87] Van Valin and LaPolla, *Syntax*, 9.
[88] Matthews, *Grammatical Theory*, 23.
[89] Chomsky, *Syntactic Structures*; Chomsky, *Aspects*.
[90] Chomsky, *Syntactic Structures*, 93; and Chomsky, *Aspects*, 3.
[91] E.g., George Lakoff, "On Generative Semantics," in *Semantics: An Interdisciplinary Reader in Philosophy, Linguistics and Psychology*, ed. Danny D. Steinberg and Leon A. Jakobovits (Cambridge: Cambridge University Press, 1971), 232–96, followed by a number of others. See Randy Allen Harris, *The Linguistics Wars* (Oxford: Oxford University Press, 1993), 101–59, for a recounting of the semantics debate. For a different reading of this development within Chomskyan linguistics, see Dirk Geeraerts, *Theories of Lexical Semantics* (Oxford: Oxford University Press, 2010), 101–23, who attributes the shift to an article published in 1963 by Jerrold J. Katz and Jerry A. Fodor, "The Structure of a Semantic Theory," *Language* 9 (1963): 170–210.
[92] See Pius ten Hacken, *Chomskyan Linguistics and Its Competitors* (Sheffield: Equinox, 2007).
[93] Chomskyan linguistics has had a greater effect within ancient Hebrew than Greek studies. See Stanley E. Porter, "Linguistic Theory in Greek and Hebrew Language Study," in *Putting the Pieces Together: Formalizing Units and Relations in the Biblical Languages*, ed. Stanley E. Porter, Christopher D. Land, and Francis G. H. Pang, MNTS (Eugene, OR: Pickwick, forthcoming).

He wrote a major monograph on syntax and exegesis, in which he utilized a form of Chomsky's standard theory to create thirty-seven rules for the syntax of New Testament Greek, as well as publishing a number of articles on generative grammar.[94] The last one published, so far as I can determine, reflects Wonneberger's later concerns with electronic data processing, in which he attempts to unite data processing and generative grammar in Greek syntax.[95] Wonneberger (unfortunately for his legacy) wrote most of his work in German and he has not had lasting influence on English-language scholarship probably at least in part due to restricted access.

Schmidt wrote a brief monograph on complementation using Chomsky's extended standard theory including both transformational and lexicalist hypotheses to describe nominalizations.[96] In this work, Schmidt notes that his work is part of a larger research project on a transformational-generative grammar of Hellenistic Greek—to my knowledge a project that never went beyond local photocopies.[97] Louw utilizes what appears to be his own form of constituent structure analysis that is similar to Chomsky's phrase structure grammar, with the explicit admission that "meaning" is a prerequisite of analysis, not a claim that Chomsky would have made at an equivalent time.[98] The tree diagrams that Louw produces are highly syntactical rather than phrase structural in orientation, and include his clausal colon analysis. Louw is probably best known within current New Testament Greek language study for his colon analysis approach to discourse analysis, which seems to constitute a semantic extension beyond the colon or clause, used as an interpretive device to group together emerging larger semantic patterns.[99] Palmer had a predecessor in the work of Funk,[100] who was influenced by American structuralism, in particular the constituent analysis of Bloomfield as interpreted by Gleason.[101] Palmer drew upon slightly later developments in Chomsky (later abandoned in the minimalist program), including both his lexicalist hypothesis regarding transformations acting upon constituents and the supposition of intermediate levels of syntactic structure. This resulted in x-bar theory or a theory of projection of elements, to provide a formalist description of phrase structure in Greek, used by Palmer in his study of the Gospel of Luke.[102]

Most recently, Crellin has studied the historical semantic development of the perfect tense-form using Chomskyan linguistics and Neo-Davidsonian semantics, indebted to

---

[94]Reinhard Wonneberger, *Syntax und Exegese: Eine generative Theorie der griechischen Syntax und ihr Beitrag zur Auslegung des Neuen Testaments, dargestellt an 2. Corinther 5.2 und Römer 3.21-26*, BBET 13 (New York: Peter Lang, 1979); Wonneberger, "Der Beitrag der generativen Syntax zur Exegese: Ein Beispiel (2.Kor 5,2f) und neun Thesen," *Bijdragen* 36 (1975): 312–17; and Wonneberger, "Generative Stylistics: An Algorithmic Approach to Stylistic and Source Data Retrieval Problems based on Generative Syntax," in *Bedeutung, Sprechakte und Texte: Akten des 13. Linguistischen Kolloquiums*, 2, ed. Willy Vandeweghe and Marc Van de Velde (Tübingen: Niemeyer, 1979), 389–99.

[95]Reinhard Wonneberger, "Greek Syntax: A New Approach," *LLC* 2.2 (1986): 71–9.

[96]Daryl Dean Schmidt, *Hellenistic Greek Grammar and Noam Chomsky*, SBLDS 62 (Chico, CA: Scholars Press, 1981).

[97]Schmidt, *Hellenistic Greek Grammar*, ix, 41.

[98]Louw, *Semantics of New Testament Greek*, 67–89.

[99]A similar approach is found in John Beekman, John Callow, and Michael Kopesec, *The Semantic Structure of Written Communication*, 5th ed. (Dallas: Summer Institute of Linguistics, 1981), but has not, to my knowledge, resulted in a monograph using this method in New Testament studies.

[100]Funk, *Beginning-Intermediate Grammar*.

[101]H. A. Gleason Jr., *An Introduction to Descriptive Linguistics*, rev. ed. (New York: Holt, Rinehart & Winston, 1961).

[102]Micheal W. Palmer, *Levels of Constituent Structure in New Testament Greek*, SBG 6 (New York: Peter Lang, 1995); cf. Palmer, "How Do We Know a Phrase Is a Phrase? A Plea for Procedural Clarity in the Application of Linguistics to Biblical Greek," in *Biblical Greek Language and Linguistics: Open Questions in Current Research*, ed. Stanley E. Porter and D. A. Carson, JSNTSup 80 (Sheffield: JSOT Press, 1993), 15–86.

analytic philosophy.[103] Crellin's study appears to be an attempt at creating a positivist analysis according to syntactic and semantic rules, but it also seems to be far removed from being a study of how languages actually function. He also is primarily concerned with what is usually called lexical aspect rather than grammatical or morphological aspect, thus limiting the scope of his discussion to individual lexemes rather than the Greek verbal network.

This is not the place to provide a thorough critique of Chomskyan linguistics, a task that has been performed by numerous others both internally and externally to the school of linguistics. Chomskyan theory in general has been subject to criticism over the years, as have major components of Chomskyan linguistics. Apart from the implicit (and sometimes explicit) criticisms of other schools of linguistics (or their simple dismissal), major criticisms of Chomsky arguably began with Charles Hockett. Hockett, an American descriptivist and so in many ways positioned to be sympathetic to Chomsky, was one of the first to object to Chomsky's approach, attacking the major foundations of Chomskyan theory focusing especially upon Chomsky's early *Aspects*. Hockett addressed Chomsky's perceived failings in a short book subsequently largely neglected by other linguists.[104] Since then, there has been regular, even if only occasional, criticism by others,[105] with perhaps the most active critic through the years being the British linguist Geoffrey Sampson.[106] Sampson addresses most of the major tenets of Chomskyan theory, offering a variety of arguments in response. In particular, Sampson questions such Chomskyan notions as language creativity as defined by Chomsky,[107] grammaticality, language hierarchy, transformations, and Universal Grammar (and with it the snowflake analogy that Chomsky has used, in which each language is different but they share a common structure).[108] As a result, the Chomskyan notion of Universal Grammar, the emphasis upon competence over performance, Chomsky's conception of creativity of language as being no more than its additive ability, and language interference are all called into serious question. Most of these works by Sampson (and others), nevertheless,

---

[103] Robert Crellin, *The Syntax and Semantics of the Perfect Active in Literary Koine Greek* (New York: Wiley Blackwell, 2016). For Donald Davidson (1917–2003), he cites Davidson, "The Logical Form of Action Sentences" (1967), repr. in Davidson, *Essays on Actions and Events* (Oxford: Clarendon, 1980), 105–22, with responses (122–48). The major problem with use of Davidson (besides those raised by others) is that he is only concerned with the logical form of the statement (a very restricted form of meaning), and nothing beyond this, as he admits (105–6). This is certainly an approach consistent with Chomsky's early linguistic theories.

[104] Charles F. Hockett, *The State of the Art*, JLSMi 78 (The Hague: Mouton, 1968).

[105] E.g., Rudolf P. Botha, *Challenging Chomsky: The Generative Garden Game* (Oxford: Blackwell, 1989).

[106] Geoffrey Sampson, *The Form of Language* (London: Weidenfeld and Nicolson, 1975); Sampson, *Liberty and Language* (Oxford: Oxford University Press, 1979); Sampson, *Making Sense* (Oxford: Oxford University Press, 1980); Sampson, *Empirical Linguistics* (London: Continuum, 2001); and Sampson, *Linguistics Delusion*, 23–78.

[107] Chomsky's argument regarding creativity in language is supposedly evidenced by the ability of competent users to create new, understandable sentences that have never been heard or used before. The fact that users do this in their language is not open to dispute. See the explanation in Noam Chomsky, "Linguistic Theory," a lecture reprinted in *Noam Chomsky: Selected Readings on Transformational Theory*, ed. J. P. B. Allen and Paul van Buren (Oxford: Oxford University Press, 1971 [1965]), 152–9, esp. 153–4; and Chomsky, *Topics in the Theory of Generative Grammar* (The Hague: Mouton, 1971), 11, both cited in Sampson, *Linguistics Delusion*, 23–34 (in particular 24). Sampson, however, disputes this notion of creativity. He contends that there is nothing more creative to language in Chomsky's theory than there is in the addition function. The numbers may be large but the creativity is still very limited.

[108] On Universal Grammar in particular, see Geoffrey Sampson, *The "Language Instinct" Debate*, rev. ed. (London: Continuum, 2005 [1997]) and Fiona Cowie, *What's Within? Nativism Reconsidered* (Oxford: Oxford University Press, 1999).

have garnered relatively little significant response from the Chomskyan community, so far as I can tell.[109]

After an initial flurry, surprisingly little significant research has been done using Chomsky and Chomskyan linguistic theories in description of the Greek of the New Testament. This is somewhat surprising as the kinds of formalist descriptions that are found in these treatments are in some ways well-suited to the limitations of knowledge of an ancient language, in which we have access to the morphosyntactic elements in a more immediate way than we do the semantics. One reason may be that semantics (however this term is defined and extended to include or encompass pragmatics) is always at play in linguistic description, even if the analysis does not readily concede this. How one identifies syntagmatic units and their constituents and their relationships is as much semantic as it is syntactic. Another reason that Chomskyan theories may not be used is that the functions of language are at least as important as the structures of language, even if they are related to each other in admittedly diverse ways. There is an immediacy to learning the structures of language, as any elementary student of an ancient language realizes. However, theories that do not address the functions of language—especially in a discipline such as New Testament studies, which is less concerned with the innate language function than it is in describing the use of language—have less long-term attraction than those that ask questions of function, even if the functions are realized by formal structures. A third reason is probably the insignificance as to what had been accomplished by the previous studies. In other words, there may have been the question of "so what" that could not be answered, whether that was because the semantic or functional or some other question was not being answered.

Construction Grammar

There were a number of linguistic movements that shared Chomsky's fundamental formalist perspective but that rejected major components of his developing grammar and posited others. I realize that some might wish to place Construction Grammar—and there are many different kinds of Construction Grammar, some of which might well be better placed elsewhere—within the Cognitive Schools of linguistics, since Construction Grammar is the label often given to grammars associated with Cognitive Linguistics.[110] However, since the major dialogue partner of Construction Grammar as it is found in New Testament studies seems to be Chomskyan linguistics, I place it here as part of the Formalist School. One of the linguists who rejected Chomsky in some of his fundamental notions was Charles Fillmore (1929–2014), who taught first at Ohio State and then at UC Berkeley. Although not a student of Chomsky, Fillmore was part of the mid-1960s reaction to Chomskyan formalism initiated by Lakoff, Ronald Langacker, and others who wanted to find a place for meaning in Chomsky's grammar and led to development of

---

[109]For example, Pinker in his *Language Instinct* does not list Sampson in his index. An exception in response is Jerry Fodor, "Doing without What's Within: Fiona Cowie's *What's Within? Nativism Reconsidered*," *Mind* 110 (437; 2001): 99–148.

[110]See Laura A. Michaelis, "Construction Grammar and the Syntax-Semantics Interface," in *The Bloomsbury Companion to Syntax*, ed. Silvia Luraghi and Claudia Parodi (London: Bloomsbury, 2015), 421–35. For example, William Croft is a major figure in Cognitive Linguistics (see my further discussion) and the developer of his Radical Construction Grammar, one of the many forms of Construction Grammar. See William Croft, *Radical Construction Grammar: Syntactic Theory in Typological Perspective* (Oxford: Oxford University Press, 2001). See also Adele E. Goldberg, *Constructions: A Construction Grammar Approach to Argument Structure* (Chicago: University of Chicago Press, 1995).

generative semantics. Fillmore first proposed what he called Case Grammar in an article entitled "The Case for Case."[111] Case Grammar, as opposed to grammatical case (with which most New Testament scholars will be more familiar), was a way of identifying semantic functions of noun phrases in relation to their verbs, such as agent, patient, and instrument.[112] Fillmore's theory of case, which described semantic, thematic, or functional roles, came to be integrated into Chomskyan grammar by means of the work of Ray Jackendoff, one of the MIT linguists working with Chomsky, with its closest notion being the idea of theta roles.[113] In New Testament studies, Simon Wong used this form of Case Theory by Fillmore in his study of case in Paul,[114] but apart from a few articles by Wong (and one response to him), no more has been done in this area that I know of.[115]

Fillmore, in conjunction with others such as Lakoff at Berkeley and Paul Kay at Stanford University, developed the form of Construction Grammar that has been adopted by the New Testament Greek scholar Paul Danove, who studied at the Graduate Theological Union in Berkeley and had the opportunity to work with Fillmore.[116] Danove has been virtually unique in his use of Construction Grammar, what he calls Case Frame Analysis. Even if the school of Construction Grammar is not large in New Testament studies, however, it (or rather he) is prolific, as Danove has written a number of works using it. In virtually every monograph that he has written, Construction Grammar or Case Frame Analysis has played a role, and he continues to utilize it in his publications.[117] Case Frame Analysis, according to Danove, is a descriptive, generative, and non-transformational theory that is concerned to describe predicators, that is, words that "license" other phrasal elements called arguments and adjuncts. A Valence Description, displayed in graphic format, is the fundamental descriptive mechanism for describing the predicator, displaying such analysis in terms of three strata: syntactic function (e.g., verbal subject, predicate, complement—there are three syntactic functions plus the C function for adjuncts), semantic function (on the basis of twenty-one thematic roles that Danove has identified), and lexical information (realizations by various phrases, such as noun and verb. Danove has applied his Case Frame Analysis to a variety of linguistic situations.

---

[111] Charles J. Fillmore, "The Case for Case," in *Universals in Linguistic Theory*, ed. Emmon Bach and Robert T. Harms (New York: Holt, Rinehart & Winston, 1968), 1–88. See also Fillmore, "The Case for Case Reopened," in *Syntax and Semantics. VIII. Grammatical Relations*, ed. Peter Cole and Jerrold M. Sadock (New York: Academic Press, 1977), 59–81.
[112] See Matthews, *Grammatical Theory*, 179.
[113] Seuren, *Western Linguistics*, 132.
[114] Simon S. M. Wong, *A Classification of Semantic Case-Relations in the Pauline Epistles*, SBG 9 (New York: Peter Lang, 1997).
[115] Simon S. M. Wong, "What Case Is This Case? An Application of Semantic Case in Biblical Exegesis," *Jian Dao* 1 (1994): 49–73. Response by Stanley E. Porter, "The Case for Case Revisited," *Jian Dao* 6 (1996): 13–28.
[116] Charles J. Fillmore and Paul Kay, *Construction Grammar* (Stanford, CA: CSLI, 1999).
[117] Paul L. Danove, *The End of Mark's Story: A Methodological Study*, BINS 3 (Leiden: Brill, 1993); Danove, *Linguistics and Exegesis in the Gospel of Mark: Applications of a Case Frame Analysis and Lexicon*, JSNTSup 218, SNTG 10 (Sheffield: Sheffield Academic, 2002); Danove, *Grammatical and Exegetical Study of New Testament Verbs of Transference: A Case Frame Guide to Interpretation and Translation*, LNTS 329, SNTG 13 (London: T&T Clark, 2009); Danove, *New Testament Verbs of Communication: A Case Frame and Exegetical Study*, LNTS 520 (London: Bloomsbury, 2015); and Danove, *A Case Frame Grammar and Lexicon for the Book of Revelation*, LNTS 666 (London: T&T Clark, 2022). I use Danove, *New Testament Verbs*, 1–21, a relatively recent extensive treatment, for the description provided. He also uses it in Danove, *The Rhetoric of Characterization of God, Jesus, and Jesus' Disciples in the Gospel of Mark*, JSNTSup 290 (New York: T&T Clark, 2005) and Danove, *Theology of the Gospel of Mark: A Semantic, Narrative, and Rhetorical Study of the Characterization of God* (London: Bloomsbury, 2019). Danove has also written numerous articles using his Case Frame Analysis.

In his initial work on Mark's Gospel he uses Construction Grammar (later called Case Frame Analysis) as a corrective analog for deficiencies in previous definitions of plot; that is, plot becomes a type of syntactic description. He has also devoted volumes to verbs of communication and verbs of transference in the New Testament, and he continues to expand the repertoire of predicators he describes. In one of his most recent volumes, his theology of Mark's Gospel, Danove uses three frames: semantic, narrative, and rhetorical. He focuses upon God in various case roles, including agent, agentive benefactive, innate and originating benefactive, recipient and reciprocal benefactive, content, experiencer, goal, and instrument, and patient, source, theme, and topic. Needless to say, Danove generates an abundance not just of data but of analysis as well.

This must be one of few areas in which other New Testament scholars have not picked up an idea and developed it further, especially as Danove has been a tireless advocate for Case Frame Analysis. However, the reasons for the lack of adoption are probably related to the fact that there are a number of features of the analysis that are not readily apparent. The predicator is the unit of analysis, but the relationships among the levels of predicators are not made obvious. Predicator is usually associated with the notion of verb, but for Case Frame Analysis a predicator is any word that licenses other phrasal elements, and thus there is the potential for embedding and recursion that is not adequately theorized. There is also difficulty with the notion of function, as it is used of both syntax and semantics, where the strata are aligned. More complex syntax is provided by what Danove calls the C function (the function that is assigned to adjuncts), but that seems to take the Case Frame Analysis beyond its syntactical boundaries. Most case grammars are also more limited in the number of thematic roles that they identify, with Danove's 21 being one of the largest number that one might encounter. The number begs the questions of how one differentiates them and whether the identification of semantic roles is precise enough. A final consideration may be that it is not readily apparent how Danove's Case Frame Analysis relates to textual interpretation and hence exegesis. Danove certainly produces lists of data regarding his predicators, but their textual significance remains elusive.

Cognitive Schools

I have chosen to place Cognitive Schools of linguistics into their own category, rather than placing them with either Formalist or Functional Schools, as some other categorizations have done. One of the advantages of this tripartite division is that the separate categorization avoids the problem of having to decide where cognitivists should be placed. Some would argue that they belong with formalist theories on the basis of their origins and similarities with Chomskyan linguistics, as well as the fact that some of their important early advocates were educated by Chomsky or were highly influenced by him (e.g., Lakoff, Langacker, Kay), while others would argue that they should be placed with functionalist syntactical theories, as has been done by Van Valin and LaPolla in their common opposition to Chomsky.[118] I trust that my definition of Cognitive Schools of linguistics will show why they occupy this ostensive middle ground, even if they have some similarities with both Formalist and Functional Schools of linguistics.

---

[118] Van Valin and LaPolla, *Syntax*, 8–15.

Cognitive Linguistics

Cognitive Linguistics is probably the fastest-growing and developing area within contemporary linguistics. As I previously noted, it shares with Chomskyan formalism a cognitive base. However, the major difference between the two theories is that, whereas Chomsky and his followers have traditionally argued for a Universal Grammar in the form of a language component within the human brain, Cognitive Linguistics believes that language is used according to more general human cognitive principles. Cognitive Linguistics began to develop in the 1970s in relation to the emergence of semantics as a component in Chomskyan grammar (see previous discussion on the rise of generative semantics).[119] It became far more robust in the 1980s and continues to be a vibrant area of linguistic study, while at the same time being a highly diverse area of linguistics that is often viewed more as an orientation to language than as a defined school of linguistic thought.

The great diversity within Cognitive Linguistics means that there are almost as many definitions of it as there are advocates.[120] My purpose here is not to survey the various definitions but to see if we can identify enough common features so as to understand its basic contours. A standard introduction to Cognitive Linguistics by the cognitive linguists William Croft and Alan Cruse states that "three major hypotheses" guide Cognitive Linguistics. These three hypotheses are:

Language is not an autonomous cognitive faculty

Grammar is conceptualization

Knowledge of language emerges from language use.[121]

One can immediately see why Cognitive Linguistics is sometimes placed alongside Functional Schools, as it too is concerned with language use (although I would also say that language use and language function may mean two different things in such definitions), as the third principle affirms. Croft and Cruse note how the first principle distances Cognitive Linguistics from Chomskyan generative grammar and its autonomous language module or Universal Grammar (but without rejecting the idea that humans have innate language capacity). They also observe how the second proposal opposes truth-conditional semantics, and the third opposes reductionism in the first two on the basis of use.[122] As a result, linguistic knowledge in Cognitive Linguistics becomes what is sometimes referred to as "conceptual structure," whether phonological, morphological, or syntactical. Furthermore, cognitive language ability is similar to other kinds of cognitive ability and is part of the human cognitive capacity.[123]

---

[119]Vyvyan Evans and Melanie Green, *Cognitive Linguistics: An Introduction* (Edinburgh: University of Edinburgh Press, 2006), 3, state that Cognitive Linguistics grew out of "dissatisfaction with formal [i.e., Chomskyan] approaches to language."

[120]A fundamental work is Ronald W. Langacker, *Foundations of Cognitive Grammar, Volume 1: Theoretical Prerequisites* (Stanford, CA: Stanford University Press, 1987). For the related area of typology, see John R. Taylor, *Linguistic Categorization: Prototypes in Linguistic Theory*, 2nd ed. (Oxford: Clarendon, 1995 [1989]).

[121]William Croft and D. Alan Cruse, *Cognitive Linguistics*, CTL (Cambridge: Cambridge University Press, 2004), 1.

[122]Croft and Cruse, *Cognitive Linguistics*, 1. Ronald N. Langacker, *Cognitive Grammar: A Basic Introduction* (Oxford: Oxford University Press, 2008), 5, refers to grammar as working through symbolic relationships.

[123]Croft and Cruse, *Cognitive Linguistics*, 2.

A second, though in some ways similar, definition of Cognitive Linguistics is offered by two further cognitive linguists, Vyvyan Evans and Melanie Green. They contend that Cognitive Linguistics holds to two fundamental commitments. These two fundamental commitments were first articulated in an article by Lakoff, one of the founders of the field who was also instrumental in the rise of generative semantics.[124] These two commitments are: the generalization commitment and the cognitive commitment. The generalization commitment assumes that "there are common structuring principles that hold across different aspects of language, and that an important function of linguistics is to identify these common principles."[125] These common features by which language may be organized include: categorization, polysemy, and metaphor. Categorization according to these common principles is based upon such concepts as centrality, representativeness, and family resemblances. Polysemy, the idea that elements of language have multiple meanings, applies to both lexis (where it is usually discussed) and syntax. Finally, metaphor, a topic that has become immensely important in Cognitive Linguistics, is a means of extending meaning for both the lexicon and syntax. The cognitive commitment, the second of the two commitments, holds "that principles of linguistic structure should reflect what is known about human cognition from other disciplines, particularly the other cognitive sciences (philosophy, psychology, artificial intelligence and neuroscience)."[126] The cognitive commitment relies upon language profiling using fuzzy boundaries, as well as metaphor, hence its relationship to prototype theory, which is used in a variety of ways in Cognitive Linguistics. Evans and Green also note that a further central notion in Cognitive Linguistics is the "embodied mind."[127] Rather than the mind being distinct from the body (as per Descartes and Chomsky, who appears to follow in Descartes' line), Cognitive Linguistics emphasizes embodied experience by an embodied mind participating in real experiences.

Many areas of Cognitive Linguistics provide avenues of potential interest for New Testament scholars. One of these is frame theory, where there has already been some published research, or even semantic primitives if they may be placed here.[128] However, New Testament scholars have tended to follow most enthusiastically those cognitive linguists who have developed the area of conceptual metaphor theory and its derived extensions. One of the leading figures in this area is, again, Lakoff, who has worked with the philosopher Mark Johnson to develop notions of metaphor that draw upon human

---

[124]George Lakoff, "The Invariance Hypothesis: Is Abstract Reason Based on Image-Schemas?" *Cognitive Linguistics* 1.1 (1990): 39–74. See also Lakoff, *Women, Fire, and Dangerous Things: What Categories Reveal about the Mind* (Chicago: University of Chicago Press, 1987).
[125]Evans and Green, *Cognitive Linguistics*, 28. Discussion is found on 28–40.
[126]Evans and Green, *Cognitive Linguistics*, 40. Discussion is found on 40–4.
[127]Evans and Green, *Cognitive Linguistics*, 44. For a full study of this concept, see George Lakoff and Mark Johnson, *Philosophy in the Flesh: The Embodied Mind and Its Challenge to Western Thought* (New York: Basic, 1999).
[128]See, for example, Yoon Man Park, *Mark's Memory Resources and the Controversy Stories (Mark 2:1–3:6): An Application of the Frame Theory of Cognitive Science to the Markan Oral-Aural Narrative*, LBS 2 (Leiden: Brill, 2010); or Anna Wierzbicka, *What Did Jesus Mean? Explaining the Sermon on the Mount and the Parables in Simple and Universal Human Concepts* (Oxford: Oxford University Press, 2001), following her extensive previous work on semantic primitives, such as Wierzbicka, *Understanding Cultures through Their Key Words: English, Russian, Polish, German, Japanese* (New York: Oxford University Press, 1997). Geeraerts, *Theories of Lexical Semantics*, 124–37, places Wierzbicka within neostructural semantics, but recognizes some similarities with Cognitive Linguistics. I place her here for convenience of classification.

embodiment.[129] Conceptual metaphor theory essentially contends that all language is based upon mapping semantic domains or conceptual spheres upon each other, especially more remote domains upon more familiar ones. An example of such mapping would be mapping the remote upon something as familiar as the human body, etc. As a result we get metaphors regarding the "head of the class" or the "foot of the bed." Early versions of conceptual metaphor theory have been extended to encompass a range and mix of metaphors. These include primary metaphor theory, metonymy, and conceptual blending or integration theory,[130] the latter of which expands the range of metaphor by blending various metaphors together into larger conceptual constructs, all thus falling within the larger scope of conceptual blending or integration theory.[131]

There has been a growing number of significant works in conceptual metaphor and related (and other) theories of metaphor within New Testament studies (worth noting here, even if not strictly falling within Cognitive Linguistics), but not all of them are what one might call studies of Greek language. In fact, few of them are. They are instead conceptual studies of images or figures or metaphors within the Bible, often assuming other theories of Greek language when used. These include works by Jacobus Liebenberg on comparing the parabolic metaphors in the Synoptic Gospels and the Gospel of Thomas,[132] Bonnie Howe on 1 Peter,[133] David Downs on Paul's use of metaphor in speaking of the collection,[134] Nijay Gupta on Paul's cultic metaphors,[135] Beth Stovell on kingship in John's Gospel (although she also uses other linguistic theories, such as SFL),[136] Jennifer McNeel on 1 Thessalonians and the infancy/nursing mother metaphors,[137] Frederick Tappenden on resurrection in Paul (plant and "body is house" metaphors),[138] William

---

[129] George Lakoff and Mark Johnson, *Metaphors We Live By* (Chicago: University of Chicago Press, 1980); and Lakoff and Mark Turner, *More than Cool Reason: A Field Guide to Poetic Metaphor* (Chicago: University of Chicago Press, 1989). They have been followed by numerous other volumes on conceptual metaphor. On embodiment, see Lakoff and Johnson, *Philosophy in the Flesh*.

[130] Evans and Green, *Cognitive Linguistics*, 304–10; Alice Deignan, "The Cognitive View of Metaphor: Conceptual Metaphor Theory," in *Metaphor Analysis: Research Practice in Applied Linguistics, Social Sciences and the Humanities*, ed. Lynne Cameron and Robert Maslen (Sheffield: Equinox, 2010), 44–56, esp. 50–1; Gilles Fauconnier and Mark Turner, *The Way We Think: Conceptual Blending and the Mind's Hidden Complexities* (New York: Basic, 2002). For a good history of the development of cognitive metaphor theory, see Zoltán Kövecses, *Metaphor: A Practical Introduction* (Oxford: Oxford University Press, 2002).

[131] The notion of space is fundamental to conceptual integration theory, in which various concepts occupy space and are brought into relation with each other. Space is an important concept in Cognitive Linguistics as a whole. See, for example, Terry Regier, *The Human Semantic Potential: Spatial Language and Constrained Connectionism* (Cambridge, MA: MIT Press, 1996); Paul Bloom et al., eds., *Language and Space* (Cambridge, MA: MIT Press, 1996); and Gilles Fauconnier, *Mappings in Thought and Language* (Cambridge: Cambridge University Press, 1997).

[132] Jacobus Liebenberg, *The Language of the Kingdom and Jesus: Parable, Aphorism, and Metaphor in the Sayings Material Common to the Synoptic Tradition and the Gospel of Thomas*, BZNW 102 (Berlin: de Gruyter, 2001).

[133] Bonnie Howe, *Because You Bear This Name: Conceptual Metaphor and the Moral Meaning of 1 Peter*, BINS 81 (Leiden: Brill, 2008).

[134] David J. Downs, *The Offering of the Gentiles: Paul's Collection for Jerusalem in Its Chronological, Cultural, and Cultic Contexts* (Tübingen: Mohr Siebeck, 2008; repr., Grand Rapids: Eerdmans, 2016).

[135] Nijay K. Gupta, *Worship that Makes Sense to Paul: A New Approach to the Theology and Ethics of Paul's Cultic Metaphors*, BZNW 175 (Berlin: de Gruyter, 2010).

[136] Beth M. Stovell, *Mapping Metaphorical Discourse in the Fourth Gospel: John's Eternal King*, LBS 5 (Leiden: Brill, 2012).

[137] Jennifer McNeel, *Paul as Infant and Nursing Mother: Metaphor, Rhetoric, and Identity in 1 Thessalonians 2:5-8* (Atlanta: SBL Press, 2014).

[138] Frederick S. Tappenden, *Resurrection in Paul: Cognition, Metaphor, and Transformation* (Atlanta: SBL Press, 2016).

Robinson on Romans 8 and "spirit-life is a journey,"[139] Erin Heim on adoption and sonship metaphors,[140] Robert Von Thaden who utilizes conceptual integration theory in relationship to embodiment,[141] Gregory Lanier on a variety of Old Testament metaphors (e.g., horn, appearing, bird, stone),[142] Judith Stack on sin and evil,[143] Clifford Winters on the use of the "argument is war" metaphor in Revelation (he also uses Relevance Theory; see my subsequent comments),[144] Kai-Hsuan Chang on conceptual metaphor and embodiment in Paul,[145] and Oscar Jiménez on conceptual metaphors in Ephesians.[146] There are no doubt other studies than these. Most of these studies, with the noteworthy exception of Stovell, are not directly concerned with the Greek language or study of it as one might typically conceive of linguistic research, but with what might be more typically characterized as figurative language, with a modest appeal to some discussion of conceptual metaphor theory or the like. Stovell's concern with Greek emerges from her use of a different linguistic theory (SFL; see later in this chapter).

There has been much work in the school of Cognitive Linguistics, but that raises the very question of whether this is in fact a school of linguistics. Evans and Green themselves state that "Cognitive linguistics is described as a 'movement' or an 'enterprise' because it is not a specific theory. Instead, it is an approach that has adopted a common set of guiding principles, assumptions and perspectives which have led to a diverse range of complementary, overlapping (and sometimes competing) theories."[147] As one will have noted in the previous brief discussion, many if not most of the categories that are used within Cognitive Linguistics, such as centrality, representation, family resemblance, are either very difficult to define or have been called into question. For example, the notion of family resemblance—attributed to Ludwig Wittgenstein[148]—is no longer as widely regarded as it once was. The appearance of a family resemblance, as many have pointed out, does not necessarily indicate that there is a family relationship. A further example of the limitations of Cognitive Linguistics may be found in its failure to develop a working model of grammar, at least as many if not most linguists would conceive of grammar. Cognitive Linguistics seems to give more attention to thought than it does to language.[149]

---

[139] William E. W. Robinson, *Metaphor, Morality, and the Spirit in Romans 8:1-17* (Atlanta: SBL Press, 2016).

[140] Erin M. Heim, *Adoption in Galatians and Romans: Contemporary Metaphor Theories and the Pauline Huiothesia Metaphors*, BINS 153 (Leiden: Brill, 2017).

[141] Robert H. Von Thaden Jr., *Sex, Christ, and Embodied Cognition: Paul's Wisdom for Corinth* (Atlanta: SBL Press, 2017).

[142] Gregory R. Lanier, *Old Testament Conceptual Metaphors and the Christology of Luke's Gospel*, LNTS 591 (London: Bloomsbury, 2018).

[143] Judith V. Stack, *Metaphor and the Portrayal of the Cause(s) of Sin and Evil in the Gospel of Matthew*, BINS 182 (Leiden: Brill, 2020).

[144] Clifford T. Winters, *Argument Is War: Relevance-Theoretic Comprehension of the Conceptual Metaphor of War in the Apocalypse*, LBS 18 (Leiden: Brill, 2020), who brings together Cognitive Linguistics and the following cognitive model, Relevance Theory.

[145] Kai-Hsuan Chang, *The Impact of Bodily Experience on Paul's Resurrection Theology*, LNTS 655 (London: T&T Clark, 2022).

[146] Oscar Jiménez, *Metaphors in the Narrative of Ephesians 2:11-22: Motion towards Maximal Proximity and Higher Status*, LBS 20 (Leiden: Brill, 2022). Cf. Joel B. Green and Bonnie Howe, eds., *Cognitive Linguistic Explorations in Biblical Studies* (Berlin: de Gruyter, 2014), for a collection of essays using Cognitive Linguistics; and William A. Ross and Steven E. Runge, eds., *Postclassical Greek Prepositions and Conceptual Metaphor: Cognitive Semantic Analysis and Biblical Interpretation* (Berlin: de Gruyter, 2022), for essays on Greek prepositions from a Cognitive Linguistic perspective.

[147] Evans and Green, *Cognitive Linguistics*, 3.

[148] Ludwig Wittgenstein, *Philosophical Investigations*, trans. G. E. M. Anscombe, 2nd ed. (Oxford: Blackwell, 1958), pars. 65–69, in the context of language games.

[149] Deignan, "Cognitive Metaphor," 55.

Langacker's notion that grammar is symbolic means simply—at least for him—that the relation between elements that form more complex structures is entirely symbolic, and not syntactic or even semantic, as one might find in other linguistic schools of thought.[150] There is the further problem that the concept of domain is very difficult to define, and this impedes the ability to equate domains if we are not even certain what the domains are. There is a final problem of the relationship of conceptual metaphors to language itself and how it is that one is able to move from language to metaphor.[151]

Sampson, the outspoken critic of Chomsky, has also criticized Cognitive Linguistics on several fronts. These include its making generalizations about human language based upon a limited array of evidence, that evidence primarily being English, when such generalizations have not been tested and established over a sufficiently wide array of languages. For example, he notes that Chinese does not use metaphor in the same way as does English, thus calling conceptual metaphor theory into question as following general cognitive principles. Cognitive metaphors in English may be describing a feature of how English speakers create metaphor, not how metaphor represents human cognition. That some languages might draw upon the world around them for their metaphors is hardly a deep or unique insight in any case. Sampson also points out that once one moves beyond the notion of "embodiment" the situation becomes less clear, especially as one moves into other languages and attempts to characterize human language usage.[152] Perhaps in that respect it is better to think of Cognitive Linguistics as an approach or orientation, and one that is confined to English until we can establish its basis in other languages. The fact that it may have heuristic value in English does not mean that it has similar value in ancient Greek. Whatever value there may be in the New Testament works mentioned here, what is clear is that they are not really indicating something substantial about theories of linguistics so much as theories of cognition, arguably very different categories both definitionally and phenomenologically.

Relevance Theory

To be located also in this area of cognition is Relevance Theory. This theory has emerged within linguistics and especially translation studies as a theory of importance, even if it is not as central as some others. It has been adopted by some scholars within biblical studies, to the point where we may identify it as a school, even if not a large one and even if it might not have such status in other fields where it has nevertheless had an influence. The origins of Relevance Theory are in philosophical thought, especially ordinary language philosophy. In 1957, H. Paul Grice (1913–88) the Harvard philosopher published an article entitled "Meaning," in which he laid the basis of inferential rather than code-based communication.[153] In other words, he was interested less in meaning in language as reflected or institutionalized in a formalized code, a view inherited by linguistics since Saussure, than in meaning as something that is inferred by users. Later, in 1975, Grice published an article entitled "Logic and Conversation."[154] This article outlined his theory

---

[150]Langacker, *Cognitive Grammar*, 5.
[151]Deignan, "Cognitive Metaphor," 54–6.
[152]Sampson, *Linguistics Delusion*, 77–87.
[153]H. Paul Grice, "Meaning," repr. in Paul Grice, *Studies in the Way of Words* (Cambridge, MA: Harvard University Press, 1989), 213–23. This article was originally published in *The Philosophical Review* 66 (1957): 377–88.
[154]Grice, "Logic and Conversation," repr. in *Studies*, 22–40. This article was originally published in *Syntax and Semantics, Volume 3, Speech Acts*, ed. Peter Cole and Jerry L. Morgan (New York: Academic Press, 1975), 41–58.

of conversational implicatures that developed further his notion of inferential meaning. He categorized these implicatures under what he called the Cooperative Principle, and then he laid out several sub-categories related to quantity, quality, relation, and manner in communication. According to Grice, these are the implicatures of successful conversation: they fulfill expectations regarding these categories.

At around the same time as Grice published his second article, the linguists Daniel Sperber and Deirdre Wilson began working on the field within linguistics called pragmatics and, along with it, inferential communication.[155] In 1986, they published a volume simply entitled *Relevance*. In this volume, their stated goal is to answer the following questions: "What is needed is an attempt to rethink, in psychologically realistic terms, such basic questions as: What form of shared information is available to humans? How is shared information exploited in communication? What is relevance and how is it achieved? What role does the search for relevance play in communication?"[156] The answer to these questions is Relevance Theory. Relevance Theory is a cognitive theory that rejects code theories of language to argue for what is called a "principle of relevance," that is, that "[h]uman cognitive processes ... are geared to achieving the greatest possible cognitive effect for the smallest possible processing effort."[157] The communication that results is based upon what Sperber and Wilson call ostensive-inferential communication. Ostensive behavior is defined as providing evidence of what one is thinking so that others may draw inferences from it.[158] In other words, the communicator signals and the communicatee determines meaning.[159] Relevance Theory has become widely used in translation studies, where it continues to attract interest. The Bible translator Ernest-August Gutt has applied Relevance Theory to translation in several different volumes,[160] and the notion of relevance has had a significant impact upon the Bible translation movement.

Relevance Theory has been applied to New Testament studies in a variety of ways other than in translation. The linguist and biblical scholar Margaret Sim has written a very basic introduction to the topic for use by biblical scholars in exegesis.[161] She begins with a chapter that defines Relevance Theory, in which she identifies such features of language as the underdeterminacy of meaning, the role of inference, the function of metarepresentation (how elements are otherwise represented),[162] and the role of ostension (drawing attention to elements of communication, as opposed to inference). All of these are important for establishing relevance. She then applies Relevance Theory

---

[155] Many linguistic theories differentiate semantics (meaning of a word or form in itself) and pragmatics (meaning of a word or form in context). Not all schools of linguistics find this distinction useful, including SFL. For a general introduction to pragmatics, see Jacob L. Mey, *Pragmatics: An Introduction*, 2nd ed. (Oxford: Blackwell, 2001).

[156] Dan Sperber and Deirdre Wilson, *Relevance: Communication and Cognition*, 2nd ed. (Oxford: Blackwell, 1995 [1991]), 38. See also Wilson and Sperber, "Relevance Theory," in *The Handbook of Pragmatics*, ed. Laurence R. Horn and Gregory Ward (Malden, MA: Blackwell, 2006), 607–32.

[157] Wilson and Sperber, *Relevance*, vii.

[158] Wilson and Sperber, *Relevance*, 50–4.

[159] See Geoffrey Leech and Jenny Thomas, "Language, Meaning and Context: Pragmatics," in *An Encyclopaedia of Language*, ed. N. E. Collinge (London: Routledge, 1990), 173–206, esp. 201–4 (202) on Relevance Theory.

[160] Ernst-August Gutt, *Translation and Relevance: Cognition and Context* (repr., Manchester: St. Jerome, 2010). Cf. also Gutt, *Relevance Theory: A Guide to Successful Communication in Translation* (Dallas: SIL and UBS, 1992).

[161] Margaret G. Sim, *A Relevant Way to Read: A New Approach to Exegesis and Communication* (Eugene, OR: Pickwick, 2016).

[162] See Deirdre Wilson, "Metarepresentation in Linguistic Communication," in *Metarepresentations: A Multidisciplinary Perspective*, ed. Deirdre Wilson (Oxford: Oxford University Press, 2000), 411–48.

to several specific situations: re-presentation, irony, particles, and conditional sentences. This introduction follows upon Sim's earlier work on the use of the Greek particles ἵνα and ὅτι.[163] Several other scholars who have used Relevance Theory in their research are Stephen Pattemore, Joseph Fantin, Nelson Morales, and Sarah Casson. Pattemore applies Relevance Theory to the book of Revelation in both of his volumes.[164] Fantin treats the Greek imperative in one volume and applies Relevance Theory to the confession "Jesus is Lord" in another.[165] Morales examines how the book of James uses the Old Testament on the basis of Relevance Theory and especially its theory of metarepresentation.[166] Casson, in work similar to that of Sim, examines the use of the particle γάρ as an important signpost in establishing the cohesion of the book of Romans.[167] In one of his two works, Fantin combines Relevance Theory with Neuro-Cognitive Stratificational Linguistics (NCSL), a direct and not-too-different descendant of Stratificational Grammar.[168] It is debatable whether the use of NCSL's stratal approach actually aids in identifying the pragmatics of the imperative based upon Relevance Theory. As Fantin himself admits, however, it is highly questionable whether Relevance Theory is even a theory of linguistics (being arguably more a theory of communication, and the examples that Sperber and Wilson use tend to confirm this), and NCSL, despite its stratal view of language and emphasis upon language as comprising systems of relationships into a network, is an attempt to model the way that the brain functions rather than model language.[169]

Despite the uses of Relevance Theory in translation studies, the same kinds of questions arise as were offered regarding Cognitive Linguistics. Even an advocate such as Fantin must admit that it is arguable whether Relevance Theory is a linguistic theory or whether it is a theory of communication. It is perhaps better seen as an orientation than it is a method or even a linguistic school. In New Testament studies, there tends to be more examination of language in Relevance Theory than in Cognitive Linguistics, but clearly the emphasis is not upon language even if it is upon communication. There is the further question of whether Relevance Theory has a sufficiently robust apparatus to answer the kinds of questions that linguists wish to ask of language. The generalizations that drive Relevance Theory—such as relevance itself, underdeterminacy, and inference—may well provide a foundation for pragmatic understanding, but questions remain whether these generalizations are sufficient without a more robust linguistic theory—such as Fantin incorporates—to provide suitable and sufficient linguistic description. There is the final issue of whether these generalizations are in fact pertinent to matters of language or only to the instances in which they have been used.

---

[163]Margaret G. Sim, *Marking Thought and Talk in New Testament Greek: New Light from Linguistics on the Particles* ἵνα *and* ὅτι (Eugene, OR: Pickwick, 2010).
[164]Stephen Pattemore, *Souls under the Altar: Relevance Theory and the Discourse Structure of Revelation* (New York: UBS, 2003); Pattemore, *The People of God in the Apocalypse: Discourse, Structure and Exegesis*, SNTSMS 128 (Cambridge: Cambridge University Press, 2004).
[165]Joseph D. Fantin, *The Lord of the Entire World: Lord Jesus, a Challenge to Lord Caesar?*, NTM 31 (Sheffield: Sheffield Phoenix, 2011); Fantin, *The Greek Imperative Mood in the New Testament: A Cognitive and Communicative Approach*, SBG 12 (New York: Peter Lang, 2010).
[166]Nelson R. Morales, *Poor and Rich in James: A Relevance Theory Approach to James's Use of the Old Testament* (University Park, PA: Eisenbrauns, 2018).
[167]Sandra H. Casson, *Textual Signposts in the Argument of Romans: A Relevance-Theory Approach* (Atlanta: SBL Press, 2019).
[168]This is based upon the work of Sydney Lamb, *Outline of Stratificational Grammar* (Washington, DC: Georgetown University Press, 1966), with some minimal developments. Lamb's later work is entitled *Pathways of the Brain: The Neurocognitive Basis of Language* (Amsterdam: John Benjamins, 1999).
[169]Fantin, *Imperative*, 333, 334.

Functional Schools

There are a several different Functional Schools of linguistics that have flourished in the past and that some current biblical scholars might be aware of. These include Tagmemics and various forms of Functionalism (whether West Coast or Continental or otherwise). At one time, Tagmemics was a major school of linguistics outside and within biblical studies. Kenneth Pike, professor at the University of Michigan and early leader of the Summer Institute of Linguistics, developed Tagmemics as a stratified and unified theory of human behavior, including language, invoking such notions as the tagmeme, slot and filler organization, and widely used distinction between etic and emic representation.[170] Pike's major volume on the subject incited much subsequent work, especially in the fellow SIL member and linguist, Robert Longacre (1922–2014). Longacre developed his own linguistic approach that was based upon Tagmemics but moved increasingly away from it.[171] Although Longacre wrote a number of articles in New Testament, he did not write a book exemplifying Tagmemics and few recently seem to have followed him down this path.[172] I will instead focus upon two much more active linguistic schools within the Functional Schools that continue to generate productive scholarship.

Cognitive-Functionalism

The first school of linguistics that I will discuss is what has come to be called cognitive-functional linguistics. Before I outline its major tenets, I must note some reservations with my inclusion of it here. This approach could have been discussed previously under Cognitive Schools, and in some ways perhaps should have been, but I place it here because it appears to be (or perhaps desires to be) more functionalist in nature, even though it makes wide appeal to cognitive concepts. I concentrate upon two major books that reflect this school of thought. Neither of the books uses the label "cognitive" in an overt way, but the first, by the SIL linguist and translator Stephen Levinsohn, often refers to a book that he wrote with a colleague, where their method is explicitly referred to as being "functional and cognitive."[173] The second volume in New Testament studies, by Steven Runge, also uses concepts that are cognitively defined and employed.[174] Since these two works that I will discuss also fashion themselves as directed toward discourse, one might also question whether this approach should instead be called discourse-functional (as it is on the back cover of Runge's book). One might further question whether such an approach to discourse should be included at all within the linguistic schools being discussed here, as it draws upon such schools to formulate its overall discourse analytic approach. My answer to these questions will become evident in my exposition of it. A final consideration is that this approach is very light on theoretical foundations, especially when compared to

---

[170] Pike, *Language in Relation to a Unified Theory*.
[171] Robert E. Longacre, *The Grammar of Discourse*, 2nd ed. (New York: Plenum, 1996).
[172] SIL has followed a number of different approaches to linguistics in its various educational centers (I owe this observation to Martin Culy), but most of these have not been developed into linguistic schools within New Testament Greek studies, apart from those noted in this essay.
[173] Robert A. Dooley and Stephen H. Levinsohn, *Analyzing Discourse: A Manual of Basic Concepts* (Dallas: SIL International, 2001), back cover and vii, although it also describes itself as a "'grab bag' of diverse methodologies" (vii).
[174] I have also found reference to this theory as cognitive-functional in the title of a paper by Steven Runge delivered at the ETS annual meeting in 2013, entitled "The Greek Article: A Cognitive-Functional Approach," and on his blogsite.

the theoretical apparatus found in the other schools presented here. The major work in cognitive-functional linguistics by Levinsohn devotes only four (admittedly large) pages to establishing its linguistic foundation, and the subsequent volume by Runge does not contain much more theoretical information. Nevertheless, I will treat this approach as a school of linguistic thought.

The approach of Levinsohn, followed in most if not all significant respects by Runge, is found in Levinsohn's major book, entitled *Discourse Features of New Testament Greek*, with the subtitle *A Coursebook on the Information Structure of New Testament Greek*.[175] When describing his theoretical approach, Levinsohn states that his position is one of "descriptive linguistics."[176] This is a problematic term to use. Sampson has a chapter devoted to what he calls the Descriptivists.[177] In that chapter, he focuses in particular upon Boas and Bloomfield, two major North American linguists who began their careers describing indigenous Native American languages, and this descriptivism characterized their general approach and that of their followers. Bloomfield was influenced by the New Grammarians and held to many of their tenets throughout his career, to the point of taking a behaviorist view or what he calls a mechanistic view of language. Such a position defines meaning as "the situation in which the speaker utters it and the response which it calls forth in the hearer," in other words a matter of stimulus and response.[178] I am pretty sure that Levinsohn does not mean this, but his use of the term "descriptive" and his statement that he simply wishes to treat the Greek New Testament as he would any other text leaves him open to such misunderstanding, if it is indeed a misunderstanding.

Levinsohn offers four italicized words or statements to describe his approach. The first is that he specifically labels his approach as "eclectic." By this he means exactly what one might imagine—that he draws upon various linguistic theories in his descriptions—to the point where he freely admits to drawing opposite conclusions from these theories as do their originators. One of those he specifically mentions (in fact the only one he mentions, thus calling into question the notion of what it means to be eclectic) is Talmy Givón, who is associated with West Coast Functionalism.[179] Levinsohn also specifically mentions that his approach is "functional" in that it attempts to describe the uses of linguistic structures, and it is "structural" in that it describes linguistic structures (he does not call it cognitive). In particular relation to functionalism, Levinsohn notes that he ascribes to the principle that "choice implies meaning," indicating that when authors exercise choice

---

[175] Stephen H. Levinsohn, *Discourse Features of New Testament Greek: A Coursebook on the Information Structure of New Testament Greek*, 2nd ed. (Dallas: SIL International, 2000), vii–ix (the first edition appeared in 1992), from which the description used here is taken; Steven E. Runge, *Discourse Grammar of the Greek New Testament: A Practical Introduction for Teaching and Exegesis* (Peabody, MA: Hendrickson, 2010), 5–16, the basis of the subsequent description. As surprising as it may seem, the entire framework of their approach is laid out in these few pages by Levinsohn, not much better developed in Runge.

[176] Levinsohn, *Discourse Features*, vii. Levinsohn describes the origins of his approach in Stephen H. Levinsohn, "Discourse Analysis: Galatians as a Case Study," in *Linguistics and New Testament Greek: Key Issues in the Current Debate*, ed. David Alan Black and Benjamin L. Merkle (Grand Rapids: Baker, 2020), 103–24, esp. 103–5.

[177] Sampson, *Schools of Linguistics*, 57–80.

[178] Bloomfield, *Language*, 139. Bloomfield appears to have developed a fuller sense of meaning later in his career. See Bloomfield, "Meaning," *MDU* 53 (1943): 101–6, repr. in *A Leonard Bloomfield Anthology*, ed. Hockett, 400–5.

[179] Levinsohn cites two works by Talmy Givón in his bibliography: *Topic Continuity in Discourse* (Philadelphia: John Benjamins, 1983) and *Syntax: A Functional-Typological Introduction*, 2 vols. (Amsterdam: John Benjamins, 1984–90). Givón is not apparently mentioned in Levinsohn, "Discourse Analysis."

they are also expressing a difference in meaning.[180] He says that this is a characteristic of functionalism, although it is actually one of the tenets of structuralism. If one were to take these characteristics—descriptive, eclectic, functional, structural, and choice implies meaning—one would probably conclude that this is an approach to linguistics that has elements in common with the continental structuralists, such as the Prague Linguistic Circle, or possibly even the Copenhagen School. There is something to this, as Levinsohn then gives special attention to markedness, one of the legacies of the Prague School, and the differentiation between what he calls "semantic meaning" and "pragmatic effects," a distinction between semantics and pragmatics that has its place in many different linguistic schools, including Prague.

Steven Runge, Levinsohn's closest follower, takes a similar approach.[181] He states that his approach is "cross-linguistic," by which he presumably means eclectic but in more contemporary language. He further states that he is interested in "how languages tend to operate rather than just focusing on Greek," a tendency seen in much recent discussion of typology. He finally states that his approach is "function-based."[182] Runge states that he "presupposes three core principles." These are: "choice implies meaning," "Semantic or inherent meaning should be differentiated from pragmatic effect," and "Default patterns of usage should be distinguished from marked ones."[183] He then adds a feature not found in Levinsohn (the other three are apparently directly taken from Levinsohn), that prominence and contrast capture a fundamental pragmatic implication. These two features also seem to be derived from Levinsohn.

The major problem with the cognitive-functional approach presented here is that it is not a linguistic theory at all, even if it may be a school. It is founded upon a relatively small set of generalizations and assertions mostly from structuralist linguistics, with very little that appears cognitive. Levinsohn treats a limited number of discourse features, all oriented to information structure. These include constituent order, sentence conjunctions, patterns of reference, backgrounding and highlighting, reporting of conversation, and

---

[180]I note that this wording appears to be based upon but is reformulated from the wording "*meaning* implies *choice*" by Bazell, *Linguistic Form*, 81, endorsed in the latter form by numerous linguists (cf. John Lyons, *Structural Semantics: An Analysis of Part of the Vocabulary of Plato* [Oxford: Blackwell, 1963], 25–30; Lyons, *Introduction to Theoretical Linguistics* [Cambridge: Cambridge University Press, 1968], 413–19; M. A. K. Halliday, *Language as Social Semiotic: The Social Interpretation of Language and Meaning* [London: Edward Arnold, 1978], 137, in which "Text is meaning and meaning is choice"; and Halliday, *An Introduction to Functional Grammar* [IFG1] [London: Edward Arnold, 1985], xiv, in which he states that SFL "is a theory of meaning as choice"). The difference might be that this reflects a bottom-up approach by Levinsohn, in which the language potential is found in forms realized in meanings, whereas the other reflects a top-down approach in which meanings are realized in systemic choices. Both might be true, but they reflect a difference in linguistic theories.

[181]Some have claimed that Steven E. Runge and Christopher J. Fresch, eds., *The Greek Verb Revisited: A Fresh Approach for Biblical Exegesis* (Bellingham, WA: Lexham, 2016), has presented a coherent approach to the matter of the Greek verb. Nothing could be further from the truth. There are at least six different linguistic theories, as well as traditional grammatical approaches, in evidence in the volume. These include cognitive-functional (Levinsohn, Runge), Role and Reference Grammar (Michael and Rachel Aubrey), Cognitive Linguistics (Nicholas Ellis), Relevance Theory (Randall Buth), prototype theory (Buth?, Christopher Fresch), descriptivism (Robert Crellin?), historical linguistics (Amalia Moser), as well as a number of possible others. See the review of this volume in Stanley E. Porter, "Revisiting the Greek Verb: An Extended Critique," *FN* 31 (2018): 3–16.

[182]Runge, *Discourse Grammar*, xviii. He also states that his approach is not language specific but shows "how humans are wired to process language" (5), using the terminology of Cognitive Linguistics.

[183]Runge, *Discourse Grammar*, 5.

boundary features. Runge is in fact even more limited in the features of his discourse grammar. After treating conjunction in a chapter in his foundations section, he treats forward-pointing devices, information structuring devices, and thematic highlighting devices. One notices that all the elements treated in both of these works are concerned with information structure or the textual dimension. In that sense, both of them follow in a limited way the pattern set by the Prague School, which first developed markedness and information structure with its notions of theme and rheme and the Functional Sentence Perspective. The linguistic descriptions that Levinsohn as well as Runge provides often result in judgments being made that imply much more than a descriptive framework, for which there is nothing explicit in their approach that lays the foundation for such analysis (is this an appeal to cognition?). This bottom-up approach seems to be wooden in design, although the wide range of exegetical descriptions offered suggests that there are several unstated (and perhaps unrecognized or unassimilated) assumptions also at play. At best, this school seems to provide a limited set of relatively insecure and not theoretically rigorous generalizations about some features of the Greek language.

Systemic Functional Linguistics

SFL is the most well-developed linguistic theory of what Sampson calls the London School of linguistics.[184] The major inaugural figure in the London School was Firth, who developed some of the ideas of the anthropologist Malinowski, from whom are derived such terms as "context of situation" and "context of culture" to refer to the situatedness of language that influences its function.[185] Firth is associated with a number of fundamental ideas regarding the social function and context of language. One of Firth's students was Michael Halliday.[186] In the 1960s, Halliday, who began his linguistic study by describing Chinese, first developed his scale and category grammar, which was based upon paradigmatic and syntagmatic axes. Under the influence of the functions of language of Bühler of the Prague School, Halliday developed a stratal description that moved (reciprocally) from expression to content to context, with each stratum realizing the three (or four, depending upon Halliday's developing thought) metafunctions (functions of language).[187] SFL has continued to be further developed by not only Halliday and his followers but also by those of the Sydney School and the Cardiff School.[188]

---

[184] Sampson, *Schools of Linguistics*, 212–35.
[185] Malinowski, "Problem of Meaning"; and besides his *Papers* and *Selected Papers*, see J. R. Firth, "A Synopsis of Linguistic Theory, 1930–1955," in *Studies in Linguistic Analysis* (Oxford: Blackwell, 1957), 1–32. On Firth, see Beaugrande, *Linguistic Theory*, 187–222. On the early stages of the London School, see D. Terence Langendoen, *The London School of Linguistics: A Study of the Linguistic Theories of B. Malinowski and J. R. Firth* (Cambridge, MA: MIT Press, 1968).
[186] On Halliday, see Beaugrande, *Linguistic Theory*, 223–64.
[187] Besides his IFG1 (now in its fourth edition, *Halliday's Introduction to Functional Grammar* [IFG4], rev. Christian M. I. M. Matthiessen, 4th ed. [London: Routledge, 2014]), see M. A. K. Halliday, *Explorations in the Functions of Language* (London: Edward Arnold, 1973); Halliday, *Halliday: System and Function in Language*, ed. G. R. Kress (Oxford: Oxford University Press, 1976); and Halliday, *Language as Social Semiotic*. Halliday's papers have been collected in multiple volumes. Halliday also wrote with Hasan (1931–2015), *Language*, among other works.
[188] For the Sydney School, see J. R. Martin, *English Text: System and Structure* (Amsterdam: John Benjamins, 1992); and for the Cardiff School, see Robin P. Fawcett, *Invitation to Systemic Functional Linguistics through the Cardiff Grammar: An Extension and Simplification of Halliday's Systemic Functional Grammar*, 3rd ed. (London: Equinox, 2008).

As a result, there are a variety of definitions of SFL available, including many suggested by Halliday himself, but one of the best summaries of the broad tenets of the theory is found in the linguist Margaret Berry's (1938–2020) introduction, which I draw upon but supplement here. There are seven important relatively widely accepted notions that she puts forth that will serve as a useful definition and introduction to the theory. (1) SFL places a high emphasis upon the sociological or communicative aspects of language. Rather than being a formal grammar or concentrating upon hypothetical sentences constructed for analysis, SFL sees language as the most important social tool, and so emphasizes the functions of language within communicative contexts. (2) As a result, SFL sees language as a form of linguistic behavior rather than as a form of knowledge of a language, thus viewing Saussure's *langue* as the language potential that is realized in *parole*. SFL thus dissolves the barrier between the two, or at least shifts the emphasis from *langue* to *parole*, as one construes reality through language.[189] (3) SFL utilizes a number of matrices for describing language, including clines, ranks, strata, and levels, often reflecting degrees of delicacy, from broad to narrow. As a result, the SFL model of language is a complex matrix of various dimensions of language, seen to be necessary to capture the relationships between abstract systems of language and how these are realized in instances of actual language. (4) SFL utilizes the notion of text as a semantic unit whose instances are used to verify the various linguistic hypotheses, often through corpus linguistic means (the linking of the two has existed for some time, seen in Halliday's probabilistic grammar, that is, that various patterns appear probabilistically). The notion of semantics pervades SFL, even if there is some ambiguity how semantics and the lexicogrammar relate to each other. Therefore, semantics is used to encompass a major level or stratum of language use, going way beyond the word or sentence to the notion of text. (5) SFL recognizes the varying features of different languages and differentiates varieties of language according to situational use (the powerful notion of register). Most linguistic modeling of SFL has occurred with English, but SFL accepts (at least in theory) that other languages will be modeled differently, as their language reflexes vary according to their uses of language. (6) SFL emphasizes the function of language in terms of three metafunctions that realize the components of situational context. These three metafunctions bisect the strata that extend from context to expression. The concept of metafunctions provides one of the few major generalizations of SFL in relation especially to formal grammars, as these metafunctions transverse the various strata of language. (7) Finally, SFL recognizes two axes of system and structure, while emphasizing system networks as the primary means of modeling language.[190] System networks comprise a network of related systems within the language as system. Many linguistic theories emphasize syntax (structure), whereas SFL attempts to combine both into networks of systems that provide both syntagmatic and paradigmatic choice options within the language.

---

[189] SFL reflects a social constructivist sociological theory consistent with the origins of linguistics in phenomenology. See Peter L. Berger and Thomas Luckmann, *The Social Construction of Reality: A Treatise in the Sociology of Knowledge* (New York: Doubleday, 1966); cf. Ruth A. Wallace and Alison Wolf, *Contemporary Sociological Theory: Expanding the Classical Tradition*, 5th ed. (Upper Saddle River, NJ: Prentice Hall, 1999), 254-8.

[190] Margaret Berry, *Introduction to Systemic Linguistics*, 2 vols. (London: Batsford, 1975-7), 1:22-32; cf. Christopher S. Butler, *Structure and Function: A Guide to Three Major Structural-Functional Theories*, 2 vols. (Amsterdam: John Benjamins, 2003), 1:43-8, whose definition, even after nearly thirty years, is surprisingly similar (emphasizing communication, function, semantics and pragmatics as central, and context, along with raising questions about cognition and typology). Cf. Halliday, IFG1, xiii-xvi, but which notes that this volume does not include linguistic systems, added in subsequent editions.

Since SFL was introduced in 1985 to New Testament Greek studies,[191] there have been many significant monographs that have drawn directly upon it. These include major monographs by a variety of scholars (as well as articles too numerous to mention), but they can only be summarized here to give evidence of the breadth of their explorations. As mentioned in Chapter One, I utilized system networks to describe the Greek verbal system in my major monograph on verbal aspect, and followed that with an intermediate Greek grammar utilizing SFL, a volume on linguistic analysis of the Greek New Testament with a number of chapters on SFL, and a linguistic commentary on the book of Romans using register discourse analysis as its explicit interpretive method, and most recently have published a linguistic assessment of New Testament theology using SFL as a counter-proposal.[192]

Many other studies have also been written based upon SFL. Brian Blount uses Halliday as the basis of his cultural interpretation.[193] Jeffrey Reed provides a summary of Hallidayan SFL organized by metafunctions and draws them into discussion of the debate over literary integrity in Philippians.[194] Gustavo Martín-Asensio examines transitivity in Acts as a means of indicating foregrounding.[195] Edward Adams uses a form of critical linguistics indebted to Halliday and SFL in his study of Paul's cosmological language.[196] Stephanie Black treats conjunctions in Matthew, supplemented by Relevance Theory.[197] Ray Van Neste examines the cohesion of the Pastoral Epistles, drawing upon Halliday and Hasan's fundamental work in this area.[198] Todd Klutz offers what he called a sociostylistic reading of the exorcism stories in Luke–Acts, emphasizing the sociolinguistic elements of SFL.[199] Cynthia Long Westfall utilizes a version of SFL discourse analysis to examine the form and meaning of Hebrews.[200] Matthew Brook O'Donnell utilizes various elements of SFL as a part of his study of corpus linguistics, illustrating their close connection as already mentioned.[201] Ivan Kwong examines word order patterns in Luke's Gospel

---

[191] See Nigel J. C. Gotteri and Stanley E. Porter, "Ambiguity, Vagueness and the Working Systemic Linguist," *SWPLL* 2 (1985): 105–18.

[192] Porter, *Verbal Aspect*; Porter, *Idioms*; Porter, *Linguistic Analysis of the Greek New Testament: Studies in Tools, Methods, and Practice* (Grand Rapids: Baker, 2015); Porter, *The Letter to the Romans: A Linguistic and Literary Commentary*, NTM 37 (Sheffield: Sheffield Phoenix, 2016); and Porter, *New Testament Theology*; among many other works.

[193] Brian K. Blount, *Cultural Interpretation: Reorienting New Testament Criticism* (Minneapolis: Augsburg Fortress, 1995), esp. 8–16.

[194] Jeffrey T. Reed, *A Discourse Analysis of Philippians: Method and Rhetoric in the Debate over Literary Integrity*, JSNTSup 136 (Sheffield: Sheffield Academic, 1997); along with numerous articles.

[195] Gustavo Martín-Asensio, *Transitivity-Based Foregrounding in the Acts of the Apostles: A Functional-Grammatical Approach to the Lukan Perspective*, JSNTSup 202, SNTG 8 (Sheffield: Sheffield Academic, 2000); as well as several important articles.

[196] Edward Adams, *Constructing the World: A Study in Paul's Cosmological Language* (Edinburgh: T&T Clark, 2000).

[197] Stephanie L. Black, *Sentence Conjunctions in the Gospel of Matthew: καί, δέ, τότε, γάρ, οὖν and Asyndeton in Narrative Discourse*, JSNTSup 216, SNTG 9 (London: Sheffield Academic, 2002).

[198] Ray Van Neste, *Cohesion and Structure in the Pastoral Epistles*, JSNTSup 280 (London: T&T Clark, 2004). Cf. M. A. K. Halliday and Ruqaiya Hasan, *Cohesion in English* (London: Longman, 1976).

[199] Todd Klutz, *The Exorcism Stories in Luke-Acts: A Sociostylistic Reading*, SNTSMS 129 (Cambridge: Cambridge University Press, 2004).

[200] Cynthia Long Westfall, *A Discourse Analysis of the Letter to the Hebrews: The Relationship between Form and Meaning*, LNTS 297 (London: T&T Clark, 2005).

[201] Matthew Brook O'Donnell, *Corpus Linguistics and the Greek of the New Testament*, NTM 6 (Sheffield: Sheffield Phoenix, 2005).

as a means of foregrounding.[202] Jae Hyun Lee provides a discourse analysis of Romans 1–8, supplemented by some elements from Robert Longacre's version of Tagmemics.[203] Beth Stovell, as previously noted, discusses metaphor in John's Gospel, in conjunction with conceptual metaphor theory.[204] Gregory Fewster draws upon SFL's definition of grammatical metaphor as a means of treating creation language in Romans 8.[205] Wally Cirafesi re-visits verbal aspect theory in Synoptic parallel passages to explain their relationships.[206]

Ronald Peters examines the Greek article in relation to relative pronouns, or what he calls ὁ-items (rather than wh-items).[207] David Lamb interprets the community hypothesis in John's Gospel on the basis of theories of register and Halliday's notion of antilanguage.[208] Christopher Land utilizes SFL to examine the cohesion and integrity of 2 Corinthians by examining different potential situations.[209] Bryan Dyer examines the notion of context of situation in Hebrews.[210] David Yoon utilizes the notion of register as a form of discourse analysis to examine Paul's letter to the Galatians, bringing his findings to bear on the question of the New Perspective on Paul.[211] Roque Albuquerque examines the function and semantics of the participle.[212] Angela Costley draws heavily upon SFL in her model of discourse analysis that she applies to Hebrews.[213] James Dvorak examines the interpersonal metafunction, concentrating upon appraisal theory to study Paul's language in 1 Corinthians 1–4.[214] David Mathewson has reconceptualized the voice and mood systems of Greek using SFL.[215] Chiaen Liu uses the concept of register from SFL to examine the Petrine texts in the New Testament.[216] Zachary Dawson uses linguistic stylistics, a form of SFL oriented to the study of literature, to analyze the Jerusalem Council in the Acts of the Apostles.[217] Finally, Alan Kurschner examines Rev. 19:11–20:6 in terms of cohesion.[218] There are also other works that could also be included within such a list.

---

[202] Ivan Shin Chun Kwong, *The Word Order of the Gospel of Luke: Its Foregrounded Messages*, LNTS 298 (London: T&T Clark, 2006).
[203] Jae Hyun Lee, *Paul's Gospel in Romans: A Discourse Analysis of Rom 1:16–8:39*, LBS 3 (Leiden: Brill, 2010).
[204] Stovell, *Mapping Metaphorical Discourse*.
[205] Gregory P. Fewster, *Creation Language in Romans 8: A Study in Monosemy*, LBS 8 (Leiden: Brill, 2013).
[206] Wally V. Cirafesi, *Verbal Aspect in Synoptic Parallels: On the Method and Meaning of Divergent Tense-Form Usage in the Synoptic Passion Narratives*, LBS 7 (Leiden: Brill, 2013).
[207] Ronald D. Peters, *The Greek Article: A Functional Grammar of ὁ-items in the Greek New Testament with Special Emphasis on the Greek Article*, LBS 9 (Leiden: Brill, 2014).
[208] David A. Lamb, *Text, Context and the Johannine Community: A Sociolinguistic Analysis of the Johannine Writings*, LNTS 477 (London: Bloomsbury, 2014). On antilanguage, see M. A. K. Halliday, "Anti-Languages," AA 78 (1976): 570–84.
[209] Christopher D. Land, *The Integrity of 2 Corinthians and Paul's Aggravating Absence*, NTM 36 (Sheffield: Sheffield Phoenix, 2015).
[210] Bryan R. Dyer, *Suffering in the Face of Death: The Epistle to the Hebrews and Its Context of Situation*, LNTS 568 (London: Bloomsbury, 2017).
[211] David I. Yoon, *A Discourse Analysis of Galatians and the New Perspective on Paul*, LBS 17 (Leiden: Brill, 2019).
[212] Roque N. Albuquerque, *Presupposition and [E]motion: The Upgraded Function and the Semantics of the Participle in the New Testament* (New York: Peter Lang, 2020).
[213] Angela Costley, *Creation and Christ: An Exploration of the Topic of Creation in the Epistle to the Hebrews*, WUNT 2/527 (Tübingen: Mohr Siebeck, 2020).
[214] James D. Dvorak, *The Interpersonal Metafunction in 1 Corinthians 1–4: The Tenor of Toughness*, LBS 19 (Leiden: Brill, 2021).
[215] David L. Mathewson, *Voice and Mood: A Linguistic Approach*, Essentials of Biblical Greek Grammar (Grand Rapids: Baker, 2021).
[216] Chiaen Liu, *Register Variation in the New Testament Petrine Texts*, LBS 21 (Leiden: Brill, 2022).
[217] Zachary K. Dawson, *The Message of the Jerusalem Council in the Acts of the Apostles: A Linguistic Stylistic Analysis*, LBS 22 (Leiden: Brill, 2022).
[218] Alan E. Kurschner, *A Linguistic Approach to Revelation 19:11–20:6 and the Millennium Binding of Satan*, LBS 23 (Leiden: Brill, 2022).

The several factors that these SFL-based studies have in common are their incredible diversity and variety, yet all written within various parameters of SFL as a linguistic theory. Some of them are very broad in presenting a full and robust model of SFL (such as Reed), while others are much more focused in their examination of individual elements (e.g., verbal structure, conjunction, the article, a single metafunction). Some treat SFL as a linguistic theory of syntax or semantics (e.g., Martín-Asensio, Kwong, Dvorak), while others conceive of it as a form of discourse analysis (e.g., Westfall, Porter in Romans, Yoon, Dawson).[219] A number of studies have drawn upon the productive notion of register, a linguistic category to which SFL has given a particular definition, while others hint at ways to examine literature (most recently Dawson). There have also been studies that have utilized SFL along with other linguistic approaches in an attempt to address questions for which SFL has not seemed, at least to the authors, to have adequate theoretical potential or power (e.g., Black on conjunctions or Stovell on conceptual metaphor).[220]

SFL, so far as I can determine and the evidence indicates, has been the most productive school of linguistics in New Testament Greek studies—apart perhaps and regrettably from traditional grammar. Numerous monographs and journal articles have been written within this school of linguistics, but the number compared to those writing on Greek language still remains relatively low. This raises the question of why more scholars are not using it. Another way to examine it might be to ask why it is that so many have used it so far, when SFL is, by all estimations, a very complex linguistic theory to learn. There is no doubt that SFL is complex and difficult, especially as it was developed for English and hence does not readily encompass within its architecture questions regarding non-configurational or aspectual languages such as ancient Greek, including that of the New Testament.[221] The major reasons for its intensive utilization, however, appear to be its integrated system that encompasses the strata from expression to context. Such an encompassing theory makes great demands upon its practitioners, demands that are not easily met with haphazard application. SFL is one of few linguistic schools that includes such a robust concept of context. SFL thereby connects language with situational context and hence models context in an explicit fashion, thus lending SFL to itself being a discourse analytic model. It has been productively used in all of these areas of linguistic investigation.

---

[219] The encouragement to treat SFL as a form of discourse analysis is found in Halliday, IFG1, ix, where Halliday notes that the volume grew out of a small set of lectures for a course in "functional grammar and discourse analysis." See also M. A. K. Halliday and John J. Webster, *Text Linguistics: The How and Why of Meaning* (Sheffield: Equinox, 2014).

[220] There have been several New Testament scholars who have pursued various areas of sociolinguistics (SFL has some characteristics of sociolinguistics). A variety of sociolinguistic theories are used in such studies. For examples of works that utilize sociolinguistics in study of the New Testament, besides sections in Porter, *Verbal Aspect*, esp. 111–56, see Jonathan M. Watt, *Code-Switching in Luke and Acts*, Berkeley Insights in Linguistics and Semiotics 31 (New York: Peter Lang, 1997); Stanley E. Porter, *The Criteria for Authenticity in Historical-Jesus Research: Previous Discussion and New Proposals*, JSNTSup 191 (Sheffield: Sheffield Academic, 2000); Porter, ed., *Diglossia and Other Topics in New Testament Linguistics*, JSNTSup 193, SNTG 6 (Sheffield: Sheffield Academic, 2000); Hughson T. Ong, *The Multilingual Jesus and the Sociolinguistic World of the New Testament*, LBS 12 (Leiden: Brill, 2015); and Ong, *Sociolinguistic Analysis of the New Testament: Theories and Applications*, BINS 195 (Leiden: Brill, 2021); along with numerous articles by these and other authors.

[221] On non-configurational languages, see Kenneth Hale, "Walpiri and the Grammar of Non-Configurational Languages," *Natural Language and Linguistic Theory* 1 (1983): 5–47. Configuration refers to the placement of the subject in relation to the verb phrase in phrase structure grammar, and so is constituent oriented. However, the term is useful to refer to languages that do not conform to such patterns, as does English.

IMPLICATIONS REGARDING LINGUISTIC SCHOOLS AND NEW TESTAMENT STUDY

In light of this discussion, one might well ask what the implications are regarding linguistic schools of thought in New Testament Greek language study. There are several observations that one might make based on the evidence previously discussed.[222]

The first observation is that there are many linguistic schools that apparently have not been explored in New Testament studies. The list provided by Van Valin and LaPolla in chapter one includes a number even within the communication-and-cognition category that has not been used in New Testament Greek studies. It is possible that some of these theories—if they continue to prove to be robust—might be explored in the future. However, there has also been exploration of other earlier models, such as Case Grammar or even Chomskyan formalism, that have resulted in very little recent productive research, even if there was initial enthusiasm. The question to ask is why it is that some schools of linguistics seem to attract more attention than others. There seems to be no clear correlation between theoretical complexity and adaptability, as SFL is as complex as any theory—at least so far as its nomenclature is concerned—and this has not detracted from its garnering numerous adapters, at least in comparison to other schools.

The second observation is that the number of linguistic schools that have been adopted in New Testament Greek study is still relatively limited, when compared to the schools of linguistic thought available, regardless of how these are singled out or lumped together. The two major ones are various Cognitive Schools, such as Cognitive Linguistics with its conceptual metaphor theory, and SFL. There appears to be a growing number of explorations of conceptual metaphor within New Testament studies (note that the Society of Biblical Literature has published a good number of these recent studies in conceptual metaphor), with some of these explorations examining a particular metaphor while others explore the notion of metaphor more broadly. This increased interest is consistent with a more widespread growth in interest in Cognitive Linguistics within the field of linguistics itself and cognitive science as a discipline. Cognitive Linguistics appears to be one of the fastest-growing fields of linguistics, especially as it is linked to the wider field of cognitive science and a host of related disciplines with which it is interacting. The other school of thought is SFL. Many, but clearly not all, of those who are using SFL in New Testament studies appear to be associated with McMaster Divinity College either directly or by influence. This is perplexing, but there is nothing particularly biblical about SFL. SFL as a linguistic theory has been far more widely utilized, especially in the area of education, in various cultures where there is not a high emphasis upon biblical studies (e.g., Australia, China), whereas the cognitive sciences are thriving in North America where there still remains vibrant study of the New Testament within the church and ostensibly a more Christian culture.

The third observation is that the cognitive-functional school represented by Levinsohn seems to lack theoretical or even practical or applied robustness. The theory-developing proposals are relatively limited, and its results, at least as it is currently evidenced, are generally conformative. There is some continuing publication of journal and chapter literature that explores various individual studies utilizing this theory, but such studies are rarely the kinds of significant studies that are found in monographs. The two major

---

[222] Butler, *Structure and Function*, provides a comparison of SFL, Functionalism (both Continental and West Coast), and Role and Reference Grammar, one of few works to perform such a task at significant length.

works that have been published by Levinsohn and by Runge are both styled as discourse oriented. Levinsohn's is addressed to informational structure and Runge's to discourse grammar. However, as previously noted, the contents of the volumes indicate that the scope of their exploration is relatively limited, being confined to what SFL would label as the textual metafunction. Even in this area, there is a fairly narrow construal of the term that excludes some of the major important categories within the metafunction, such as cohesive harmony.

The fourth observation is to examine what it is that SFL provides that has allowed it to develop as widely and as robustly as it has as a school of linguistic thought. There appear to be a number of considerations. The first consideration is that the linguistic approach itself is wide and diverse, and it provides plenty of scope for a variety of explorations, as has already been exemplified. A second is that the theory itself is subject to diversity of conception that lends itself to continuing development. For example, SFL is currently divided into at least three major camps, with some smaller ones. These are the Halliday School, the Sydney School, and the Cardiff Grammar. All these approaches would generally agree with the description previously offered (that's why I offered such a general one) even if they would disagree over such things as the nature and number of the strata (Sydney) or the number of metafunctions (Cardiff) or the ways to draw system networks (formal or functional or both). These areas themselves offer room for further refinement. A third consideration is that SFL attempts to model language through a variety of helpful heuristic means. Several of these have been mentioned already, including system networks, strata that differentiate semantics from the lexicogrammar (note that it is not called syntax, to avoid the syntax versus semantics opposition and to create a pattern of realization and activation between strata), the concept of register, to name just a few. There are even instances of theoretical dispute where SFL is amenable to a variety of positive proposals. For example, SFL purports to be a constituency grammar but its use of constituency has many characteristics of dependency and is compatible with a dependency framework as well (if such a distinction can be made in this environment).

A further consideration is that SFL embraces a form of the Sapir-Whorf hypothesis on linguistic determinism, and, at least in theory (though clearly not in practice in many instances, where linguistic modeling is highly dependent upon English and English alone), recognizes the differences among and particularities of various languages, to the point that one must model each language individually, even if one adopts generalized categories such as the metafunctions. For example, one might well believe that the metafunctions constitute a type of semantic universal, and so attempt to describe one's chosen language in terms of the metafunctions in the different strata. However, one might well find that the lexicogrammatical features realized for a given metafunction might arguably be different from one language to another (just as there have been differences of this sort even for English within SFL) or that one might even need to posit additional metafunctions depending upon the modeling of that language. A fifth and final consideration is that the contextual dimension of language—previously noted as its sociological or communicative dimension—is more explicitly modeled in SFL than in many if not most other linguistic theories, some of which do not even consider context. This provides a particularly powerful means of linking text to context, and register and its components are often the means of doing this. The notion of register as a type of language use, and register analysis as a means of drawing upon the resources of register study for description of texts, provides a means of extending linguistic analysis well beyond the lexicogrammar and even the semantic stratum so as to place language within its situational context. In New

Testament studies, all these features are to be welcomed as tasks to be performed in more robust ways and by more robust methods. In the chapters that follow, I explore a select few of the topics to which SFL makes a significant contribution to linguistic modeling.

CONCLUSION

There are many possible conclusions that one might draw from this broad discussion. Some of these are that, on the one hand, there are a surprisingly large number of different linguistic schools that are viable in New Testament Greek studies, including traditional grammar (if it should be considered as a school) within which fall rationalism and comparative historicism, Chomskyan formalism, Construction Grammar, Cognitive Linguistics, Relevance Theory, cognitive-functionalism, and SFL. Each one has had proponents, even though some of them have been more vibrant than others. On the other hand, I note that, compared to the wider field of modern linguistics, the number of linguistic schools—if one can compare these schools with the varieties of approaches found in contemporary linguistics—is relatively limited. There are numerous variations on Chomskyan formalism, many different nuances on Cognitive Linguistics, and quite a few functional models that have not been explored, at least to the degree that they have established themselves as linguistic schools as I have defined the term.

A perhaps even more important question concerns the relationship among these linguistic schools. In other words, how should we view these schools? There is a tendency in New Testament studies—one that I suspect has helped to dilute the effectiveness and clear-headedness of the field—to practice a widespread linguistic eclecticism. By this, I mean that scholars have tended—and not just in matters of language—to feel free to draw from a wide range of possibilities in their formulations of methods. In the survey that I have offered, we see those who practice a more methodologically pure and a more methodologically eclectic approach. Cognitive-functionalism is eclectic by definition and presentation, while Chomskyan formalism is much more purist in orientation. More to the point, however, is whether these various theories are commensurable or incommensurable. In other words, must the lines between these various schools be rigorously maintained, or is there room for conceptual blending (to use a convenient term)? I think that this depends upon the schools of linguistics that are involved. If one is working within one of the major schools—Formalist, Cognitive, or Functional Schools—there is probably room for methodological interchange and enhancement. For example, most of the various cognitive theories have a significant amount of overlap, and the same seems to be true in cognitively-oriented New Testament Greek studies. The same might, at least to some extent, be claimed for formalist theories and possibly even functional theories. I do not think that one can cross these school boundaries so easily, however, and that is perhaps why I find it difficult to accept the cognitive-functional model, since it straddles boundaries. However, I suspect that even within these major school divisions there is somewhat limited commensurability. One may be able to tweak some of the extensions of a theory, but I doubt that many of the core principles of any school are able to be harmonized with those of other models. Thus, SFL may be able to debate over issues of stratification (as it indeed has) but stratification remains central to the nature of the theory itself.

I believe that if we learn anything of importance from this survey of schools of linguistics it is that there must be the recognition that schools of linguistic thought are fundamental to our understanding and conceptualization of the Greek language. Those who think that they are simply examining the language probably hide much more than they reveal about their knowledge of Greek, almost assuredly adopting traditional grammatical models that are now outmoded in their approach. There is plenty of scope for further theoretical development within the field of linguistics, including in the study of New Testament Greek, but those who are more explicit in their recognition of various linguistic theories at least show awareness that the study of the Greek New Testament demands that we attempt to think clearly and critically about major issues in language using the best available linguistic tools.

This chapter has thus attempted to form a bridge between developments within New Testament Greek studies and some linguistic approaches. I have attempted to place such work within the wider field of linguistic theory to show both the limitations and possibilities for further research. The evidence indicates that there are a variety of ways that one might approach the study of the Greek New Testament. On the one hand, there are many possibilities open to further exploration. On the other, not all theories appear to be equal as some have clearly been more profitable and productive than others. Whereas we wish to encourage the development and use of a variety of linguistic theories, we must also attend to those that offer the most potential for further continuing and productive textual study. I happen to think—for many good and convincing reasons—that SFL offers the most persuasive and coherent linguistic theory. I have tried to be fair in my presentations throughout these first two chapters, but I have also tried to show how SFL provides a firm linguistic platform for further insightful linguistic modeling. For this reason, I as a practitioner of SFL will offer in part two four further studies using SFL in relation to other schools of thought to explore a variety of topics in contemporary linguistic and New Testament studies. Each of these chapters focuses upon one area where SFL has made a significant linguistic contribution and explores in more detail how that contribution can help clarify some other linguistic questions and provide avenues of inquiry into the Greek of the New Testament.

PART TWO

Systemic Functional Linguistics and New Testament Study

CHAPTER THREE

Metaphor in the New Testament: Expressing the Inexpressible through Language within a Systemic Functional Linguistics Perspective

INTRODUCTION

All language is metaphorical. I realize that that is a controversial statement—and it is one that I do not necessarily wish to debate in this chapter,[1] except to note that explicit recognition of the metaphorical nature of language has been lacking in much New Testament studies over the last approximately one hundred years. Over this period, New Testament studies has emphasized what I consider to be a rather flat-world view of language (to use a metaphor to describe it). By this, I mean that much New Testament studies has been shackled by a limiting and constraining literalism—or at least what purports to be literalism—that wishes to equate words with things and to give such words status as if they were things. This has resulted in an emphasis upon the "thingness" of the ancient world and its texts, rather than on the "howness," that is, rather than on how language is used to reflect upon and even create the world in which the ancients existed. Even some of the most enduring movements within the field of New Testament studies—such as the Biblical Theology movement, both the old form and its recent reinvigoration—have been slow to grasp the importance of metaphor—even though such recognition would appear to have great potential for opening up its conceptual and theological horizons. Only recently, with the use of Cognitive Linguistics and conceptual metaphor theory, has metaphor made a belated appearance in New Testament studies, even if a limited one (upon which see discussion in Chapter Two).

---

[1] For a similar view, see George Lakoff and Mark Johnson, *Metaphors We Live By* (Chicago: University of Chicago Press, 1980), 3–4; cf. Colin Murray Turbayne, *The Myth of Metaphor*, rev. ed. (Columbia: University of South Carolina Press, 1970), who appreciates the importance of metaphor in language that wishes to communicate deeply. Contrary to Eileen Cornell Way, *Knowledge Representation and Metaphor*, Studies in Cognitive Systems (Dordrecht: Kluwer, 1991), 17, who claims that such a statement is trivial (in a philosophical sense), although she also must admit that it is also in a sense true, as language only mirrors and stands for and reflects reality.

The result of such a narrow view of human experience and use of language is the failure to appreciate the nature and complexity of language itself. We see the evidence of this at its most fundamental level in the continuing utilization of theories of language as if they represent "the way that language and the world are," rather than recognizing that these theories of language are themselves metaphorical approximations of language form and function. We now are living in what I consider to be a relatively unimaginative time in New Testament studies, because we fail to take the linguistic nature of New Testament research into account—and with it to appreciate the role and function of metaphor. Fundamental to interpretation is recognition of the role that language plays in human experience, and from that grow all of the other helpful means by which we analyze texts—especially those from the ancient world whose representation is mediated only through epigraphia.

From the comments I have just made, one might well expect me to undertake a re-examination of the entire field of New Testament studies. In many ways, this might well be a desideratum. I believe that many of the areas of New Testament studies merit re-assessment, as they continue to function within outmoded paradigms that hinder rather than foster further constructive research. However, in the four chapters that follow, I have the much more modest aim of examining four specific areas to which I believe that Systemic Functional Linguistics (SFL) can speak. In this chapter, I wish to confine myself to the major topic of the use of metaphor in the New Testament and its relationship to SFL. I will examine theories of metaphor briefly to see what they help us to understand about language. Then I will treat metaphor from a SFL standpoint as it functions within the New Testament. In this section, I think that I can make some new observations regarding metaphor and how it not only functions in but opens up understanding of the New Testament.

THEORIES OF METAPHOR AND WHAT THEY CONTRIBUTE TO OUR UNDERSTANDING

One of the major surprises regarding the traditional lack of attention to metaphor in New Testament studies is that major theories of metaphor go back to the ancients themselves—and their influence has been tremendous and enduring, even if they are probably too narrow and constrained in their definitions. The study of metaphor as a trope within classical rhetoric is certainly well known to most and has traditionally formed the basis for most discussion of metaphor, at least until recently. But perhaps that is part of the problem. Aristotle (384–322 BC) and his classical successors, such as Cicero (106–43 BC), Quintilian (c. AD 35–100), and the *Rhetoric ad Herennium* (late first century AD), had what might be called the "this is that" or word-based theory of metaphor familiar to most school children from their learning about metaphor, and they tended to view its purpose as "decorative" (e.g., to provide vividness, brevity, emphasis, minimization, embellishment, or to serve as a circumlocution for the explicit statement).[2] This view

---

[2] Terence Hawkes, *Metaphor*, Critical Idiom (London: Methuen, 1972), 14, citing in particular Aristotle, *Poet.* 21–5; *Rhet.* 3; Cicero, *De Or.* 3.35.155ff., Quintilian, *Institutio oratoria* (no references), and *Rhetoric ad Herennium* 4. I draw directly upon Hawkes for this concise history of the development of metaphor. The term "this is that" is mine, not his (although I think that someone else must have used the phrase before me to describe this view of metaphor). For a history and integration of theories of metaphor, see Beth M. Stovell, *Mapping Metaphorical Discourse in the Fourth Gospel: John's Eternal King*, LBS 5 (Leiden: Brill, 2012), 31–71; and William E. W. Robinson, *Metaphor, Morality, and the Spirit in Romans 8:1–17* (Atlanta: SBL Press, 2016), 17–43. Most of the treatments of metaphor in the New Testament (see Chapter Two) do not have extensive discussions of metaphor theory. For the differentiation of word, semantic (sentence), and discourse metaphor, see Paul Ricoeur, *The Rule of Metaphor: Multi-disciplinary Studies of the Creation of Meaning in Language*, trans. Robert Czerny with Kathleen McLaughlin and John Costello (Toronto: University of Toronto Press, 1975), 4.

continued through the Middle Ages, until the French humanist and rhetorician Peter Ramus (1515–72) narrowed its scope even further by giving it an ornamental value within the performance area of rhetoric (elocution and delivery).[3] Metaphor did not recover until the Romantic period, when metaphor was once more seen as an organic part of language, drawing upon the notion of Platonic organic unity (it is questionable whether they actually understood Plato on this point), and developing what came to be known as poetic language.[4] The major insight of this period is attributed to the poet Samuel Taylor Coleridge (1772–1834), who recognized the creative and formative influence of the mind and how it is realized in linguistic form.[5]

The twentieth century, however, saw the greatest developments in significant theories of metaphor. This is not the place to describe all of them but merely an opportunity to chronicle the important events in its theoretical growth. I divide the theories into three helpful categories: philosophical, literary, and linguistic.

I am least concerned with philosophical theories of metaphor, because they are not as concerned with language in use as I am. Nevertheless, there have been many philosophers interested in metaphor; in fact, the history of philosophy is arguably a debate over meaning and hence metaphor, especially in the Continental philosophical tradition. Two major figures in the relatively recent discussion, however, are Max Black (1909–88) and his interaction theory of metaphor, representing the analytical tradition, and Paul Ricoeur (1913–2005) and his synthetic view of metaphor, based in Continental philosophy. Black's interaction theory[6] is a tensive theory of metaphor that posits that there is an "emotional tension generated by the juxtaposition of anomalous referents."[7] Black's theory of metaphor is what Ricoeur calls a sentence (semantics)-based theory of metaphor, as opposed to a semiotic (word) or discourse theory of metaphor.[8] One might well question Ricoeur's formulation of the opposition, but his observation is well-made nonetheless. This tension, Black contends, caused by the juxtaposition of anomalous entities, results in the generation of new knowledge. Ricoeur himself attempts a synthetic view of metaphor that begins with acknowledging the role of word-based metaphor in the ancients but extends it to sentence and then discourse-based metaphor, consistent with his own differentiation already noted. However, Ricoeur also notes that when we reach the discourse level, we are back at the fundamental understanding of Aristotle regarding language's creativity emerging from the merging of myth and imitation, which Ricoeur sees in the metaphorical use of the copula verb, "be," to indicate both similarity and difference. In other words, Ricoeur also endorses the tensive theory of metaphor.[9]

---

[3]Hawkes, *Metaphor*, 25. For a more detailed study, see James J. Murphy, *Rhetoric in the Middle Ages: A History of Rhetorical Theory from St. Augustine to the Renaissance* (Berkeley: University of California Press, 1974).
[4]Hawkes, *Metaphor*, 34–5. For a contrary view on at least some of the rationalists, see Nicolaas T. Oosthuizen Mouton, "Metaphor, Empiricism and Truth: A Fresh Look at Seventeenth-Century Theories of Figurative Language," in *Tropical Truth(s): The Epistemology of Metaphor and Other Tropes*, ed. Armin Burkhardt and Brigitte Nerlich (Berlin: de Gruyter, 2010), 23–49.
[5]Hawkes, *Metaphor*, 43–4. See Samuel Taylor Coleridge, *Biographia Literaria*, ed. Nigel Leask (London: Dent, 1997), 184–5; cf. I. A. Richards, *Coleridge on Imagination*, 3rd ed. (London: Routledge & Kegan Paul, 1962).
[6]Max Black, *Meaning and Metaphor: Studies in Language and Philosophy* (Ithaca, NY: Cornell University Press, 1962).
[7]Earl R. MacCormac, *A Cognitive Theory of Metaphor* (Cambridge, MA: MIT Press, 1985), 24. MacCormac also defines the controversion and deviance theories of metaphor. I will return to deviance theories later in this chapter.
[8]Ricoeur, *Rule of Metaphor*, 4. Ricoeur's opposition appears to wish to oppose word to sentence, but then also involves discourse.
[9]Ricoeur, *Rule of Metaphor*, 7.

More productive for the discussion, I believe, are various literary and linguistic theories of metaphor.[10] I begin with the literary theory of the literary scholar I. A. Richards (1893–1979), who recognized "the importance of the role any account of language's function in society must assign to metaphor."[11] Richards took a discourse-oriented view of language, in which meanings are not things in themselves but contextually situated and created by language. As a result, language is conventional and ambiguous, by which humans shape and create their world of experience. In that way, all language is metaphorical. This leads to Richards's description of metaphor as involving both "tenor," the general idea that is meant to be conveyed, and "vehicle," the linguistic expression that conveys the tenor. Richards has been followed in his tensive view by many, including among others his student William Empson (1906–84) in his *Seven Types of Ambiguity*, "which strongly reinforces the notion that ambiguity is the necessary aspect of language enabling the process of metaphor to operate most fruitfully."[12]

As one can imagine, theories of metaphor have been important to linguists from the earliest days of the discipline. There are two major streams in this linguistic development. The first is the functional track and the second is the cognitive track. This division follows a similar kind of division as we have discussed in Chapter Two between linguistic schools.

Functional linguistics has produced several theories of metaphor that grow directly out of literary theories of metaphor (and I will return to these later in this chapter). These theories seem to begin with the question of the relationship between "poetic" language and "ordinary" language. Jan Mukarovsky (1891–1975), one of the seminal figures in the Prague Linguistic Circle and associated with its literary/linguistic interface (see Chapter Two), posits the question of the relationship in one of his most important essays, on the difference between standard and poetic language. In the essay, he concludes that "The function of poetic language consists in the maximum of foregrounding of the utterance … it is not used in the services of communication, but in order to place in the foreground the act of expression, the act of speech itself."[13] This conclusion opens up numerous linguistic insights related to such areas as markedness theory (i.e., theories of deviation) and semantics (sentence)-based metaphor (including theories regarding collocation). One important insight from this formulation is the difference between live and dead metaphors, in which live ones, because of their persistent "deviation," retain

---

[10] I include what Hawkes calls "anthropological" theories within the linguistic.
[11] So Hawkes, *Metaphor*, 57. See I. A. Richards, *The Philosophy of Rhetoric* (London: Oxford University Press, 1936), esp. 89–138. For a treatment along these lines, see Janet Martin Soskice, *Metaphor and Religious Language* (Oxford: Clarendon, 1985).
[12] Hawkes, *Metaphor*, 63. See William Empson, *Seven Types of Ambiguity* (London: Hogarth, 1984 [1930]) (it would be intriguing to examine the influence of Empson upon Richards, as Empson's work, originating in an undergraduate dissertation written under Richards, was apparently completed and published before Richards's work). Others with similar views include Owen Barfield, *Poetic Diction: A Study in Meaning* (New York: McGraw-Hill, 1964 [1938]), 60–76 and Philip Wheelwright, *The Burning Fountain: A Study in the Language of Symbolism*, rev. ed. (repr., Gloucester, MA: Peter Smith, 1982 [1968]), 81–4, 115–19, and Wheelwright, *Metaphor and Reality* (Bloomington: Indiana University Press, 1962), esp. 45–79. Essays representing the range of thought are to be found in Sheldon Sacks, ed., *On Metaphor* (Chicago: University of Chicago Press, 1979).
[13] Hawkes, *Metaphor*, 73, citing Jan Mukarovsky, "Standard Language and Poetic Language," in *A Prague School Reader on Esthetics, Literary Structure, and Style*, ed. Paul L. Garvin (Washington, DC: Georgetown University Press, 1964), 17–30, here 19. It is interesting to note that Mukarovsky speaks of the "maximum of foregrounding," with the distinct indication that foregrounding is not a singular plane but a broad expanse, ranging from minimal to maximal foregrounding. This concept of foregrounding is discussed more fully in Stanley E. Porter and Matthew Brook O'Donnell, *Discourse Analysis and the Greek New Testament: Text-Generating Resources*, T&T Clark Library of New Testament Greek 2 (London: T&T Clark, 2023), ch. 5.

their semantic force, while "dead" ones are still operative but as part of the background use of language—an important insight. This same pattern is found in standard language. In fact, metaphor is not just part of standard language, according to these linguists, but the metaphorical quality of the language defines the language itself.

In their theory of linguistic determinism, Edward Sapir (1884–1939) and Benjamin Lee Whorf (1897–1941) indicate that there is an integral relationship between one's language and one's perception of the world.[14] This perception of the world is both created and limited by one's linguistic resources. In other words, a user of a language perceives the world by means of the characteristics of one's language. This is expressed at every level, including (to use my previous terms) words, sentences, and discourses. Terence Hawkes (1932–2014), writing in 1972, describes this configuration in prescient wording that we will revisit later in this chapter:

Our metaphors also unconsciously reflect a particular 'reality'. We speak of 'reaching' a 'point', 'coming to' or 'drawing' a conclusion, 'higher' education, without recognizing the implicitly linear notion of movement, along a graduated path or 'up' a scale and 'towards' a 'goal', which these and similar structures metaphorically presuppose. And yet these presuppositions affect our lives as part of a 'reality' which exists, concretely, 'brutally' and 'out there' beyond us. But it is not a question, ultimately, of there being different 'realities'. What is at issue is the existence of different perceptions of the *same* reality brought about ultimately by differences in metaphor.[15]

In similar functional linguistic thought, the role of metaphor in language was noted by another Prague School linguist, Roman Jakobson (1896–1982), in his studies of aphasia or impediments in the ability to use language. According to Jakobson, the two major types of aphasia, similarity disorder and contiguity disorder, appear to be related to metaphor and metonymy.[16] Jakobson takes what is called a substitution theory of metaphor. He uses two axes, a vertical and a horizontal axis, as the defining dimensions of his theory of language, in which there is a paradigmatic (metaphorical) and a syntagmatic dimension (metonymic; an axial distinction to which I will return). Despite the usefulness of these two dimensions, Jakobson's view has been criticized for its using substitution as the means of reinforcing resemblance.[17] This limitation is perhaps seen in a more extreme form in the early transformational-generative approach to metaphor, which saw metaphor in terms of deviance. Drawing upon the distinction between grammatical and ungrammatical

---

[14]See, for example, Edward Sapir, "The Status of Linguistics as a Science," in *Selected Writings in Language, Culture, and Personality*, ed. David G. Mandelbaum (Berkeley: University of California Press, 1949), 160–6; and Benjamin Lee Whorf, "An American Indian Model of the Universe," in *Language, Thought and Reality: Selected Writings of Benjamin Lee Whorf*, ed. John B. Carroll, Stephen C. Levinson, and Penny Lee, 2nd ed. (Cambridge, MA: MIT Press, 2012), 73–82, among other works by these two scholars. For further discussion, see Chapter Two.
[15]Hawkes, *Metaphor*, 85. Hawkes anticipates conceptual metaphor theory in his formulation.
[16]Roman Jakobson, "Two Aspects of Language and Two Types of Aphasic Disturbances," in Jakobson and Morris Halle, *Fundamentals of Language*, JLSMi 1 (The Hague: Mouton, 1956), 55–82. See also Jakobson, "Closing Statement: Linguistics and Poetics," in *Style in Language*, ed. Thomas A. Sebeok (Cambridge: MA: MIT Press, 1960), 350–77.
[17]Ricoeur, *Rule of Metaphor*, 5. However, see Kathryn Allan, *Metaphor and Metonymy: A Diachronic Approach*, Publications of the Philological Society 42 (Malden, MA: Wiley-Blackwell, 2008), 13, who notes that metaphor and metonymy are a cline, as Jakobson recognized.

sentences, transformationalists posited that metaphors were instances of "anomalies if not contradictions."[18] There have been attempts to resolve this apparent problem, with some scholars contending that the grammatical versus ungrammatical distinction is the difference between nonmetaphorical and metaphorical language. In any case, at least in these relatively early versions of transformational-generative grammar, metaphor is defined "as the intentional misuse of language to present a new insight or to propose a new hypothesis," but is also seen as evidence of the "difficulty of developing grammatical rules for the production and interpretation of metaphors."[19] This theory does not seem to offer a satisfactory explanation of semantic innovation or the ubiquity of metaphor in language.

Cognitive Linguistics—which is to be distinguished from transformational-generative grammar on a number of fronts (especially regarding Universal Grammar), as we discussed in Chapter Two—has probably made the single largest contribution to recent developments in theories of metaphor.[20] Cognitive Linguistics, believing that there is no distinction between literal and figurative language, has defined metaphor based upon the mappings of various types of so-called "perceived resemblances."[21] The most well-known manifestation of this theory is conceptual metaphor theory, developed especially by the linguist George Lakoff and philosopher Mark Johnson, and its several extensions.[22] As I noted in Chapter Two, conceptual metaphor theory essentially contends that all language is based upon mapping semantic domains or conceptual spheres upon each other, especially more remote domains upon more familiar ones. An example of such mapping would be mapping the remote upon something as familiar as the human body. The semantic domains of conceptual metaphor theory are formulated around a relatively fixed and finite set of conceptual spheres (such as the human body). Some of the most common features of conceptual metaphor theory are belief in the unidirectionality of metaphor (i.e., from the source to the target domain), noting the entailments and inferences of metaphors based upon their conceptual spheres, the possibilities of formation of metaphor systems

---

[18] MacCormac, *Cognitive Theory*, 31, citing Robert J. Matthews, "Concerning a 'Linguistic Theory' of Metaphor," *Foundations of Language* 7 (1971): 413–25, esp. 424 and 417.
[19] MacCormac, *Cognitive Theory*, 31.
[20] See the list of works that use cognitive metaphor theory in the discussion of Cognitive Linguistics in Chapter Two. The works by Stovell and Robinson noted earlier in this chapter belong in this category.
[21] Vyvyan Evans and Melanie Green, *Cognitive Linguistics: An Introduction* (Edinburgh: Edinburgh University Press, 2006), 293. See also William Croft and D. Alan Cruse, *Cognitive Linguistics*, CTL (Cambridge: Cambridge University Press, 2004). My discussion is directly dependent upon Evans and Green, with some influence of Croft and Cruse.
[22] Lakoff and Johnson, *Metaphors We Live By*. See also, continuing in this line, George Lakoff, *Women, Fire, and Dangerous Things: What Categories Reveal about the Mind* (Chicago: University of Chicago Press, 1987); Lakoff and Mark Turner, *More than Cool Reason: A Field Guide to Poetic Metaphor* (Chicago: University of Chicago Press, 1989); Turner, *The Literary Mind: The Origins of Thought and Language* (New York: Oxford University Press, 1996); Mark Johnson, *Moral Imagination: Implications of Cognitive Science for Ethics* (Chicago: University of Chicago Press, 1993), 32–77; and Gilles Fauconnier, *Mappings in Thought and Language* (Cambridge: Cambridge University Press, 1997). Useful summaries are found in Zoltán Kövecses, *Metaphor: A Practical Introduction* (Oxford: Oxford University Press, 2002); and Alice Deignan, "The Cognitive View of Metaphor: Conceptual Metaphor Theory," in *Metaphor Analysis: Research Practice in Applied Linguistics, Social Sciences and the Humanities*, ed. Lynne Cameron and Robert Maslen (Sheffield: Equinox, 2010), 44–56. Further work on semantic domains is provided in Eva Feder Kittay, *Metaphor: Its Cognitive Force and Linguistic Structure* (Oxford: Clarendon, 1987). An attempt to establish the semantic domains on a corpus basis is found in Allan, *Metaphor and Metonymy*.

(resembling schemata), certain fixed patterns that restrain metaphors, and an inevitable process of both hiding and highlighting features of the target domain when the domains are mapped upon each other.[23] Most of these features are related to the tensive and word-based (though framed as conceptual) approach of conceptual metaphor theory.

Conceptual metaphor theory has developed in several different ways, including those of primary metaphor theory, metonymy, and conceptual blending metaphor theory. Each of these is designed to correct some of the perceived shortcomings of conceptual metaphor theory. Primary metaphor theory is designed to address the issue of invariance, distinguishing between two types of metaphor, primary and compound metaphor. Primary metaphors are fundamental, and compound metaphors are the accumulation of several primary metaphors.[24] Metonymy has been part of the discussion of metaphor from the outset, but has recently been revived in "the notion that all metaphors are ultimately derived metonymically from our direct, physical experience of the world," and is thus part of what is meant by embodiment.[25] Conceptual blending theory is related to (some would say dependent upon) mental spaces theory.[26] Conceptual blending theory attempts to overcome the limitation of bringing two semantic domains into play in conceptual metaphor theory by "blending" three or more domains (e.g., to handle an instance where the two domains brought together have no apparent negative implications, yet the metaphor is negative, as in "the surgeon is a butcher"), which requires that mental space theories (such as generic and blended space) be incorporated.[27] These solutions appear to draw upon various types of resolutions, some more focused and others more inclusive within the cognitive framework, to address pertinent problems in conceptual metaphor theory.

I relate these theories for several reasons. The first is to show how the various strands of discussion of metaphor theory are more closely related than one might at first suspect, especially if we are used to being exposed to them as isolated accounts of various metaphorical theories. The second reason is to note that several fundamental issues are involved in definitions of metaphor. These issues revolve around the construction of metaphors, that is, the mechanisms by which they are formulated; the components of metaphors, that is, what exactly are the respective entities that are involved in metaphors; the nature of metaphors, that is, how it is that they function, whether tensively, substitutionally, or deviationally; and, finally, the scope of metaphors, that is, whether they are primarily word, sentence, or discourse based. With this background, we now turn to metaphor in SFL and the New Testament.

---

[23]Evans and Green, *Cognitive Linguistics*, 296–304; Croft and Cruse, *Cognitive Linguistics*, 194–204.
[24]Evans and Green, *Cognitive Linguistics*, 304–10.
[25]Deignan, "Cognitive View," 51.
[26]Gilles Fauconnier and Mark Turner, *The Way We Think: Conceptual Blending and the Mind's Hidden Complexities* (New York: Basic, 2002). Cf. Evans and Green, *Cognitive Linguistics*, 400; Croft and Cruse, *Cognitive Linguistics*, 207–9.
[27]Evans and Green, *Cognitive Linguistics*, 400–10; Croft and Cruse, *Cognitive Linguistics*, 207–9.

METAPHOR IN SYSTEMIC FUNCTIONAL LINGUISTICS AND THE NEW TESTAMENT

SFL is *not* a cognitive theory of language, although the differences between the two are sometimes overdrawn for the sake of identity formation and reinforcement, thereby neglecting the common elements.[28] Nevertheless, there are major differences, some of them seen in metaphor theory. Whereas others have attempted to integrate SFL with various other theories of metaphor, such as cognitive theories,[29] I here am more concerned with defining metaphor in a modified form of SFL (what this means will become clearer as I proceed), showing their points of similarity as a means of exploring their differences. There are two types of metaphor that I wish to discuss within a SFL framework: lexical metaphor and grammatical metaphor, with the second, grammatical metaphor, including an analysis (though not necessarily an endorsement) of interpersonal metaphor and a presentation of a more robust form of ideational metaphor suitable for examination of the Greek of the New Testament.[30]

---

[28] So intimates Michael A. K. Halliday, *An Introduction to Functional Grammar* (IFG1) (London: Edward Arnold, 1985), xxviii–xxix (this introduction removed in subsequent editions). See also Halliday and Christian M. I. M. Matthiessen, *Construing Experience through Meaning: A Language-Based Approach to Cognition* (London: Continuum, 1999), 2 and passim, which addresses many issues related to Cognitive Linguistics.

[29] This has been done by both biblical scholars and linguists. See Stovell, *Mapping Metaphorical Discourse*, 39–65; and L. David Ritchie and Min Zhu, "'Nixon Stonewalled the Investigation': Potential Contributions of Grammatical Metaphor to Conceptual Metaphor Theory and Analysis," *Metaphor and Symbol* 30.2 (2015): 118–36.

[30] The bibliography on metaphor in SFL is large. Some of the fundamental works are Michael A. K. Halliday, IFG1, 319–45; Halliday, "On the Language of Physical Science," in *Registers of Written English: Situational Factors and Linguistic Features*, ed. Mohsen Ghadessy (London: Pinter, 1988), 162–78 (repr. in Halliday, *The Language of Science*, ed. Jonathan J. Webster, CWMH 5 [London: Continuum, 2004], 140–58); Halliday, "Things and Relations: Regrammaticising Experience as Technical Knowledge," in *Reading Science: Critical and Functional Perspectives on Discourse of Science*, ed. J. R. Martin and Robert Veel (London: Routledge, 1998), 185–235 (repr. in Halliday, *Language of Science*, 49–101); Halliday and J. R. Martin, *Writing Science: Literacy and Discursive Power* (London: Falmer Press, 1993); J. R. Martin, *English Text: System and Structure* (Amsterdam: John Benjamins, 1992), 406–17; Halliday, *Halliday's Introduction to Functional Grammar* (IFG4), rev. Christian M. I. M. Matthiessen, 4th ed. (London: Routledge, 2014), 698–731; and Halliday and Matthiessen, *Construing Experience*, 227–96. For other works of importance, see Halliday, "Grammatical Metaphor in English and Chinese" (1984), repr. in Halliday, *Studies in Chinese Language*, ed. Jonathan J. Webster, CWMH 8 (London: Continuum, 2006), 325–33, where Halliday appears to make the claim to create the term "grammatical metaphor" (325); Louise Jane Ravelli, "Grammatical Metaphor: An Initial Analysis," in *Pragmatics, Discourse and Text*, ed. Erich H. Steiner and Robert Veltman (Norwood, NJ: Ablex, 1988), 133–47; Ravelli, *Metaphor, Mode and Complexity: An Exploration of Co-Varying Patterns* (Nottingham: Nottingham Trent University, 1999); Anne-Marie Simon-Vandenbergen, Miriam Taverniers, and Louise Ravelli, eds., *Grammatical Metaphor: Views from Systemic Functional Linguistics* (Amsterdam: John Benjamins, 2003), esp. Ravelli, "Renewal of Connection: Integrating Theory and Practice in Understanding of Grammatical Metaphor," 37–64, and Liesbet Heyvaert, "Nominalization as Grammatical Metaphor: On the Need for a Radically Systemic and Metafunctional Approach," 65–99; Geoff Thompson, *Introducing Functional Grammar*, 2nd ed. (London: Hodder Education, 2004), 218–37; Taverniers, "Grammatical Metaphor and Lexical Metaphor: Different Perspectives on Semantic Variation," *Neophilologus* 90 (2006): 321–32; Devo Y. Devrim, "Grammatical Metaphor: What Do We Mean? What Exactly Are We Researching?" *Functional Linguistics* 2.3 (2015): 1–15; and Winfred Wenhui Xuan and Shukun Chen, "A Synthesis of Research on Grammatical Metaphor: Meta-Data and Content Analysis," *WORD* 65.4 (2019): 213–33.

There have been previous grammars of metaphor or grammatical treatments of metaphor.[31] In fact, many of the theories of metaphor that I have surveyed have a grammatical component to them. Some of them are based upon the word (such as classical theory and conceptual metaphor theory), some on the sentence (such as Black's theory), and some on the discourse (such as Richards's and conceptual blending theory), while others recognize the paradigmatic and syntagmatic dimension of language (such as Jakobson's). Those familiar with SFL will recognize that these categories are in fact fundamental distinctions made within the SFL architecture of language. SFL utilizes the rank scale (word to word group to clause), strata of exponence (expression to content to context), and the fundamental organizational framework of structure (syntagm) and system (paradigm) as the primary means of describing language. These provide the larger framework for understanding metaphor.

Lexical Metaphor

Discussion of metaphor in SFL has concentrated upon the syntagmatic dimension, to the neglect of the paradigmatic dimension. This is made clear in Halliday's *Introduction to Functional Grammar* (IFG), which has in many ways left paradigmatic discussion behind, at least so far as metaphor is concerned, so that it emphasizes two types of grammatical metaphor, interpersonal and ideational. I believe that this is not just a shortcoming of IFG, but a shortcoming of much recent work in SFL, which has tended to focus upon particular elements of systemic functional grammar to the neglect of others (e.g., the neglect of register). This neglect is also reflected in some of the other treatments that are designed to explicate the approach in IFG.

To find a reasonable definition and exemplification of lexical metaphor, one must go to Halliday and Matthiessen's *Construing Experience through Meaning*—although this is an ambivalent treatment of lexical metaphor that endorses grammatical metaphor (as I will point out, this is not entirely well grounded).[32] Despite the historical significance of lexical metaphor, as previously noted in my survey, this is one of few works that discusses the topic in any detail.[33] In true SFL fashion (which endorses various perspectives on language), Halliday and Matthiessen differentiate two types of metaphor, examination of an expression "from below" and examination "from above," that is, from the lexis or from the grammar.[34] Lexical metaphor concerns wording or lexis in this scheme and involves a difference in meaning. Thus, the word *flood* has either the literal (congruent)[35] meaning of "an inundation of water" or a metaphorical sense of "an intense emotion," such as a *flood of relief*. Examination from above would start with the question of how

---

[31]Besides some of those already mentioned, Hawkes (*Metaphor*, 67–70) cites Christine Brook-Rose, *A Grammar of Metaphor* (London: Secker and Warburg, 1958).
[32]Halliday and Matthiessen, *Construing Experience*, 232–4; cf. Halliday, IFG1, 319–20.
[33]See also Anne-Marie Simon-Vandenbergen, "Lexical Metaphor and Interpersonal Meaning," in *Grammatical Metaphor*, ed. Simon-Vandenbergen, Taverniers, and Ravelli, 223–55; Taverniers, "Grammatical Metaphor," 326–31; and Antonella Luporni, "Grammatical Metaphor through the Lens of Software? Examining 'Crisis' in a Corpus of Articles from *The Financial Times*," in *Systemic Functional Linguistics in the Digital Age*, ed. Sheena Gardner and Siân Alsop (Sheffield: Equinox, 2016), 260–75.
[34]Cf. Simon-Vandenbergen, "Lexical Metaphor," 224–8, who surveys similarities and differences between lexical and grammatical metaphor.
[35]Halliday and Matthiessen, *Construing Experience*, 232, tend to use the language of "literal" vs. "metaphorical." The term "literal" is problematic. A better opposition is congruent vs. incongruent (metaphorical). This was apparently the language of Halliday, IFG1, 321.

emotion might be expressed and use either the literal expression *she felt greatly relieved* or the metaphorical expression *she felt a flood of relief.*

Grammatical metaphor, however, involves a difference in expression, not meaning. In other words, in some ways, they are the same, differing only in perspective. However, Halliday and Matthiessen then go on to give two different examples of lexical and grammatical metaphor that are not as readily interchangeable as the previous example. They cite the example of lexical metaphor involving the literal (congruent) *applauded loudly* and the metaphorical *applauded thunderously*, in which the "lexico-semantic domain of 'volume' has been mapped onto the lexico-semantic domain of 'metereological commotion.'" A lexico-semantic domain is not defined but is presumably a domain of meaning that organizes lexical items. Grammatical metaphor, by contrast, involves the congruent *applauded loudly* and metaphorical *loud applause*, in which "the grammatico-semantic domain of 'figures' [configuration of elements] has been mapped onto the grammatico-semantic domain of 'participants,'"[36] in other words, in which a process has been rendered as an entity (nominalization), an instance of ideational grammatical metaphor.[37] A grammatico-semantic domain, also not defined, is presumably a domain of meaning that organizes grammatical features. This difference between lexical and grammatical metaphor, according to Halliday and Matthiessen, is one of "delicacy," not kind, as "they are both aspects of the same general metaphorical strategy by which we expand our semantic resources for construing experience."[38] They do this by reconstruing one domain in terms of another, with grammatical metaphor doing this in a general way and lexical metaphor in a more delicate way (as lexis is the most delicate grammar).[39]

There are a number of problems, however, with this formulation. In their attempt to find congruence between grammatical and lexical metaphor (probably because of the emphasis placed upon grammatical metaphor at the expense of lexical metaphor throughout the development of IFG), several terms are used ambiguously, possibly even ambivalently, and almost assuredly confusedly. These include, first, the notion of domain. A lexico-semantic domain is different from a grammatico-semantic domain by their own tacit admission (otherwise we would not need the different terms to describe them), and because of this they have various content and ways in which they are used. Halliday and Matthiessen only allude to such differences. The second is the failure to note the fundamental difference between paradigmatic and syntagmatic organization. This difference is what Halliday and Matthiessen have described. In effect, the different types of metaphor might be better labeled paradigmatic (lexical) and syntagmatic (grammatical) metaphor, as this makes clear both the types of congruence involved and the different elements involved. This axial differentiation also involves the difference between the different ranks. Lexical metaphor occurs at the word level and grammatical metaphor at the clause (sentence) level.

---

[36] Halliday and Matthiessen, *Construing Experience*, 232.
[37] See Halliday, IFG4, 707–31, esp. 710.
[38] Halliday and Matthiessen, *Construing Experience*, 233.
[39] See Ruqaiya Hasan, "The Grammarians' Dream: Lexis as Most Delicate Grammar," in *New Developments in Systemic Linguistics, Volume 1: Theory and Description*, ed. M. A. K. Halliday and Robin P. Fawcett (London: Pinter, 1987), 184–211. This is an important dimension of SFL's conception of lexicogrammar.

Making such distinctions allows us to understand two further characteristics of lexical metaphor that are noted by Halliday and Matthiessen (though I realize their use of the terms does run the risk of increasing confusion). They note that lexical metaphor (though it is paradigmatic in nature) does have the characteristic of being "syntagmatic": this means that "lexical metaphors tend to occur in regular clusters," which they call "syndromes."[40] Thus, if one were to invoke lexico-semantic metaphors regarding *congregation* as *flock*, one might also refer to a religious official as a *shepherd*, and a group of believers as a *fold*, etc. The second characteristic is that lexical metaphor is also "paradigmatic": for them this means that "lexical metaphors typically involve a shift towards the concrete, a move in the direction of 'objectifying.'"[41] I believe that these formulations involve unfortunate uses of terms, perhaps motivated by the overwhelming desire to make lexical metaphor into grammatical metaphor. There is an unfortunate tendency here to use the hammer of grammatical metaphor to see everything as a nail. There is, however, nothing syntagmatic about clusters of lexico-semantic metaphors, as each of them constitutes an individual lexical metaphor. I think that it is appropriate to note that they tend to cluster or occur in syndromes, but I believe that this is based upon the invocation not simply of a single lexical metaphor but an entire lexico-semantic domain that includes a variety of lexical items (as we will see in the subsequent examples). Furthermore, there is nothing paradigmatic about lexical metaphors tending toward being concrete. This is only the case, perhaps, if one wishes to make lexical metaphor more like grammatical metaphor, which in its ideational form tends to make processes into entities (something we will discuss further as well). In any case, I do not believe that this is in fact necessarily true, or at least true in a particularly helpful linguistic sense.

In regard to my second point regarding paradigmatic lexical metaphor, however, Halliday and Matthiessen note that they

> do not yet have a general description of lexical metaphorical syndromes or of the location of metaphorical domains within the overall ideation base. But it is possible to discern that a central resource for metaphor is human bodily experience; and that the human body itself, concrete phenomena located in space-time, and features of daily social life are the most favoured metaphorical motifs.[42]

They cite work that has found that, so far as English is concerned, 87 percent of the metaphorical entries in a dictionary of metaphor are accounted for by thirty-seven of these types of motifs, including: the human body (23 percent), animals (9 percent), sport, food and drink, war and military, buildings, geography, clothes, nautical items, religion and biblically based, transport, plants, meteorology, science and medicine, colors, commerce, and manufacturing.[43] One might well note the similarities of this finding with the categories identified by Lakoff and Johnson, as do Halliday and Matthiessen.[44]

---

[40] Halliday and Matthiessen, *Construing Experience*, 233.
[41] Halliday and Matthiessen, *Construing Experience*, 233.
[42] Halliday and Matthiessen, *Construing Experience*, 233.
[43] Halliday and Matthiessen, *Construing Experience*, 233 note 1. I note, however, that the motifs that they identify do not add up to 87 percent, but only 74 percent, with the other categories being at 1 percent or lower.
[44] Halliday and Matthiessen, *Construing Experience*, 233 note 1, citing Lakoff and Johnson, *Metaphors We Live By*.

I believe, however, that Halliday and Matthiessen have missed the fact that lexical metaphor does not work simply by invoking metaphorical domains but by the invoking of lexico-semantic domains in non-congruent ways. There is a difference. There may be tendencies for any number of reasons, but the issue is not metaphorical domains but lexico-semantic domains used metaphorically. Furthermore, I believe that they have not made clear that lexico-semantic domains in SFL are something other than the conceptual domains within Cognitive Linguistics (which themselves are difficult to define). Conceptual domains within Cognitive Linguistics are cognitively organized clusters of information, usually organized around various spatial, temporal, and related categories.[45] This is not the only way to think of lexico-semantic domains in SFL. They can be organized according to a variety of means, including both paradigmatic and syntagmatic features (as they probably would be in a SFL lexicon). In this sense, we are greatly aided in the study of the New Testament, because we already have a major advance on other languages (including English, the language Halliday and Mathiessen are using for their illustrations) through the Louw-Nida semantic domain lexicon.[46] This lexicon allows us to think in terms of semantic domains that may or may not be invoked by a given author when lexical metaphorization occurs. I realize that there are some cognitive elements to the Louw-Nida lexicon; however, I think that, without thinking of it as a perfect tool, there are other elements based upon such features as frequency, collocation, and syntax that allow it to be used in other than simply cognitive contexts.

As examples of the use of lexical metaphor, I wish to examine two passages in the New Testament, the conversation between Jesus and the Samaritan woman in John 4 and the conversation between Jesus and Martha regarding her brother Lazarus in John 11. I begin with the episode in John 4 with the Samaritan woman.[47] Let me recount the story in a way that establishes the thrust of what I wish to examine. On his own in Samaria, in a town called Sychar, Jesus is tired and sits by a well. When a Samaritan woman approaches to draw water, Jesus says to her, "Give me something to drink" (Jn 4:7).[48] We see that the major lexico-semantic domains of the discourse are going to include particular individuals (Names of Persons and Places, LN domain 93), water from a well (Natural substances, LN domain 2; and possibly Constructions, LN domain 7), and acquisition of it (Physiological Processes and States, LN domain 23). The woman responds by at first pursuing the issue of persons and places, but she relates these persons and places to Jesus's asking her for a drink (v. 9).[49] Jesus addresses both of these. He acknowledges that if she had known the gift of God[50] and his identity as the one requesting the drink, she would, instead, have asked him for "living water" (ὕδωρ ζῶν; v. 10). The introduction of living water is grammatical metaphorization of the notion of "water flows." However, this is a relatively standard grammatico-semantic metaphor of the ancient world as a way of talking about flowing rather than standing water. The woman understands this "stock" metaphor and

---

[45]See Evans and Green, *Cognitive Linguistics*, 14–15; Croft and Cruse, *Cognitive Linguistics*, 15–16.
[46]Johannes P. Louw and Eugene A. Nida, *Greek–English Lexicon of the New Testament Based on Semantic Domains* (LN), 2 vols. (New York: United Bible Societies, 1988), esp. their introduction, vi–xx.
[47]For another treatment of this passage, see Stanley E. Porter, *Linguistic Analysis of the Greek New Testament: Studies in Tools, Methods, and Practice* (Grand Rapids: Baker, 2015), 302–6.
[48]The NIV11 interprets the command as a polite request. One might well think of this as interpersonal grammatical metaphor in English, but that is beyond the scope of my study here.
[49]One notes that the woman apparently construes the command of v. 7 as a request.
[50]The "gift of God" is an instance of ideational grammatical metaphor (see later in this chapter for a definition and explanation of this type of metaphor). She did not know that God was giving her a gift.

pursues it in her comments (it is found in much other literature, such as *Did.* 7:3), while Jesus construes the grammatical metaphor so as to pursue the lexico-semantic metaphor on a spiritual level.

In this instance, the lexical metaphor is a more delicate form of metaphor, because it takes the "living water" grammatical metaphor and develops it as a lexical metaphor. However, the way that the lexical metaphor works here is not according to how we have seen it described earlier. The metaphor is not moving to a more concrete entity but to a more abstract entity involving theological concepts. Furthermore, the lexical metaphor is not substituting other lexico-semantic domains for "living" or "water," but reconstruing the metaphor by means of a spiritual lexico-semantic domain. The way that it is construed here is in terms of juxtaposing the literal (congruent) lexico-semantic domain of physical flowing water with a theological lexico-semantic domain of spiritual transformation. There is no specific domain with this semantic designation in the Louw-Nida lexicon (the closest they probably come is LN domain 40, Reconciliation, Forgiveness, or LN domain 88, Moral and Ethical Qualities and Related Behavior), but that is because the Louw-Nida lexicon mostly is, as it should be, a lexicon of congruent semantic representation, not incongruent metaphorical ones (though it does include "standard" or "dead" metaphors, because of their congruent meaning on the basis of repeated usage).[51] The lexical metaphors are created by the reconstrual of one domain by another, in this case giving theological metaphorical significance to the domain of "living water." In that sense, one of the opportunities of lexical metaphor is the reconstrual of any lexico-semantic domain with another based upon the reconstrual of meaning.

The woman continues the discussion by accepting the metaphor of "living water" as indicating flowing water and not static water, but she retains the fact that this is a metaphor about qualities of water, nothing more. In a sense, she makes the metaphor into a dead metaphor, so far as she is concerned. She queries Jesus's ability to draw such water from the well. However, she does recognize that Jesus has made a claim about himself by his statement about being able to provide such "living water." Jesus does not accept this offer to discuss his identity, but instead pursues the lexico-semantic metaphor of "living water" as spiritual transformation. His comments are all addressed to this spiritually vital provision: unlike the well-water (the "living water" as normally construed), this water that he is speaking of permanently slakes thirst, that is, permanently satisfies spiritual longing, to the point that what it means for this water to be "living" is that it becomes itself a spring of water welling up to eternal life (another instance of grammatical metaphor, reconstruing the "spring wells up with water" to a "spring welling up") (Jn 4:14). The word for "well" is the same as "spring" (πηγή). Even though the Louw-Nida lexicon places these uses in separate semantic domains, here we see that the dialogue is playing on the use of the same word (if the lexeme is not to be understood as "well" in the second instance, also a possibility). The "well" is reconstrued by the lexico-semantic domain as a life-giving spiritual source ("spring"). At the conclusion of this sub-episode, the woman only partly grasps the spiritual transformative significance of the dialogue with Jesus. She has grasped that this is water unlike other water in that by partaking of it she will no longer thirst, but she still equates the water with that which is drawn from the well.

---

[51]See LN 1, xvii. An example would be LN domain 90 subdomain M Experiencer, with the example of γεύομαι, "(a figurative extension of meaning of 'to taste') ... to experience." There are others like this in this section, such as with ὁράω, ἐμπλέκομαι, ἐκχέομαι.

The second episode occurs in John 11, when Jesus arrives in Bethany and meets Lazarus's sister, Martha. In this episode, Martha comes out to meet Jesus, and when she states that, if Jesus had been there, Lazarus would not have died (a congruent statement), Jesus answers, "Your brother can expect to rise again (ἀναστήσεται)" (Jn 11:23). Martha responds by acknowledging that "he can expect to rise again (ἀναστήσεται) in the resurrection (ἀναστάσει) in the last day" (v. 24). Jesus says that he himself is "the resurrection (ἀνάστασις) and the life (ζωή)," and that "the one who believes in me can expect to live (ζήσεται), even if he might die, and everyone who lives (ζῶν) and believes" (not "lives by believing," as the NIV11) in him will not ever die (v. 25). The conversation is left at this point, but Jesus then goes on to raise Lazarus from the dead, so that he physically comes from the tomb.

What appears at first glance to be a conversation of missed meanings, in which the meanings produced by Jesus and Martha are at cross purposes regarding such things as "resurrection" and "life," is, instead, I believe, a complex set of lexico-semantic metaphorical interactions. In the example in John 4, we observed that both grammatical and lexical metaphors were used. In this second example, we have a similar set of metaphorical usages. As we will examine further, grammatical metaphor occurs when the process of *rising* is transformed into the entity *resurrection*, but also (and I will discuss this kind of example in subsequent comments) the entity of *life* is transformed into the process of *living*. However, despite this use of grammatico-semantic metaphor, there are instances of congruent and incongruent usage at the lexico-semantic metaphorical level in John 11. We must bear in mind that Martha and Jesus are both using grammatical metaphor, but that there is also lexical metaphorization occurring. Martha understands the congruent construction of a person rising from the dead at the final resurrection, a notion based upon Jewish resurrection thought that had developed in the Second Temple period.[52] We are right in seeing this as in some sense metaphorical usage, but it has become a standard, congruent usage also (a dead metaphor). Jesus, however, shifts the lexico-semantic domain from wordings about a standard view of Jewish eschatology and applies the words metaphorically to himself. The domain is reconstrued from the lexico-semantic domain of Jewish eschatology to another theological lexico-semantic domain related to Jesus's theological belief in himself as the one who is able to resurrect a human being, such as performing an actual individual resurrection. Martha is speaking about Jewish belief in corporate resurrection at the end of time, and Jesus has metaphorically reconstrued the language of resurrection and life into personal qualities that he believes he himself is able to bestow now.

In these episodes, we have what I think are good examples of lexico-semantic metaphor that illustrate the importance of developing a robust theory of lexical metaphor. There are several reasons for this. The first is that this use of lexical metaphor is, indeed, more delicate than grammatical metaphor, as Halliday and Matthiessen indicate. Lexical metaphor focuses upon the paradigmatic axis, not upon the syntagmatic axis. The paradigmatic axis provides for levels of lexico-semantic metaphorization. In the example in John 11, there may well be several levels here, including various types of spiritual or corporate resurrection, as well as individual resurrection. The second reason is that lexical metaphor reconstrues the congruent or literal domain by means of a metaphorical

---

[52]See Stanley E. Porter, "Jesus and Resurrection," in *Jesus in Continuum*, ed. Tom Holmén, WUNT 289 (Tübingen: Mohr Siebeck, 2012), 323–54. Modern humans may construe this as entirely metaphorical, but the ancients clearly did not.

domain. However, in these instances there is not any substitution that occurs, but the metaphorical reconstrual of the lexis by means of the metaphorical domain of theological signification. A third reason is that these instances of lexical metaphor also involve instances of grammatical metaphor, some of which I have identified in these particular episodes. This observation is not surprising in light of the relationship between the two, as we already noted. They appear in similar co-texts but they are used for different purposes. The use of lexical metaphor is not simply a word-level substitution, but it is a lexico-semantic domain level reconstrual, in which there are new meanings created through what must be seen as the tensive character of metaphor.

Lexical metaphor remains significant, even if it is not as widely discussed or well developed in SFL treatments of metaphor. The examples provided—and there are many more that could be cited in the New Testament—attest to the productivity of lexical metaphor in ancient Greek in the New Testament.

Grammatical Metaphor

The second type of metaphor, as we have already observed, is grammatical metaphor. Grammatical metaphor (sometimes referred to in the literature as GM) dominates discussion of metaphor within SFL studies, to the point that one might believe that there is no other form of metaphor worth discussing. As we have seen, that is not the case. However, that does not diminish its importance or the fact that SFL has made a major contribution to linguistics by defining and developing the notion of grammatical metaphor. There have, however, been only relatively few studies of New Testament Greek that explore the possibilities of grammatical metaphor.[53]

There are two types of grammatical metaphor that have been widely identified by Halliday and others working within SFL, interpersonal metaphor and ideational metaphor.[54] These forms of grammatical metaphor are defined in relation to the metafunctions, that is, the way that SFL characterizes the "basic functions of language."[55] The interpersonal metafunction is concerned with how language "enact[s] our personal and social relationships," while the ideational metafunction is concerned with how language "construe[s] human experience."[56] These metafunctions are "extended" by means of metaphor.[57] In both interpersonal and ideational metaphor, there is a transferred semantic configuration or a transference that occurs. This transference occurs when a congruent

---

[53] See Wally V. Cirafesi, "ἔχειν πίστιν in Hellenisic Greek and its Contribution to the πίστις Χριστοῦ Debate," *BAGL* 1 (2012): 5–38; Gregory P. Fewster, *Creation Language in Romans 8: A Study in Monosemy*, LBS 8 (Leiden: Brill, 2013), esp. 73–93, who provides one of the best short introductions to grammatical metaphor as a prelude to his defining lexicogrammatical metaphor (combining lexical and grammatical metaphor); and Fewster, "Metaphor Analysis with Some Help from Corpus Linguistics: Contextualizing 'Root' Metaphors in Ephesians and Colossians," in *Modeling Biblical Language: Selected Papers from the McMaster Divinity College Linguistics Circle*, ed. Stanley E. Porter, Gregory P. Fewster, and Christopher D. Land, LBS 13 (Leiden: Brill, 2016), 339–61.
[54] A few SFL linguists have proposed a textual grammatical metaphor. See Martin, *English Text*, 416–17; Thompson, *Introducing Functional Grammar*, 235–6, but neither with a robust discussion or exemplification. Halliday did not introduce it in IFG1 and denies it altogether in IFG4: "While some scholars have explored the possibility of grammatical metaphor within the textual metafunction, we do not see any evidence that the textual metafunction engenders metaphor" (731 n. 6). However, Halliday is not always right on issues of metaphor, as I point out later in this chapter. Halliday, IFG4, 715–18, does discuss the textual effects of grammatical metaphor.
[55] Halliday, IFG4, 30.
[56] Halliday, IFG4, 30.
[57] Halliday, IFG4, 698.

meaning is transferred into a non-congruent or metaphorical meaning.[58] Transference in this sense is different from transcategorization, in which a shift in category may not be metaphorical but may merely indicate a shift in rank that is part of the productive capacity of language.[59]

There are two ways that metaphorical transference has been modeled within SFL grammatical metaphor theory.[60] The first approach is stratal, in which there is said to be a tension between strata (stratal tension), the lexicogrammatical and discourse-semantic strata, caused by the metaphorization.[61] The second approach is semantic, in which a "semantic junction" occurs as the result of shifts that join two semantic categories, such as "process thing," and result in an instance of grammatical metaphor.[62] There are some clear differences in how grammatical metaphor is described in these two renderings, one utilizing the SFL strata of language and the other levels of semantic categories. In the stratal view, grammatical metaphor creates a tension between the lexicogrammar and the semantics because the lexicogrammar is incongruent and the semantic is congruent, whereas in the semantic view, metaphorical transference occurs between semantic categories, even if they are realized in the lexicogrammar. However, the stratal and semantic are nevertheless very similar in conception and both involve semantics, with movement between levels (including the semantic stratum) or semantic categories that create the metaphorical transference. Most of the discussion within SFL of grammatical metaphor assumes the stratal view. I do not believe that it is important for my discussion here to make much of the difference in conception.

Interpersonal Grammatical Metaphor

I turn first to interpersonal metaphor. Interpersonal metaphor is one of two categories of grammatical metaphor identified and developed by Halliday. There are two major types of interpersonal metaphor in the scheme that he defines: (1) expansion by projection and (2) speech functions.

(1) Expansion by projection. The first form of interpersonal grammatical metaphor is a form of expansion by projection that is used to address the issue of mood. As Halliday states, "the semantic domain of modality is extended through grammatical metaphor to include explicit indications of subjective and objective orientation: a modal proposition or proposal is realized, as if it was a projection sequence, by a nexus of two clauses …"[63]

---

[58]See Halliday, IFG1, 321; Halliday and Martin, *Writing Science*, 258; Ravelli, "Renewal of Connection," passim.
[59]Halliday and Matthiessen, *Construing Experience*, 259.
[60]See Devrim, "Grammatical Metaphor," esp. 1–5, whose characterization I rely upon in my description. According to Devrim, the major works that take a stratal view are: Halliday, IFG1, 319–45; Halliday, "Language of Physical Science"; Halliday, "Things and Relations"; Martin, *English Text*, 406–17; and Halliday and Martin, *Writing Science*. The major work that takes a semantic view is Halliday and Matthiessen, *Construing Experience*, 227–96. One cannot help but wonder how much of the difference, if there is a significant one, is due to this being the contribution of Matthiessen, rather than the concepts of Halliday. As Devrim, "Grammatical Metaphor," 1, states, "the semantic model is a development of the stratal model … grammatical metaphor examined in the semantic model can be viewed as the result of transference and/or transcategorization of GM discussed in the stratal model …" The two seem to converge in Halliday, IFG4, which was revised by Matthiessen. See my subsequent comments.
[61]See Halliday, "Things and Relations," 144: "Thus grammatical metaphor, like metaphor in its traditional, lexical sense, is a realignment between a pair of strata: a remapping of the semantics on to the lexicogrammar." There have been other ways of speaking of this relationship, such as seeing multiple lexicogrammatical realizations. See Ravelli, *Metaphor*, 55; Ravelli, "Grammatical Metaphor," 86.
[62]Halliday and Matthiessen, *Construing Experience*, 244. Cf. Halliday, "Things and Relations," 162, where he lays out the order of semantic downgrading.
[63]Halliday, IFG4, 698.

METAPHOR

An example that Halliday uses involves the following two clauses (spaced so as to visualize the point being made here):

Probably	that pudding will never be cooked
I don't believe	that pudding ever will be cooked

He states that the

> cognitive mental clause *I don't believe* is a metaphorical realization of probability: the probability is realized by a mental clause as if it were a figure of sensing. Being metaphorical, the clause serves not only as the projecting part of a clause nexus of projection, but also as a mood Adjunct [if one were to analyze the interpersonal clausal structure, I do not believe that it should be analyzed as an adjunct; see my further comments], just as *probably* does.[64]

According to Halliday, the "representation of grammatical metaphor in such [interpersonal metaphorical representations] shows how the metaphor is embodied in the structural organization as an increase in the layers of meaning and wording. But there is, of course, also a systemic effect. Systemically, metaphor leads to an expansion of the meaning potential: by creating new patterns of structural realization."[65] Halliday also enumerates a number of other wordings that he says represent *I believe*, a major metaphorical modal projecting clause, such as *it is obvious that*, *nobody tries to deny that*, *there can be no doubt*, etc.[66] For Halliday, "The reason for regarding this as a metaphorical variant is that the proposition is not, in fact, 'I think'; the proposition is 'it is so.'" He claims that the tag for such a statement as *I think it's going to rain* is *isn't it?*, not *don't I?* "In other words the clause is a variety of *it's probably going to rain (isn't it?)* and not a first-person equivalent of *John thinks it's going to rain*, which does represent the proposition 'John thinks' (tag *doesn't he?*)."[67] Halliday summarizes how expansion by projection works: "The metaphoric strategy is to **upgrade** the interpersonal assessment from group rank to clause rank—from an adverbial group of prepositional phrase serving within a simple clause to a clause serving within a clause nexus of projection."[68]

The type of metaphor that Halliday defines is confined to a relatively small number of clausal constructions (especially mental clauses) that involve what he calls modal adjuncts and their relationship to metaphorical reconstruals by means of a projective clausal nexus. I believe, however, that Halliday is probably wrong concerning this dimension of interpersonal metaphor on a number of different points. The major mistake that he makes, I think, is to confuse what he contends is the proposition with something that has some kind of linguistic status apart from the person making the statement and that person's degree of involvement in it. This involvement is reflected in the role of being the subject of the major clause that projects the projected clause in the clausal nexus. In other words, the congruent interpersonal statement is the statement of belief or thought or feeling made by the speaker, of which the projected clause is not the proposition, but merely the content of the thought

---

[64] Halliday, IFG4, 687.
[65] Halliday, IFG4, 699.
[66] Halliday, IFG4, 689–90.
[67] Halliday, IFG4, 687.
[68] Halliday, IFG4, 700 (emphasis original).

(contra his statement that it is not *I think* but *it is so*). The interpersonal grammatico-semantics reside with the formulation on the basis of the one making the statement. The proposition is not *it is so*, but *a person believes that it is so*.[69] Every statement is to be understood this way, whether the projecting clause is present or not. In that sense, whether or not one uses the tag *isn't it?* or *don't I?* (I find this an unconvincing test of the semantics of the clause, and arguably incorrect), the projection is of some type of thinking, belief, feeling, etc., which the speaker is claiming in the projected clause. Therefore, the alternative constructions that he gives are not the same as *I think*, but in fact metaphorical ways of reconstruing *I think*, by metaphorically embedding the speaker within the projection itself, which takes on an enhanced status. Thus, the metaphorical statement is the one with the modal adjunct (e.g., probability), as a way of metaphorically reconstruing the proposition by including the speaker as a part of the construction, usually as an adjunct that indicates the manner or means of the proposition. As Halliday virtually admits, when we see the use of *probably* in a statement as its modal adjunct, it is a way of saying *I believe with some degree of certainty that* ...[70] The result is often to give the statement clausal status when this is instead a metaphorical proposition-like statement of what is congruently seen as belief or thought. The further result of this type of interpersonal grammatical metaphor is, as we will see when we discuss ideational metaphor, a downgrading from clausal nexus to clause, from projecting statement to projection.

This type of interpersonal grammatical metaphor, nevertheless, is found within the New Testament. Rom. 7:7-25 is an excellent example of the use of congruent and metaphorical statements—but mostly congruent statements. For example, Paul says that "I do not know sin apart from through law, and I did not know desire unless the law said, 'You will not covet,'" τὴν ἁμαρτίαν οὐκ ἔγνων εἰ μὴ διὰ νόμου, τήν τε γὰρ ἐπιθυμίαν οὐκ ᾔδειν εἰ μὴ ὁ νόμος ἔλεγεν, οὐκ ἐπιθυμήσεις (Rom. 7:7). This is opposed to Paul stating something like "sin was unknown apart from through law" and "desire was unknown ..." Then by means of interpersonal grammatico-semantic metaphor (in particular, personification) sinning becomes a participant that takes advantage of an opportunity provided by the commandment to accomplish every desire "in me," ἐν ἐμοί in which Paul is reconstrued as an adjunct of the clause: "sin through the commandment accomplished in me every desire" ἡ ἁμαρτία διὰ τῆς ἐντολῆς κατειργάσατο ἐν ἐμοὶ πᾶσαν ἐπιθυμίαν (v. 8). Paul says "I was alive apart from the law then," ἐγὼ δὲ ἔζων χωρὶς νόμου ποτέ (v. 9), but (again using interpersonal metaphor) "when the commandment came sin came to life," ἐλθούσης δὲ τῆς ἐντολῆς ἡ ἁμαρτία ἀνέζησεν (v. 9). "I died" ἐγὼ ... ἀπέθανον (v. 10), "and the commandment that was designed for life was found 'in me' to lead to death," καὶ εὑρέθη μοι ἡ ἐντολὴ ἡ εἰς ζωὴν αὕτη εἰς θάνατον (v. 10). The grammatico-semantic metaphorical structure continues until v. 14, when Paul returns to congruent constructions: "For we know that the law is spiritual, and I am fleshly, sold under sin," οἴδαμεν γὰρ ὅτι ὁ νόμος πνευματικός ἐστιν, ἐγὼ

---

[69] I find it intriguing—and perhaps inconsistent—that Halliday, whom I believe to be a social constructivist, would claim that a statement represents what is so, when at most one can claim that one thinks that something is so. On social constructivism, see Peter L. Berger and Thomas Luckmann, *The Social Construction of Reality: A Treatise in the Sociology of Knowledge* (New York: Doubleday, 1966); cf. Berger, *Invitation to Sociology: A Humanistic Perspective* (Garden City, NY: Doubleday, 1963). See also Margaret M. Poloma, *Contemporary Sociological Theory* (New York: Macmillan, 1979), 196–205; and George Ritzer, *Contemporary Sociological Theory*, 3rd ed. (New York: McGraw-Hill, 1992), 248–53, within a discussion of phenomenological sociology and related to ethnomethodology. Halliday's social constructivism is consistent with his views on linguistic determinism.

[70] Halliday, IFG4, 687. Though he does not say this explicitly, this seems to be what he is indicating in his statements.

δὲ σάρκινός εἰμι, πεπραμένος ὑπὸ τὴν ἁμαρτίαν (v. 14). "I do not know what I am doing, for I do this that I do not wish but what I hate I do this …," ὃ γὰρ κατεργάζομαι οὐ γινώσκω, οὐ γὰρ ὃ θέλω τοῦτο πράσσω, ἀλλ' ὃ μισῶ τοῦτο ποιῶ (v. 15). And so it continues. One of the factors that probably have not been taken fully into account in discussion of this passage is not the metaphorical personification of sin and death but the congruent and hence "literal" grammaticalization of Paul himself throughout much of this passage.

(2) Speech functions. The second type of interpersonal grammatical metaphor discussed by Halliday is the use of interpersonal metaphor to explicate speech functions. The question of speech functions within SFL is very complex and cannot be explained in detail here. Speech functions are, in essence, the various functions that commands, statements, offers, and questions have at the semantic rather than lexicogrammatical level.[71] Some speech functions in English are congruent with their lexicogrammatical realization, as when a statement is realized by a declarative clause or a question is realized by an interrogative clause. For example, *She sent the letter on Tuesday* is a statement realized by a declarative clause, and *Is this the book you ordered?* is a question realized by an interrogative clause. So much makes sense. However, there are times when they are incongruent. A statement may be realized by other clauses. For example, in a heated exchange the interrogative clause *Do you think I am stupid?* may function as a statement, *I am not stupid, despite how you are treating me*. A question may be realized by a declarative clause. For example, the declarative clause *I'm waiting* may realize the question, *Are you going to act/speak?* Halliday attempts to explain these as involving interpersonal metaphor. This is a major way that he attempts to explain apparent discrepancies between what are sometimes called sentence and utterance meanings or are treated elsewhere as indirect speech acts. The classic example is the declarative clause *It's hot in here*, and whether this is a statement or a command.

Halliday identifies two major types of reconstruals of speech functions by means of interpersonal grammatical metaphor (these are identified as attempting to address questions raised by speech act theory).[72] The first type involves reconstrual by means of a propositional clause.

> The command 'vote against …' is realized metaphorically by a hypotactic clause nexus; it is realized as if it was a report of what the speaker says. This is just like the metaphorical realization of modality of the explicitly subjective orientation. Thus the reported command can be tagged: *I urge you to vote against … will you?* In other words, just like modality, speech function can be represented as a substantive proposition in its own right; and this proposition is a figure of sensing or saying that projects the original … proposal or … proposition.[73]

The second type "involves a shift in the realizational domain of commands from 'imperative' to 'indicative' clauses. The 'indicative' clause can be either 'declarative' or 'interrogative.'"[74] This is typified by what are sometimes called indirect speech acts, as

---

[71] I have discussed these in more detail in Stanley E. Porter, "Systemic Functional Linguistics and the Greek Language: The Need for Further Modeling," in *Modeling Biblical Language*, ed. Porter, Fewster, and Land, 9–47. See Chapter Four for further discussion.
[72] Halliday, IFG4, 707.
[73] Halliday, IFG4, 701.
[74] Halliday, IFG4, 705.

previously introduced. Indirect speech acts involve instances where an indicative clause such as *It is hot in here* is to be interpreted as realized by the imperative clause *Open the window* (or interrogative clause *Would you open the window?*).

Such instances of grammatical metaphor may have some application in the Greek of the New Testament. There are, however, problems with this formulation of grammatical metaphor. I am not convinced that this is in fact a type of grammatical metaphor, at least as Halliday describes it. The attempt to deal with the problem of sentence and utterance meaning is not as easily alleviated simply by appeal to metaphor since there is clearly more at play than merely examination of the clause and its speech function. The even more pressing underlying issue, however, is the difficulty of determining the speech function when there is supposed incongruity. A relatively straightforward example from New Testament Greek illustrates the problem. We are all familiar with discussions of whether certain instances in New Testament Greek are, for example, commands (imperative mood form) or declarations (indicative mood form). In Romans 6, is Paul saying "thus indeed you consider (λογίζεσθε) yourselves dead to sin but alive to God in Christ Jesus" or "indeed consider (λογίζεσθε) yourselves …" (v. 11), the first a declaration (indicative) and the second a command (imperative); or is Paul saying "being free from sin and enslaved to God, you have (ἔχετε) your fruit that leads to holiness, of which the end is eternal life" or "being free … and enslaved …, have (ἔχετε) your fruit …," the first a declaration (indicative) and the second a command (imperative) (v. 22)? We cannot determine whether the form is an indicative or imperative, to say nothing of whether the statement is a Greek command or a declaration.

The beseeching formulas that Paul uses represent a type of statement that captures both of the problems. For example, in Rom. 12:1, Paul appears to be saying this: "I encourage (παρακαλῶ) you, therefore, brethren, through the compassions of God, to establish your bodies as a sacrifice, living, holy and pleasing to God, your reasonable service." The question is whether this "indicative" formulation is a declaration or a command. Is Paul encouraging the Romans to take a course of action, in which case it is a declaration, or is he issuing a command for them to follow? I do not think that we can tell simply based upon the formulation. I think that, instead, determination of the semantics of the speech function is determined not on the basis of the clausal construal but on the basis of a variety of factors, including lexical choice, clausal semantics, and discourse semantics, of which speech functions, congruent and otherwise, are a part.[75] However, I would also argue that the statement we have in Rom. 12:1 is the congruent statement, whatever we decide the incongruent statement might be (see Rom. 6:13, for a construal of the command using the imperative form).

Ideational Grammatical Metaphor

I turn now to the second type of grammatical metaphor, ideational metaphor. We have considered interpersonal grammatical metaphor and found that it is not without certain problems in SFL, especially in relationship to Greek. Ideational metaphor is more straightforward for the most part (though not entirely, as I will discuss further). As Halliday states, "the general tendency for ideational metaphor is to 'downgrade' the domain of grammatical realization of a semantic sequence, figure or element—from

---

[75] The importance of context in its various dimensions in such interpretation is explored further in Stanley E. Porter, *Hermeneutics, Linguistics, and the Bible: The Importance of Context*, T&T Clark Library of New Testament Greek 3 (London: T&T Clark, forthcoming), esp. chs. 4–6.

clause nexus to clause, from clause to group/phrase, and even from group/phase [sic] to word."[76] Halliday uses this as an example:

> Slate was once shale. But over millions of years, tons and tons of rock *pressed* down on it. *The pressure* made the shale very *hot*, and the *heat and pressure* changed it into slate ...

This example "contains two nominalizations, one verbal nominalization (*press* > *pressure*) and one adjectival nominalization (*hot* > *heat*). These nominalizations are in fact examples of ideational metaphors where processes and qualities are construed as if they were entities—they are reified ..."[77]

There are various types of construals that can occur through grammatico-semantic metaphor. These include the movement, along a cline, from relator > circumstance > process > quality > entity.[78] The two examples Halliday cited in the previous paragraph indicate movement from process > entity in *press* > *pressure*, and quality > entity in *hot* > *heat*. However, these movements are not equally probabilistic within grammar. Halliday observes that "Nominalizing is the single most powerful resource for creating grammatical metaphor. By this device, processes (congruently worded as verbs) and properties (congruently worded as adjectives) are reworded metaphorically as nouns; instead of functioning in the clause, as Process or Attribute, they function as Thing in the nominal group."[79] Halliday contends, as he does for lexical metaphor, that grammatical metaphors occur in "syndromes," or "clusters of interrelated transformations that reconfigure the grammatical structure as a whole."[80] This does not appear to be the case with interpersonal grammatical metaphor, but there is a sense in which there are clusters of ideational grammatical metaphors in the New Testament. Whether that is a property of metaphors or a characteristic of the author's idiolect or a property of the text remains a question still to be decided.

The New Testament, nevertheless, is full of instructive examples of ideational grammatical metaphors, in which the grammatico-semantic potential is expanded by use of the incongruent expression. A good example is Rom. 5:9-11 and its discussion of reconciliation. Paul says,

> much more, therefore, having been justified now in his blood, we shall be saved through him from wrath. For if, being enemies, we *were reconciled* (κατηλλάγημεν; verb in the aorist passive indicative first person plural form, as predicator of a secondary clause) to God through the death of his son, much more, *having been reconciled* (καταλλαγέντες; verb in the aorist passive participle masculine nominative plural form, as predicator of a secondary embedded clause), we shall be saved in his life; and not only this, but indeed boasting in God through our Lord Jesus Christ, through whom now we receive *reconciliation* (καταλλαγήν; noun in the feminine accusative form, as the head term of a nominal group).

---

[76] Halliday, IFG4, 719.
[77] Halliday, IFG4, 710.
[78] This list is from Halliday, "Things and Relations," 162.
[79] Halliday, IFG4, 729. One notes that at this point the stratal and semantic views of grammatical metaphor seem to have merged for all intents and purposes. Halliday was far from the first to make this realization regarding nominalization. See Otto Jespersen, *Essentials of English Grammar* (London: George Allen & Unwin, 1933), 73. Ravelli, "Renewal of Connection," 38, cites others as well. Halliday may have been unduly influenced in his view of nominalization by scientific prose. See Halliday, "Language of Physical Science," esp. 155–6.
[80] Halliday, "Things and Relations," 165.

In the two instances of the use of the verb forms, each of the verbs serves as the predicator of its own clause. In the first instance, the finite form of the verb is the predicator of a secondary clause as part of the protasis of a conditional construction ("if we were reconciled, then we shall be saved"), preceded by an adjunct participle clause ("being enemies"). The second instance picks up this conditional protasis as a participial adjunct of the primary clause of the same conditional ("much more, having been reconciled …"), in which the participle is the predicator of this secondary embedded clause. The process of *reconciling* is then grammatico-semantically metaphorically reconstrued as the entity *reconciliation* in the metaphorical statement. The noun, "reconciliation," is used as the complement of the predicator, "receive."

In this example, we see all the major elements of ideational grammatical metaphor. There is the reconstrual of a process into an entity, in this case *reconciling* into *reconciliation*. There is also a downgrading that occurs, in which the clausal construction becomes a word group; that is, the verb functioning as a predicator in its own clause (whether a secondary or secondary embedded clause) is reconstrued as the noun functioning as the head term of a complement in the metaphorical reconfiguration. The major result is that a process becomes an entity, a reification occurs, through the process of nominalization and takes on the characteristics of thingness—the process by which we are reconciled with God becomes the entity of reconciliation itself.

With this, I could be done describing grammatical metaphor in SFL. However, I believe that there is an element that Halliday has missed, and that is the reverse process from the one that I have just described. Halliday in fact states that such a reverse process cannot occur. After having described the movement from process to entity and other such moves in his ordered hierarchy (see previous discussion), he states: "But not the other way round: entities cannot be construed as if they were processes; and so on."[81] I am not the only one who finds this concept hard to accept. David Ritchie and Min Zhu express what surely has been thought by others (although I can't find any who express it): "It is difficult to know what to make of this, since it is easy to find counterexamples."[82] They cite the English example of the noun, *stone*, and the verb *to stone*, the noun *stonewall* (noun *stone* + noun *wall*) that then is used as a verb *to stonewall*.[83] I think that the same occurs in Greek, what might legitimately be called verbalization.[84] There is a process of grammatico-semantic metaphorical reconstrual that takes entities (and possibly qualities) and makes them into processes, especially (but not only) when this involves the use of participles. In other words, there is not a necessary downgrading of the domain of grammatical realization, but an expansion of the grammatico-semantic potential through reconstrual of entities or attributes as processes (i.e., an upgrading).

There are several possible preliminary objections to such a consideration, besides the apparent fact that it is done, at least in English. One objection is that such instances might be seen to involve (unhelpful) upgrading, that is, the expansion of the grammatical expression, so that the force of the metaphor is lost. However, I do not think that this is what necessarily happens, as I hope to show. Another objection is that this occurrence is perhaps better

---

[81] Halliday, "Things and Relations," 162. Halliday associates the movement from process to entity with the process of concreteness found in traditional views of metaphor.
[82] Ritchie and Zhu, "'Nixon Stonewalled the Investigation,'" 122.
[83] Ritchie and Zhu, "'Nixon Stonewalled the Investigation,'" 122.
[84] Cf. Heyvaert, "Nominalization as Grammatical Metaphor," 66–7, 76–85 with the gerundive.

described as what is usually referred to as grammaticalization, the "process whereby lexical items and constructions come in certain linguistic contexts to serve grammatical functions, and, once grammaticalized, continue to develop new grammatical functions."[85] In one sense, or at least so far as the first half of this definition is pertinent, I am in some ways describing grammaticalization, but I am not insofar as the second part is concerned. The kinds of grammatico-semantic metaphorical reconstruals that I am describing are created by particular authors as a process of expanding their semantic potential, and do not necessarily become a part of the continuing development of new grammatical functions, especially as these are typically defined in studies of grammaticalization (e.g., the downgrading of semantic features and levels associated with most types of grammaticalization, which often result in types of semogenesis). Instead, I think that instances of this other type of ideational grammatical metaphor expand the semantic possibilities, especially because of the range of semantic features encoded in verbs in ancient Greek. The verb encodes features such as aspect (realized by tense-form), attitude (realized by mood form), causality (realized by voice form), person, and number, with the participle having aspect, causality, number, gender, and case. In this type of grammatical metaphor, we often see entities turned into processes, especially participial-verb processes, which expand the semantic function of the entity by attributing verbal properties.

To illustrate this type of grammatico-semantic ideational metaphor, I use a passage with similarities to the previous one, 2 Cor. 5:18-20. In this passage, Paul says, "all things are from the God who *reconciles* (καταλλάξαντος; aorist active participle masculine genitive singular, defining God) us to himself through Christ and who gives to us the ministry of *reconciliation* (καταλλαγῆς; noun in the feminine genitive singular, as a qualifier of the noun group, 'the ministry of reconciliation')" (v. 18). So far, this may be seen as an instance of ideational metaphor in which a process is reconstrued as an entity—the process of God reconciling results in a ministry of reconciliation. The process of *reconciling* becomes the entity *reconciliation*. In the first construction, the participle is the predicator of a secondary embedded clause that serves as the definer of "God" within a nominal word group, "the God who reconciles," while in the second construction, the noun is downgraded to a qualifying constituent of a nominal word group, in which this entity qualifies the type of ministry.

We also note, however, that there are certain semantic features that are lost in this process of metaphorization. The concord of gender, case, and number provided by the verb is lost, as well as the features of causality and aspect. Paul continues: "that is, in Christ, God was *reconciling* (καταλλάσσων; present active participle masculine nominative singular, part of a periphrastic construction with God as the subject) the world to himself, not counting their transgressions against them, and placing in us the word of *reconciliation*" (καταλλαγῆς; v. 19).[86] We see a similar movement here in this verse. The first use is congruent with the use of the process of *reconciling* as part of the predicator of the primary clause, and the process is reconstrued as an entity, *reconciliation*, which in this instance qualifies the "word." There is in this verse, as in the previous one, a shift from the more complex structure to the downgraded structure, here as the main verb of a predicator of a primary clause to a qualifier in a nominal word group. I would argue again that something is lost in

---

[85]Paul J. Hopper and Elizabeth Closs Traugott, *Grammaticalization*, CTL (Cambridge: Cambridge University Press, 1993), xv. See also Traugott and Bernd Heine, eds., *Approaches to Grammaticalization*, 2 vols., Typological Studies in Language 19 (Amsterdam: John Benjamins, 1991), esp. the introduction by the editors in 1:1–14.
[86]See Stanley E. Porter, Καταλλάσσω *in Ancient Greek Literature, with Reference to the Pauline Writings*, Estudios de Filología Neotestamentaria 5 (Córdoba: Ediciones El Almendro, 1994), esp. 125–44.

the process of ideational metaphorization. Paul continues: "on behalf of Christ, therefore, we are representatives as if God were appealing through us: we implore on behalf of Christ, *be reconciled* (καταλλάγητε; aorist passive imperative second person plural) to God" (v. 20). In this climactic discourse structure, Paul ends his "reconciliation" language with the imperative form in a command. He does not simply speak of a ministry of *reconciliation* or a word of *reconciliation*. Instead, he changes these entities into a process, that of *being reconciled*, that encodes important information about causality and person (and aspect).

While this movement does reverse the process of downgrading the structure, we see that this upgraded structure is contained within what is itself a secondary clausal unit. Paul acts as an ambassador, the ambassador implores his audience (note use of the second person plural), and the command to be reconciled is the content of that command (indirect external agency with passive voice form). Thus, even though the process is the predicator of a clause, this clause is the projection of a request that is the message of Paul the ambassador. The grammaticalized process expresses mood—imperative used here in its commanding function; voice—the passive used to focus the Corinthians as the grammatical subject though not the agent of the action (that is implicitly God, because the agency is indirect and external and does not require specification); aspect—perfective used here of the entire act of reconciliation; person—second person directly addressed to the Corinthians; and number—plural including all of them. The predicator also takes a complement as the recipient of the action—reconciliation is focused upon God.

A final example will help to illustrate the importance of ideational grammatical metaphor of this upgrading type even further. In 1 Cor. 6:12, Paul makes the following statement: "All things to me are permitted (ἔξεστιν), but all things are not profitable. All things to me are permitted (ἔξεστιν), but I myself will not be mastered (ἐξουσιασθήσομαι) by anything [or anyone]."[87] There is much metaphorical wordplay in this verse. This verse has instances of both interpersonal grammatical metaphor and ideational grammatical metaphor. The first, the interpersonal metaphor, is the congruent expression "I think that all things are permitted." This is grammatico-semantically metaphorically reconstrued by embedding the interpersonal feature in the clausal adjunct, "to me." This construction is used by Paul twice: "All things to me are permitted." However, in the second major instance of metaphor, rather than reconstruing the process as an entity, that is, ἔξεστιν ("it is permitted") does not become ἐξουσία ("the right to act," often translated "authority"), but the process is instead reconstrued as a different type of process using the cognate ideational verbal form based upon the participle of the first verb (ἔξεστιν > ἐξουσία > ἐξουσιάζω, "control someone's rights or master them").[88]

In this instance, we see the reconstrual of the grammatico-semantic domain from one process to a more semantically encoded process. The verb ἔξεστιν has a number of characteristics, including its being aspectually and causally vague, impersonal fixed

---

[87] I wish to thank Anthony C. Thiselton, *The First Epistle to the Corinthians*, NIGTC (Grand Rapids: Eerdmans, 2000), 461, for this reference. He recognizes the wordplay and hints at the metaphorical analysis that I offer, when he states that "The noun ἐξουσία often *authority* [sic], but means no less *the right to act* because the agent possesses ἐξουσία in the sense of freedom of choice." However, I think that he misunderstands the role of metaphor here, and his translation, in its effort to re-enforce the quotation used by Paul, misses the point ("'Liberty to do all things'; but not everything is helpful. 'Liberty to do anything'; but I will not let anything take liberties with me," p. 458).

[88] See Thiselton, *First Corinthians*, 461.

usage, and what is often termed a verbal operator or "light verb" because of its reduced semantic weight.[89] However, semantic weight is added to the verb through the process of metaphorical reconstrual, in which aspect (for aspectual verbs), causality, person, and number (among possibly other semantic features) become part of its grammatico-semantic potential. This metaphorization allows Paul to move from the interpersonal metaphor to an ideational metaphor, in which through the future form he specifies expectative semantic force,[90] indirect external agency (passive voice form) with a causal adjunct (by anyone/anything), and first person singular with reference to himself. Regardless of whether Paul is citing a Corinthian slogan in this verse, through the process of metaphorical reconstrual of experience he transforms the interpersonal metaphor into an ideational metaphor that expands significantly not only the semantic potential but the interpretive significance of the verse. Paul is no longer simply citing an impersonal statement about permissibility, but he is denying any personal mastery of this force of which he speaks.

At this point, let me provide some further examples where ideational grammatical metaphor is used in the New Testament and provides a means of shaping and forming interpretation. Paul's letters are replete with ideational metaphors. I have drawn upon his letters frequently in this chapter. I have found similar use of metaphor in some of his other letters, what Halliday would probably call syndromes of metaphors. I will offer some further examples from Colossians and Ephesians. There are many theories about the possible relationships between Colossians and Ephesians, but for the sake of this discussion the more interesting observation is that, despite theories of their relationship and dependence and their both relatively frequent use of metaphors, they appear to use different metaphors.[91]

Colossians has numerous ideational grammatical metaphors. They are used for various apparent purposes within the text. I will begin with some examples of nominalization. In Col. 2:11, Paul says the Colossians "were circumcised with a circumcision made without hands (περιετμήθητε περιτομῇ ἀχειροποιήτῳ)" in putting off the fleshly body, in or by the "circumcision of Christ (τῇ περιτομῇ τοῦ Χριστοῦ)." The process of circumcision is reconstrued as the entity circumcision, first of the Colossians, where it is defined, and then of Christ, where it is qualified with the genitive modifier. The nominalization downgrades the construction from the predicator of a relative clause to the head term (Halliday's Thing) of the nominal group as adjunct. This allows for it to be modified in two different ways, one by means of a definer and the other by a qualifier.

In Col. 2:19, Paul similarly speaks of the head, from which the entire body, through ligaments and sinews that supply and hold it together, "can expect to grow with respect to the growth of God (αὔξει τὴν αὔξησιν τοῦ θεοῦ)." The process of growth as predicator of the secondary clause is transferred to the complement as recipient of this growth. The process has been reconstrued as an entity through nominalization, qualified as the "growth of

---

[89] See Thompson, *Introducing Functional Grammar*, 51; Donna Jo Napoli, *Syntax: Theory and Problems* (New York: Oxford University Press, 1993), 98.
[90] The future form is aspectually vague, though it has expectative semantics. See Stanley E. Porter, *Verbal Aspect in the Greek of the New Testament, with Reference to Tense and Mood*, SBG 1 (New York: Peter Lang, 1989), 403–39.
[91] I will assume the kind of information on the letters found in Stanley E. Porter, *The Apostle Paul: His Life, Thought, and Letters* (Grand Rapids: Eerdmans, 2016), 354–75 on Colossians and 384–404 on Ephesians.

God."[92] There are also a large number of examples of verbalization. In Colossians 1, Paul expresses his desire that the Colossians be filled with knowledge in "all" (πάσῃ) wisdom (v. 9), bearing fruit in "each" (παντί) good work and growing in knowledge of God (v. 10), and "in each power, being empowered (ἐν πάσῃ δυνάμει δυναμούμενοι)" on the basis of (κατά) the strength of his glory for (εἰς) "every" (πᾶσαν) endurance and patience, with (μετά) joy (v. 11). Paul is clearly speaking in extremes and inclusive language regarding the totality of wisdom, good works, power, etc. He expands the semantic potential when he reconstrues power from an entity (δυνάμει) into a process (δυναμούμενοι), upgrading the construction from the head term in an adjunct to a predicator of a participle clause. The metaphorical reconfiguration allows for modification and development appropriate for a verb as predicator, such as taking three adjuncts (all three prepositional phrases).

In Col. 1:29, Paul speaks of every person being established in Christ, a task, he says, that he is working to fulfill, working hard on the basis of (note the preposition κατά) "his [Christ's] energy that energizes in me in power (τὴν ἐνέργειαν αὐτοῦ τὴν ἐνεργουμένην ἐν ἐμοὶ ἐν δυνάμει)." This transference metaphorizes the entity energy as the process of energizing. This interesting example involves both semantic upgrading and downgrading. The head term of the prepositional phrase is the noun ἐνέργειαν, which is reconstrued as the process of energizing. Even though the participle is the predicator of an embedded participle clause, it functions as a definer within the nominal group with ἐνέργειαν as its head term. Thus, the process is both upgraded and downgraded. The metaphorization is apparently used to emphasize the verbal properties of the middle voice with indirect internal agency. Paul reconstrues Christ's energy, an entity, as a process that is active in a particular way within him.

In the Christological passage in Col. 2:9-11, Paul states that in Christ "all the fullness" (πᾶν τὸ πλήρωμα) of godness bodily dwells (v. 9), and, presumably because of this, "you are in a fulfilled state (ἐστὲ ... πεπληρωμένοι)" in him (v. 10). The entity of the divine fullness is reconstrued as the process of a filled state, with the noun as head term of a nominal group becoming the predicator in the periphrastic construction. The participle encodes aspect (especially stative aspect of the perfect participle) and causality (indirect external agency), as well as gender, case, and number. The entity as a complete thing (all fullness) is reconstrued as a stative process that, through the periphrastic construction, is enacted by the Colossians (second person plural, you). In Col. 3:15, Paul commands the Colossians, "become thankful" (εὐχάριστοι γίνεσθε), and then, after elucidating what this may entail, he concludes by stating that they should do everything in the name of the Lord Jesus, "giving thanks (εὐχαριστοῦντες)" to God the father through him. This metaphorical transference transfers the quality to a process. The quality is that of being thankful (εὐχάριστοι), but when it comes to enacting this thankfulness, Paul reconstrues it as a process that as predicator of a clause takes its own complement (to God) and adjunct (through him).

In Ephesians, we see similar examples, especially in the second half of the letter. In Eph. 4:4, Paul tells the Ephesians that "you were called in one hope of your calling (ἐκλήθητε ἐν μιᾷ ἐλπίδι τῆς κλήσεως ὑμῶν)." This example, similar to Col. 1:9 and 2:11 previously cited, reconstrues the process of calling as the entity calling. The process is the predicator

---

[92]Some might be tempted to label this as a cognate accusative, and perhaps attribute it to Semitic language enhancement. There may be some Semitic language enhancement, but that does not change the description. In fact, it suggests that much more might be done to examine the metaphorical transference in Hebrew.

of the primary clause, whereas the entity is a qualifier of a nominal group in an adjunct, and thus thoroughly downgraded according to Halliday's progression. A similar example is also found in the Old Testament quotation of Ps. 68:18 in Eph. 4:8: "he took captive the captive (ᾐχμαλώτευσεν αἰχμαλωσίαν)."[93] The process of captivity is reconstrued as the entity captivity. This entire quotation is about the results of actions (taking captives and giving gifts) and so the nominalization metaphorizes this emphasis by reconstruing the process as an entity.

A very interesting example occurs at the beginning of the thanksgiving portion of Ephesians (Eph. 1:3-23). In Eph. 1:3, the opening verse, Paul begins the thanksgiving with a complex set of metaphorical reconfigurations. He states that "Blessed (εὐλογητός)" is the God and father of our Lord Jesus Christ, "the one who blessed us in every spiritual blessing in the heavenlies in Christ (ὁ εὐλογήσας ἡμᾶς ἐν πάσῃ εὐλογίᾳ πνευματικῇ ἐν τοῖς ἐπουρανίοις ἐν Χριστῷ)" (Eph. 1:3). There appear to be two metaphorizations here, one that moves from the quality to a process (*blessed* > *one who blessed*) and a second. But what is the second? Is it one that moves from a quality to an entity (*blessed* > *blessing*) or one that moves from a process to an entity (*one who blessed* > *blessing*)? Perhaps it does not matter, since the movement, as Halliday suggests, is normal in metaphorization, the process of nominalization (from either quality or process to entity). The result is, first, that the verbalization allows for the head term of the nominal group as subject to be the participle (εὐλογήσας), which has a complement (ἡμᾶς) and two adjuncts (both prepositional phrases). The first of these adjuncts contains the second metaphorical reconstrual. In the second grammatical metaphor, the entity is the head term of the prepositional phrase and is able to be defined by two definers, "all" and "spiritual." In Eph. 3:19 (cf. Col. 2:9-10 and Eph. 1:23 just cited), Paul tells the Ephesians that the purpose of knowing the love of Christ is so that "you may be filled into all the fullness of God (πληρωθῆτε εἰς πᾶν τὸ πλήρωμα τοῦ θεοῦ)." The process of filling is reconstrued as the entity fullness through nominalization.

There is an abundance of verbalizations in Ephesians and they seem to follow a regular pattern in which an entity is expanded by means of reconfiguration, and there is thus transference to a process. In Eph. 1:6 Paul speaks of the praise of the glory of "his [Christ's] grace of which he graced us in the one he loved (τῆς χάριτος αὐτοῦ ἧς ἐχαρίτωσεν ἡμᾶς ἐν τῷ ἠγαπημένῳ)" (cf. the use of the noun again in v. 7). The metaphorization enables Paul to reconstrue the entity as a process with all of the semantic properties of a verb: an agent acts upon recipients. In Eph. 1:19-20 (cf. Col. 1:29), Paul speaks of God's greatness and power for believers, on the basis of the "energy (ἐνέργειαν)" of his strong power, which "he energized (ἐνήργησεν)" in Christ by raising him from the dead. The verbalization reconstrues the entity as a process, with the attributes of a process, such as a (implicit) subject and adjuncts. In Eph. 1:21, Paul details Christ's cosmic location as surpassing every other power and "every name being named (παντὸς ὀνόματος ὀνομαζομένου)." As mentioned before, this example represents both lexicogrammatical downgrading and upgrading in the transference from entity to process. The process is reworded as a verb as the predicator of a participle clause, but the entire clause functions as a definer of the

---

[93] I recognize that this verse may be translated in a variety of ways. Many translations translate the complement in the plural as a collective noun.

nominal group head term, ὀνόματος. The use of the participle, however, encodes more information that can express the verbal meaning and hence semantically more fully define the head term.

A similar pattern is found in Eph. 1:23. This relative clause identifies Christ's body as "the fullness of the one who fulfills all things in all things (τὸ πλήρωμα τοῦ τὰ πάντα ἐν πᾶσιν πληρουμένου)." The movement from entity to process expands the possibilities of qualifying the "fullness." The process reworded as a verb is the predicator of a participle clause that indicates causality (indirect internal agency of the middle voice) and takes a complement and adjunct, both reinforcing the completeness and totality of the fulfilling. In Eph. 2:4, Paul speaks of "his [God's] great love which he loved us (τὴν πολλὴν ἀγάπην αὐτοῦ ἣν ἠγάπησεν ἡμᾶς)," with the ideational grammatical metaphor, reconstruing the entity as a process, in the enhancing relative clause. In Eph. 5:2, Paul uses a construction as in Eph. 2:4: "walk in love as indeed Christ loved us (περιπατεῖτε ἐν ἀγάπῃ καθὼς καὶ ὁ Χριστὸς ἠγάπησεν ἡμᾶς)," with reconstrual from entity to process. We may wish to go back to Eph. 5:1, where Paul speaks of "beloved children (τέκνα ἀγαπητά)," in which the movement is from quality to entity and then to process. In Eph. 6:18, Paul instructs the Ephesians in prayer: "through every prayer and request praying in every time in the Spirit (διὰ πάσης προσευχῆς καὶ δεήσεως προσευχόμενοι ἐν παντὶ καιρῷ ἐν πνεύματι)." The prepositional phrase is an adjunct of the clause with the participle προσευχόμενοι as the predicator. Adjuncts as non-mandatory clausal components may appear in a variety of places within the clause but the adjunct with the prepositional phrase appears to be thematized here. The result is that the entity precedes the process in the configuration. This appears to be intentional so that the metaphorization upgrades the construction from head term of the nominal group in the adjunct to predicator of the clause so as to expand the statement regarding prayer by means of verbal properties.

In an unusual instance in Eph. 4:29 and 32, Paul speaks of God giving "grace (χάριν)" to those who hear. He then later commands the Ephesians to "become kind to one another, compassionate, being gracious to each other as indeed God in Christ is gracious to you" (γίνεσθε εἰς ἀλλήλους χρηστοί, εὔσπλαγχνοι, χαριζόμενοι ἑαυτοῖς καθὼς καὶ ὁ θεὸς ἐν Χριστῷ ἐχαρίσατο ὑμῖν)." This follows the pattern of verbalization, but there are several complicating factors that indicate that metaphorization has intentionally occurred. Paul reconstrues the entity of "grace" as the process "being gracious (χαριζόμενοι)" apparently so as to be able to create the participle clause and to expand what he wishes to say by means of clausal properties (e.g., taking a complement, clausal complexing). However, the use of the participle χαριζόμενοι is not lexicogrammatically equivalent to the two previous clauses. The first clause is the primary clause "become kind (γίνεσθε … χρηστοί)," with a predicator and complement (and adjunct, "to one another"), with the complement a nominal group with adjective as head term. The second clause is apparently elliptical for "become compassionate (γίνεσθε … εὔσπλαγχνοι)." The participle construction is grammatically an adjunctive use of a secondary participle clause. However, it appears that lexicogrammatical upgrading was necessary to express the desired meaning by means of a clause for which only a verbal construction would suffice.

There are many more examples that could be cited. Metaphorization is an important element of the expression of meaning in language, and the Greek of the New Testament is no exception. We can see from these few examples that metaphorization, especially verbalization, opens up the language potential by means of often upgrading the semantic pattern so as to expand upon textual meaning. I believe that grammatical metaphor has much more potential than has previously been realized in textual analysis of the Greek New Testament. Only a few preliminary studies have utilized it as it can be used. However, I also believe that definitions of grammatical metaphor may need to undergo thorough scrutiny in relation to the linguistic features of particular languages—in this case in relation to ancient Greek—in order to maximize their full semantic and interpretive potential.

CONCLUSION

I am far from having said the last word on metaphor, whether lexical, grammatical, or otherwise. I have made no such attempt. What I have attempted to accomplish, however, are several more modest goals. The first goal is to develop metaphor within a SFL framework as a means of understanding some of the features of metaphor as an essential part of linguistic description. One of the strengths of some recent theories of metaphor, such as conceptual metaphor theory, is to help us understand that metaphors are fully integrated within our everyday use of language, and that it is difficult to use language without invoking varied semantic domains that expand the communicative capacity of language. I have tried to show that SFL has potential to expand some of the capacities of metaphor theory. Various types of lexical and grammatical metaphor must be taken into consideration as well, as a further resource for the creative communicative function of language. The second goal is to develop an operative and appliable theory of metaphor based upon SFL for the interpretation of the Greek of the New Testament and, with it, its texts. Despite the fact that relatively little use of SFL theories of metaphor has been applied to study of the New Testament, I hope that I have shown in this chapter that there are still many possibilities for both lexical and grammatical metaphor. Lexical metaphor has suffered at the hands of uncertain definition for millennia, but I believe that some linguistic clarity can help to revive study and utilization of lexical metaphor. However, SFL is also correct that there is a relationship between lexical and grammatical metaphor and that the most challenging and potentially productive results will lie in the use of grammatical metaphor. Interpersonal grammatical metaphor begs for further qualification and refinement, although there are clear potentials to be realized. However, ideational grammatical metaphor offers numerous insightful possibilities for describing and understanding the Greek of the New Testament.

CHAPTER FOUR

Rhetoric and Persuasion in the New Testament from a Systemic Functional Linguistics Perspective

INTRODUCTION

The field of rhetoric studies has made significant inroads into many different areas of academic discourse,[1] and this is especially true of New Testament studies over the last thirty or so years. The results have been the development of various kinds of scholarly works that undertake various types of rhetorical analysis. I will briefly trace the history of the discipline of rhetoric as a field, in particular in regard to it as a field within New Testament studies, in the next major section of this chapter. To introduce this subject, however, I wish simply to note that rhetoric as a discipline or even as a sub-discipline within New Testament studies, much to its own detriment, has unfortunately taken on a character of its own that has disengaged it in many respects from important supportive and fundamental relationships. Rhetoric, whether conceived of as ancient or modern, traditional or new, is to be found to be operative within every situational context in which humans use language for communicative purposes.

As a result, rhetoric must always be examined in relation to two major considerations: its purpose and its language. Its purpose is concerned with both its macro-analytic persuasive function and the individual micro-analytic functions found within individual instances of rhetoric, regardless of the configuration of such instances. The language of rhetoric is related to the instantiation of these various macro- and micro-analytic functions, first to persuade and then to perform a number of other tasks for which "rhetorical language" is appropriate. Thus, the examination of rhetorical language must address both the semantics and the lexicogrammar of rhetoric. Therefore, studies of rhetoric that will move beyond simple exercises in labeling or the provision of sterile taxonomies have the potential to address the linguistics of rhetoric. In this brief introduction, I have conceptualized

---

[1] For a recent overview of the field of rhetorical studies, see Michael J. MacDonald, ed., *The Oxford Handbook of Rhetorical Studies* (Oxford: Oxford University Press, 2017). Parts One to Four treat the ancient to Renaissance periods, and Parts Five and Six the modern and contemporary periods. For a historical treatment, see Winifred Bryan Horner, ed., *The Present State of Scholarship in Historical and Contemporary Rhetoric*, rev. ed. (Columbia: University of Missouri Press, 1990).

rhetoric within the framework of Systemic Functional Linguistics (SFL). Even though there is not a formalized rhetoric within SFL, this linguistic framework is suitable for and highly adaptable to formulation of a linguistically based rhetoric.

In this chapter, I wish to provide a basic formulation of a SFL rhetoric that addresses both the use and function of rhetoric within a linguistic framework but, more than that, finds a linguistic means of conceptualization of such a linguistic rhetoric. To set the stage for such a conceptualization, I first offer a brief history of the field of rhetoric, telling the story from the standpoint of New Testament studies and linguistics. This will provide the necessary interpretive framework for development of a SFL rhetoric suitable for ancient Greek and examination of the New Testament. In the next section, I will offer a sketch of such a rhetoric. This is not an easy task for two major reasons. The first is that, in some noticeable ways, SFL is already a rhetorical linguistic theory and so the mechanisms are already in place for conceptualization of rhetoric within its overall linguistic framework. The second is that, despite this, SFL requires much more of rhetoric than is usually demanded of such a theory (at least within New Testament studies) and hence raises a number of questions for such a rhetorical formulation. I will provide such a conceptualization by means of examples from the Greek of the New Testament, so that any positive findings will have relevance for study of the New Testament.

A BRIEF HISTORY OF RHETORIC AND NEW TESTAMENT STUDIES

Rhetoric, at least as normally conceived, goes back to the ancient Greeks. The emergence of rhetoric occurs in conjunction with the rise of democracy and the emergence of civilian over military institutions in sixth-century BC Athens. Rhetoric is seen in such impromptu contexts as speeches given at the funerals of fallen soldiers and within judicial practices. The founder of rhetoric is said to be Empedocles of Agrigentum (Sicily), who taught the fellow Sicilian sophist Gorgias, who came to Athens in 427 BC. The first teachers of Greek rhetoric were Corax and Tisias (or one person, Tisias, called Corax), who lived in the first half of the fifth century BC. From these early teachers and practitioners emerged ancient Greek rhetoric as we know it. This rhetoric was preserved mostly through the learning of rhetorical discourses in what became rhetorical education and practiced in the institutions of Athenian society, such as in the courts and on various civic occasions. At this stage there were no rhetorical handbooks, even though instructors, such as the Sophists, developed various figures of usage and rules of practice. Credit is given to the fourth-century BC orator Isocrates for playing the most important role in developing rhetorical education, through his teaching and writing out his speeches, a pattern that became widespread, and his expanding rhetoric beyond the confines of law. One of the first significant handbooks to rhetoric was written by Theodorus of Byzantium, mentioned by Aristotle, but others were written as well, especially Aristotle's own lectures, *On Rhetoric*, thought to be the most important theoretical (and philosophical) work of rhetoric of ancient Greece. Another early handbook is the fourth-century BC *Rhetoric for Alexander*.

Aristotle (384–322 BC) defined the three major types of oratory: judicial (forensic), political (deliberative), and ceremonial (epideictic) (*Rhet.* 1:3). Though some have thought that judicial rhetoric was the first, there is good reason to think that all three were important from the start. Judicial rhetoric is treated as the most complex by the handbooks, and ceremonial rhetoric as the least detailed in its characteristics. The ten

Attic orators became the canon of orators used in the rhetorical curriculum, and their use of rhetoric in the fourth century BC set the continuing standard for later Greco-Roman rhetoric, as they were frequently used and cited in later works on rhetoric, including Quintilian's (c. AD 35–100) *Institutio oratoria*, but others as well, which came to have a practical and applied or technical approach. The later rhetorical curriculum further developed sets of preliminary exercises for students before they studied the orators (called *progymnasmata*, by such authors as Aelius Theon [first century AD], Hermogenes of Tarsus [second century AD], and Aphthonius of Antioch [fourth century AD]) and focused upon declamation, characteristic of the Second Sophistic, that period from the first to third centuries AD when there was a revival of Greek rhetoric and learning.

There were other subsequent developments within rhetoric as well. Some later rhetoricians attempted to imitate the earlier models, but even those within the ten Attic orators were not identical in their language and style, as evidenced in the particularities of the language of Demosthenes (384–322 BC) (e.g., his use of abstract noun groups such as the articular infinitive and marked word order). A number, especially those outside of Athens, attempted to develop their own style of rhetoric (some of it in reaction to the fiercely pro-Athenian Demosthenes). Those in the east developed a less periodic style that utilized its own prose features (sometimes called Asianism), while others reacted by insisting upon the language standards of fourth-century BC Athens (sometimes called Atticism). Both show the development of the language of rhetoric as it spread outside the direct control of Athens. The same is true of Roman rhetoric, in many ways imitative of the Greeks. In true inclusive Roman fashion, the Roman rhetoricians typically defined three styles of rhetoric (e.g., *Rhetoric ad Herennium*, Cicero [106–43 BC], Quintilian), although Demetrius in the first century BC (the date of his work *On Style* is debated) defined a fourth, all of which were further developed in later thought.[2]

The Middle Ages continued this rhetorical tradition as inherited from the Greco-Roman world, especially the prescriptive tendencies found in the later rhetorical handbooks. The major additional factor was the attempt to bring ancient rhetoric and Christianity together. This tendency was seen in several early church authors, such as John Chrysostom (c. AD 347–407) and Augustine (AD 354–430), among others. There was also an expansion of the scope of rhetoric, until it came to encompass not only its classical uses especially as described in Cicero, but also the writing of poetry, the writing of letters, and the art of preaching (all of which engendered treatises), to the point of losing the sense of unity of rhetoric and concentrating mostly upon practice and technique.[3] The Renaissance indeed fostered a revival of rhetoric within the Western world. The renewal of classical learning brought interest in the classical authors, especially when significant manuscripts of their

---

[2] The opening of this section is dependent upon Stanley E. Porter, "Applied Rhetoric and Stylistics in Ancient Greece," in *Rhetorik und Stilistic/Rhetoric and Stylistics: Ein internationales Handbuch historischer und systematischer Forschung/An International Handbook of Historical and Systematic Research*, ed. Ulla Fix, Andreas Gardt, and Joachim Knape, Handbücher zur Sprach- und Kommunikationswissenschaft/Handbooks of Linguistics and Communication Science 31.1 (Berlin: de Gruyter, 2008), 284–307. See also George A. Kennedy, *The Art of Persuasion in Greece* (Princeton: Princeton University Press, 1963); Kennedy, "Historical Survey of Rhetoric," in *Handbook of Classical Rhetoric in the Hellenistic Period, 330 B.C.–A.D. 400*, ed. Stanley E. Porter (Leiden: Brill, 1997), 3–41, with a summary of all of the rhetorical handbooks; and M. L. Clarke, *Rhetoric at Rome: A Historical Survey*, rev. D. H. Berry (London: Routledge, 1996). For other histories of rhetoric, see Brian Vickers, *In Defense of Rhetoric* (Oxford: Clarendon, 1988); and Jennifer Richards, *Rhetoric*, New Critical Idiom (London: Routledge, 2008).
[3] James J. Murphy, *Rhetoric in the Middle Ages: A History of Rhetorical Theory from St. Augustine to the Renaissance* (Berkeley: University of California Press, 1974), 3–42.

works were rediscovered. However, there was an even further narrowing of the scope of rhetoric, notably under the influence of the early Renaissance scholar Peter Ramus (1515–72).[4] Rhetoric became focused upon elocution, that is, eloquence, and the source of eloquence was the use of the tropes of the language, and hence a narrow definition of style resulted. This is the origin of the notion that rhetoric is primarily concerned with ornamentation. By the end of the era, in the eighteenth and the nineteenth centuries, rhetoric had come to be associated not just with one narrow use of it, style, but with composition in the proper style, and hence with criticism, which was then applied to the reading and criticism of literature. Shakespeare (1564–1616) became a major target of such readings, and this led directly to rhetoric being later associated with departments of English literature. Despite a backlash against such a definition of rhetoric by the Romantics, who rejected such rhetorical language (artificial because of its style) for the language of the common person, and believed in the power of the sublime over the sterile practice of rhetoric, rhetoric entered the twentieth century as a narrow branch of critical studies.[5]

Rhetoric experienced a revival, at least in two arenas of thought, in the twentieth century, and through these its impact has been felt across a range of disciplines. The first rejuvenation was a rebirth into a new form, sometimes called the New Rhetoric (also called this by its rejectors), and the other was into an ancient-inspired form, sometimes called classical rhetoric. There are many interesting interconnections among all of those involved.

The development of the New Rhetoric is usually attributed to the English literary scholar I. A. Richards (1893–1979).[6] Richards rejected the traditional definition and treatment of rhetoric, especially as found in its critical scientific form, and promoted a new rhetoric that understood the nature of language not merely as the wordings in which thought was dressed (related to the ornamental view), but in terms of the conventional and arbitrary nature of language (the result of Saussurian structuralism). Richards reflected the thought of Ferdinand de Saussure (1857–1913) regarding the arbitrariness of the sign (there is no inherent relation between the sign and what is signified),[7] so that it is not words that mean but the users of words that mean. As a result, Richards uses metaphor as an example of how language is inherently ambiguous, rather than, like Aristotle, treating language as scientific and metaphor as the exception.[8] Richards was followed by a number of scholars in development of what is called the New Rhetoric, this attempt to formulate a new view of how language functions to persuade. Some of the best known in the emergence of this tradition include the American literary and rhetorical theorist Kenneth Burke (1897–1993) and the philosophers Chaim Perelman (1912–84) and Lucie Olbrechts-Tyteca (1899–1987).[9] For Burke, the use of language constitutes "symbolic action," by which is meant that it is "a resource that can be drawn upon by individuals

---

[4] Terence Hawkes, *Metaphor*, Critical Idiom (London: Methuen, 1972), 22–3.
[5] J. Richards, *Rhetoric*, passim, but esp. 102–13.
[6] See I. A. Richards, *The Philosophy of Rhetoric* (London: Oxford University Press, 1936), among some other works, such as C. K. Ogden and I. A. Richards, *The Meaning of Meaning: A Study of the Influence of Language upon Thought and of the Science of Symbolism*, 3rd ed. rev. (New York: Harcourt, Brace, 1930 [1923]).
[7] Ferdinand de Saussure, *Course in General Linguistics*, ed. Charles Bally and Albert Sechehaye, with Albert Riedlinger, trans. Wade Baskin (New York: Philosophical Library, 1959 [1916]), 114–20.
[8] See Hawkes, *Metaphor*, 57–8; cf. J. Richards, *Rhetoric*, 116–17.
[9] Kenneth Burke, *Grammar of Motives* (Berkeley: University of California Press, 1945); Burke, *Rhetoric of Motives* (Berkeley: University of California Press, 1950); Chaim Perelman and Lucie Olbrechts-Tyteca, *The New Rhetoric: A Treatise on Argumentation*, trans. John Wilkinson and Purcell Weaver (Notre Dame, IN: University of Notre Dame Press, 1969 [1958]).

to act on or persuade others ... [b]ut it also shapes our values and beliefs in ways that we are not always aware of."[10] As Jennifer Richards aptly summarizes Burke, whose views have much in common with the work of Edward Sapir (1884–1939) and Benjamin Lee Whorf (1897–1941) (who heavily influenced Michael Halliday [1925–2018]), "we are constituted in language, but we are not determined by it."[11] That is, language plays a formative role in what it means to be and to act human, but it does not set the limits of what humans are.[12]

The New Rhetoric was influential on various theories of argumentation in a number of fields,[13] although it does not seem to have become as widely utilized in literary and related circles, probably due to the more radical reaction caused by structuralism and poststructuralism in the second half of the twentieth century.[14] Another way to frame this would be to say that the New Rhetoric was not rhetorical enough for some, who wished to create their own newer rhetoric. Such figures include Roman Jakobson (1896–1982), Gérard Genette (1930–2018), Roland Barthes (1915–80), Jacques Derrida (1930–2004), and Paul de Man (1919–83), among others.[15] Heavily influenced by and reacting to Saussure, they progressively and thoroughly rejected the notion of the place of rhetorical theory and trained rhetoricians. Jakobson reduces rhetoric simply to his theory of metaphorical substitution. Genette continues this line of thought by criticizing the continuing reductionism of rhetorical thought through the ages (as previously noted). Barthes rejects rhetoric for its failure to teach how to be persuasive because of its overwhelming preoccupation with the teaching of details, failing to take into account that it was a tool used by the cultural elites. Derrida unravels the language of rhetoric itself,

---

[10] J. Richards, *Rhetoric*, 162; cf. 161–75. See Kenneth Burke, *Language as Symbolic Action: Essays on Life, Literature, and Method* (Berkeley: University of California Press, 1966).

[11] J. Richards, *Rhetoric*, 163. See, for example, Edward Sapir, *Selected Writings in Language, Culture, and Personality*, ed. David G. Mandelbaum (Berkeley: University of California Press, 1949); and Benjamin Lee Whorf, *Language, Thought and Reality*, ed. John B. Carroll, Stephen C. Levinson, and Penny Lee, 2nd ed. (Cambridge, MA: MIT Press, 2012), among other works by these two scholars; and at least since 1966 in a major way in Michael A. K. Halliday, *Grammar, Society and the Noun* (London: H. K. Lewis for University College London, 1967); repr. in Halliday, *On Language and Linguistics*, ed. Jonathan J. Webster, CWMH 3 (London: Continuum, 2003), 50–73.

[12] See Sonja K. Foss, Karen A. Foss, and Robert Trapp, *Contemporary Perspectives on Rhetoric*, 3rd ed. (Long Grove, IL: Waveland, 2002), who offer their own provocative list of new rhetoricians. These include I. A. Richards, Ernesto Grassi (1902–91), Perelman and Olbrechts-Tyteca, Stephen Toulmin (1922–2009), Richard M. Weaver (1910–63), Burke, Jürgen Habermas (1929–), bell hooks (1952–2021), Jean Baudrillard (1929–2007), and Michel Foucault (1926–84). Whereas arguably all these scholars have an interest in rhetoric, communication, and symbolic action, with some of these terms more comfortable for some than others, many of these scholars probably would not identify with the field of rhetoric as strongly as others. However, many of them have had an influence on the field, either directly or indirectly. They are all concerned with how humans persuade, describe, and explain the world around them.

[13] See Frans H. van Eemeren, "Rhetoric and Argumentation," in *Oxford Handbook of Rhetorical Studies*, ed. MacDonald, 661–71.

[14] See J. Richards, *Rhetoric*, 121.

[15] E.g., Roman Jakobson, "Two Aspects of Language and Two Types of Aphasic Disturbances," in Jakobson and Morris Halle, *Fundamentals of Language*, JLSMi 1 (The Hague: Mouton, 1956), 55–82; Roland Barthes, *The Semiotic Challenge*, trans. Richard Howard (Oxford: Blackwell, 1988), esp. "The Old Rhetoric: An Aidemémoire," 11–94; Paul de Man, *Allegories of Reading: Figural Language in Rousseau, Nietzsche, Rilke, and Proust* (New Haven: Yale University Press, 1979), esp. the essay "Semiology and Rhetoric," 3–19, which first appeared in *Diacritics* 3.3 (1973): 27–33; Jacques Derrida, *Dissemination*, trans. Barbara Johnson (London: Continuum, 2004), esp. 63–171; and Gérard Genette, "La rhétorique restreinte," in *Figures III* (Paris: Éditions du Seuil, 1972), 21–40; ET in Genette, *Figures of Literary Discourse*, trans. Alan Sheridan (Oxford: Blackwell, 1982), 103–24.

with an attack on language itself. Finally, de Man reduces rhetoric to something other than what it was in earlier times and sees it as nothing more than tropes of language.[16] By that time, much of rhetoric had disappeared as anything resembling classical rhetoric.

At the same time, however, there was a revival of classical rhetoric by a number of scholars who continued to draw upon the classical sources, especially Aristotle's *On Rhetoric*, to continue the tradition and make it applicable in modern contexts. This revival of rhetoric includes its uses both for constructive persuasive purposes, as in the writing of various types of essays, and in the critical rhetorical analysis of various types of literature. This movement was in some ways supported by Terry Eagleton's call for the use of rhetoric, or rather the return to rhetoric, as a way of examining literature, despite the advances of poststructuralism already identified.[17] Some of the major figures in this persistent yet revivalist tradition, still often referred to in departments of English and their teaching of "composition," are T. S. Eliot (1888–1965), Cleanth Brooks (1906–94), Robert Penn Warren (1905–89), W. K. Wimsatt Jr. (1907–75), Heinrich Lausberg (1912–92), Edward P. J. Corbett (1919–98), James L. Kinneavy (1920–99), Wayne Booth (1921–2005), and Brian Vickers, among others.[18] The Nobel laureate and literary critic Eliot, in anticipation of the revival of rhetoric, looks to Shakespeare as a master rhetorician, not an ornamentalist. Brooks and Warren, two very influential literary critics, wrote an enduring textbook on modern rhetoric, drawing roughly on the categories of ancient rhetoric. Wimsatt draws upon classical rhetoric and extends it to literary analysis. Lausberg directly bases his handbook upon Quintilian. Corbett wrote a very successful rhetoric textbook based upon the complex rhetorical handbook of Aristotle, as an aid in constructing persuasive language for everyday life. He also edited a book on how rhetorical analysis could be used to examine modern literature. Kinneavy frames his view of rhetoric in larger terms of discourse analysis (see later in this chapter). Booth wrote a work that treated "technique as rhetoric" grounded in the classical tradition. And Vickers shows how rhetoric might be used in various ways to analyze literature from the perspective of classical rhetoric. There are to this day works used in undergraduate courses in North America (and perhaps elsewhere) entitled Rhetorical Criticism that are formulated around ancient techniques of persuasion, such as the tropes and organization.[19]

---

[16] J. Richards, *Rhetoric*, 121–56.
[17] Terry Eagleton, *Literary Theory: An Introduction* (Oxford: Blackwell, 1983), esp. 205–6. See J. Richards, *Rhetoric*, 156–7; Peter Dixon, *Rhetoric*, Critical Idiom (London: Methuen, 1971), esp. 71–5.
[18] T. S. Eliot, "'Rhetoric' and Poetic Drama" (1919), in Eliot, *Selected Essays*, 3rd ed. (London: Faber and Faber, 1941), 37–42; Cleanth Brooks and Robert Penn Warren, *Modern Rhetoric* (New York: Harcourt Brace Jovanovich, 1949); W. K. Wimsatt Jr., *The Verbal Icon: Studies in the Meaning of Poetry* (New York: Noonday, 1958), esp. "Rhetoric and Poems: Alexander Pope," 169–85; Heinrich Lausberg, *Handbook of Literary Rhetoric: A Foundation for Literary Study*, ed. David E. Orton and R. Dean Anderson, trans. Mathew T. Bliss, Annemiek Jansen, and David E. Orton (Leiden: Brill, 1998 [1960]); Edward P. J. Corbett, *Classical Rhetoric for the Modern Student*, 3rd ed. (New York: Oxford University Press, 1990 [1965]); Corbett, *Rhetorical Analyses of Literary Works* (New York: Oxford University Press, 1969); James L. Kinneavy, *A Theory of Discourse: The Aims of Discourse* (New York: Norton, 1971); Wayne C. Booth, *The Rhetoric of Fiction* (Chicago: University of Chicago Press, 1961; 2nd ed., 1983), preface (second unnumbered page in 1st ed.; xiv in 2nd ed.); and Vickers, *In Defense of Rhetoric*. For a sympathetic assessment of such work, especially since Corbett, see Kathleen E. Welch, *The Contemporary Reception of Classical Rhetoric: Appropriations of Ancient Discourse* (Hillsdale, NJ: Lawrence Erlbaum, 1990).
[19] See, for example, Gerard A. Hauser, *Introduction to Rhetorical Theory* (Prospect Heights, IL: Waveland, 1986; 2nd ed., 2002); Sonja K. Foss, *Rhetorical Criticism: Exploration and Practice* (Longwood, CO: Waveland, 1989; 3rd ed., 2004); and Roderick P. Hart, *Modern Rhetorical Criticism* (New York: HarperCollins, 1990).

The use of rhetoric in New Testament studies, and to a lesser extent Old Testament studies, emerged out of the revival of interest in ancient rhetoric.[20] Hans Dieter Betz and George Kennedy are often attributed with the recent revival of ancient rhetoric within New Testament research.[21] Betz wrote a commentary on Galatians that drew upon the principles of speech organization (classical arrangement) to posit that the Pauline book was an instance of an apologetic letter and hence judicial rhetoric. Kennedy's work in reviving rhetoric in classical studies preceded his work in New Testament studies by some time. He began by reviving ancient rhetoric within classical studies through a series of volumes on Greek and Latin rhetoric before turning to the New Testament. Both of these scholars have influenced a large number of students and other scholars who have gone on to promote classical rhetorical studies in various ways.[22] There has also been a backlash against the use of classical rhetoric in New Testament studies (see, for example, Carl Joachim Classen [1928–2013], Jeffrey T. Reed, Philip Kern, and Stanley Porter, among a number of others).[23] This rejection of the use of the categories of classical rhetoric has been formulated, first, on the basis that there has been a mistaken appropriation of a tool that was never designed for such a purpose and, second, on the grounds that the analyses are more taxonomies than they are explanations of the persuasiveness of a text. There have also been a few scholars who have attempted to bring various forms of the New Rhetoric or adaptations of it into New Testament studies, especially that of Burke and Perelman.[24] This has been carried out to the point where Vernon Robbins has devised what

---

[20] In Old Testament studies, ancient rhetoric came into play under the influence of James Muilenburg's article on moving beyond form criticism, although what he defines as rhetoric is probably better understood as literary criticism, of the sort mentioned in the previous note. See Muilenburg, "Form Criticism and Beyond," *JBL* 88 (1969): 1–18. See also Phyllis Trible, *Rhetorical Criticism: Context, Method, and the Book of Jonah*, GBS (Minneapolis: Fortress, 1994).

[21] Hans Dieter Betz, *Galatians: A Commentary on Paul's Letter to the Churches in Galatia*, Hermeneia (Philadelphia: Fortress, 1979), esp. 14–25, and subsequent work; George A. Kennedy, *New Testament Interpretation through Rhetorical Criticism* (Chapel Hill: University of North Carolina Press, 1984), as well as numerous other works by Kennedy both before and after especially in the area of classical rhetoric. For a recent history and assessment, see Stanley E. Porter, "Rhetoric and New Testament Studies," in *Oxford Handbook of Rhetorical Studies*, ed. MacDonald, 649–59.

[22] It is difficult to single out just a few from among a large group, but contributions have been made by Richard N. Longenecker, *Galatians*, WBC 41 (Dallas: Word, 1990); Duane F. Watson, *Invention, Arrangement and Style: Rhetorical Criticism of Jude and Second Peter* (Atlanta: Scholars Press, 1988); and Ben Witherington III, *New Testament Rhetoric: An Introductory Guide to the Art of Persuasion in and of the New Testament* (Eugene, OR: Cascade, 2009); among others.

[23] E.g., Carl Joachim Classen, *Rhetorical Criticism of the New Testament*, WUNT 128 (Tübingen: Mohr Siebeck, 2000); Jeffrey T. Reed, "Using Ancient Rhetorical Categories to Interpret Paul's Letters: A Question of Genre," in *Rhetoric and the New Testament: Essays from the 1992 Heidelberg Conference*, ed. Stanley E. Porter and Thomas H. Olbricht, JSNTSup 90 (Sheffield: Sheffield Academic, 1993), 292–324 (with essays by Classen, Porter, and Dennis Stamps also in this volume, all calling into question the application of classical rhetoric); Philip H. Kern, *Rhetoric and Galatians: Assessing an Approach to Paul's Epistle*, SNTSMS 101 (Cambridge: Cambridge University Press, 1998); and Stanley E. Porter, "Paul of Tarsus and His Letters," in *Handbook of Classical Rhetoric*, ed. Porter, 533–86 (also with essays by Reed and Stamps).

[24] For example, see Lauri Thurén, *Argument and Theology in 1 Peter: The Origins of Christian Paraenesis*, JSNTSup 114 (Sheffield: Sheffield Academic, 1995); Christopher D. Stanley, *Arguing with Scripture: The Rhetoric of Quotations in the Letters of Paul* (New York: T&T Clark International, 2004), who follows the work of Eugene E. White, one of Perelman's followers; and James D. Hester and J. David Hester, eds., *Rhetorics in the New Millennium: Promise and Fulfillment* (London: T&T Clark, 2010). Cf. Eugene E. White, *The Context of Human Discourse: A Configurational Criticism of Rhetoric* (Columbia: University of South Carolina Press, 1992).

he calls social-rhetorical criticism.²⁵ This is a form of rhetorical criticism that attempts to place early Christian writings within their social context and then examines their various "textures." In its latest manifestation, socio-rhetorical criticism (or interpretation) adds dimensions of cognitive science. There have been a number of works produced using variations on Robbins's form of rhetorical criticism.²⁶

The use of rhetoric in New Testament studies is probably not much different than it is in other academic fields, such as in English departments and speech departments. There is a strong acknowledgment of its place, but there is also a lack of significant work that has provided convincing interpretive results of the benefits of its use.

RHETORIC AND PERSUASION IN SYSTEMIC FUNCTIONAL LINGUISTICS AND THE NEW TESTAMENT

I have taken this somewhat lengthy path to get to the use of rhetoric and persuasion within the New Testament because of the obvious difficulties that it has faced. The question is, with all that has been said before, how can we define a useful and productive role for rhetoric within New Testament studies? I think that the solution to this dilemma rests with an approach that has not been widely used in rhetorical studies. Rhetoric has been examined from a variety of angles, but rarely has it been seen to be part of a larger linguistic system.²⁷ If anything, rhetoric has been seen as opposed to or in competition with various theories of language. Within some linguistic circles, discourse analysis is seen as the modern equivalent of ancient rhetorical analysis, in the sense that discourse analysis avails itself of the latest thoughts regarding language function in its discussion of texts, rather than simply invoking categories of thought utilized by the ancients.²⁸ To some extent, this is the approach I am taking in this chapter. I see linguistic analysis as the contemporary interpretive framework that comes closest to realizing the goal of providing a linguistically sensitive and informed way of approaching texts, including ancient texts, that benefits from the insights gained by more recent language study. I wish to pursue this more fully by attempting to locate the rhetorical function of language within SFL, and then bring some of these findings to bear on specific texts of the New Testament.

---

²⁵Vernon K. Robbins, *The Tapestry of Early Christian Discourse: Rhetoric, Society and Ideology* (London: Routledge, 1996).
²⁶As examples, see Roy R. Jeal, *Exploring Philemon: Freedom, Brotherhood, and Partnership in the New Society*, Rhetoric of Religious Antiquity 2 (Atlanta: SBL Press, 2015); and Vernon K. Robbins, Robert H. von Thaden Jr., and Bart B. Bruehler, eds., *Foundations for Sociorhetorical Exploration: A Rhetoric of Religious Antiquity Reader*, Rhetoric of Religious Antiquity 4 (Atlanta: SBL Press, 2016). For a more inclusive treatment of major figures in New Testament rhetorical criticism, see Troy W. Martin, ed., *Genealogies of New Testament Rhetorical Criticism* (Minneapolis: Fortress, 2014), who includes treatment of Betz, Kennedy, Wilhelm Wuellner (1927–2004), Elisabeth Schüssler Fiorenza, and Robbins.
²⁷I made a preliminary venture in this regard in Stanley E. Porter, "Linguistics and Rhetorical Criticism," in *Linguistics and the New Testament: Critical Junctures*, ed. Stanley E. Porter and D. A. Carson, JSNTSup 168, SNTG 5 (Sheffield: Sheffield Academic, 1999), 63–92, where I discuss rhetoric in relationship to various grammars, including transformational grammar; Tagmemics; communication theory; sociolinguistics, including SFL; and discourse analysis in its various forms.
²⁸See, for example, Robert de Beaugrande and Wolfgang Dressler, *Introduction to Text Linguistics* (London: Longman, 1981), 15. Cf. Teun A. van Dijk, "Introduction: Discourse as a New Cross-Discipline," in *Handbook of Discourse Analysis*. I. *Disciplines of Discourse*, ed. Teun A. van Dijk (London: Academic Press, 1985), 1–10, esp. 13.

As previously noted, most of the rhetorical schools of thought, even those that are part of the New Rhetoric and claim some type of linguistic heritage, are theoretically poor regarding their linguistics. Most of the work in the New Rhetoric (at least that I have read) approaches the topic either literarily or classically. Even Robbins in his approach, though he has many linguistically oriented insights, does not ground his approach within any definable linguistic theory.[29]

Having said that, I do not think that most linguistic theories have done a better job of locating a specifically rhetorical component within their linguistic frameworks. Within SFL, there have been several explorations of rhetoric. Most are not lengthy, but they provide a framework for our discussion. Halliday himself places rhetoric within the textual metafunction, by which he means that the persuasive function is in some ways realized by the organizational and structural resources of language.[30] This would include such elements as the conjunction of clauses, cohesion, and information structure. There are other linguistic theories that have rhetorical elements to them that have pursued this textual component as the home of rhetoric. This would include Rhetorical Structure Theory, which is an attempt to find the overriding and overarching rhetorical groupings within a coherent text and how they are conceptually related to one another to constitute an entire whole.[31] This theory, developed for computer-based text analysis, posits a hierarchy of conceptual groupings as a means of describing textual coherence. The theory has not apparently caught on in a significant way in SFL studies, despite its promotion in IFG4, to the point that it can be said to constitute the rhetorical component of SFL. Some various attempts at Exchange Structure also have elements of rhetoric to them, as they are concerned with how the participants in any given exchange engage in their interaction—

---

[29]For a thorough critique that argues for SFL as the heir to rhetorical criticism, see Gustavo Martín-Asensio, "Hallidayan Functional Grammar as Heir to New Testament Rhetorical Criticism," in *The Rhetorical Interpretation of Scripture: Essays from the 1996 Malibu Conference*, ed. Stanley E. Porter and Dennis L. Stamps, JSNTSup 180 (Sheffield: Sheffield Academic, 1999), 84–107.

[30]See Michael A. K. Halliday, *Language as Social Semiotic: The Social Interpretation of Language and Meaning* (London: Edward Arnold, 1978), 233; and Halliday in Halliday and Ruqaiya Hasan, *Language, Context, and Text: Aspects of Language in a Social-Semiotic Perspective*, 2nd ed. (Oxford: Oxford University Press, 1989), 12.

[31]See, for example, William C. Mann and Sandra A. Thompson, "Rhetorical Structure Theory: A Theory of Text Organization," *ISI Reprint Series* (June 1987): 1–82; Mann and Thompson, "Rhetorical Structure Theory: Toward a Functional Theory of Text Organization," *Text* 8.3 (1988): 243–81; and Mann, Christian M. I. M. Matthiessen, and Thompson, "Rhetorical Structure Theory and Text Analysis," in *Discourse Description: Diverse Linguistic Analyses of a Fund-Raising Text*, ed. William C. Mann and Sandra A. Thompson (Amsterdam: John Benjamins, 1992), 39–79, incorporated into M. A. K. Halliday, *Halliday's Introduction to Functional Grammar* (IFG4), rev. Christian M. I. M. Matthiessen, 4th ed. (London: Routledge, 2014), 657–8. See also Christian M. I. M. Matthiessen, "Interpreting the Textual Metafunction," in *Advances in Systemic Linguistics: Recent Theory and Practice*, ed. Martin Davies and Louise Ravelli (London: Pinter, 1992), 37–81, esp. 61–2 and 71–2, who also places Rhetorical Structure Theory within the textual metafunction (as it is within IFG4). One can clearly see where the cognitive influence on Halliday comes from, as reflected in the work of Matthiessen. One also notes that this approach has similarities to South African colon analysis developed by J. P. Louw (1932–2011) (see Andrie du Toit, "Exploring Textual Structure: Discourse Analysis," in *Focusing on the Message: New Testament Hermeneutics, Exegesis and Methods*, ed. Andrie du Toit [Pretoria: Protea, 2009], 217–65), and what is sometimes called arcing developed by Daniel Fuller (Daniel Fuller, "Hermeneutics" [unpublished manuscript, 1969; 5th ed., 1978]; Thomas R. Schreiner, *Interpreting the Pauline Epistles* [Grand Rapids: Baker, 1990], 97–126; cf. also David E. Johnson and Paul M. Postal, *Arc Pair Grammar* [Princeton: Princeton University Press, 1980]).

although so far such exchange structure analysis has not progressed very far, with most attention still confined to the textual metafunction.[32]

James Martin and Peter White have developed an entire specialized area of linguistics within SFL called Appraisal Theory, focusing upon but not confined to the interpersonal metafunction.[33] Appraisal Theory is an attempt to account for evaluative comments that are made either explicitly or implicitly within a text. So far as it has been developed and applied to English, Appraisal Theory has primarily concentrated upon lexis, with very little to do with the grammar. Recently, however, Appraisal Theory has been modeled for New Testament Greek, where the role of grammar, especially with regard to the mood system, has been developed to have a more significant role in the theory.[34] I will say more about Appraisal Theory under the topic of evaluation when I discuss it later in this chapter.

There are no doubt other linguistic theories that have a rhetorical component as part of their model of language. The examples already treated, however, suffice to make some generalizations. What some of these approaches suggest is that rhetoric is deeply and integrally embedded within a sector of the content stratum of language; that is, it is part of the semantics and lexicogrammar of the language. However, others of these approaches suggest that rhetoric occupies a place of its own within the language structure, either as a metafunction of its own, that is, as a particular function to which language is put, realized by particular lexicogrammatical features, or as a stratum or sub-stratum of its own, perhaps located either between the semantics and lexicogrammar or between the context and the content.[35]

---

[32] For example, J. R. Martin and David Rose, *Working with Discourse: Meaning beyond the Clause*, 2nd ed. (London: Continuum, 2007), 244–51. An exception on its limitations is Margaret Berry, who extends Exchange Structure to all three metafunctions. See, for example, Margaret Berry, "Systemic Linguistics and Discourse Analysis: A Multi-Layered Approach to Exchange Structure," in *Studies in Discourse Analysis*, ed. Malcolm Coulthard and Martin Montgomery (London: Routledge & Kegan Paul, 1981), 120–45. For an expanded form of the model applied to study of the Greek texts of the New Testament, see Stanley E. Porter and Matthew Brook O'Donnell, *Discourse Analysis and the Greek New Testament: Text-Generating Resources*, T&T Clark Library of New Testament Greek 2 (London: T&T Clark, 2023), ch. 3.

[33] J. R. Martin and P. R. R. White, *The Language of Evaluation: Appraisal in English* (London: Palgrave Macmillan, 2005).

[34] See James D. Dvorak, *The Interpersonal Metafunction in 1 Corinthians 1–4: The Tenor of Toughness*, LBS 19 (Leiden: Brill, 2021); Dvorak, "'Prodding with Prosody': Persuasion and Social Influence through the Lens of Appraisal Theory," *BAGL* 4 (2015): 85–120; Dvorak, "To Incline Another's Heart: The Role of Attitude in Reader Positioning," in *The Language and Literature of the New Testament: Essays in Honor of Stanley E. Porter's 60th Birthday*, ed. Lois K. Fuller Dow, Craig A. Evans, and Andrew W. Pitts, BINS 150 (Leiden: Brill, 2017), 599–624; Dvorak, "Ask and Ye Shall Position the Readers: James's Use of Questions to (re-)Align His Readers," in *The Epistle of James: Linguistic Exegesis of an Early Christian Letter*, ed. James D. Dvorak and Zachary K. Dawson, LENT 1 (Eugene, OR: Pickwick, 2019), 196–245; Zachary K. Dawson, "Language as Negotiation: Toward a Systemic Functional Model for Ideological Criticism with Application to James 2:1-13," in *Modeling Biblical Language: Selected Papers from the McMaster Divinity College Linguistics Circle*, ed. Stanley E. Porter, Gregory P. Fewster, and Christopher D. Land, LBS 13 (Leiden: Brill, 2016), 362–90; Dawson, "The Rules of 'Engagement': Assessing the Function of the Diatribe in James 2:14-26 Using Critical Discourse Analysis," in *Epistle of James*, ed. Dvorak and Dawson, 155–95.

[35] It appears that so far as rhetorical studies are concerned, M. A. K. Halliday and Ruqaiya Hasan, *Cohesion in English* (London: Longman, 1976), has had the most influence, as it has had a lasting impact upon how cohesion is defined within rhetoric. See Irwin Weiser, "Linguistics," in *Encyclopedia of Rhetoric and Composition: Communication from Ancient Times to the Information Age*, ed. Theresa Enos (London: Routledge, 1996), 386–91, esp. 390–1.

I wish here to return to a suggestion that I made a number of years ago and suggest that rhetoric is best situated, not within the textual metafunction but within the interpersonal metafunction of language—even if there are relations to the other metafunctions.[36] Of the SFL models already discussed, I, therefore, find the most potential in Appraisal Theory, though there are still interpersonal moves made in language pertaining to rhetoric that fall outside of appraisal—namely, those akin to the moves described in various forms of Exchange Structure (see previous comments).[37] (I am not including here the so-called tropes, which can mostly be seen as instances of grammatical metaphor.)[38] I am concerned here with positioning what is typically referred to as rhetoric—the attempt to persuade—within the linguistic resources of the Greek language.

If language is organized into strata, we have contextual, content, and expression strata. The contextual strata include both the overriding context of culture that establishes the broad parameters of the cultural setting and constraints within which language use occurs, such as setting, behavioral environment, and the use of language itself, and the prototypical context of situation that describes an instance of language use. The context of situation is typified by the field (what the context is about and who is involved in it and how), tenor (the relationships and roles of the participants), and mode (the means by which the previous two are expressed as a text). A situational context is described by a contextual configuration of field, tenor, and mode. This constitutes a register. The major components of the context of situation—field, tenor, and mode—are each realized within the content stratum by a particular metafunction, the ideational, interpersonal, and textual metafunctions. These metafunctions are then realized by instances of language within the lexicogrammar, typically at or around the clausal level. The field is realized by the ideational metafunction, which includes the lexis of the discourse, the transitivity patterns of the relationships among the entities and their processes, described in terms of such relations as the actors, goals, and circumstances (of various kinds), the types of processes (material, mental, behavioral, verbal, relational, and existential), and the logical relations. The clause here functions to convey the message of the discourse. The mode is realized by the textual metafunction and functions around and beyond the clause, in which the clause acts as a means of representation. The textual metafunction is realized by cohesion, conjunction, and information flow including theme and rheme analysis. The tenor is realized by the interpersonal metafunction, which includes the participant relations, person, mood, evaluation, and comment. The clause here functions as a means of exchange of meanings.

---

[36]See Stanley E. Porter, "Dialect and Register in the Greek of the New Testament: Theory" and "Register in the Greek of the New Testament: Application with Reference to Mark's Gospel," in *Rethinking Contexts, Rereading Texts: Contributions from the Social Sciences to Biblical Interpretation*, ed. M. Daniel Carroll R., JSOTSup 299 (Sheffield: Sheffield Academic, 2000), 190–208, 209–29, used throughout this section. See esp. "Dialect and Register," 203–4.

[37]See Berry, "Systemic Linguistics," 120–45. Martin and Rose, *Working with Discourse*, have been interpreted as modeling two interpersonal systems, Appraisal and Negotiation (25–71, 219–54). See Dawson, "Language as Negotiation," 362–90. It is possible to conceive of these as independent systems (if Negotiation is, in fact, such a system), as they do, but rhetoric, defined essentially as the means of persuasion, necessarily involves considering how both these systems cooperate in text to achieve their interpersonal aims.

[38]See Chapter Three.

As Geoff Thompson states, "We tell other people things for a purpose: we may want to influence their attitudes or behaviour, or to provide information that we know they do not have, or explain our own attitudes or behaviour, or to get them to provide us with information, and so on."[39] Rhetoric is concerned with the purposes of discourse (which I have called persuasion), such as influencing others, dealing with participant relations, for example, the relation of teacher to pupil, of politician to polis, of lawyer to jury, since persuasion, teaching, and description—the typical functions of rhetoric—seem to be functions of mood, and it is designed to be evaluative by making comment upon behavior. Therefore, I think that rhetoric is perhaps best modeled as a part of the interpersonal semantic component.[40]

In what follows, I wish to offer several instances of how the tenor of a discourse is realized by the interpersonal metafunction and elements of the lexicogrammar of Greek, as a means of illustrating how rhetoric might become integrated within a Greek linguistic framework. One caveat before proceeding, however, is that virtually all the linguistic features that I will mention are part of the structure of the Greek language, and not particular to rhetoric—as if such a thing would even be possible, according to how I am framing the analysis (it cannot, because rhetoric must, I believe, be part of the linguistic system). One can interpret and hence treat these linguistic features in one of two ways. One is to attempt to differentiate rhetorical from non-rhetorical uses of the same features. The problem with this approach is that there is no component of the language that allows such a differentiation. Another is simply to claim that, because all the features are elements of the Greek language, all language is rhetorical and hence when these features are used language is simply being used rhetorically. I would prefer to say that in some sense, even if one not worth making all the time, language is always rhetorical, that is, functioning for various explicit purposes. With an integrated rhetorical component within a linguistic framework, language can legitimately be discussed as always exemplifying some rhetorical function. In what follows I will discuss three major rhetorical components of the interpersonal metafunction: speech functions, participant relations, and evaluation.

Speech Functions

Greek speech functions are based around the resources available to Greek users to speak about and convey meanings about their real, imagined, and constructed experience, including the exchange of information, feelings, goods, or services.[41] In Greek, the

---

[39]Geoff Thompson, *Introducing Functional Grammar*, 2nd ed. (London: Hodder Education, 2004), 45.

[40]Porter, "Dialect and Register," 203–4. For other important works on register in SFL, see the selection of essays in J. R. Martin and Y. J. Doran, eds., *Systemic Functional Linguistics*, 5 vols. (London: Routledge, 2015), 4:11–122, with essays by J. R. Firth (1890–1960), Michael Gregory, J. Ellis and J. N. Ure, Halliday, and Matthiessen; Halliday, *Language as Social Semiotic*, 62–4, 115–20, 143–5, 222–3; Halliday and Hasan, *Language, Context, and Text*; Mohsen Ghadessy, ed., *Register Analysis: Theory and Practice* (London: Pinter, 1993); Helen Leckie-Tarry, *Language and Context: A Functional Linguistic Theory of Register*, ed. David Birch (London: Pinter, 1995). For a discussion in relation to the Greek New Testament, see Porter and O'Donnell, *Discourse Analysis*, ch. 3. Some examples of New Testament register analysis are Stanley E. Porter, *The Letter to the Romans: A Linguistic and Literary Commentary*, NTM 37 (Sheffield: Sheffield Phoenix, 2015); and David I. Yoon, *A Discourse Analysis of Galatians and the New Perspective on Paul*, LBS 17 (Leiden: Brill, 2019).

[41]On speech functions in Greek, see Stanley E. Porter, "Systemic Functional Linguistics and the Greek Language: The Need for Further Modeling," in *Modeling Biblical Language*, ed. Porter, Fewster, and Land, 9–47, esp. 20–32, in response to Halliday etc. I rephrase Halliday's notion of speech functions as primarily concerning information and goods and services because it is too limited (and reflects his materialistic view of reality). See Halliday, IFG4, 134–9. I would now partially reframe my discussion of exchange roles in light of a re-assessment of these categories (Porter, "Systemic Functional Linguistics," 29).

fundamental semantic differentiation is not between assertion and direction (as one would believe from Halliday regarding English), but between assertion and non-assertion. The result is several speech functions in Greek that are not found, for example, in English (the language upon which most modeling of SFL is based). That is, Greek grammaticalizes a different set of speech functions than does English. The major Greek speech functions may be configured in the following systemic network of attitude (Figure 4.1):

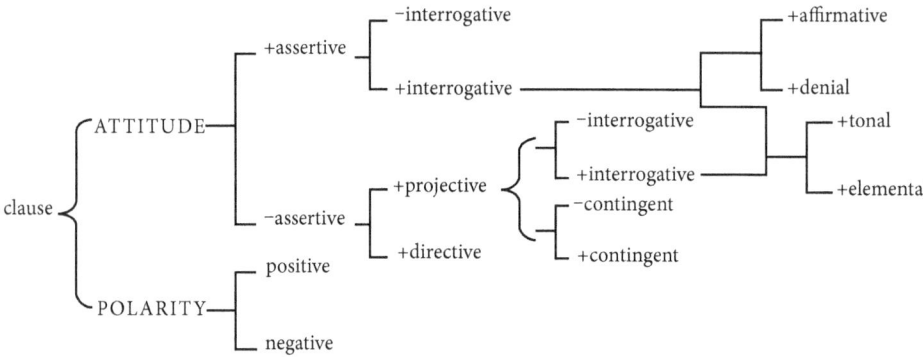

FIGURE 4.1 Systemic network of attitude including potential realizations of speech functions.[42]

This system network results in the following exchange roles within the Greek language (Table 4.1):

TABLE 4.1 Major Greek speech functions[43]

Exchange Role	Goods and Services	Information
Giving	Open question	Declaration
Projecting	Projective question	Projective statement
Wishing	Projective cont. statement	Positive/negative question
Demanding	Command	τ-Question
Inquiring	Projective cont. question (?)	Projective (cont.) τ-question (?)

---

[42]Porter, "Systemic Functional Linguistics," 27. This system network incorporates elements of the attitude semantic system, previously proposed in Stanley E. Porter, *Verbal Aspect in the Greek of the New Testament, with Reference to Tense and Mood*, SBG 1 (New York: Peter Lang, 1989), 109; and further refined in Stanley E. Porter and Matthew Brook O'Donnell, "The Greek Verbal Network Viewed from a Probabilistic Standpoint: An Exercise in Hallidayan Linguistics," *FN* 14 (2001): 3–41, esp. 40. For the semantic terminology and definitions, see Porter, *Verbal Aspect*, 163–77. This system network is not to be taken as definitive and is offered for exemplary purposes. For example, the [+tonal] does not indicate that we know the sound system of ancient Greek, but that we believe that tonal patterns were involved in some way. See also David L. Mathewson, *Voice and Mood: A Linguistic Approach*, Essentials of Biblical Greek Grammar (Grand Rapids: Baker, 2021), 95–135.

[43]Porter, "Systemic Functional Linguistics," 29. The categories of "information" and "goods and services" should be read as including expansive notions of these ideas that encompass all the things that can be accomplished by means of language. This includes stating feelings, thoughts, and anything else that can be expressed by means of language, and performing any and all non-language tasks. Halliday is clearly too limited in his conception, due to his materialist (Marxist) view of reality. This is surprising in light of his views of language and social constructivism (see Chapter Three for previous mention).

As a result, we have more than simply the four functions: statements, commands, offers, and questions. In Greek, we have ten different speech functions: declarations, projective statements, commands,[44] questions (six different types),[45] and projective contingent statements.[46] As in English (for the most part), these are directly linked with the various mood forms of the language. In other words, the speech functions of Greek are more numerous and differentiated than they are in English because of the more complex verbal structure of Greek than of English.

I will return to the same figure and table (Figure 4.1 and Table 4.1) in the next chapter on cognition, where I will refer to them for a different purpose than here. As already stated, there is nothing inherently rhetorical about the use of any of these speech functions in and of themselves. Each use, however, is part of the rhetorical effect of the given text and can be understood to function in this way. There are also particular configurations of such speech functions that seem to emphasize this rhetorical effect. I offer several instances here.

Romans 5:1-2. The rhetorical effect of the interpersonal metafunction can be seen in the example of how to interpret Rom. 5:1-2.[47] The text-critical question is whether the verb translated "have" is an indicative (ἔχομεν) or a subjunctive (ἔχωμεν) mood form. The dispute between these readings has an intriguing history. Before the middle of the twentieth century, most scholars endorsed the subjunctive reading, at which point the indicative reading became the more prominent, almost to the point of forcing the other from consideration. The argument shifted from reliance upon the external evidence, which is overwhelmingly for the subjunctive reading, to reliance upon supposed internal evidence.[48] There are numerous discussions of the effect of the use of the indicative or the subjunctive in the passage, with many rejecting the subjunctive because of the supposed theological uncertainty that this reading brings to the text. They suppose that it would mean something like, "Having been justified by faith, we *may* have peace with God ..." I believe that this is a misinterpretation of the use of the subjunctive, and that a better understanding would be, "Having been justified by faith, *let us have* peace with God ..." This debate is clearly ongoing and the major commentaries may be consulted for further discussion (although much of it is repetitive of the same arguments, with very few new ideas presented).

---

[44]For a description of Greek commands and the imperative mood (directive attitude) as it is conceived in light of the interpersonal metafunction of SFL, see James D. Dvorak, "'Evidence That Commands a Verdict': Determining the Semantics of Imperatives in the New Testament," *BAGL* 7 (2018): 201–23. Cf. Stanley E. Porter, "Aspect and Imperatives Once More," *BAGL* 7 (2018): 141–72, esp. 142–4 and 159–64.

[45]For a recent work that demonstrates the potential the six types of questions as they are grammaticalized in Greek have for persuasive means, see Dvorak, "Ask and Ye Shall Position," 196–245.

[46]There are various ways that these speech functions could be named. I have avoided the unmodified term *statement* because of its potential ambiguity with the way that I use it elsewhere. There are other ways that the labels could be formulated as well (e.g., projection, contingent projection).

[47]For treatment of this passage within the entire book of Romans, see Porter, *Letter to the Romans*, 114.

[48]See Stanley E. Porter, "The Argument of Romans 5: Can a Rhetorical Question Make a Difference?" *JBL* 110 (1991): 655–77; repr. and rev. in Stanley E. Porter, *Studies in the Greek New Testament: Theory and Practice*, SBG 6 (New York: Peter Lang, 1996), 213–38. The only possible early witness to the indicative reading is 0220, but despite the *vid* reading by the editors (and the NA and *UBSGNT* critical apparatuses), this reading is highly speculative. The varied shapes and spacing of the letters and the condition of the parchment make it only slightly more plausible for the indicative than the subjunctive reading.

What is rarely if ever considered, however, is the rhetorical effect of the shift between the indicative and subjunctive forms so far as the speech function within Paul's argument. The difference would be between a declaration, "Having been justified by faith, we have peace with God," and the projective statement being used in an exhortative way, "Having been justified by faith, let us enter into or let us enjoy peace with God ..." I believe that the subjunctive reading is the better reading for both especially external but also internal reasons, not least because of the rhetorical effect. Paul, having finished his exposition of what it means to be made righteous by God (Rom. 3:22–4:25), now turns from the legal predicament and legal solution of the human condition to the relational situation, in which humanity is alienated from and at enmity with God (Rom. 5). He says that, now that we are justified by faith, "let us (also) enter into and enjoy peace with God through our Lord Jesus Christ, through whom we also are in a state of having access by faith into this grace in which we stand, and let us enter into boasting upon the hope of the glory of God." I take the verb translated "boast" (καυχώμεθα) as a subjunctive as well (the form can be identified as either a subjunctive or indicative mood form, depending upon how one interprets the verb "have" in v. 1). Paul continues: "not only this, but indeed let us enter into boasting in our tribulations, knowing that ..." and he continues with his step progression that leads from tribulation to hope that is grounded in the love of God. The progression continues in Rom. 6:1 and 15.

1 Corinthians 1:13. A second example is found in 1 Cor. 1:13. The body of 1 Corinthians begins in 1:10 and extends until 4:21. In the opening section of the body of this letter, Paul is exhorting the Corinthians regarding divisions among them and wanting them to be of the same mind and joined together. In 1 Cor. 1:12 he says, "I say this, that each of you says, 'I am of Paul,' and 'I am of Apollos,' and 'I am of Cephas,' and 'I am of Christ.'" (It is just possible that these are to be taken as questions—"each of you says, 'am I of Paul?,' and 'am I of Apollos?,' and 'am I of Cephas?,' and 'am I of Christ?'"—but I leave that matter aside.) Paul is clearly concerned with divisions and schisms within the Corinthian church. However, does he then say, "Christ stands divided" or "Does Christ stand divided?" The Greek text reads thus: μεμέρισται ὁ Χριστός (I intentionally do not close with punctuation). The *UBSGNT* and NA text punctuates this as a question, along with a number of other translations and versions, and thus: μεμέρισται ὁ Χριστός; However, Westcott and Hort take this as a declaration, μεμέρισται ὁ Χριστός. The NEB takes it as an exclamation, "Surely Christ has not been divided among you!" So far as I know Greek does not have a mark of punctuation to indicate this interpretation.[49]

The Greek text is susceptible to any of these three renderings, especially if one were to derive the third based upon the use of the stative aspect of the perfect tense-form (rather than the polar negative question). The rhetorical impact is the difference between taking the speech function as a declaration, a strong declaration (here exclamation), or

---

[49]This example poses an interesting problem in relation to the Greek text that supposedly stands behind the NEB, prepared by R. V. G. Tasker, *The Greek New Testament: Being the Text Translated in The New English Bible 1961* (Oxford: Oxford University Press; Cambridge: Cambridge University Press, 1964), 257, where the Greek text reads: μὴ μεμέρισται ὁ Χριστός; The NEB committee accepts a textual variant found in P46 and a number of later manuscripts with the negation. This textual variant is not to be accepted in this clause. The evidence against including it includes the other early majuscule manuscripts (e.g., ℵ A B C D) and many others, as well as the later textual tradition. The effect of accepting the variant is to make this a polar negative question (a question expecting a negative answer), translated in this instance with the strong assertion (often such questions expecting a negative answer are translated with a tag, such as "has he?" and not the thematically placed strong adjunct).

an open question. The rest of v. 13 is clearly a question, as it is formulated as a polar negative question (with the negation expecting a negative answer, μή). So much is perhaps adequately explained by usual exegetical comment. However, we must also consider the rhetorical effect of these various textual interpretations. There are two major effects to consider. The first possible effect is to see the clause in 1 Cor. 1:13a as a concluding declaration, "Christ stands divided." Paul comments upon the situation as he sees it among the Corinthian Christians, before he turns to questions in which he formulates the expected negative answer that, in fact, Paul was not crucified for them and they were not baptized into Paul's name. The second possible rhetorical effect is to see 1 Cor. 1:13a as an initiating question, "Does Christ stand divided?" This question then leads to the questions that expect a negative answer.

John 21:15-17. This example involves the dialogue between Jesus and Peter in John 21. This is a well-known passage that is often confined to discussion over whether the two different verbs often translated with the English "love" (ἀγαπάω and φιλέω) are contextual synonyms. The formulation is usually not quite as simple as that, as there is often confusion among commentators over the nature of synonymy and other issues. I have argued elsewhere that these words clearly are not true synonyms, as each one has a distinct sense (ἀγαπάω being vertical regarding esteem and the other, φιλέω, horizontal regarding affection). More than that, they are not contextual synonyms either, as is, I believe, made clear in the nature of the dialogue and the shift in usage in the third question and answer set (see the passages discussed further in this chapter).[50] That issue, however, is not the point of my including this example here. The reason for this example is to note the difference in rhetorical effect between the clauses by Jesus being taken as questions or declarations. The Greek is susceptible to either interpretation, and the rhetorical difference is to be noted. If they are taken as questions, Jesus asks Peter three times, "Simon Peter, do you love (ἀγαπᾷς) me more than these?," "Simon son of John, do you love (ἀγαπᾷς) me?," and "Simon son of John, do you love (φιλεῖς) me?" If they are taken as declarations, Jesus then states to Peter three times, "Simon Peter, you love (ἀγαπᾷς) me more than these," "Simon son of John, you love (ἀγαπᾷς) me," and "Simon son of John, you love (φιλεῖς) me."

In each case, we note that Peter always responds with a form of the verb φιλέω. By the third time, he is clearly in some way disconcerted. Let's explore the difference in rhetorical effect of the two different ways of understanding this exchange between Jesus and Peter. If these are questions, then Peter is apparently perplexed with Jesus over several matters: one is the fact that, even though he responds positively to Jesus's question, Jesus asks him another one, up to three times in total; and the other is that Jesus does not appear to accept Peter's answer each time but asks him a slightly different question in the following question, persisting in probing the issue. However, if these are declarations, then Peter's perhaps being confused, which appears to be the case whether questions or declarations are made, is confusion of a slightly different sort. Peter meets Jesus's declarations with similar, if not stronger, declarations in response. Peter uses the asseverative, "Yes" (ναί), the first two times, and then the stative aspect verb (perfect tense-form of the verb of knowing, οἶδας) with the emphatic personal pronoun, "you" (σύ), the third time. Yet each time, Jesus makes a similar statement as the one before as if he has not even heard

---

[50] For treatment of this passage in more detail, see Stanley E. Porter, *Linguistic Analysis of the Greek New Testament: Studies in Tools, Methods, and Practice* (Grand Rapids: Baker, 2015), 298–301, where I defend the view proposed here.

Peter's answer. In the first construal, with questions, Peter is perhaps perplexed, but in the second, with declarations, he is probably frustrated.

Mark 1:40-41. This final example involves Jesus's episode of cleansing of a leper in Mk 1:40-44. A leper comes to Jesus and begs him on bended knee for healing. Jesus complies with his request. However, I wish to note how the leper frames his request. He does so, not by means of a question or a command, but by means of a conditional clause complex to make a declaration: "If you are willing, you are able to heal me (ἐὰν θέλῃς δύνασαί με καθαρίσαι)" (Mk 1:40). The leper uses two devices with rhetorical effect. The first device, in the protasis of a third-class conditional construction, is the subjunctive mood form indicating a projective statement. The leper does not use a first-class conditional construction with an indicative verb and hence make a declaration but uses a third-class conditional. He frames the approach in projective rather than assertive terms. Then, in the apodosis of the conditional construction, he uses a catenative construction: "you are able to heal me (δύνασαί με καθαρίσαι)." I note that, in this part of the construction, the leper continues the use of a modulated formulation. Rather than using an imperative as a command or something similar ("heal me"), he phrases his imploration to be healed as a declaration about Jesus's abilities. Further, he uses a catenative construction with a verbal operator (some would call it a "light verb") and a related predicator rather than simply a predicator.[51] On both clausal accounts, the protasis and the apodosis, the leper, despite his physical condition and needy state, frames his desire to be healed in constructions that avoid the kinds of statements that one might expect. Jesus is filled with compassion and reaches out his hand and touches the man and says to him: "I agree (θέλω); be healed (καθαρίσθητι)" (Mk 1:41). Jesus reformulates the man's imploring into the kinds of straightforward statements that the man himself avoids. Jesus uses a declaration in response to the protasis of the man's conditional construction in direct refutation of its conditionality. He then uses the imperative as a direct command that the man so clearly avoided by use of the catenative construction. With that, the man is healed, and the leprosy is gone. The contrast in speech functions and lexicogrammatical formulations contrasts the rhetorical impact of the two sets of statements, by the leper and by Jesus.

Participant Relations

The primary participants (or sometimes called interactants) in a discourse are part of the field of a discourse; that is, they are the ones who are engaged in the discourse itself. Social relationships among participants may be established through extra-linguistic information (such as the difference between God and humanity) or these relationships may be entirely intra-linguistic. The first are defined apart from the use of language, even though language must be used in relation to these relationships, and the second are defined by the linguistic system itself. However, the grammaticalized relations among the participants are part of the interpersonal metafunction and hence implicit in the rhetorical effect of the use of language. The tenor component of the situational context is concerned with participant relations, and indicates who is taking part in the discourse, the relationships that exist between the participants, and indications of their status, permanence, and role relationships, all realized linguistically. These involve the

---

[51]See Thompson, *Introducing Functional Grammar*, 51; Donna Jo Napoli, *Syntax: Theory and Problems* (New York: Oxford University Press, 1993), 98.

relationships that exist within a text among such figures as the informer, questioner, and responder (in exchange structure). All the interpersonal semantic options of the language system are part of the interpersonal metafunction and are clausal or lower structural features.

There are three major ways that participant relations may be expressed in the Greek language that I am concerned with. The first means is through the grammaticalization of person as either first, second, or third person. First and second person includes either the speaker (first person) or addressee (second person) as participants [+participants] but third person includes neither [-participants]. Whereas first person includes the speaker, whether the addressee is envisioned or not, the second person directly includes the addressee, as well as the speaker. The third person includes neither and therefore serves as a means of linguistically creating distance in a discourse between speaker–addressee and others–events, since there is a grammaticalized differentiation and distancing of any specific participant-role in the text.[52] The second way that participant relations are indicated is through grammaticalization of participants by means of full forms, reduced forms, or implied forms. Full forms include such devices as names or other word groups (e.g., "Paul," "the author of Romans," "the apostle to the Gentiles") (there is no doubt a hierarchy to such full forms), reduced forms include pronouns of various types (intensive, personal, demonstrative, etc.), and implied forms are those indicated by monolectic verbs (e.g. the person designation on a verbal form). The semantics of participants within the interpersonal metafunction are indicated by these two important lexicogrammatical devices. The third means of indicating participant relations concerns case usage and is related to causality realized by the voice system (especially seen in what Halliday calls ergativity).[53] The participants can be grammaticalized in various ways based upon their functions within the clause, according to whether they function as subject, complement, or adjunct. Those functioning as subject are usually grammaticalized in the nominative case, those as the complement in either the accusative (predominantly) or sometimes the dative or genitive cases, and the adjunct usually in the dative or sometimes genitive cases. This establishes a functional hierarchy of clausal function, with the subject taking precedence over the complement over the adjunct.[54] The subject is the grammaticalized subject of the clause and usually linked ideationally to the actor of the process, whereas the complement is usually linked to its goal, and the adjunct to the circumstances (correlating clausal components of the interpersonal and ideational metafunctions).

As already mentioned, participant relations are not of themselves rhetorical. However, from the previous description, one can see that there are interpretive possibilities of examining participant relations and their rhetorical effect within the Greek of the New Testament. I cite two examples that illustrate the rhetorical effectiveness of participant relations in Greek.

---

[52] See Stephen C. Levinson, *Pragmatics*, CTL (Cambridge: Cambridge University Press, 1983), 69; Porter, "Register in the Greek," 223; and Porter and O'Donnell, *Discourse Analysis*, ch. 5, where a much fuller exposition of person involvement is offered. For general comments (not all of them to be relied upon for the Greek of the New Testament), see Anna Siewierska, *Person*, CTL (Cambridge: Cambridge University Press, 2004).

[53] Halliday, IFG4, 336–55. For discussion of ergativity in the Greek verbal system (in particular how it applies to the middle and passive voice forms), see Porter and O'Donnell, "Greek Verbal Network"; and extended further in Mathewson, *Voice and Mood*, 25–50; Bryan W. Y. Fletcher, *Voice in the Greek of the New Testament* (PhD diss., McMaster Divinity College, 2020).

[54] See Porter and O'Donnell, *Discourse Analysis*, ch. 5.

The "son of man." One of the most noteworthy instances in the New Testament to examine the possible rhetorical effect of participant reference is the nominal group "son of man." There has been much debate about this word group.[55] These questions have revolved around whether it is or is not a recognizable Greek phrasing, its relationship to Aramaic meanings and usage, the classification of examples, the likelihood that Jesus used one or more of these types of uses, and what Jesus might have meant by using this nomenclature, if he indeed did use it. This is not the place to go into detail regarding the use of "son of man" phrasing within the Gospels, except to say that the phrase may be unusual in the collocation of these specific lexemes, but the syntactical configuration is recognizable and in fact standard Greek (it follows the pattern of the so-called adjectival attributive genitive).[56] If there is a consensus to be found on the issues, it is that, in at least some of the instances, Jesus used this phrasing and that, in at least some of these instances, he was referring to himself and, finally, that in at least some of these self-referring instances, he was invoking imagery of the one like a son of man in Dan. 7:13.

Whether these conclusions are right or whether the entire issue should be formulated in this way, I leave aside at this point. However, the rhetorical linguistic effect of such usage has probably not been as fully appreciated as it might be. There has been some discussion on whether this is a circumlocution that Jesus uses to refer to himself. At least in part, this discussion asks the question of the rhetorical effect of the use of the phrasing. There is, however, much more to this usage than that. We know from some Synoptic parallels that Jesus is recorded as referring to himself with the first-person pronoun where other parallels use the term "son of man" (Mt. 16:13 and Mt. 8:27; Lk. 6:22 and Mt. 5:11; Lk. 12:8 and Mt. 10:32). This shift between third person and first person stands at the heart of much of the discussion of the meaning and use of this word group—although most who debate the usage do not discuss it in relation to the interpersonal metafunctional implications.

For the sake of discussion, let us agree that Jesus uses the phrasing "son of man," even if he is referring to himself as the one who is the "son of man." By doing so, he refers to himself in the third person.[57] As I already noted, the use of the third person distances the participant from the speaker and other participants. This is a means of creating linguistic distance in the text between the speaker–addressee and others. One might well ask what the rhetorical effect of such a formulation might be, even with Jesus using such language. In Mk 14:62 (and parallels), we have a good example of the possible explicit rhetorical formulation and its response. In Jesus's trial before the Sanhedrin, the high priest asks

---

[55] I discuss some of this in Stanley E. Porter, *Sacred Tradition in the New Testament: Tracing Old Testament Themes in the Gospels and Epistles* (Grand Rapids: Baker, 2016), 51–77, where support is given for some of the exegetical decisions; and Porter, *New Testament Theology and the Greek Language: A Linguistic Reconceptualization* (Cambridge: Cambridge University Press, 2022), 246–78.

[56] See Stanley E. Porter, "The Adjectival Attributive Genitive in the New Testament: A Grammatical Study," *TJ* NS 4 (1983): 3–17; and now Porter, *New Testament Theology*, 259–77.

[57] On some possible theological implications of illeism, see Roderick Elledge, *Use of the Third Person for Self-Reference by Jesus and Yahweh: A Study of Illeism in the Bible and Ancient Near Eastern Texts and Its Implications for Christology*, LNTS 575 (London: Bloomsbury T&T Clark, 2017).

him, "Are you the Christ/Messiah, the son of the blessed one [that is, God]? (σὺ εἶ ὁ Χριστὸς ὁ υἱὸς τοῦ εὐλογητοῦ;)" (Mk 14:61).[58] Jesus answers him, "I am (ἐγώ εἰμι)" (Mk 14:62). We note Jesus's use of the first person singular personal pronoun (at least in the Greek text, which we are discussing). This use makes clear that Jesus is including himself as direct participant in the positive response to the high priest. However, he then goes on to cite a combination of Ps. 110:1 and Dan. 7:13: "and you can expect to see the son of man seated at the right hand of power and coming with the clouds of heaven (καὶ ὄψεσθε τὸν υἱὸν τοῦ ἀνθρώπου ἐκ δεξιῶν καθήμενον τῆς δυνάμεως καὶ ἐρχόμενον μετὰ τῶν νεφελῶν τοῦ οὐρανοῦ)" (Mk 14:62). Jesus uses the phrasing "son of man" (τὸν υἱὸν τοῦ ἀνθρώπου) because that is what is found in Dan. 7:13 (with the New Testament's typical formulation as articular nominal group ὁ υἱὸς τοῦ ἀνθρώπου, "the son of the man," in the accusative case). However, I think that we might well see that the rhetorical impact is (so to speak) to place Jesus, on the basis of his use of "I am," firmly on the shoulders of the "son of man," who is riding triumphantly on God's right hand as he comes to judge the world. Even though the use of the third person distances the participant linguistically, in this case, the distance creates a more powerful effect because of the image that is created of one coming in triumph to judge humanity, God's co-equal in position and power. I cannot prove this, but I think that if Jesus had reformulated this as "you will see me seated at the right hand of power," the effect would have been reduced, because the inclusion of the image with the speaker would have detracted from its apocalyptic visionary dimension. What I do know is that, at least according to the Gospel account (found in all the Synoptics), the high priest realizes the claim that is being made. He tears his robe and accuses Jesus of blasphemy.

Letter form. A second example of participant reference is found in the letter form. I will use an example from one of Paul's letters, although this pattern is followed in similar ways in the other letters of the New Testament as well. In all the openings of his letters, Paul refers to himself (whether he includes a co-sender or not) in a full reference in the nominative case, often expanded by means of elaboration. For example, in Rom. 1:1, Paul styles himself as "Paul, servant of Christ Jesus, called apostle, designated for the gospel of God … (Παῦλος δοῦλος Χριστοῦ Ἰησοῦ, κλητὸς ἀπόστολος, ἀφωρισμένος εἰς εὐαγγέλιον θεοῦ)." In 1 Cor. 1:1, the opening ascription is "Paul, called apostle of Christ Jesus through the will of God, and Sosthenes the brother … (Παῦλος κλητὸς ἀπόστολος Χριστοῦ Ἰησοῦ διὰ θελήματος θεοῦ, καὶ Σωσθένης ὁ ἀδελφός)." There is a similar pattern in all thirteen Pauline letters. However, the way that the recipients are grammaticalized varies. In the personal letters, such as 1 Timothy, 2 Timothy, Titus, and Philemon, the address is made to the respective recipient using the dative case with the full reference by name.[59] Thus, the letter is written from Paul "to Timothy (Τιμοθέῳ)" (1 Tim. 1:2; 2 Tim. 1:2), "to Titus (Τίτῳ)" (Tit. 1:4), and "to Philemon … and Aphia … and Archippus … and the church in your house (Φιλήμονι … καὶ Ἀπφίᾳ … καὶ Ἀρχίππῳ … καὶ τῇ κατ' οἶκόν

---

[58] I note that the clause could be a declaration rather than a question. This reflects an interpretive decision. For the sake of discussion, I treat it as an open question. My decision is probably well-grounded as it is unlikely that the high priest wishes to make such an assertion unless it is done ironically or sarcastically.
[59] See further discussion of this feature of Paul's letters in Stanley E. Porter, *The Pastoral Epistles: A Commentary on the Greek Text* (Grand Rapids: Baker, forthcoming), loc cit.

σου ἐκκλησίᾳ)" (Phlm. 1-2), with various kinds of elaboration of the name. However, in the church letters, the recipients are grammaticalized with slight variation in wordings as either "the church of or in ..." or "those who are in ..."

There are three important points to note here related to rhetorical effect. The first is that Paul uses salutations that are very similar to the epistolary style of the first century AD, in which the formula was "X to Y, greetings." Paul expands either the designation of himself or occasionally of the recipients, but the basic form is the same, so there is an expectation created based upon the commonality. The second observation is that there is a rhetorical effect of the shift from the nominative case of the sender to the dative case of the recipient. The effect of the shift in grammatical case is to downgrade in some way the status of the recipient. The one in the nominative is the subject who is the addresser. The addresser in the nominative is addressing the addressee or respondent in the dative, who is the recipient. The third point to note is that the phrasing used of the recipients also downgrades some of the recipients further by the phrasing itself. This is seen in the phrase "those who are in ..." Rather than referring to them as the church or churches in a particular city or area, they are seen simply as those who "are," with their city designation as a modifier of the head term of the nominal word group.

Evaluation

Evaluation is concerned with comment upon and evaluation of the participants and processes involved in the discourse as realized in the text. Evaluation is a difficult category, as it has taken on a wider scope in SFL than other semantic features realized in the lexicogrammar. Appraisal Theory, as it has been developed by Martin and White (previously mentioned), includes semantic systems realized by both grammatical and especially lexical features and is closely related to what I am calling evaluation but is probably better treated as parts of several different metafunctions (and hence is a much broader concept). Appraisal Theory is a recent addition to the repertoire of SFL, and so it has not been widely incorporated into New Testament research and exegesis. The first monograph-length study that I know of is James Dvorak's *The Interpersonal Metafunction in 1 Corinthians 1–4*. In this important volume, he defines a form of interpersonal discourse analysis based around the interpersonal metafunction in SFL. He draws upon Appraisal Theory to be able to analyze the intersubjective stance within a text. This involves modeling the three systems of attitude, engagement, and graduation within the theory, drawing upon both grammatical and especially lexical elements. With this framework in place, Dvorak then studies 1 Corinthians 1–4 according to its epistolary organization to see how Paul "takes up stances relative to the entities, propositions, or proposals referenced in the text."[60] Zachary Dawson emphasizes modality (the mood system) in modeling what he calls Negotiation (see previous comments), among other features.[61] There will no doubt be much more development of Appraisal Theory and related areas in New Testament Greek studies.

---

[60]Dvorak, *Interpersonal Metafunction*, 94. See also Dvorak, "Prodding with Prosody," 85–120; Dvorak, "To Incline Another's Heart," 599–624; Dvorak, "Ask and Ye Shall Position," 196–245.
[61]Dawson, "Language as Negotiation," 362–90; and Dawson, "Rules of 'Engagement,'" 155–95.

My focus here, however, is upon the narrower concept of evaluation, for the sake of clarity and precision. I do not attempt to provide a survey of all the possible ways in which appraisal may be made within a Greek text. I think that evaluation, if it is to be used most effectively, must be thoroughly integrated into the semantics and lexicogrammar of the language, and in particular into the interpersonal metafunction. I will attempt to do that here, even if in a brief way, by concentrating on evaluation that does not depend upon lexis. As a part of the lexicogrammaticalization of rhetoric, evaluation involves several different types of constructions. Evaluation "can be simply defined as the indication of whether the speaker thinks that something (a person, thing, action, event, situation, idea, etc.) is good or bad."[62] The speaker may be the biblical author or may be a participant in the biblical account, especially in the Gospels. There have not been many attempts to define scales of evaluation (as there have been for appraisal), but unless these can be firmly embedded within the lexicogrammar, they are often based simply upon subjective evaluation of the posited force of various lexemes (probably better handled within the ideational metafunction).[63] So, here I am concerned with various lexicogrammatical means of evaluation that are not necessarily fully integrated as components within the clausal structure, but that are used to comment upon or evaluate what is said in the clausal construction (whether major or minor). In other words, such elements are often not part of the core components (subject, predicator, and complement) of a clause. These include qualitative evaluation by means of a supplemental clausal adjunct, intensification by means of a supplemental clausal adjunct, or subjective evaluation by means of empty clauses (e.g., "it is necessary," "it is lawful/permitted"). These means of evaluation often draw upon linguistic resources found within the Louw-Nida lexicon in LN domain 70, Real, Unreal; LN domain 71, Mode; LN domain 72, True, False; LN domain 73, Genuine, Phony; LN domain 78, Degree; and LN domain 88, Moral and Ethical Qualities and Related Behavior.[64] I will give examples of each of the three types of evaluation to illustrate their relation to rhetoric.

Qualitative Evaluation

Qualitative evaluation is used by the author/speaker to render a qualitative comment or evaluation of an event, usually good or bad.

---

[62]Thompson, *Introducing Functional Grammar*, 75. Thompson is actually referring to appraisal, which he places within the interpersonal metafunction, but I have appropriated his quotation for evaluation.

[63]In Appraisal Theory, scales of evaluation are handled within the sub-system of Graduation, which concerns how meanings can be up-scaled and down-scaled. Meanings can be scaled in terms of their force (i.e., intensity or amount) or their focus (i.e., preciseness). Martin and White explain that graduation "operates as phenomena are scaled by reference to the degree to which they match some supposed core or exemplary instance of a semantic category" (*Language of Evaluation*, 137). According to Dvorak, as he has modeled Appraisal Theory for New Testament Greek, the rhetorical effect of scaling pertains to the language user's commitment to the value position at hand so that up-scaling the intensity or precision around propositions or proposals construes the writer as highly committed to the value position being advanced, and down-scaling in the same ways indicates the writer is less invested in the value position ("Prodding with Prosody," 102–3). Cf. Dvorak, *Interpersonal Metafunction*, 86–90.

[64]See Johannes P. Louw and Eugene A. Nida, *Greek–English Lexicon of the New Testament Based on Semantic Domains* (LN), 2 vols. (New York: United Bible Societies, 1988). However, not all the elements listed within each of these domains are pertinent, especially if they are adjectives used in nominal word groups. I make use of examples cited in the lexicon.

Matthew 15:7: καλῶς ἐπροφήτευσεν περὶ ὑμῶν Ἡσαΐας. "Isaiah *accurately/correctly/ rightly* (καλῶς) prophesied concerning you," or "Isaiah was right when he prophesied about you" (LN trans.). In this instance, the adverb as adjunct is thematized as prime by being placed first in the clausal structure (preceded only by a vocative element that falls outside of clausal structure). The result is to provide a positive evaluation of Isaiah's prophesying.

Galatians 4:17: ζηλοῦσιν ὑμᾶς οὐ καλῶς. "They are zealous for you, but *not well* (οὐ καλῶς)," with the adjunct providing a negative qualitative comment on their good or bad intentions. The clausal construction may be analyzed several ways. οὐ καλῶς may be a polar negative adjunct with the negated adverb and used almost as a tag to the clause provided by the author to evaluate the claim of zealousness. But it may also be a polar negative minor clause, negatively elaboratively evaluating the primary clause.

Acts 25:10: ὡς καὶ σὺ κάλλιον ἐπιγινώσκεις. "As you yourself know *exceedingly well* (κάλλιον)," with the comparative form of the adjective as head term of an adjunct indicating the evaluative circumstances and heightening the degree of evaluative comment.

1 Corinthians 15:34: ἐκνήψατε δικαίως καὶ μὴ ἁμαρτάνετε. "Come to your senses, *rightly* (δικαίως), and don't sin," with the adverb as adjunct providing an evaluative comment on the right course of action.

Philippians 1:17: οἱ δὲ ἐξ ἐριθείας τὸν Χριστὸν καταγγέλλουσιν, οὐχ ἁγνῶς. "Some out of strife proclaim Christ, *not sincerely* (οὐχ ἁγνῶς)." As in the earlier example (Gal. 4:17), the clausal construction may be variously analyzed. οὐχ ἁγνῶς may be a polar negative adjunct with the negative adverb used as a tag to evaluate this proclamation. But it may also be a polar negative minor clause, negatively elaboratively evaluating the primary clause.

Matthew 15:22: ἡ θυγάτηρ μου κακῶς δαιμονίζεται. "My daughter is demon-possessed, *badly* (κακῶς)," with the father interjecting his own commentary on the condition of his daughter by means of the adverb as adjunct.

Intensification

Intensification is used by the author/speaker to render an emphatic comment or evaluation of an event. There are varying degrees of intensity, but most instances of them provide means of endorsing by singling out the event for emphatic comment. There is also the use of various lexicogrammatical devices to de-intensify an event. Both are exemplified here.

1 Corinthians 5:1: ὅλως ἀκούεται ἐν ὑμῖν πορνεία. "Porneia is, *indeed/really/actually* (ὅλως), reported among you," which use of the evaluative adverb as adjunct rhetorically intensifies the observation regarding the report. The adjunct is thematized in prime position.

Mark 4:41: τίς ἄρα οὗτός ἐστιν …; "Who *indeed* (ἄρα) is this one?," with the particle used intensively to provide the speaker's/author's evaluation of the event. This particle is often used conjunctively, but even in doing so it is often intensive.

Matthew 24:45: τίς ἄρα ἐστὶν ὁ πιστὸς δοῦλος …; "Who *indeed* (ἄρα) is the faithful servant …?" with the particle used as in Mk 4:41.

Acts 12:18: τί ἄρα ὁ Πέτρος ἐγένετο. "What *indeed* (ἄρα) Peter had done," with the particle intensifying the clause, and not just the reference to Peter.

Luke 20:13: πέμψω τὸν υἱόν μου τὸν ἀγαπητόν· ἴσως τοῦτον ἐντραπήσονται. "I will send my beloved son; *equally* (ἴσως) will they respect him," with the use of the adjunct thematized in prime position indicating high probability by the speaker.

Acts 28:4: πάντως φονεύς ἐστιν ὁ ἄνθρωπος οὗτος. "This person is *completely* (πάντως) a murderer," with the adjunct with the adverbial form of the adjective thematized in prime position for intensification.

Romans 5:7: μόλις γὰρ ὑπὲρ δικαίου τις ἀποθανεῖται· ὑπὲρ γὰρ τοῦ ἀγαθοῦ τάχα τις καὶ τολμᾷ ἀποθανεῖν. "For, *hardly*, for a good person will someone die; for the good person someone may, *possibly/perhaps* (τάχα), dare to die." There are two uses of de-intensification in these two clauses. The first is thematized as the prime, while the second follows the thematized prepositional phrase in prime position. One sees that de-intensification is a form of intensification, by intensifying the minimizing of the event.

Matthew 5:18: ἀμὴν γὰρ λέγω ὑμῖν ... "For, *truly*, (ἀμήν) I say to you ...," with the use of the fixed form ἀμήν as thematized and prime position adjunct to indicate a strong endorsement by Jesus and hence by the author.

John 1:51: ἀμὴν ἀμὴν λέγω ὑμῖν ... "*Truly truly* (ἀμὴν ἀμήν), I say to you ...," or perhaps "I am telling you the solemn truth" (LN trans.). The Johannine author often uses the doubled fixed form, also thematized in prime position, to intensify a statement.

Matthew 2:16: τότε Ἡρῴδης ἰδὼν ὅτι ἐνεπαίχθη ὑπὸ τῶν μάγων ἐθυμώθη λίαν. "Then Herod, seeing that he had been deceived by the magi, became angry, *indeed* (λίαν)," with the particle as adjunct used to intensity the emotion.

Acts 20:38: ὀδυνώμενοι μάλιστα ἐπὶ τῷ λέγῳ. "Being grieved, *very much so* (μάλιστα), at the word," in which the adverb as adjunct indicates the intensification of the grief.

Acts 20:12: ἤγαγον δὲ τὸν παῖδα ζῶντα, καὶ παρεκλήθησαν οὐ μετρίως. "They took the child alive, and were comforted, *not moderately* (οὐ μετρίως)." The polar negative adjunct intensifies the degree of comfort, with the adjunct placed almost as a tag of the clause.

Luke 23:10: εἱστήκεισαν ... εὐτόνως κατηγοροῦντες αὐτοῦ. "They stood ... accusing him *vigorously/vehemently/strongly* (εὐτόνως)." The adverb itself is intensified with its prefix.

Acts 18:28: εὐτόνως γὰρ τοῖς Ἰουδαίοις διακατηλώγχετο δημοσίᾳ. "He refuted the Jews *vigorously/vehemently/strongly* (εὐτόνως) in public," with the author providing evaluative comment upon Apollos's actions. This example shows the difference between an adjunct used to intensify (εὐτόνως) and one used to indicate local circumstance (δημοσίᾳ).

Matthew 2:10: ἐχάρησαν χαρὰν μεγάλην σφόδρα. "They were made to rejoice with great joy, *exceedingly* (σφόδρα)," or "they rejoiced even more exceedingly" (LN trans.). The adjunct functions to intensify the entire statement, while the defining adjective "great" (μεγάλην) only provides positive comment on the size of the joy.

Revelation 16:21: ὅτι μεγάλη ἐστὶν ἡ πληγὴ αὐτῆς σφόδρα. "Because her plague is great, *exceedingly* (σφόδρα)," with the authorial comment upon it. This example is similar to a previous one (Mt. 2:10), but with the adjective as complement in the clause and only providing comment upon the plague.

Luke 11:53: ἤρξαντο οἱ γραμματεῖς καὶ οἱ Φαρισαῖοι δεινῶς ἐνέχειν. "The scribes and the Pharisees began to criticize *terribly/frightfully* (δεινῶς)," indicating intense criticism.

1 Corinthians 15:6: ἔπειτα ὤφθη ἐπάνω πεντακοσίοις ἀδελφοῖς ἐφάπαξ. "Then he was seen at one time by five hundred brothers, *in fact more than* (ἐπάνω)," with the use of the adjunct commenting upon the degree of intensification. There is a contrast between the adjunct used to intensify (ἐπάνω) and the one used to indicate circumstantial frequency (ἐφάπαξ).

The so-called conditional particle, ἄν (and occasional variant ἐάν), is used to de-intensify an event.[65]

Mark 6:56: ὅπου ἂν εἰσεπορεύετο εἰς κώμας ἢ εἰς πόλεις. "*Wherever* (ἄν) he was entering into villages or into cities," where the use of ἄν as adjunct with the adjunct ὅπου used of place de-intensifies the specificity of the reference.

Matthew 23:16: ὃς ἂν ὀμόσῃ ἐν τῷ ναῷ. "*Whoever* (ἄν) might swear in the temple," where the use of ἄν with the relative pronoun de-intensifies the reference so as to form what is sometimes called a conditional-like protasis statement.

Luke 7:39: οὗτος εἰ ἦν προφήτης, ἐγίνωσκεν ἄν. "This one, if he were a prophet, *would* know (ἄν)," with the particle used to formulate the second-class conditional evaluation—this is contrary to fact (a sub-class with less certainty than the first class).

1 Corinthians 16:6: ἵνα ὑμεῖς με προπέμψητε οὗ ἐὰν πορεύωμαι. "So that you yourself might send me *wherever* (ἐάν) I might go," with the use of ἐάν with the subjunctive.

Subjective Evaluation

Subjective evaluation is provided by empty clauses that provide either positive or negative evaluation by the speaker/author of an event. Several verbs are used in this way to indicate possibility and levels of obligation, according to the perspective of the speaker/author.

Acts 2:29: ἐξὸν εἰπεῖν μετὰ παρρησίας πρὸς ὑμᾶς περὶ τοῦ πατριάρχου Δαυίδ. "*It being possible* (ἐξόν) to speak with boldness to you concerning the patriarch David." The possible accusative absolute of the verb often translated "it is possible/permissible" (ἔξεστι) is used to mark the author/speaker's evaluation of the advisability of speaking boldly about what he thinks the audience should know.

Matthew 12:2: οἱ μαθηταί σου ποιοῦσιν ὃ οὐκ ἔξεστιν ποιεῖν ἐν σαββάτῳ. "Your disciples are doing *what is* not *permitted* (ἔξεστιν) to do on the Sabbath," that is, the evaluation is provided for what is or is not allowed on the Sabbath.

Luke 12:12: τὸ γὰρ ἅγιον πνεῦμα διδάξει ὑμᾶς ἐν αὐτῇ τῇ ὥρᾳ ἃ δεῖ εἰπεῖν. "For the Holy Spirit will teach you in this hour what *it is necessary* (δεῖ) to say," that is, "what you should say," subjectively evaluated as positive or necessary.

---

[65] See Stanley E. Porter, *Idioms of the Greek New Testament*, 2nd ed. (Sheffield: Sheffield Academic, 1994), 206, on why this is better called a conditional than a modal particle.

Matthew 18:33: οὐκ ἔδει καὶ σὲ ἐλεῆσαι τὸν σύνδουλόν σου …; "*Was it not necessary* (ἔδει) for you to show mercy to your fellow servant …?," with the empty clause providing a subjective evaluation of the action as merited: "should you not have …?"

Matthew 23:23: ταῦτα ἔδει ποιῆσαι κἀκεῖνα μὴ ἀφιέναι. "*It was necessary* (ἔδει) to do these things and not to neglect those things," that is, "you ought to do this …"

Acts 27:21: ἔδει μέν, ὦ ἄνδρες, πειθαρχήσαντάς μοι, μὴ ἀνάγεσθαι ἀπὸ τῆς Κρήτης. "*It was necessary* (ἔδει), men, being obedient to me, not to sail from Crete," that is, "you should have been obedient …"

James 3:10: οὐ χρή, ἀδελφοί μου, ταῦτα οὕτως γίνεσθαι. "*it is not necessary* (χρή), my brothers, that these things should come about," that is, "these things should not happen."

1 Corinthians 4:8: καὶ ὄφελόν γε ἐβασιλεύσατε. "And *would that* (ὄφελον) you were ruling," with the use of the participle form as an empty clause to indicate subjective desire.

2 Corinthians 11:1: ὄφελον ἀνείχεσθέ μου μικρόν τι ἀφροσύνης. "*Would that* (ὄφελον) you were sharing with me a little foolishness," that is, "I wish that you were …"

There are three types of evaluation that I have identified for their rhetorical evaluative function within the interpersonal metafunction of Greek. There no doubt may be more, and they are separate from other forms of evaluative language based upon lexical meaning. Each one of the examples that I have used here is a means of either qualifying, intensifying, or subjectively evaluating the participants and processes of a clause in its interpersonal semantics.

CONCLUSION

This chapter has attempted to examine rhetoric and persuasion from a linguistic perspective, in particular to model its place within SFL, and to explore some of its implications for interpretation of the New Testament. Even though both rhetoric and linguistics have purportedly been primarily concerned with the functions of language, the two fields have been studiously kept separate within most academic and intellectual discourse. Rhetoric has been a topic of widespread attention within New Testament studies over the last thirty to forty years, as well as continuing to be important within other textual studies. Although initial enthusiasm for various types of rhetorical criticism has apparently abated in more recent New Testament scholarship, that does not mean that there is not a place for consideration of questions of rhetoric. Rhetoric is primarily concerned with persuasion, a function of language that may be expressed by various lexicogrammatical means. Some scholars within SFL have made a conscious attempt to bring the two, rhetoric and linguistics, into a form of interpretive harmony. This has not been easy, because of definitional and applicational problems. SFL has found it difficult to place rhetoric within SFL architecture. More problematic, however, is that SFL has had a developing and expanding conception of the role of various rhetorical functions, such as appraisal and negotiation. I believe that we should reconceive the notion of rhetoric and model it within the interpersonal metafunction. As I have attempted to show in this chapter, a SFL approach to rhetoric demands that rhetoric be stratified, and even structuralized, within the language hierarchy, so that we can understand the role that it plays within the situational context, the semantics, and lexicogrammar of the language. Even though I have on previous occasions opposed the application of categories of ancient rhetoric within New Testament studies, and continue to do so, I believe that there is a place, if it is rightly conceived and modeled, for a robust theory of rhetoric within a linguistic framework of interpretation, especially that of SFL.

CHAPTER FIVE

Defining Cognition through Systemic Functional Linguistics System Networks and the Greek of the New Testament

INTRODUCTION

The relationship of cognition to Systemic Functional Linguistics (SFL) and hence to the study of the New Testament has been a relatively underexplored area, at least until recently.[1] The major reason is that SFL is a functional approach to language, quite possibly one of the most strictly functional theories that has been developed.[2] Functional linguistics, at least traditionally, has placed its emphasis upon the notion of language in use, that is, upon how language is used by speakers as it is found in naturally occurring instances within a variety of actual contexts. The result is the development of a variety of linguistic theories, some of them more and some less pertinent for some languages, because of the recognition that functional theories of language are based upon actual usage, with all its intriguing and provocative anomalies. Thus, functional linguistics is opposed to various types of so-called formal linguistic theories in which linguistic competence is given priority over linguistic performance. Linguistic performance, with all its necessary and unavoidable messiness, is not as highly valued in formal linguistics for the insight that it might provide into what constitutes linguistic competence. Competence, for much formal linguistics, is directly related to the innate language capacity that is shared by every human being. Hence, according to formal linguists, various formal linguistic

---

[1] The major work in SFL that addresses cognition, or perhaps better inserts cognition into SFL in an explicit way, is M. A. K. Halliday and Christian M. I. M. Matthiessen, *Construing Experience through Meaning: A Language-Based Approach to Cognition* (London: Continuum, 1999). This volume has had an influence upon the general direction of some major parts of SFL. See Chapter Three for discussion of some of those related to grammatical metaphor.
[2] See Robert D. Van Valin Jr. and Randy J. LaPolla, *Syntax: Structure, Meaning and Function*, CTL (Cambridge: Cambridge University Press, 1997), 12, where they characterize Systemic Functional Grammar as "perhaps the most radical discourse-pragmatic view, a 'top-down' analytic model which starts with discourse and works 'down' to lower levels of grammatical structure."

structures may have differences in surface expression, but numerous language universals, in fact a Universal Grammar, underlie these surface anomalies. The primary interest for formal linguistics is in the underlying common grammar, sometimes represented as being a universal grammar that is hard-wired into every human being. There are of course different functional approaches to language, and they all have differences among them. Nevertheless, some of the major lines of difference between functionalism and formalism can be seen in this brief description (see Chapter Two for more detailed discussion).

I use this opposition between SFL and Chomskyan linguistics to address the question of cognition and linguistics. To do so, I begin with a short summary of some major elements of Cognitive Linguistics, because Cognitive Linguistics has come to be associated, at least in the minds of many (including many biblical scholars), with language and cognition. I wish to challenge that cognition is the rightful domain only of Cognitive Linguistics and suggest that there are other ways of thinking of cognition that involve SFL. To do this, I will briefly discuss Cognitive Linguistics and then turn to the broader question of what constitutes cognition. These topics provide the basis for my suggestions of how SFL may provide a better linguistic theory for addressing questions of cognition and language.

THE RISE OF COGNITIVE LINGUISTICS AND THE QUESTION OF COGNITION

Cognitive Linguistics emerged in the 1970s out of growing dissatisfaction with especially formal linguistics, although in many ways Chomskyan-derived linguistics is cognitive in nature (some would perhaps say that it is psychological in nature). What became Cognitive Linguistics was developed out of the rise of the cognitive sciences in the 1960s and 1970s (as well as earlier Gestalt psychology, which dates back to the first half of the twentieth century).[3] There were a number of linguists who helped to pioneer what has come to be known as Cognitive Linguistics, although Cognitive Linguistics is less a clear theory of language as one might find in formal linguistics than it is what has been called a "movement" or an "enterprise."[4] The major intellectual figure who is credited with defining the major contours of Cognitive Linguistics is the linguist Ronald Langacker, who wrote an important, fundamental two volume work, *Foundations of Cognitive Grammar* (1987, 1991).[5]

---

[3]See, for example, the essays in Lila R. Gleitman and Mark Liberman, eds., *An Invitation to Cognitive Science: Language*, 2nd ed. (Cambridge, MA: MIT Press, 1995); cf. James P. Spradley, ed., *Culture and Cognition: Rules, Maps, and Plans* (San Francisco: Chandler, 1972); Lucia Vaina and Jaakko Hintikka, eds., *Cognitive Constraints on Communication: Representations and Processes* (Dordrecht: Reidel, 1984); and Jan Nuyts and Eric Pederson, eds., *Language and Conceptualization* (Cambridge: Cambridge University Press, 1997). For principles of Gestalt psychology, see Wolfgang Köhler, *Gestalt Psychology: An Introduction to New Concepts in Modern Psychology* (New York: Liveright, 1947), where he treats, among others, such subjects as dynamism (rather than mechanistic views of behavior), organization of the senses, and entities, behavior, association, and recall, all of which have correlates in Cognitive Linguistics.

[4]Vyvyan Evans and Melanie Green, *Cognitive Linguistics: An Introduction* (Edinburgh: Edinburgh University Press, 2006), 3. I am dependent on their introduction for my brief introduction here (3–4). Cf. William Croft and D. Alan Cruse, *Cognitive Linguistics*, CTL (Cambridge: Cambridge University Press, 2004), 1–4. For more discussion of Cognitive Linguistics, see Chapter Two.

[5]Ronald W. Langacker, *Foundations of Cognitive Grammar*, 2 vols. (Stanford, CA: Stanford University Press, 1987–91). See also Langacker, *Cognitive Grammar: A Basic Introduction* (Oxford: Oxford University Press, 2008).

Cognitive Linguistics has come to be categorized by several major defining principles, each of which helps to distinguish the cognitive linguistic movement from formal linguistics. According to one account of these fundamental notions, there are two widely held principles: the Generalization Commitment and the Cognitive Commitment. The Generalization Commitment is firmly opposed to the kind of categorization that is found in formal linguistics, in which language is divided into discrete components, such as phonology, morphology, syntax, semantics, and pragmatics, each one with theoretically basic structures and quite possibly different rules operating on each. Cognitive Linguistics instead sees overriding principles operative across language, to the point that there are lots of fuzzy boundaries and family resemblances among categories, with the result that polysemy characterizes human language. As a consequence, metaphor is a central notion in Cognitive Linguistics, as it unites and extends across various features of language.[6] The Cognitive Commitment holds that views of linguistics should reflect the latest findings in the areas of the cognitive sciences with regard to the functioning of the human brain. One of the most important of these views is that Cognitive Linguistics rejects the Chomskyan notion of a separate language module within the human brain.[7] Thus the structures of language are not formal as part of this module but are symbolic structures associated with cognitive processing, which can understand similar things in a variety of ways. The role of metaphor has become one of the best known areas of Cognitive Linguistics, following work pioneered by George Lakoff, Mark Johnson, and others.[8]

Cognitive Linguistics has made significant inroads into a variety of areas of research, including biblical studies, besides the general field of linguistics.[9] There are several points of potential overlap between Cognitive Linguistics and SFL. They have in common their emphases upon: (1) both the communicative function of language and the social functions of language, in which language is first a means of communication to perform various social functions before it is a set of rules; (2) the grammatical features of a language reflecting the functions to which it is put; (3) an integrated approach to the structure of language, including semantics and grammar, rather than a modular approach that distinguishes these structural categories; (4) what has been called a functional-typological approach to language rather than arguing for Universal Grammar, in which the use of language dictates the typology; (5) some form of linguistic determinism (the Sapir-Whorf hypothesis), although SFL probably has a stronger form of it than does Cognitive Linguistics (both reject the strong or hard form of linguistic determinism); and (6) any language universals

---

[6] Evans and Green, *Cognitive Linguistics*, 28–40. Cf. Croft and Cruse, *Cognitive Linguistics*, 1, who refer to three guiding principles: "language is not an autonomous cognitive faculty," "grammar is conceptualization," and "knowledge of language emerges from language use."

[7] Evans and Green, *Cognitive Linguistics*, 40–3.

[8] The work that concretized and incited discussion within Cognitive Linguistics, and within a much broader sphere of inquiry, is George Lakoff and Mark Johnson, *Metaphors We Live By* (Chicago: University of Chicago Press, 1980). For discussion of other important works in conceptual metaphor theory and its various progeny, see Chapter Three.

[9] Besides the extensive list of works cited in Chapter Two in my survey of linguistic schools, see Ellen van Wolde, *Reframing Biblical Studies: When Language and Text Meet Culture, Cognition, and Context* (Winona Lake, IN: Eisenbrauns, 2009).

being regularized patterns or generalizations based upon usage, rather than being based upon universal rules.[10] As a result, there has been some research inside and outside of New Testament studies that has explored some of these intersections, but these are the exception rather than the rule. For example, though Michael Halliday (1925–2018) and Christian Matthiessen frame their *Construing Experience through Meaning* as making a contribution to general linguistics, and in particular cognitive science, they also make sure that they mark out differences between their approach and Cognitive Linguistics.[11]

I do not wish to undertake in this chapter such an integrative endeavor between Cognitive Linguistics and SFL or even to venture into Cognitive Linguistics per se. I wish to engage in the much more confined and circumscribed task of exploring how SFL might play a role in defining cognition, at least as I am defining it. I will do this by drawing upon the notion of system networks within SFL. System networks are a fundamental part of SFL architecture, and I believe they have a larger role to play simply than as a heuristic device to display language potential. But first I must define cognition. After defining cognition, I will examine the role of SFL system networks, and then I will apply this networking to some examples in the New Testament.

WHAT IS COGNITION?

Before I can undertake to see how SFL system networks might play a role in examining the notion of cognition, we must undertake to define cognition. I am not a cognitive linguist, so I am sure that much of what I have said and have to say about it is subject to question, or at least suspicion. However, I think that if we reverse the process of conceptualizing the question—from the assumption of moving from cognition to language to the opposite of moving from language to cognition—we might be able to make some progress.

I begin with a few necessary generalizations (most of which are probably highly debatable, but I do not have space to argue them here). The first is that I do not deny that humans have brains, but I also think that they have minds, and that the relationship between them is one that we are far from understanding. As a result, I reject the various ways in which we have attempted to metaphorize the mind/brain relationship, including the latest major one: that the human brain (which often ends up subsuming the mind into a single entity) is a computer. The study of the metaphors used to describe the human brain is an intriguing one that I do not have space or inclination to recount, except to say that our latest metaphorization is merely the last in a series that goes back at least as far as the ancient Greeks and has involved many of the great thinkers from Augustine to Freud and beyond.[12] That the current metaphor of "brain as computer" is firmly embedded in our thinking, including that of Cognitive Linguistics, is found in the "processing" metaphor that we use to speak of what humans do when they deal with various phenomena, including language: they process it. I do not believe that the human mind/brain is a giant processor,

---

[10] Evans and Green, *Cognitive Linguistics*, 758–61. Cf. John R. Taylor, *Linguistic Categorization: Prototypes in Linguistic Theory*, 2nd ed. (Oxford: Clarendon, 1995 [1989]).

[11] Halliday and Matthiessen, *Construing Experience*, 2; cf. 565–601. Cf. Beth M. Stovell, *Mapping Metaphorical Discourse in the Fourth Gospel: John's Eternal King*, LBS 5 (Leiden: Brill, 2012), who draws upon both Cognitive Linguistics and SFL, but differentiates them as theories and their usefulness for her purposes of interpretation.

[12] See the intriguing book by Charles Hampden-Turner, *Maps of the Mind: Charts and Concepts of the Mind and Its Labyrinths* (New York: Macmillan, 1981), but who precedes the computerization of the brain.

but that, instead, computer processors are small-scale electronic devices designed to mimic the human mind/brain. Thus, I do not believe that cognition is the "processing" of information by the human being (whether brain, mind, or both).[13]

Cognition, I believe, is the human capacity to make perceptions of experience into various types of meaningful representations—in particular through human language— along with the means by which these perceptions and representations occur and are perceived and understood.[14] Thus, these meaningful representations of human language offer the reciprocal ability to determine the meaningful perceptions of experience that are responsible for them, and hence result in communication.[15] As indicated by this definition of cognition (dependent upon those in Cognitive Linguistics), there are three parts to cognition. One involves the perception of experience, including both extra-linguistic and linguistic perception, the transference of this perception into meaningful representations, that is, representations such as human speech or other examples of human language and communication, and the responsive mechanisms by which these transfers take place and are then perceived and understood. Once these transfers of experience become language, the language becomes a representation of the meaningful nature of that perception and experience.

I do not pretend that this provides a definitive, and certainly not a technical, definition of cognition. However, apart from the fact that it is more explicit than most of the definitions that I have seen, it serves my purpose of capturing cognition's essential characteristics. These are sufficient to enable us to examine cognition within a SFL framework.

SYSTEMIC FUNCTIONAL LINGUISTICS SYSTEM NETWORKS

One of the defining features of SFL is its system networks. System networks were an early means developed by Michael Halliday and others to capture and display in graphic form the meaningful paradigmatic choices made in language use. Such system networks were widely used in much SFL work until *An Introduction to Functional Grammar* was first published in 1985—without a single system network in it.[16] This marked a shift in SFL from its previous balanced paradigmatic (system) and syntagmatic (structure) approach to one that emphasized structure. I have commented elsewhere on what I think are the harmful effects that this move had on the development of SFL, including its ability (or lack thereof) to deal with several features of language.[17] I do not need to repeat those comments here. I wish instead to return to the strengths of the system networks and entertain their possible role in talking about cognition.

---

[13]As an illustration of how this metaphor can come to dominate our discussion, see Evans and Green, *Cognitive Linguistics*, 240–1. They speak of how "cognition operates *off-line*. In other words, cognitive *processing* employs mental representations (concepts) that are *stored in memory*, and thereby frees itself from the *process* of experiencing a particular phenomenon every time that experience is *accessed* and *manipulated*" (I italicize all the computer language that I am aware of; bold in original eliminated).
[14]This definition is inspired to some extent by Evans and Green, *Cognitive Linguistics*, 240.
[15]I resist using the term "reverse-engineer," for obvious reasons. Some might prefer to use the term "redound."
[16]M. A. K. Halliday, *An Introduction to Functional Grammar* (IFG1) (London: Edward Arnold, 1985).
[17]See Stanley E. Porter, "Systemic Functional Linguistics and the Greek Language: The Need for Further Modeling," in *Modeling Biblical Language: Selected Papers from the McMaster Divinity College Linguistics Circle*, ed. Stanley E. Porter, Gregory P. Fewster, and Christopher D. Land, LBS 13 (Leiden: Brill, 2016), 9–47, upon which some of which follows is dependent.

SFL has distanced itself from many other linguistic theories, as already noted in previous chapters (including much of Saussurian structuralism), but the concept of system (paradigm) remains fundamental. Within a given language, any meaningful component is part of a system of similar available choices, and these systems of choices are arranged into a network that displays the language potential. As Halliday says, "The system network is the grammar."[18] SFL sees language as a network that specifies the choices available in a given system and displays them graphically.[19] These choices are meaningful and hence SFL endorses the notion that meaning is choice.[20] Robin Fawcett, one of the formative scholars in SFL and the motivating force behind the so-called Cardiff School, calls these networks "the expression of knowledge as procedures," in which "the availability of such a [systemic] choice is always dependent on the selection of a logically prior feature."[21] There are a number of features of these system networks to note. First, movement through a network system does not imply temporal progression, but it does display a set of selected semantic features. Despite various conceivable ways of drawing the same network, each network ideally is elegant; that is, it captures the generalizations of the language and breaks them down into their constituents in the most economical and symmetrical fashion. To use a given language a speaker or writer makes certain increasingly specific semantic choices; that is, the progression is from broader to more delicate, and these constitute the necessary conditions for subsequent choices, until a specific realization is arrived at. A realization statement for a network consists of a selection expression of semantic features (therefore hierarchy is very important in systemic linguistics).[22] Second, in any given system network, not all choices are always available. Certain choices either are not possible or have never been thought necessary by the speakers of a given language. Displaying the choices in a network graphically allows the implications of choice to be grasped more firmly. Third, to display a system network is not to say that a speaker or writer actually makes a conscious choice at every juncture or node, although in some instances this might be the case, any more than any user of a language is consciously aware of everything that the user does on every occasion. This does not mean, however, that choices are not being made within the system network.

Two types of networks are to be differentiated within SFL, formal and semantic. Strictly formal networks, called by Nigel Gotteri "bogus" networks, are not bogus in the sense that they do not have validity.[23] To the contrary, their primary validity is to provide integrated networks of the formal (paradigmatic) choices available within the language

---

[18]M. A. K. Halliday, "A Brief Sketch of Systemic Grammar," in *Halliday: System and Function in Language*, ed. Gunther R. Kress (Oxford: Oxford University Press, 1976), 3–6, esp. 3.

[19]Stanley E. Porter, *Verbal Aspect in the Greek of the New Testament, with Reference to Tense and Mood*, SBG 1 (New York: Peter Lang, 1989), 8–9 for what follows.

[20]This is a statement often attributed to Charles E. Bazell, *Linguistic Form* (Istanbul: Istanbul Press, 1953), 81, and many linguists since. See Chapter Two for further discussion, especially in regard to SFL.

[21]Robin P. Fawcett, *Cognitive Linguistics and Social Interaction: Towards an Integrated Model of a Systemic Functional Grammar and the Other Components of a Communicating Mind* (Heidelberg: Julius Groos; Exeter: Exeter University, 1980), 19.

[22]See Nigel J. C. Gotteri, "Towards a Comparison of Systemic Linguistics and Tagmemics: An Interim Report and Bibliography," *Journal of the Midland Association for Linguistic Studies* NS 7 (1982): 31–42, here 34.

[23]N. J. C. Gotteri, "When Is a System Network Not a System Network? And Is That a Fair Question? Fragments from a Continuing Discussion," *Occasional Papers in Systemic Linguistics* 1 (1987): 5–14, esp. 7. They may be considered as displays of possible forms in the lexicogrammar but not as semantic systems. I note that Gotteri's work on this was done before Halliday's system networks were incorporated into his IFG3, published in 2004. Gotteri provides unique insights into system networks, whether semantic or lexicogrammatical or formal.

(e.g., the Greek tense-forms or mood forms). However, they are bogus in that they are not to be confused with "genuine" networks, including lexicogrammatical ones, based upon the semantic choices of the language, even if formally realized. Semantic networks graphically display as options the semantic potential of a given system. In this sense, system networks represent the language potential. The traditional strength of SFL has been in differentiating the two, but in emphasizing the semantic system networks over the formal graphic displays.

For the purposes of this exercise, I am going to return to a system network that I used in the previous chapter when I was discussing the topic of rhetoric and SFL. I could draw upon any number of other system networks, because these system networks are integral to SFL architecture. However, I return to the system network for Greek attitude, as I have expanded it for discussion of speech functions, because of its familiarity and usefulness for the topic here, cognition. The Greek system network for attitude is presented in Figure 5.1:

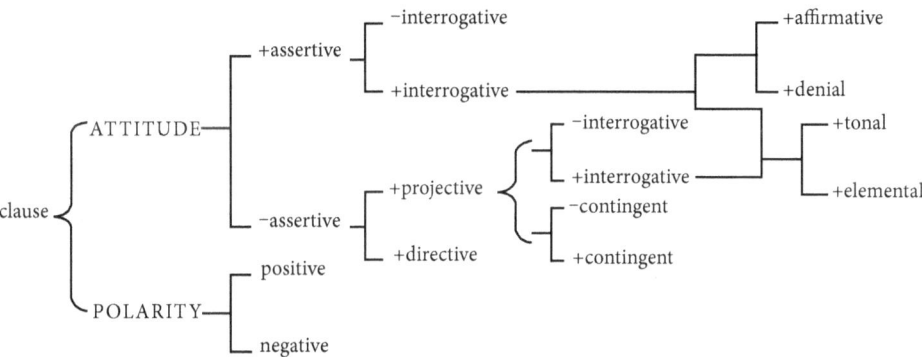

FIGURE 5.1 Systemic network of attitude including potential realizations of speech functions.[24]

I will briefly explain some of the features of this system network, because they are pertinent to our discussion of cognition. First of all, I note that I do not include realization statements for this network, although it is fairly easy to see what they might be. [+directive] is realized by the imperative, [+affirmative] by the indicative, [+projection: +contingent] by the optative, and [+projective: −contingent] by the subjunctive. The other pathways through the network provide such indications as questions ([+interrogative], and the six different varieties). There are ten major speech functions that can be derived from the attitude system expanded to indicate speech functions. Second, the formulation of this attitude system network is the system network for the lexicogrammar of the Greek language. The speech functions that are based upon them constitute the semantic stratum. Both these strata are part of the content stratum of the Greek language. Third, this system network is formulated around principles that, I believe, are important for linguistic theory-building. These include elegance, such as non-duplication of systems and single

---

[24]This system network incorporates elements of the attitude semantic system, previously proposed in Porter, *Verbal Aspect*, 109; and further refined in Stanley E. Porter and Matthew Brook O'Donnell, "The Greek Verbal Network Viewed from a Probabilistic Standpoint: An Exercise in Hallidayan Linguistics," *FN* 14 (2001): 3–41, esp. 40. For the semantic terminology and definitions, see Porter, *Verbal Aspect*, 163–77. This system network is not to be taken as definitive and is offered for exemplary purposes.

realization statements for each network pathway, and economy, such as no unnecessary systems or redundant systems and as few possible systems with exclusionary or non-realizable forms. They also include binarism, formulated around the idea that any system consisting of three or more terms can be reformulated more elegantly and hierarchically by means of sets of binary systems, which are both more expressive and more accurate approximations of definable semantic choices.[25]

This attitudinal semantic system network provides the lexicogrammatical realization of the Greek speech functions. These speech functions may be represented in the following tentative way (Table 5.1):

TABLE 5.1 Major Greek speech functions[26]

Exchange Role	Goods and Services	Information
Giving	Open question	Declaration
Projecting	Projective question	Projective statement
Wishing	Projective cont. statement	Positive/negative question
Demanding	Command	τ-Question
Inquiring	Projective cont. question (?)	Projective (cont.) τ-question (?)

I will not go into the relationships among these, except to say that the realization statement for each of the pathways through the lexicogrammatical system corresponds with the speech functions represented in this chart and provides the basis for the descriptions used here.

At this point, I wish to turn to the relationship of this system network (or any system network) to cognition as I have defined it in this chapter. The moderate form of the Sapir-Whorf hypothesis, or moderate linguistic determinism (shared in some way by both Cognitive Linguistics and SFL),[27] posits that thought is not wholly constrained by language, nor does language construe thought in a strongly determinative way. If strong determinism were to be the case, then there would be very little chance, for example, of interlingual translation between widely disparate languages, or of users of one language understanding a concept for which there is not a word in their language, or of those with limited lexical choices understanding or recognizing more widely variegated phenomena (such as color terms), or any number of other differing phenomena. However, having said that, both Cognitive Linguistics and SFL recognize that the lexicogrammatical resources

---

[25] I realize that not all systemicists follow the principle of binarism in this way. However, in most systems, I believe that such a principle can be productively applied and probably should be for the sake of elegance and clarity.

[26] Porter, "Systemic Functional Linguistics," 29. As noted in Chapter Four, the categories of "information" and "goods and services" should be read as including expansive notions of these ideas that encompass all the things that can be accomplished by means of language. This includes stating feelings, thoughts, and anything else that can be expressed by means of language, and performing any and all non-language tasks.

[27] See Evans and Green, *Cognitive Linguistics*, 95–101; and, among many occasional references, M. A. K. Halliday, *Language as Social Semiotic: The Social Interpretation of Language and Meaning* (London: Edward Arnold, 1978), 25. For discussion of the Sapir-Whorf hypothesis and references to pertinent secondary works, see Chapter Two. See also Stanley E. Porter, *Hermeneutics, Linguistics, and the Bible: The Importance of Context*, T&T Clark Library of New Testament Greek 3 (London: T&T Clark, forthcoming), ch. 5.

of a language do and do not facilitate expression and hence have a relationship to understanding. The resources of the language do constrain not the ability to communicate but the means by which communication occurs. Some languages, in other words, make some things easier to communicate than do others, because of their differing linguistic resources. As an example, languages with specific terminology for differentiating familial relations enable easier and sometimes clearer communication regarding whether an "aunt" or an "uncle" is matrilineal or patrilineal—although sometimes, when such information is redundant, the necessity of using such terminology may make some languages less efficient than others, at least in some instances.

Thus, the semantic system network for attitude, which reflects meaningful semantic choices in the Greek language, is the major semantic system within the interpersonal metafunction and thus captures the choices available in participant relations, or how one chooses to relate interpersonally. The attitude system network encodes these semantic choices within its mood system that is realized in indicatives, imperatives, subjunctives, and optatives, etc. (see Chapter Four). There is a relationship between the attitudinal system, that is, how one creates and poses questions (and their types), formulates declarations, makes projections and contingent projections, etc., and the formal realizations within the language. We may say that this is a functional cognitive relationship. It is cognitive in that, so far as we can tell, the linkage between the two, the attitude system network and the formal mood system, exists in the mind/brain, even if it is not a self-conscious one or one that requires further probing. It is functional in that the use of language functions as a tool for communication. In this way, there is a sense in which the system network of attitude thus expresses the cognitive processes that are encoded by the attitudinal system and realized by the Greek mood-form system and how they are understood and responded to. Other systems within the Greek language could be analyzed similarly. The implications of this relationship, however, are what I wish to explore in some examples from the New Testament.

SYSTEM NETWORKS AND CONCEPTUALIZING THE GREEK NEW TESTAMENT

In the previous sections, I have both defined a functional view of cognition and described systemically the attitude semantic system and the mood-form system that realizes these semantics within ancient Greek. In this section, I wish to examine three major passages within the New Testament that illustrate how the attitude system indicates the cognitive processes that were occurring in the language user and perceiver, at least insofar as this can be predicated and described based upon the linguistic resources of the language as found within its semantic systems. In other words, the supposition is that the use of language reveals cognition (however this is defined), but that our only meaningful access to this is constrained by the resources of the language system.

Philippians 3:1-2

The first example I wish to examine is Phil. 3:1-2, as a section within Phil. 3:1-11. The passage reads as follows: τὸ λοιπόν, ἀδελφοί μου, χαίρετε ἐν κυρίῳ, τὰ αὐτὰ γράφειν ὑμῖν ἐμοὶ μὲν οὐκ ὀκνηρόν, ὑμῖν δὲ ἀσφαλές. βλέπετε τοὺς κύνας, βλέπετε τοὺς κακοὺς ἐργάτας, βλέπετε τὴν κατατομήν (Phil. 3:1-2). These two verses have been the subject of a variety of interpretations. Several of the interpretive issues are important for understanding, not only of the larger section, but of the entire book of Philippians. These verses have implications for questions of the unity of Philippians, the nature of the opponents, and Paul's relationship with the Philippian Christians, among others.[28] There are four varying interpretations of these verses that I wish to discuss as they relate to cognition.

(1) The usual understanding of these verses is to interpret them as making sense within the argument of Philippians. The NIV11 translates Phil. 3:1-2 in this way: "Further, my brothers and sisters, rejoice in the Lord! It is no trouble for me to write the same things to you again, and it is a safeguard for you. Watch out for those dogs, those evildoers, those mutilators of the flesh."[29] Paul is thankful for the Philippians and their support, so he instructs them to rejoice in the Lord. But he then commands them to be on the lookout for outside agitators or opponents. Even though the three commands in Phil. 3:2 translated as "watch out" appear to be at odds with the encouraging command in Phil. 3:1 of "rejoice," these sets of commands are seen to be part of the overall complexity of Paul's relationship with the Philippians. This interpretation is probably the standard view of how to understand these two verses harmoniously within their context. This understanding of the Greek, however, is predicated upon several factors that are related to the attitude system that I previously discussed. In Phil. 3:1, the verb translated "rejoice" (χαίρετε) can be analyzed as either a present tense-form indicative or imperative mood form. Likewise, in Phil. 3:2, the three instances of the verb more neutrally translated "see" (βλέπετε; often translated "beware" or "watch out for," as in the NIV11, reflecting the forceful response) can also be analyzed as either present tense-form indicative or imperative mood forms. In most interpretations, as indicated in translations such as the NIV11, all four verbs are analyzed as imperative forms, and therefore functioning as types of commands. Their directive semantics is therefore seen to be commands given by Paul to the Philippians.

(2) A second understanding of these verses emphasizes some of the disjunctive elements in these two verses. For many interpreters, this passage indicates major problems with the unity of Philippians and points to the piecing together of several letters into one canonical letter.[30] Indicators of compilation are several. One is the transition τὸ λοιπόν, sometimes translated "finally" (KJV, HCSB, ESV, NASB, NRSV), in Phil. 3:1. This transition has indicated to some that it marks the conclusion to one of the individual parts of a composite book of Philippians (for those who hold to either two-letter or three-letter hypotheses). A second indicator is the wording of Phil. 3:2. Many translations and commentators translate Phil. 3:2 with strong commands: "Watch out ..." The use of the supposed strong commands in Phil. 3:2 indicates to some scholars an abrupt change in tone from the positive and encouraging earlier parts of Philippians to a harsh and stern warning that, again, marks the bringing together of a separate portion of a composite letter. These two

---

[28]For discussion of some of these issues, see Stanley E. Porter, *The Apostle Paul: His Life, Thought, and Letters* (Grand Rapids: Eerdmans, 2016), 329–54.

[29]There is widespread debate among commentators on how some of the individual lexical items should be rendered. While such issues are important, they are not my focus in this discussion.

[30]For discussion, see Peter O'Brien, *Philippians*, NIGTC (Grand Rapids: Eerdmans, 1991), 347–57; Gerald F. Hawthorne, *Philippians*, rev. Ralph P. Martin, WBC 43, rev. ed. (Nashville: Nelson, 2004), xxx–xxxiv and 171–5; and Paul Holloway, *Philippians*, Hermeneia (Minneapolis: Fortress, 2017), 147–54, with several excurses on issues. For a linguistic treatment of such issues, see Jeffrey T. Reed, *A Discourse Analysis of Philippians: Method and Rhetoric in the Debate over Literary Integrity*, JSNTSup 136 (Sheffield: Sheffield Academic, 1997).

interpretations of what at first sight appear to be relatively small elements within the text have larger interpretive implications. The interpretation of these individual elements or verses in the way that I have outlined them forms a relationship between perception of the text and our response to it, especially how we then perceive other elements of the text (e.g., whether we perceive it as a unity or not and how we then interpret other portions of the text). Likewise, the perception of the text is related to supposed interpretation of some of the characteristics of the text itself. This is part of the cognitive circle that I outlined earlier, in which cognition consists of perception that is manifested in response, and the response influences perception and hence cognition. For those who interpret these as jarring elements that disrupt the textual flow, they may well be inclined to find the letter a composite or at least a text that lacks cohesion.

These are not the only two options for understanding these two verses. In the two proposals that follow, I wish to explore several different ways to interpret these verses in their larger context within Philippians, so as to draw out their cognitive implications.

(3) I wish first to explore the cognitive implications, as I have defined them here, for taking these forms as imperatives and hence as indicating that commands are being given with directive force. This perspective, although suggesting several new ways of looking at these verses, is in harmony with some traditional interpretations of the imperatives in these verses (view 1), although it may also present evidence for the partition view of Philippians (view 2). In some of my recent linguistic research, I have been examining exchange roles and speech functions, as I have already indicated. In Greek, according to my analysis, the command realized by the imperative (such as we have in both Phil. 3:1 and 2) may be used for, among other things, demanding the delivery of goods and services (the same as it is in English, according to Halliday), in this case services.[31] Focusing upon the speech functions and possible exchange roles, rather than simply seeing the verbs as imperatives, may influence our interpretation of this passage and give us some cognitive insights.

The result when we examine the exchange role of the previous one-sided conversation (this is not a passage given to exchange structure at least at this point, but is a single-sided exchange) is that the author, Paul, says the following (using an expansive paraphrase to capture the semantics as realized by the verbal forms):

> Finally (taking this as a marker of a section in the argument), my brothers and sisters, you are to provide the service of rejoicing in the Lord. It is not problematic for me to write these things to you but they are a safeguard (as part of my further commanding language to you). You are to be observant of the dogs (probably here lexico-semantically metaphorically indicating some kind of evil-doers, as in LN domain 88.120, or possibly even a sexual pervert, as in LN domain 88.282),[32] that is, you are to provide the service of watchfulness for some kind of evil people, you are to be watchful of those who are workers of evil, and you are to be watchful of those who practice bodily mutilation through circumcision.

---

[31] M. A. K. Halliday, *Halliday's Introduction to Functional Grammar* (IFG4), rev. Christian M. I. M. Matthiessen, 4th ed. (London: Routledge, 2014), 134–9, as well as many other places in his writings and those of others within SFL.
[32] Johannes P. Louw and Eugene A. Nida, *Greek–English Lexicon of the New Testament Based on Semantic Domains* (LN), 2 vols. (New York: United Bible Societies, 1988).

After Paul's command that the Philippians rejoice, Paul seems to say that, in effect, he needs to provide this command to them, as a safeguard for them. The reason is that he wants them to be on their guard against these various types of evil influences, as represented by these several different evildoers. The interpretation of the passage as indicating commands to rejoice and then commands to be watchful against three types of evil does not indicate a semantic shift but creates a consistent speech-functional role of Paul demanding certain things of his audience.

According to this analysis, the cognitive shift seems to occur not between Phil. 3:1 and 2 (as possibly with view 1 and certainly with view 2) but between Phil. 2:30 and 3:1, and then again after Phil. 3:2. This is especially indicated after what Paul has said in Philippians 2 leading up to Phil. 3:1. After speaking of Timothy and Epaphroditus and their service to Paul, service that he believes the Philippians should have rendered him (Phil. 2:19-30), Paul shifts the argument by means of commanding language so that the Philippians will provide what has been lacking. Then, after Paul's words of warning in Phil. 3:2, what he says about himself comes as another strong contrast. Phil. 3:3 states: ἡμεῖς γάρ ἐσμεν ἡ περιτομή. Whatever was said about "them," that is, the objects of his commands of watchfulness in Phil. 3:2, is now placed in diametrical opposition to what he says about himself, represented as "we." We (Paul and possibly his companions, but not the Philippians) are the circumcision, those who serve God in spirit and boast in Christ Jesus and put confidence not (apparently as do those in Phil. 3:2) in the flesh. When we arrive at Paul's autobiography in Phil. 3:4-6, we cannot help but think that what he says about himself is in contrast with those who are characterized as perverted dogs, evildoers, and self-mutilators. The distinguishing self-characteristics that Paul lists in Phil. 3:4-6 are those things in which one might have confidence, if such confidence were warranted. With the shifts caused by the commanding language, and with the cognitive implications of such demands for service as I have indicated, I do not find it surprising that there are those who argue that these two verses, Phil. 3:1 and 2, indicate that these are transition points in the letter that possibly indicate multiple letters being compiled into a single letter to the Philippians (even if I reject the multiple letter hypothesis).

(4) There is a fourth way to interpret these two verses, Phil. 3:1 and 2, however, by which they are seen to influence our interpretation of this portion of Philippians in a significantly modified way—modified from the traditional way it is interpreted (view 1), from the way that sees discontinuity created by these two verses (i.e., for those who wish to see these verses as in some way promoting partition theories, as in view 2), and from the way that sees cognitive dissonance surrounding Phil. 3:1-2 (view 3). I find it surprising how little consideration there is of alternative understandings of these verses. There are admittedly some scholars who wish to modify the perception of Paul's supposedly strong objection in Phil. 3:2 and who introduce a variety of interpretations of who the opponents are that he addresses. However, there is very little attention given to rethinking more fundamental conceptual (and cognitive) categories, such as how to interpret the Greek used in these verses. Nevertheless, I think that such an alternative is worth consideration. Even if we do not end up finding the interpretation persuasive, I believe that the process of thinking about it gives us insight into how language and cognition can be related to each other, and hence how the system network that I have outlined in this chapter offers a means of graphically displaying the cognitive implications of choices within a semantic network.

The fourth alternative interpretation is to analyze the four verbs in Phil. 3:1 and 2 not as imperatives functioning as commands in the demand of goods and services, but as instances of indicative mood forms functioning as declarations in the giving of information (one of the possible functions of such language, as Halliday states). The reason that I have chosen this passage for exposition is that the forms can legitimately be parsed either way (imperatives or indicatives), but with significant semantic and hence cognitive interpretive implications. Rather than simply examining a given passage to explain its cognitive patterning, by examining an alternative explanation of the same passage I believe that we can recognize how system networks capture the cognitive differences encoded within the language. In this alternative interpretation, Paul offers the following (again using an expansive paraphrase for the sake of illustration):

> As for the rest (taking this transitional device not as marking a section but as a continuation of the argument so far), my brothers and sisters, you are giving me information that you are rejoicing in the Lord. It is not problematic for me to write these things to you but they are a safeguard for you (with this statement now in support of what Paul sees in the Philippians). You are in the position of giving information of your observing the dogs (still representing evildoers or even sexual perverts), you are observing those who do evil, and you are observing the mutilators of the flesh.

With the use of the declarative language, rather than the commanding, there is continuity between Philippians 2 and Phil. 3:1-2. There is, furthermore, continuity between Phil. 3:1-2 and 3:3-11. In continuing his argument, Paul turns from his statements in Phil. 2:19-30 regarding Timothy and Epaphroditus to the Philippians in Phil. 3:1-11. Even if the Philippians could not provide the service that Epaphroditus did then (which Paul appears to rebuke if the verbs in Phil. 3:1-2 are taken as commands), they are, according to the analysis of them as declarations, able to offer rejoicing and watchfulness now, or at least Paul seems to frame it this way. They are not commanded to undertake something that they may not be doing or might not be able to do, but they are declared by Paul to be doing the very thing that he desires. They are rejoicing and watchful. In Paul's further comments in Phil. 3:3-11, he then appears to be including the Philippians within those he characterizes as "we," rather than excluding them, as he may well be doing in the previous interpretation. We, including both Paul and his companions and the Philippians (not just Paul and his companions), are the circumcision, those who serve God in the spirit and who boast in Christ Jesus and who are confident but not in the flesh. Then in Phil. 3:4, Paul turns to focus upon himself. In particular, he seems to say, if anyone had confidence in the flesh, I would be the one. He then recounts the features of his autobiography. This interpretation of the verbs in Phil. 3:1-2 mitigates the disjunctive sense of the verses found in the previous three readings (whether for or against unity of the letter), and also tends to provide less evidence for the partition theory of the letter and more for its continuity, at least through these oft-times troubling few verses.

My concern here, however, is less with whether one accepts the standard interpretation (commands) or the alternative interpretation (declarations) of the verbs. My greater concern is to understand the relationship between the interpretation of the verbal forms and how they reflect on our cognitive formulations in relation to them. If we re-examine the Greek attitudinal system, we see that the choice between [+assertive] and [−assertive] is the first and hence primary semantic distinction within the attitude system network. In other words, the first binary choice required is between thinking of making an assertion or of making something else, such as a projection (realized by the subjunctive or optative) or a directive (realized by the imperative) and hence a command. These are basic and important cognitive distinctions as realized by Greek verbal forms. They are the difference between continuing to find ways of making assertions, whether they be in the form of declarations or various types of questions, and between making those types of statements that are not assertive but end up with various types of projective or directive behavior. The semantic difference also represents a different orientation to processes and their relationships to reality. The first set asserts as if reality is being affirmed, and the other does not make and cannot make a statement in and of itself about reality. There are further choices to be made in the network with cognitive implications. The distinctions regarding the [+assertive] are less important at this point and for this set of verses than the others and revolve mostly around choices of whether to make declarations or formulate questions. The analysis of Phil. 3:1-2 that parsed the verbs as indicatives indicates that Paul is simply making declarations ([+assertive: −interrogative]). However, the traditional and usual analyses indicate that Paul is choosing to be directive rather than projective. These two choices reflect different cognitive stances upon the relation of action to reality, and they constitute a secondary level of semantic (and perhaps also cognitive) differentiation. Rather than choosing to project, whether in the form of various types of declarations or questions, Paul, according to the traditional analysis, gives a command for goods and services, resulting in his use of an imperative form.

As I have attempted to show, if even only briefly, there are interpretive and hence cognitive implications of such descriptions. The traditional view (view 1) tends to promote discontinuity within the text, creating three stages to the unfolding argument, as the reader/listener shifts from the statements regarding Timothy and Epaphroditus to the disruptive commands regarding rejoicing and watchfulness to the statements that characterize Paul and those with him. The partition theories of Philippians (view 2), while not a necessary outcome of such analysis, are understandable within this disjunctive cognitive environment. In fact, as I have shown in view 3, any view of the language as commanding seems to indicate textual disjunction. The final alternative view that I have suggested (view 4) tends to promote continuity within the text, with the three stages all becoming part of a continuing, unfolding discourse progression from statements regarding Timothy and Epaphroditus to supportive declarations regarding rejoicing and watchfulness to further statements about Paul and the Philippians, until Paul singles himself out to offer his autobiography in relation to what has preceded. The partition theories of Philippians, while not necessarily excluded by such an alternative analysis, are far less plausible or understandable within this contiguous cognitive environment. More importantly, however, this cognitive environment may invite new ways of viewing Paul's argument in Philippians.

Mark 14:37-38 and 41

There are several places within Mark's Gospel where analysis of the attitudinal semantics of the passage has various cognitive implications. Of the several possible instances, I choose one passage with several examples to illustrate how attitudinal semantics are related to cognitive conceptualization. In Mk 14:32-42, after their final meal together, Jesus goes to the garden of Gethsemane with his disciples. He tells some to sit while he prays. He takes Peter, Jacob, and John with him and is overcome with grief. He returns to the three and finds them sleeping. At this point, Jesus says to Peter: Σίμων, καθεύδεις, οὐκ ἴσχυσας μίαν ὥραν γρηγορῆσαι, γρηγορεῖτε καὶ προσεύχεσθε ἵνα μὴ ἔλθητε εἰς πειρασμόν (Mk 14:37-38).

This wording raises a number of interpretive questions. There are three different ways to analyze this passage that I will mention. (1) The first option is that Jesus says, "Simon, are you sleeping (καθεύδεις)? You are not able to watch (οὐκ ἴσχυσας ... γρηγορῆσαι) one hour, are you? Watch (γρηγορεῖτε) and pray (προσεύχεσθε), so that you might not enter into temptation (or possibly: watch, and pray so that you might not enter into temptation)." In this analysis, Jesus asks Peter two questions, the first an open question and the second one expecting a positive answer, and then he issues two commands, followed by the purpose for these commands. (2) The second alternative is that Jesus asks Peter four questions: "Simon, are you sleeping? You are not able to watch one hour, are you? Are you watching and praying, so that you might not enter into temptation (or possibly: are you watching, and are you praying so that you might not enter into temptation)?" In this analysis, Jesus simply asks Peter four questions, the second framed to demand a positive answer. (3) The third alternative for what Jesus says to Peter is as follows: "Simon, you are sleeping. You are not able to watch for a single hour. You are watching and praying so that you might not enter into temptation." In this analysis, Jesus makes four declarations to Peter, but with the four declarations addressing the reason for Peter to be watching and praying, not regarding what he is actually doing.[33] Such choices are, so far as I can determine, not discussed in the commentary literature. The only question that occasionally comes up is the change from second person singular to plural. That is an interesting question, but not the one that I am examining here.

According to the first analysis, Jesus is using an open question to inquire after Peter's willingness or ability to sleep (are you able to do this? It appears that he is), and a question expecting a positive answer to express his wish for information (I wish you were able to watch, but you are not, are you?). Jesus then gives two commands, both demanding some action of Peter, his watchfulness and his prayer, for the purpose of his not entering into temptation regarding the fate of Jesus. The second analysis provides a variation on the first, in which Jesus continues his first two questions by asking a further two open questions regarding his ability to give of goods and services (Are you, Simon, watching and praying for a purpose?). The third analysis provides a different attitudinal semantics regarding Jesus's address of Peter. In the third analysis, Jesus offers four declarations that give information regarding Peter: he is sleeping, he is not able to watch, he is watching for a purpose, and he is praying for a purpose. The different sets of attitudinal semantics reflected in the three different analyses require different pathways through the system network.

The various types of questions and the declarations have in common that they indicate [+assertive] semantics as a primary semantic choice. Their more delicate secondary choices in the hierarchy then diverge. The declarations are [+assertive: −interrogative], while the questions are [+assertive: +interrogative]; the more delicate choice for the positive

---

[33] I have done an informal and unsystematic survey of over thirty different types of commentaries on this passage and have found only one that comes close, so far as I can see, to addressing some of the questions I raise here. Many accept that Jesus is rebuking Peter. However, only one I found links this to specifics of language. See Robert H. Stein, *Mark*, BECNT (Grand Rapids: Baker, 2008), 663. He states, "Jesus's words, 'Simon, are you sleeping?' (14:37c), are best understood not as a question, for Jesus already knows that Peter has been sleeping (14:38a), but as a rebuke. The second question also functions as a rebuke." Stein seems to accept the wording as a question but interprets its speech function as a rebuke. He does not suggest that it might be analyzed as a declaration. He also does not say what the relationship is between a question and a rebuke, and why a question cannot be a rebuke or why a rebuke cannot be a question. He does not appear to address any of the other constructions similarly.

question is [+affirmative]. The commands require that the primary choice in the semantic hierarchy be [−assertive] and then [−assertive: +directive]. Thus, we see that there are radically different semantics involved in the three different analyses. The first requires mixed attitudinal semantics, with two types of questions, and then two commands, while the second involves four questions, three of them open inquiries regarding what Peter might give to Jesus, and the third analysis makes four declarations. The differences in cognitive orientation are also significant. The first semantic pattern orients the scene differently than does the second or the third. In the first analysis, Jesus in relation to Peter is speaking about goods and services, the first two involving questions regarding giving of them and the second two involving demands regarding them. These involve Peter's sleeping, his inability to watch, and the purposeful need for him to watch and pray. This pattern might indicate that Jesus is surprised to see Peter acting this way (resulting in the two questions), and so he instructs him in how to behave. The second semantic pattern is one completely oriented to the asking of questions, most of them open ended. Jesus is asking mostly about what Peter might give in terms of services to him: not only are you sleeping and not able to watch, but are you watching and praying for any purpose? This pattern might indicate not only Jesus's surprise at Peter's actions, but his frustration in light of the circumstances. The third semantic pattern orients the scene in an altogether different way again, in which Jesus is simply giving information to Peter by means of his declarations: he is telling him that he is sleeping, that he is unable to watch, and that he is watching and praying for a purpose. This pattern might indicate that Jesus is simply resigned to the behavior of Peter, despite the dangers to Peter (and Jesus) involved.

This Markan scene contains a second episode that illustrates a similar possible semantic and cognitive environment. In Mk 14:41, after Jesus leaves the three disciples and goes away to continue his praying another time, he returns for the third time and he addresses them for the final time: καθεύδετε τὸ λοιπὸν καὶ ἀναπαύεσθε. There are again three potential analyses. (1) According to the first analysis, Jesus says: "Are you sleeping (καθεύδετε) therefore and resting (ἀναπαύεσθε)?," taking the clause complex as a pair of open questions. This involves two open questions about the giving of goods and services, here the question regarding the disciples' sleeping and resting. (2) According to the second analysis, Jesus says: "Sleep therefore and rest," taking the clause complex as a pair of commands. This would involve two commands about Jesus demanding goods and services of the disciples, their sleeping and resting. (3) According to the third analysis, Jesus says: "You are sleeping therefore and resting," taking the clause complex as a pair of declarations. This would involve two declarations that give information about their activities.[34] The commentators who recognize some of the interpretive and translational possibilities in this verse are more numerous than for the previous passage (about half), probably because the KJV translates the clause complex as commanding, when most subsequent interpreters interpret it as questioning. Many of the commentators simply leave the distinction as one of identification of the form of the verbs as either indicative (which could function in either a declaration or a question) or imperative in mood form, while others distinguish between command or question. Four commentators that I have

---

[34] There are several other less likely possibilities as well, such as a mix of these.

found (and I admit I may have missed some, but the point is that reference is not frequent) recognize the full range of possibilities of question, command, or declaration.[35]

As far as the attitudinal system network is concerned, the three different interpretations involve more than simply whether the two finite verbs are parsed as imperative or indicative mood forms and whether the clause complex is construed as a statement or a question complex. The open questions and the declarations have semantic features in common, as they have a similar primary semantic choice: [+assertive]. The open questions require the same pattern through the network as previously noted [+assertive: +interrogative], while the declarations have the pathway of [+assertive: −interrogative]. The commands, however, have a different primary semantic choice, involving the choice of [−assertive] and then [+directive]. What at first appears simply to be a matter of translational or even punctuational nuance has significant semantic differentiation based upon semantic choices within the Greek attitudinal system.

The implications for cognitive differences are also to be observed, based on the different semantic pathways through the system network. Roger Omanson in his analysis of the variants in the Greek New Testament, including what he calls segmentation variants, notes some of the implications of these differences (these comments are similar to some found in a few other commentators as well). His descriptions of Mk 14:41 capture well the cognitive differences. For example, he states of the first analysis, "As a question, they may indicate [Jesus'] disappointment."[36] Jesus returns and finds his disciples sleeping—again!—and so he is disappointed that they have not been able to stay awake, but are instead sleeping and resting, not taking seriously the gravity of the situation. Furthermore, Omanson states of the third analysis, "As a statement, Jesus' words may be understood as an accusation";[37] that is, Jesus's informational observations may carry the implication that he is accusing them of doing what he has expressly asked or told them not to do. Omanson also suggests that "It is also possible to understand the words as Jesus' permission to sleep since he has finished praying and no longer needs them to stay awake with him," although he also notes that Jesus's following response of "get up" does not seem to follow from this interpretation.[38] Omanson does not address the cognitive implications of the second analysis with the statements as commands, but this analysis may well involve Jesus's ironic commentary on their three-times failing to follow his instructions and to appreciate the dire situation.

---

[35]These commentators are Robert H. Gundry, *Mark: A Commentary on His Apology for the Cross* (Grand Rapids: Eerdmans, 1993), 857–8; Craig A. Evans, *Mark 8:27–16:20*, WBC 34B (Nashville: Nelson, 2001), 417, following Gundry; Stein, *Mark*, 664, although he identifies the differences based upon mood forms and has a category of "exclamatory indicatives," a category that is not transparent; and Eckhard J. Schnabel, *Mark*, TNTC (Downers Grove, IL: IVP, 2017), 366. There are some troubling comments made about this verse. Joel Marcus, *Mark*, 2 vols., AYB 27, 27A (New York: Doubleday; New Haven: Yale University Press, 1999–2009), 2:980, states that "The difference between the declarative interpretation and the interrogative one is negligible," clearly missing the semantics and probably simply examining the forms (where there is no difference). He also posits that the use of the present tense-form of the two verbs is a "conative (intentional) use of the present tense," a category without status in examination of the Greek verbal edifice. Cf. Ezra P. Gould, *A Critical and Exegetical Commentary on the Gospel according to St. Mark*, ICC (Edinburgh: T&T Clark, 1901), 271, who believes the present imperative indicates "continuance of an action already begun." These kinds of views of kind of action in the verb are disputed in Porter, *Verbal Aspect*, esp. 75–108 and 335–61; and Porter, "Aspect and Imperatives Once More," *BAGL* 7 (2018): 141–72, esp. 145–54. Some of the more detailed discussions are found in C. E. B. Cranfield, *The Gospel according to St Mark*, CGTC (Cambridge: Cambridge University Press, 1959), 435; and R. T. France, *The Gospel of Mark*, NIGTC (Grand Rapids: Eerdmans, 2002), 588.

[36]Roger L. Omanson, *A Textual Guide to the Greek New Testament* (Stuttgart: Deutsche Bibelgesellschaft, 2006), 97.
[37]Omanson, *Textual Guide*, 97.
[38]Omanson, *Textual Guide*, 97.

Each of these three different analyses cognitively orients the passage in a different way. According to these different interpretations, Jesus ranges in his possible emotions from disappointment to accusation to permission to irony. The differences in cognitive orientation shift the perception of the episode from start to finish, and influence how we as readers view Jesus, as those sent to arrest him arrive on the scene. The differentiation of these semantic functions makes a huge difference in how we reconstruct the cognitive environment of this passage.

2 Corinthians 10:7

One of the continuing items of contention regarding 2 Corinthians is how to understand the relationship between 2 Corinthians 1–9 and 10–13. Those who argue against integrity of the letter often cite what they perceive to be differences in tone between the two parts, which indicates to them that 2 Corinthians 10–13 is a separate letter or letter portion written when problems in Corinth were present and that it was written before 2 Corinthians 1–9, which seems to view the major problems as now in the past.[39] I do not intend to argue that a single re-analysis of a verse can change our entire perception of such a large issue, but I do think that large-scale and sometimes over-generalized statements are often the result of a number of smaller incremental decisions. This may be an instance of one of those small decisions that could have an impact on an overall assessment of the situation and literary integrity of 2 Corinthians. I wish to examine 2 Cor. 10:7: τὰ κατὰ πρόσωπον βλέπετε.

This initial clause of 2 Cor. 10:7 is susceptible to three different analyses. (1) The first analyzes the verb as an indicative in mood form and the clause as a declaration. Paul is saying to the Corinthians: "You are looking (βλέπετε) only on the surface of things," to cite the old NIV (the NIV11 has the less satisfactory: "You are judging by appearances"). Paul in this case is offering information by means of a declaration. (2) The second analysis interprets the verb as an indicative but the clause as a question. In this instance, Paul is asking the Corinthians: "Are you looking only on the surface of things?" Paul in this interpretation is inquiring by means of an open question regarding the giving of goods and services, that is, the considering of superficial appearances. (3) The third analysis takes the clause as a command by interpreting the verb as an imperative. In this final instance, Paul is commanding the Corinthians: "Look only on the surface things." In this case, Paul is using the command to demand goods and services, that is, the examination of the surface phenomena. Each of these is a linguistic possibility.

As noted in these possible analyses, in the interpretations that take the statements as either declarations or questions, there is a primary semantic choice within the system network of [+assertive]. However, the open question is then followed by a more delicate secondary semantic choice of [+interrogative], while the declaration concludes its pathway through the network with [−interrogative]. The third interpretation, with the command, involves a different primary semantic choice, with the semantic pathway indicating [−assertive] as its primary choice and [+directive] as its secondary choice.

---

[39]See Porter, *The Apostle Paul*, 244–90. A recent defense of integrity is found in Christopher D. Land, *The Integrity of 2 Corinthians and Paul's Aggravating Absence*, NTM 36 (Sheffield: Sheffield Phoenix, 2015). A very thorough discussion of the various views of unity is found in Margaret E. Thrall, *A Critical and Exegetical Commentary on the Second Epistle to the Corinthians*, 2 vols., ICC (Edinburgh: T&T Clark, 1994–2000), 1:3–49.

In that regard, the declaration and the question in their speech functions do reflect the semantic similarities realized by the attitudinal semantic system network. However, the command, because it realizes a significantly different pathway dependent upon different choices, results in a major semantic difference reflected in the fact that a command rather than a declaration or open question is the realized speech function.[40]

In his discussion of this passage, Omanson inadvertently draws attention not only to the interpretive differences among these analyses but also to the cognitive signification of these varying choices. Citing Jan Lambrecht, Omanson notes that taking the statement as a declaration (what he calls a statement), the first analysis proposed, has certain implications. It "implies: you ought not to see the outward appearance, but the reality below the surface."[41] If it is interpreted as a question, the second analysis, the cognitive disposition shifts. Omanson, because he conflates the statement and question on the basis of an indicative verb being used in each (he does not differentiate speech functions from lexicogrammar), states that "[i]f the verb is taken in the indicative, either as a statement or a question, Paul may be uttering a reproach: all they seem to be able to see is the superficial side of things."[42] I would contend that this analysis is more appropriate to the statement being an open question rather than a declaration. The open question is used by Paul to give goods and services, in this instance the question regarding how it is that they look on things. In the third analysis, as a command, Omanson says that this formulation "warns against a present danger (REB: 'Look facts in the face'). Taken as a command, the sense is 'let them merely look at the obvious facts that are staring them in the face' ..."[43]

If Omanson is right about the third interpretation—minus the notion regarding the present situation—then interpreting this clause in 2 Cor. 10:7 as a command, rather than as a declaration (or a question), changes the cognitive disposition of interpretation of this portion of the letter. We note from examining the attitudinal semantics that the pathway for a command is [−assertive], which it shares with projections, and hence it is not about assertions about reality, but about non-assertions that might be made about envisioned realities. This fits well with a situation in which Paul is addressing a church whose crisis has been resolved. Rather than simply observing their behavior or reproaching them for their approach, Paul instead is endorsing a particular way of making decisions. This is apparently what the NIV11 has in mind with its rendering "You are judging by appearances," although taking this as a statement does not have the sense of endorsement of the command. In a footnote, the NIV11 has: "Look at the obvious facts." The commanding speech function marks a smooth transition from Paul speaking of his ministry to an endorsement of his own belonging to Christ in the same way as others.[44] Thus, Paul is saying that he is as valid an apostle in his ministry as are others who make competing claims, and the Corinthians are invited to make a similar estimation.

---

[40]Commentators have noted some of these possibilities for some time. See Thrall, *Second Epistle to the Corinthians*, 2:618–19.

[41]Omanson, *Textual Guide*, 366, citing Jan Lambrecht, *Second Corinthians*, SP 8 (Collegeville, MN: Liturgical, 1999), 155.

[42]Omanson, *Textual Guide*, 367.

[43]Omanson, *Textual Guide*, 367, citing Thrall, *Second Epistle to the Corinthians*, 2:618. I am not sure about the basis of Omanson's statement that this is a "present danger," apart possibly from misunderstanding the function of a present imperative as in some way involving present circumstances. See Porter, *Verbal Aspect*, 335–61.

[44]See Murray J. Harris, *The Second Epistle to the Corinthians*, NIGTC (Grand Rapids: Eerdmans, 2005), 687, cited by Omanson, *Textual Guide*, 367.

CONCLUSION

In this chapter, I have concentrated upon the attitudinal semantic system network as an illustration of how such SFL system networks can give insight into cognition. I realize that some may accuse me of cherry-picking examples based upon identical morphology of some forms. I admit that I have chosen such examples. I have chosen, them, however, to provide clear examples that invite and even beg for semantic description in light of their cognitive possibilities. The interpretive possibilities of these forms are sometimes recognized by commentators, but not nearly as frequently as one might hope. Few offer suggestions that deal with speech functions and their cognitive interpretive possibilities. The results of this study, even though admittedly brief, indicate that attention to attitudinal semantics and their related speech functions offer challenging and potentially provocative insights into various episodes within the New Testament and how these episodes present various cognitive scenarios. This is not the only system network that would provide such insights into the semantic potential of Greek or its relationships to cognition. The area where much work has already been done within Greek linguistics—though not in relation to its influence upon and reflection of cognition—is the Greek verbal aspectual system.[45] Semantic choices made regarding verbal aspect also have cognitive implications, often unrealized. These are unrealized because of the misconception that verbal tense-forms grammaticalize time rather than aspect and because of the oft-seen lack of differentiation in translations of the various aspects. However, one area of further research that might be of use would be to explore the cognitive implications of differing perceptions of processes as these are grammaticalized within the Greek aspectual system. This is merely one of several systems that illustrate the importance of SFL system networks for modeling cognitive differences, as well as—and no doubt most importantly—their modeling the semantic differences captured by the networks themselves.

---

[45]See Porter, *Verbal Aspect*, 75–108, esp. 109; and Porter and O'Donnell, "Greek Verbal Network," 3–41, esp. 40.

CHAPTER SIX

Orality and Textuality and Implications for Description of the Greek New Testament from a Systemic Functional Linguistics Perspective

INTRODUCTION

Orality is given precedence over textuality in apparently most disciplines where such a distinction is made. These include orality studies, classics, folklore studies, cultural anthropology, linguistics, and New Testament studies, among possibly many others. There is a certain innate logic to such a supposition: we speak before we write. What is repeatedly and demonstrably true of individuals is also apparently true of cultures: cultures are oral before they are textual. What is culturally evident is also apparently historically the case: primary oral cultures preceded more developed textual cultures. All these patterns, however, essentially constitute a diachronic argument that attempts to describe both local and global patterns. As a result, orality studies focus upon the transformation caused by writing, both individually and societally, as people and cultures were affected by the introduction of literacy. The literary scholar Walter Ong (1912–2003) is well known for arguing for such a position.[1]

In classical studies, orality and textuality have also long been discussed. The oral-formulaic theory of Milman Parry (1902–35) and Albert Lord (1912–91) regarding oral transmission, also known as the Parry-Lord hypothesis, is still highly regarded as the basis of theories concerning the development of the Homeric poems.[2] The elaborate tales told

---

[1] Walter J. Ong, *Orality and Literacy: The Technologizing of the Word* (London: Routledge, 1982); cf. also Ong, *Interfaces of the Word: Studies in the Evolution of Consciousness and Culture* (Ithaca, NY: Cornell University Press, 1977).
[2] See John Miles Foley, *The Theory of Oral Composition: History and Methodology* (Bloomington: Indiana University Press, 1988), for a history of the development of this theory. See also Rosalind Thomas, *Literacy and Orality in Ancient Greece* (Cambridge: Cambridge University Press, 1992).

by formally illiterate Slavonic poets are seen as providing a model of how formulaically structured poems of extreme length can be recited. This theory of oral transmission was extended to a range of other epic literature, such as the Old English *Beowulf* and the Old French *Chanson de Roland*, as well as other later oral literary creations studied within the sociology of literature.[3] Other theories pervade classical studies as well regarding the transforming power of writing on Greek consciousness and thought.[4]

Folklore studies are traditionally structured around examination of the varieties of tellings and retellings of the tales of a given culture. Many cultures have been particularly productive for folklore examination, with the Russian culture perhaps being the best known through the work of Vladimir Propp (1895–1970).[5] Related to folklore studies is work in cultural anthropology, in particular research on myths. Myths are not viewed by anthropologists as fanciful or necessarily harmful or misleading stories, but traditional stories of the etiology of a culture. They are first transmitted orally, even if they are often put into writing relatively early (as were the religious texts of numerous cultures).[6] Modern linguistics has also been distinguished by the emphasis upon speaking over writing. Ferdinand de Saussure's (1857–1913) formulation of the distinction between *langue* (language) and *parole* (idiolect) is formulated around the recognition of speech providing access to language, and his major formulations deal with speech rather than writing.[7]

New Testament studies itself, so far as it can be characterized as a discipline in its own right, is highly dependent upon a wide range of theories of orality over textuality, whether these are seen in the early formulations of form criticism, some theories of Synoptic origins, dictation theories of composition, or oral performance and supplementation of even written texts. Various theories of orality have been used at various times within New Testament studies, including the Parry-Lord hypothesis (already mentioned), theories of rabbinic oral transmission, orality and folklore studies, informed controlled oral tradition theories, social or collective memory hypotheses, and the place of eyewitnesses.[8] No doubt some others could be mentioned.

---

[3] See Albert B. Lord, *The Singer of Tales* (New York: Atheneum, 1960); Lord, *Epic Singers and Oral Tradition* (Ithaca, NY: Cornell University Press, 1991); and G. S. Kirk, *The Songs of Homer* (Cambridge: Cambridge University Press, 1962). See also Berkley Peabody, *The Winged Word: A Study in the Technique of Ancient Greek Oral Composition as Seen Principally through Hesiod's Works and Days* (Albany: State University of New York Press, 1975), esp. for secondary literature; and Janet Watson, ed., *Speaking Volumes: Orality and Literacy in the Greek and Roman World*, MnS 218 (Leiden: Brill, 2001). For later literature, see Ruth Finnegan, *Oral Poetry: Its Nature, Significance and Social Context* (Cambridge: Cambridge University Press, 1977). Some scholars have doubted some of the disjunctions between orality and textuality in such studies. See, for example, Ruth Finnegan, *Literacy and Orality* (Oxford: Blackwell, 1988).
[4] See Eric A. Havelock, *Preface to Plato* (Cambridge, MA: Belknap Press, 1963).
[5] Vladimir Propp, *Morphology of the Folktale*, trans. Laurence Scott, 2nd ed. (Austin: University of Texas Press, 1968).
[6] Perhaps the most well-known study is by the structural anthropologist Claude Lévi-Strauss, *Mythologiques*, trans. John and Doreen Weightman, 4 vols. (New York: Harper & Row, 1969–81 [orig. 1964–71]). The four volumes are well known in their own right: "The Raw and the Cooked," "From Honey to Ashes," "The Origin of Table Manners," and "The Naked Man."
[7] Ferdinand de Saussure, *Course in General Linguistics*, ed. Charles Bally and Albert Sechehaye, with Albert Riedlinger, trans. Wade Baskin (New York: Philosophical Library, 1959; ET of *Cours de linguistique générale*, ed. Charles Bally and Albert Sechehaye, with Albert Riedlinger [Paris: Payot et Rivages, 1995 (1916)]).
[8] The secondary literature on these topics is immense. A book that provides a summary of many of these theories in New Testament studies is Eric Eve, *Behind the Gospels: Understanding the Oral Tradition* (London: SPCK, 2013).

The previous discussion is only a brief survey of the role that orality study has played and will no doubt continue to play in a variety of disciplines, including New Testament studies. I do not want to fall into the trap of overgeneralization or caricature, but I believe that it is fair to say that if one were to choose between orality and textuality, orality would take precedence in New Testament studies.[9] In other words, the supposed diachronic facts have become evaluative conclusions, with oral precedence indicating such values as reliability, authenticity, and the like. Without offering a judgment or evaluation of the various proposals, we can see this conclusion in such studies as the role of oral or eyewitness tradition in Synoptic studies, oral language features supposedly indicating authentic sayings of Jesus, features of oral performance indicating reliability of even written documents, and, one might even speculate, written texts that display supposed oral linguistic features having greater claims to canonical stature.[10]

In this chapter, however, I wish to call this assumption into question. Rather than see diachronic precedence indicating evaluative superiority, I wish to argue that orality and textuality are poles on a synchronic cline that does not necessarily imply evaluative judgment, only linguistic difference, accompanied by the resulting entailments of such a conclusion.[11] In order to do so, I define the features of orality and textuality as they are used within linguistics and in particular Systemic Functional Linguistics (SFL) and then perform some preliminary studies on selected portions of the New Testament to consider the results and their implications.

---

[9]This is exemplified in part by the recent rise of performance-based approaches to the narrative texts of the New Testament. See, for example, Rafael Rodríguez, *Structuring Early Christian Memory: Jesus in Tradition, Performance, and Text* (London: T&T Clark, 2010); Rodríguez, *Oral Tradition and the New Testament: A Guide for the Perplexed* (London: T&T Clark, 2013); William D. Shiell, *Reading Acts: The Lector and the Early Christian Audience* (Leiden: Brill, 2004), who posits that reading Acts as being performed orally fills interpretive gaps left by literary and rhetorical-critical studies; Whitney Shiner, *Proclaiming the Gospel: First-Century Performance of Mark* (Harrisburg, PA: Trinity Press International, 2003); Pieter J. J. Botha, "The Gospel of Mark, Orality Studies and Performance Criticism," *Religion and Theology* 25 (2018): 350–93; Richard A. Horsley, Jonathan A. Draper, and John Miles Foley, eds., *Performing the Gospel: Orality, Memory, and Mark* (Minneapolis: Fortress, 2011); and Antoinette C. Wire, *The Case for Mark Composed in Performance* (Eugene, OR: Cascade, 2011), who suggests, albeit unconvincingly, that the Gospels were "composed, not by individual authors with pens in hand, but orally in performance." Wire overstates her case in suggesting that one must choose between oral tradition and authors. For a two-part survey on "performance criticism" emerging as a discipline and a method, see David M. Rhoads, "Performance Criticism: An Emerging Methodology in Second Testament Studies," *BTB* 36 (2006): 118–33 (part 1) and 164–84 (part 2). Rhoads suggests that performance criticism can offer a paradigmatic shift in medium from written to oral, which may bring about changes in the way New Testament scholars approach the writings of the New Testament.

[10]See Eve, *Behind the Gospels*; cf. Kelly R. Iverson, "Orality and the Gospels: A Survey of Recent Research," *CBR* 8 (2009): 71–106. Besides the many works Eve and Iverson cite, one should also note: Brooke Foss Westcott, *An Introduction to the Study of the Gospels*, 7th ed. (London: Macmillan, 1888 [1851]); Bo Reicke, *The Roots of the Synoptic Gospels* (Philadelphia: Fortress, 1986); Rainer Riesner, *Jesus als Lehrer: Eine Untersuchung zum Ursprung der Evangelien-Überlieferung*, WUNT 2/7 (Tübingen: Mohr Siebeck, 1988); Eta Linnemann, *Is There a Synoptic Problem? Rethinking the Literary Dependence of the First Three Gospels*, trans. Robert W. Yarbrough (Grand Rapids: Baker, 1992); Henry Wansbrough, ed., *Jesus and the Oral Gospel Tradition*, JSNTSup 64 (Sheffield: Sheffield Academic, 1992); Armin Baum, *Der mündliche Faktor und seine Bedeutung für die synoptische Frage: Analogien aus der antiken Literatur, der Experimentalpsychologie, der Oral Poetry-Forschung und dem rabbinischen Traditionswesen* (Tübingen: Francke, 2008); and T. M. Derico, *Oral Tradition and Synoptic Verbal Agreement: Evaluating the Empirical Evidence for Literary Dependence* (Eugene, OR: Pickwick, 2016); no doubt among others.

[11]See Finnegan, *Literacy and Orality*, who also posits that orality and literacy be viewed along a continuum in a co-existing relationship. The nature of this relationship, however, is still uncertain in Finnegan's approach since orality and literacy still seem to be polarized, even though they are on the same continuum.

ORALITY AND TEXTUALITY AS A SYNCHRONIC PHENOMENON

As I have already noted, the prevailing paradigm for study of orality and textuality is diachronic. This diachronic perspective has led to a bifurcation between orality and textuality within New Testament studies. Before we can attempt to overcome this unhelpful bifurcation, I wish to examine in more detail some traditional views of orality and textuality and then define orality and textuality within a SFL framework.

Traditional Views of Orality and Textuality

Studies of differences between orality and textuality have only moderately recently begun to come into their own as an area of technical linguistic consideration. Before such studies, comments about the differences between oral and written texts were usually made based upon impressions, haphazard estimations, or perhaps a few supposedly representative linguistic features. The result was that many generalizations regarding their differences tended to favor one over the other. If one were to examine the dichotomy during the era of comparative or classical philology, the evaluation privileged textuality over orality. Oral texts may have had diachronic precedence, but they were often evaluated as products of so-called primitive cultures and hence inferior to the written products of more advanced or civilized cultures.[12] Nowhere was this seen to be more true than concerning the ancient Greek epic. Early theories of the Homeric literature examined these as written texts, not, as we do now, as the latterly written products of a process of oral transmission and development. The high point in Greek literary and linguistic development was seen to be captured in the writings of the fifth century BC Athenians, with such writers as Aeschylus at the beginning of the century and Thucydides at the end. Everything else was seen as either prelude or postlude to the Attic greats.

As previously observed, most modern linguists have reversed this set of priorities and have given precedence to orality over textuality. The result is that the following kinds of generalizations are sometimes made regarding the differences between speech, which is preferred, and writing, which is denigrated as in some way seen to be, if not inferior at least less linguistically desirable for study. For example, a recent introduction to linguistics says the following, reflecting what many perhaps think that they know about language. After discussing some of the obvious ways that written language is enscribed (e.g., punctuation), the authors state,

> Other differences between speech and writing appear lexically in the greater variety of vocabulary in writing, especially in selection of adjectives, longer versus shorter words, and Latin versus Anglo-Saxon words [remember we are speaking about English here]. Syntactically, speech is much less structured than writing, with incomplete sentences, little subordination, active declarative sentences rather than passive ones, or cleft sentences ... Writing makes use of subordination rather than coordination and marks relationships between clauses explicitly with subordinating conjunctions ... and logical connectors ... where speech uses coordinating conjunctions ... Speech is often much less explicit than writing.

---

[12] See James Paul Gee, "Orality and Literacy: From *The Savage Mind* to *Ways with Words*," *TESOL Quarterly* 20 (1986): 719–46, esp. 719. The terminology of primitive vs. civilized, etc., is clearly part of a now questionable anthropology. However, one sees how the diachronic perspective on orality and literacy has played a role in such outmoded estimations.

Written language is also more conservative than spoken language. When we write something—particularly in formal writing—we are more apt to obey the "prescriptive rules" taught in school, or to use a more formal style, than when we speak [citing dangling participles and ending sentences with a preposition as features of speaking].[13]

The authors then conclude: "A linguist wishing to describe the language that people regularly use cannot depend, therefore, on written records alone."[14] In other words, if one really wants a reliable account of the language people use, one needs to consult their speech. Such an attitude seems to pervade much New Testament studies as well, with its emphasis upon the speech of Jesus and the initial orality of Paul's letters.

A recent treatment of the issue of orality in New Testament studies addresses some of these same issues. The work is primarily addressed to responding to various theories about the orality of the Gospel of Mark and to defend the notion that the Gospel retains characteristics of orality even though it is presented in a written form. As a result, Nicholas Elder has identified what he considers three "features *characteristic* of oral and literary registers" and two criteria regarding how oral and written texts relate to tradition (what he calls "metalinguistic") in his discussion of the difference between oral and written narratives.[15] He essentially presents the same kind of criteria as do Fromkin and other linguists already mentioned.

- Criterion One: Parataxis, Apposition, and the Idea Unit
  Elder believes that oral texts are paratactic vs. written texts are hypotactic, which breaks oral texts into shorter idea units vs. longer idea units in written texts. Oral texts also use apposition.

- Criterion Two: Repetition of Syntactical Patterns, Words, Phrases, and Ideas
  Oral texts are more repetitive than written texts, including repetition in syntax, episodes, and concepts.

- Criterion Three: Verb Employment
  Oral texts use greater variety in tense-forms vs. written texts with less variety in tense-forms but more variety in voice and mood.[16] Oral narratives often switch tense-forms while written narratives are often told in the past. Written texts tend to use the passive voice.

---

[13] Victoria Fromkin et al., *An Introduction to Language: Third Canadian Edition* (Toronto: Nelson/Thomson, 2006), 604. This is one of the most widely used introductions to linguistics in North America, here in its Canadian version. See Douglas Biber, *Variation across Speech and Writing* (Cambridge: Cambridge University Press, 1988), 5, who summarizes and complexifies such views: "The general view is that written language is structurally elaborated, complex, formal, and abstract, while spoken language is concrete, context-dependent, and structurally simple. Some studies, though, have found almost no linguistic differences between speech and writing, while others actually claim that speech is more elaborated and complex than writing." Other linguists have posed other sets of criteria. See Elinor Ochs, "Planned and Unplanned Discourse," in *Discourse and Syntax*, ed. Talmy Givón (New York: Academic Press, 1979), 51–80; and Deborah Tannen, "Oral and Literate Strategies in Spoken and Written Narratives," *Language* 58 (1982): 1–21.

[14] Fromkin et al., *Introduction*, 604.

[15] Nicholas A. Elder, *The Media Matrix of Early Jewish and Christian Narrative*, LNTS 612 (London: T&T Clark, 2019), 16–28, with quotations from 16 and 23. The following five points cite Elder's categories and summarize his discussion on 16–28. Elder draws on several linguistic studies, but apparently not the work of Michael Halliday cited later in this chapter.

[16] Elder appears to be completely unaware of discussion over the last thirty years of the Greek verbal system, including tense/aspect, mood/attitude, and voice/causality. This is a serious shortcoming in his analysis, especially as he attempts to relate English to Greek.

- Criterion Four: Multiform Tradition
  Oral texts are "equiprimordial," that is, "equally original," and have "radical instability."[17]
- Criterion Five: Embedded Textuality and Intertextuality
  Oral texts embed other texts based upon memory and in a more limited way vs. written texts that can embed texts more extensively and permanently.

Elder has attempted to advance discussion by invoking metalinguistic criteria, as well as criteria based upon those suggested by linguistic discussion. Those familiar with previous New Testament study will note that his first to third criteria have been used in New Testament studies to describe New Testament texts in a variety of ways, such as identifying Semitisms. They clearly do not advance discussion. The fourth and fifth criteria are of questionable relevance to the question of language use.

Both Fromkin et al. and Elder only provide rough-and-ready linguistic criteria regarding either orality or textuality, and no clear basis for establishing a relationship between them. In other words, despite the recognition of their interconnectedness, the two remain as two ends of a polarity rather than constituting a cline. Such claims remain vague and not substantiated through linguistic analysis. They are based upon impressionistic assumptions (most of which have been observed for some time) that purport to be the intuitions of language users.

Orality and Textuality in a Systemic Functional Linguistics Framework

These assessments have been questioned and corrected especially by some linguists who use principles of SFL. Michael Halliday (1925–2018) has in fact devoted an entire book to this topic, as well as several important articles.[18] His findings, however, challenge the traditional viewpoint as represented in the two examples previously cited.

Let me say, at the outset, that Halliday does not question the fact that speaking precedes writing. He overtly recognizes that the individual's use of language parallels the development of the human species regarding language use (from protolanguage to language),[19] with speech preceding writing. Nevertheless, language is a meaning-making

---

[17] Elder, *Media Matrix*, 23–4, citing on "equiprimordial" Werner H. Kelber, "The Works of Memory: Christian Origins as MnemoHistory—A Response," in *Memory, Tradition, and Text: Uses of the Past in Early Christianity*, ed. Alan Kirk and Tom Thatcher, SemeiaSt 52 (Leiden: Brill, 2005), 221–48, here 237, and Kelber, "In the Beginning Were the Words: The Apotheosis and Narrative Displacement of the Logos," repr. in Kelber, *Imprints, Voiceprints, and Footprints of Memory: Collected Essays of Werner H. Kelber* (Atlanta: Society of Biblical Literature, 2013), 75–101, here 77–80; and on "radical instability," see P. Zumthor, *Oral Poetry: An Introduction*, trans. K. Murphy-Judy, Theory and History of Literature 70 (Minneapolis: University of Minnesota Press, 1990), 202; and Zumthor, *Essai de poétique médiévale* (Paris: Seuil, 1972), 68–72.

[18] His major work on the subject, which I rely upon extensively in this chapter, is M. A. K. Halliday, *Spoken and Written Language*, 2nd ed. (Oxford: Oxford University Press, 1989). See also Halliday, "Language and Social Man" (1974), repr. in Halliday, *Language and Society*, ed. Jonathan J. Webster, CWMH 10 (London: Continuum, 2007), 67–130; Halliday, "Differences between Spoken and Written Language: Some Implications for Literacy Teaching" (1979), repr. in Halliday, *Language and Education*, ed. Jonathan J. Webster, CWMH 9 (London: Continuum, 2007), 63–80; Halliday, "Spoken and Written Modes of Meaning" (1987), repr. in Halliday, *On Grammar*, ed. Jonathan J. Webster, CWMH 1 (London: Continuum, 2002), 323–51; and Halliday, "The Spoken Language Corpus: A Foundation for Grammatical Theory" (2002), repr. in Halliday, *Computational and Quantitative Studies*, ed. Jonathan J. Webster, CWMH 6 (London: Continuum, 2005), 157–89.

[19] Halliday, *Spoken and Written Language*, 2; cf. 9–11.

system, a semiotic system, and in that sense spoken and written language have the same purpose. However, at this point, Halliday importantly switches from a diachronic to a synchronic perspective. He notes that there are some features that spoken language possesses that written language does not. These things include what he calls prosodic (intonation, rhythm, phrasing, and pausing) and paralinguistic (tamber, tempo, loudness, and bodily movements) features.[20] The reason for spoken language having these features is not because of a difference in language but because of a difference in perspective. Spoken language is delivered for the situation, but written language is not (written language is not a happening but existence, not a process but a product), and so does not need the variety of features of oral language. Written language "is not tied to the environment in which it is produced in the way that conversation is."[21] Spoken language instead uses what came to develop into punctuation (Halliday notes that ancient Greek did not have punctuation)[22] to indicate boundaries, status, and relations, all related to various features of the language. Once the difference between spoken and written language is established, they assume other characteristics, within which are typologically related functional varieties (registers). In that sense, the difference between speaking and writing is "an instance of a more general phenomenon of variation in language, that is of register."[23] To anticipate Halliday's conclusions, he believes that spoken and written language are each complex, but complex in different ways from each other.

Halliday focuses upon two major factors in estimating the differences between spoken and written language: lexical density and grammatical intricacy.[24] The first is lexical density, and it is here that Halliday sees written language being more complex than spoken. Lexical density, he says, is that "[w]ritten language displays a much higher ratio of lexical items to total running words."[25] By lexical items, he means so-called content words, not function words,[26] in relation to the total number of words in a unit, which he elsewhere later defines as the non-embedded clause (he excludes embedded clauses, because their lexical items would need to be counted twice as being within both clauses, the non-embedded and embedded one),[27] or what we in the OpenText.org project usually refer to as primary and secondary (but not secondary embedded) clauses. He also means

---

[20] Halliday, *Spoken and Written Language*, 30.

[21] Halliday, "Differences between Spoken and Written Language," 70.

[22] Halliday, *Spoken and Written Language*, 32–3.

[23] Halliday, "Differences between Spoken and Written Language," 78; cf. Halliday, *Spoken and Written Language*, 44–5; Halliday, "Language and Social Man," 93–7. The language on register in SFL is extensive. See elsewhere in this volume, as well as: M. A. K. Halliday, *Language as Social Semiotic: The Social Interpretation of Language and Meaning* (London: Edward Arnold, 1978), 62–4, 115–20, 143–5, 222–3; Halliday and Ruqaiya Hasan, *Language, Context, and Text: Aspects of Language in a Social-Semiotic Perspective*, 2nd ed. (Oxford: Oxford University Press, 1989); Mohsen Ghadessy, ed., *Register Analysis: Theory and Practice* (London: Pinter, 1993); Helen Leckie-Tarry, *Language and Context: A Functional Linguistic Theory of Register*, ed. David Birch (London: Pinter, 1995); and Stanley E. Porter and Matthew Brook O'Donnell, *Discourse Analysis and the Greek New Testament: Text-Generating Resources*, T&T Clark Library of New Testament Greek 2 (London: T&T Clark, 2023), ch. 3.

[24] Halliday, *Spoken and Written Language*, 61–91. See also Halliday, "Spoken and Written Modes," 227–37; Halliday, "Spoken Language Corpus," 168–9.

[25] Halliday, *Spoken and Written Language*, 61; cf. 64.

[26] Halliday defines function words, at least in English, as "determiners, pronouns, most prepositions, conjunctions, some classes of adverb, and finite verbs. (Determiners include the articles.)" (*Spoken and Written Language*, 61). Finite verbs are considered content words in Greek for this exercise and perhaps as a result elevate the minimal count.

[27] Halliday, *Spoken and Written Language*, 80. This is stated from the outset more clearly in Halliday, "Spoken Language," 168: "the number of lexical items (content words) per ranking (non-embedded) clause."

by "lexical units" lexical items, that is, not just words but units of more than a single word that function in the same way as single words (they are called "lexical" because they function as lexical and not grammatical items as parts of open sets of lexemes).[28] The estimation of density is then calculated by determining the number of lexical (and grammatical) words and establishing a ratio of the lexical words in relation to the total words. The higher the ratio, the higher the lexical density, and hence the "more 'written' the language being used."[29] As the unit for examination, Halliday, as already noted, uses the clause as his basis (not the sentence). Halliday explains the "significance" of this formulation in terms of "the density with which the information is presented. Relative to each other, written language is dense, spoken language is sparse."[30] Halliday's calculations of lexical density vary to some extent. According to his original proposal, he estimates that, at least for English, spoken language has 1.5 to 2 lexical items per non-embedded clause, whereas written language ranges from 3 to 6 per clause.[31] In a later discussion, Halliday estimates that, at least for written English, there are 6 of what he calls lexical words for every ranking clause, while in spoken language there are around 2 lexical words for every such clause.[32]

The second factor is grammatical intricacy. Halliday first calls into question the notion that spoken language is in any way less structured than writing or more given to formlessness. Halliday contends that spoken language "is certainly not unstructured and superficial," as has sometimes been posited. "The 'formlessness' of speech is an artefact of the transcription; if a written text is reproduced with all the planning processes left in, then it too will appear formless."[33] The reason is that the spoken language was not designed to be written or represented in that form. As he states, "The spoken language is, in fact, no less structured and highly organized than the written."[34] To appreciate this factor, rather than comparing the transcripts of speech with written texts, Halliday claims that one should compare transcripts of speech with drafts of written texts—they reveal the same characteristics of formlessness, but the written text has been subsequently revised into the shape that one finds in the final written text.

There are, nevertheless, some differences between spoken and written texts regarding grammatical intricacy. The first difference is in relation to the first factor of lexical density. Because written language uses fewer clauses than spoken language, the number of lexical items per clause is less for spoken language, even though it tends to use the same lexical items. There are two important points to note here—that the density may be different but that the same lexical items tend to be used in both spoken and written texts. They are simply spread out over more clauses in spoken language. In this way, spoken language is less lexically dense and more lexically sparse, but written language is more

---

[28]Halliday, *Spoken and Written Language*, 63; cf. 63–4 for definition of grammatical words in terms of English, especially spelling. For our purposes grammatical words are words that occur in a closed set, such as prepositions and pronouns.

[29]Halliday, *Spoken and Written Language*, 64. Halliday suggests but does not pursue the notion of differentiating between high and low frequency lexical words (64–5).

[30]Halliday, *Spoken and Written Language*, 62.

[31]Halliday, *Spoken and Written Language*, 80. Cf. Halliday, "Spoken and Written Modes," 329 and 331, where the ranges for spoken texts are 1.8 to 3 lexical items per clause and for written texts 6.3 to 9.6 lexical items per clause.

[32]Halliday, "Spoken Language," 168, although his discussion is briefer and less detailed.

[33]Halliday, *Spoken and Written Language*, 77. Cf. Halliday, "Spoken and Written Modes," 337–41.

[34]Halliday, *Spoken and Written Language*, 79 (in bold in the original).

lexically dense based upon its grammatical intricacy. The reason that spoken language has a greater number of clauses, Halliday believes, is because "[w]ritten language represents phenomena as **products**. Spoken language represents phenomena as **processes**."[35] Nouns are used to represent entities, and verbs are used to represent processes, but in order to represent these processes they require clauses. As a result, written language has a greater ratio of lexical items per clause with its emphasis upon the product of experience, and spoken language has a lesser ratio as it represents events. In this way, Halliday contends, spoken language and written language differ in their function and the medium through which this function is represented.[36]

The second area of intricacy concerns grammatical intricacy itself, or what Halliday defines as quantification of "the number of ranking clauses in the clause complex."[37] The clause complex in spoken language is the analog of the sentence in written language. Halliday states that "[i]n spontaneous spoken language the clause complex often became extraordinarily long and intricate … If we analyse one of these in terms of its hypotactic and paratactic nexuses, we get a sense of its complexity."[38] Such complexity is not found as often in written language, at least written English (Greek may well be different in this regard with its periodic sentences). Halliday notes that these complex clauses appear to happen more in extended monological sections, as opposed to shorter dialogical sections with their minor clauses. Halliday does not attempt a numerical calculation of what it means for complex clauses to be more frequent in spoken language. However, "[w]hat one can say is, that the more intricate a given clause complex is, the more likely it is that it happened in speech rather than in writing,"[39] even if he does not provide any numerical estimations of what kind of intricacy to expect in spoken over written language. As Halliday states, "[t]he spoken language is every bit as highly organized as the written, and is capable of just as great a degree of complexity. Only, it is complex in a different way."[40] The difference is between written language that is "static and dense" and spoken language that is "dynamic and intricate."[41] Lexical density is found in written language, but grammatical intricacy is found in spoken language.

Those who are familiar with some of the studies of differences between spoken and written language will also be aware of the studies of Douglas Biber.[42] Biber's analyses are some of the most complex to approach the question of quantifying (using corpus linguistics) differences in types of language. I have used a modified form of Biberian analysis to study a number of Paul's letters.[43] However, what Biber discovered in his

---

[35]Halliday, *Spoken and Written Language*, 81 (emphasis original). Cf. Halliday, "Spoken and Written Modes," 331–5.
[36]Halliday also notes that this difference helps to account for why grammatical metaphor—the transformation of a process into an entity—is more typical of written than of spoken language. See Halliday, *Spoken and Written Language*, 93–6; Halliday, "Spoken and Written Modes," 345–9. On grammatical metaphor, see Chapter Three.
[37]Halliday, "Spoken Language," 169. This topic is also discussed in Halliday, *Spoken and Written Language*, 82–9, but with less definite conclusions.
[38]Halliday, "Spoken Language," 169. Cf. also Halliday, "Spoken and Written Modes," 331–5.
[39]Halliday, "Spoken Language," 169.
[40]Halliday, *Spoken and Written Language*, 87.
[41]Halliday, *Spoken and Written Language*, 87.
[42]Biber, *Variation*.
[43]Stanley E. Porter, "The Functional Distribution of Koine Greek in First-Century Palestine," in *Diglossia and Other Topics in New Testament Linguistics*, ed. Stanley E. Porter, JSNTSup 193, SNTG 6 (Sheffield: Sheffield Academic, 2000), 53–78.

quantification of language was not about differences between spoken and written language but the differences between texts, that is, their differences in text-types. I similarly used such findings to discuss differences in register between letters. James Libby has extended such work into questions of authorship and discovered that differences in linguistic profiles of the Pauline letters based upon complex sets of features are not attributable to authorship but to register or genre.[44] Thus, I will not use the type of analysis that I have used previously for register analysis for the issue of differentiating spoken and written language.[45] I will use Halliday's categories regarding lexical density and grammatical intricacy.

SPOKEN AND WRITTEN LANGUAGE AS MODE: CHANNEL AND MEDIUM IN SYSTEMIC FUNCTIONAL LINGUISTICS

As already indicated, this chapter argues that orality and textuality are poles on a synchronic cline which represents linguistic difference. This presents the question as to what that linguistic difference is and what determines the use of one mode over the other. In other words, what is the *function* of spoken and written language and what determines their use? Is there a linguistic situation that elicits the use of one over the other in the sense that one does something the other does not? To help identify what these linguistic differences might be, at least from a SFL standpoint, I will briefly address the linguistic phenomena of channel and medium. Channel and medium are two distinct but not unrelated notions that pertain to process sharing. The act of process sharing takes place in varying degrees and can involve the addressee in more active ways, such as in an open dialogue or debate, or in more passive ways, as in a classroom lecture. Process sharing is a complex issue when considering the mode of discourse. Grammatical intricacy is related to the modality through which the addressee encounters the message of the one creating the text, whether that message is apprehended through sound waves or as inscribed images in the form of writing.[46] As previously mentioned, spoken language tends to be less lexically dense while written language is more lexically dense based upon grammatical intricacy.

The degree that an addressee is involved in process sharing—whether in the process of creating texts or encountering the text as a finished product—is closely related to what Halliday and Ruqaiya Hasan (1931–2015) refer to as channel.[47] The two channels, as

---

[44]James A. Libby, "The Pauline Canon Sung in a Linguistic Key: Visualizing New Testament Text Proximity by Linguistic Structure, System, and Strata," *BAGL* 5 (2016): 122–201.
[45]Some other approaches to these questions are represented in, for example, Deborah Tannen, ed., *Spoken and Written Language: Exploring Orality and Literacy*, Advances in Discourse Processes 9 (Norwood, NJ: Ablex, 1982).
[46]Hasan in Halliday and Hasan, *Language, Context, and Text*, 58. Cf. Deborah Tannen, "The Myth of Orality and Literacy," in *Linguistics and Literacy: Topics in Language and Linguistics*, ed. W. Frawley (Boston: Springer, 1982), 37–50, who differentiates between involvement being associated with orality and content with literacy. Halliday would no doubt question both.
[47]Hasan in Halliday and Hasan, *Language, Context, and Text*, 58. Similar issues are discussed from a different angle in Egbert J. Bakker, "How Oral Is Oral Composition?" in *Signs of Orality: The Oral Tradition and Its Influence in the Greek and Roman World*, ed. Anne E. Mackay (Leiden: Brill, 1999), 29–47, esp. 29–33, where he includes discussion of the conception of a discourse.

Hasan refers to them, are graphic and phonic.[48] Phonic channels are the most conducive for establishing an *active* linguistic context where the addresser and addressee are both involved in the act of what Hasan calls "process sharing."[49] Addressees in graphic channels, on the other hand, tend to be more passive in the act of process sharing. It is worth noting, however, that phonic channels speak only to the *potential* of active process sharing since a variety of different factors may prevent the actualization of both parties being involved. A classroom lecture, for example, offers a phonic channel whereby a professor can interact actively with students; however, students become passive participants in the act of process sharing if the professor lectures without pausing within the established timeframe of the meeting and allowing for student response. Hasan notes that even in such instances, however, the physical presence of the addressee in phonic channels can still "provid[e] feedback on the textual processes through extra-verbal modalities, such as eye-contact, facial expression, a yawn, or body posture."[50] Graphic channels can hardly provide such feedback since the awareness a writer has of the addressee's needs is greatly diminished. One potential function of phonic channels, then, might be to involve the participation of the addressee whether actively or through some other means in process sharing. The function of graphic channels, on the other hand, concerns itself more with transmitting cultural knowledge or information without any concern for active participation from the addressee.[51] These distinctions are certainly not concrete, but serve to demonstrate that both spoken and written language differ in their function.

While *channel* refers to the degree of involvement of an addressee, *medium* refers to the "patterning [of] the wordings themselves."[52] The primary distinctions in medium are spoken and written language with attention given to the degree of lexical density and grammatical intricacy. Hasan notes that "medium is a historical product of process sharing" and that "variations in medium" (i.e., spoken vs. written language) are "a product of variation in channel" (i.e., variations in phonic vs. graphic language).[53] While there is some congruency between channel and medium, the relationship between the two can be quite complex. One might, for example, expect the active process of sharing in a dialogue to utilize the phonic channel through a spoken medium while the graphic channel is

---

[48] In earlier works, Hasan referred to these channels as *aural* and *visual* but later found the terms to be inappropriate for several good reasons. First, the terms were too oriented to the addressee. Second, while eye-contact (visual contact) might appear to be associated with the visual channel, it more normally occurs with the aural (now phonic) channel. It is also worth noting that the terms *graphic* and *phonic* to describe channel are identified by other linguists as *written* and *spoken* channels, which Hasan avoids as she believes they lead to problems when it comes to discussing *medium*. See Hasan in Halliday and Hasan, *Language, Context, and Text*, 58, where she refers to her earlier work.
[49] Hasan in Halliday and Hasan, *Language, Context, and Text*, 58.
[50] Hasan in Halliday and Hasan, *Language, Context, and Text*, 58.
[51] Halliday provides three functions that graphic channels play in the everyday lives of adults. Written language's primary functions are: (1) promoting action for social contact, (2) disseminating information, and (3) providing entertainment. He acknowledges that these functions are not always clearly differentiated and sometimes overlap. What functions as informational at the time of communication, for example, may be for entertainment later and what is for instruction may later be informational. See Halliday, *Spoken and Written Language*, 40–1.
[52] Hasan in Halliday and Hasan, *Language, Context, and Text*, 58.
[53] Hasan in Halliday and Hasan, *Language, Context, and Text*, 58.

reserved for monologues and utilizes a written medium. The degree of congruence, however, becomes disturbed when the use of one channel does not align with the expected medium. One example of this would be writing a letter to a close friend or family member where the graphic channel is utilized, but the medium used resembles that of a spoken medium rather than written one. This happens in instances where one *writes* as though they are *speaking* to their addressee. Hasan notes that the choice of *channel* and *medium* is "subservient to the choices in the field and tenor of discourse."[54]

ORALITY AND TEXTUALITY IN NEW TESTAMENT GREEK

We now turn to an examination of orality and textuality in the Greek of the New Testament based upon treatment of this topic by Halliday in SFL. There are, however, several preliminary issues that must be raised before we are able to engage in such an examination. The first preliminary question that we must ask is whether Halliday's analyses based upon English examples hold for ancient Greek.[55] We know from previous experience that SFL was developed primarily as a description of English and that this requires that the categories be reconsidered when describing ancient Greek. We must do this before we are able to apply any of these findings to the Greek New Testament.

This need for remodeling SFL poses several of its own problems. The first problem is the very one that Halliday himself addresses when he speaks of the difficulties of transcription and how one should compare transcriptions of spoken language with drafts of written language. All ancient texts from the ancient world—even those purporting to represent speech, including the documentary papyri or the plays of Aristophanes—are transcriptions that have been transformed into writing and have taken on some characteristics of writing, even if some of the characteristics of spoken language are retained. There are no accurate transcriptions of speech from the ancient world that have not been transmitted by means of writing. The ancients implicitly recognized the difference. We have various uneducated people represented in ancient literature, such as in Aristophanes, where for example the sausage seller in *The Knights* speaks in his rustic ways. Thucydides includes numerous speeches in his account of the Peloponnesian war, but there is a major question of how close to the original spoken words these speeches are, and further questions of whether they are even the words of those who purportedly spoke them.[56] Demosthenes and other ancient orators delivered their speeches, but some of them also wrote speeches for others. In such instances, even if these were delivered orally, they were oral readings of written language, and possibly memorized so as to be as fluent

---

[54]Hasan in Halliday and Hasan, *Language, Context, and Text*, 59. Field and tenor are two situational contextual variables concerned with the "what" and "who" of the text. See Halliday in Halliday and Hasan, *Language, Context, and Text*, 12; cf. Porter and O'Donnell, *Discourse Analysis*, ch. 3.

[55]See Ji Hoe Kim, "A Hallidayan Approach to Orality and Textuality and Some Implications for Synoptic Gospel Studies," *BAGL* 8 (2019): 111–39, whose article offers promising results on this front and suggests that Mark's Gospel is more akin to spoken language in comparison to the other three Gospels. This conclusion conceivably supports the view that Mark's Gospel is the earliest of the four and thus bears the most likeness to the oral tradition out of which it arose.

[56]See Stanley E. Porter, "Thucydides 1.22.1 and Speeches in Acts: Is There a Thucydidean View?" *NovT* 32 (1990): 121–42; repr. in Porter, *Studies in the Greek New Testament: Theory and Practice*, SBG 6 (New York: Peter Lang, 1996), 173–93.

(and written-like?) as possible. A similar question to that of Thucydides has been raised by the speeches in Acts, which in virtually all significant instances are probably written summaries of much longer speeches, if they are the words of the speakers recorded. There is no easy way around this problem as we have no ancient Greeks to interrogate and no recordings—digital, magnetic, or otherwise—to access for the original words. In other words, the channel of all ancient texts is graphic, even if the medium is spoken.

There is the further complication, at least with the words of Jesus, and possibly of some others, of the language used when the words were spoken. If they were delivered in Aramaic, then the words that we have are doubly problematic, being translated and written. That is, the medium is spoken then translated with the channel graphic.[57] If they were delivered in Greek, as will be discussed later in this chapter, then the words are only written, not translated also. But the medium remains spoken and the channel graphic. Even if we believe that we have a faithful account of the words spoken, we do not have accurate transcriptions that include all the information typically found in such transcriptions. We simply do not have—to my knowledge—such information from the ancient world, at least the world of ancient Greek. Therefore, there is an inherent incapability of making a genuine comparison of spoken and written language for ancient Greek. Does this mean the task is impossible? In one sense, it is. However, in another it is not. Even if we must admit that we do not have direct access to spoken language, we probably have written language that has preserved some of the features of spoken language, even in its graphic channel. Halliday himself seems to intimate this when he notes that grammatical intricacy—that is, a higher number of clauses within a clause complex—probably indicates origins in spoken rather than written language. Since we are discussing relative differences, not differences in kind, according to Halliday (the differences fall along a cline; they are not a disjunction), there is no inherent reason why we cannot work with the material that we have, perhaps with the working assumption that the degrees of difference as indicated may shift but the basic distinctions still hold.

The second problem concerns the applicability of English-based linguistic categories to Greek. Here we must admit that several of Halliday's assumptions and conclusions are at least subject to question and in need of re-modeling. For example, we may begin with the assumption that the numerical values of lexical density in English are appropriate for Greek, but we must test these numbers on our available corpus. A further issue is the nature of embedding. For Halliday, embedded clauses include relative clauses as well as participle and infinitive clauses,[58] whereas for Greek embedded clauses are constructed primarily although not entirely around participle and infinitive clauses. Another issue is the characterization of the difference in grammatical intricacy between spoken and written language. The problem is highlighted by the fact that we have been told that Greek written language—at least of the high Attic era—is periodic in style, meaning that it has high grammatical intricacy, with numerous hypotactic structures. Parenthetically, this

---

[57]This translation process, however, may have been nearly instantaneous, in that those who heard Jesus speak in Aramaic were functional multilinguals who transmitted Jesus's words in Greek. See Allan Bell, "The Early Greek-Language Tradition behind the Gospels," in *Holding Forth the Word of Life: Essays in Honor of Tim Meadowcroft*, ed. John de Jong and Csilla Saysell (Eugene, OR: Wipf & Stock, 2020), 229–42, esp. 235.

[58]See M. A. K. Halliday, *Halliday's Introduction to Functional Grammar* (IFG4), rev. Christian M. I. M. Matthiessen, 4th ed. (London: Routledge, 2014), esp. 490–508.

hypotactic feature, however, may offer some insights into koine Greek. If koine Greek is the regularized Great Attic Greek utilized across virtually all social, economic, and educational strata during the Hellenistic and Roman periods,[59] its decrease in periodicity and increase in parataxis in the written language may indicate changes to the written language effected by the spoken language. After all, the periodic style of classical Greek is reflected in the instances of literary written language. In this sense, koine Greek may well, if Halliday's supposition is correct, indicate through the reverse the very motivating factor he notices. Rather than grammatical intricacy indicating origins in spoken language for English, the relative lack of grammatical intricacy, compared to Attic (or Atticistic) Greek, indicates origins in the koine spoken language, even if conveyed through the graphic channel.

In any case, all these factors indicate that we must turn to some sample texts of the New Testament to determine both lexical density and grammatical intricacy, the two major factors in determining the difference between spoken and written language.

SAMPLES FROM THE GREEK NEW TESTAMENT AS INDICATORS OF SPOKEN OR WRITTEN LANGUAGE

In this section, I analyze three sets of samples from the Greek New Testament as indicators of spoken or written language. The three passages are the Sermon on the Mount, two passages of narrative in Acts, and two passages from Pauline letters. Halliday does not give any indication of a reasonable sample size for making his comparisons. Some of the examples that he uses are relatively small.[60] As a result, I am going to use sample sizes of varying lengths to compare results over different lengths. However, all of the examples exceed the lengths that Halliday appears to use.

Matthew 5–7

I have chosen Matthew 5–7 (Mt. 5:3–7:27) because, despite various views on the origin of the material contained within these three chapters, many if not most scholars who have studied the issue believe that these words were spoken by Jesus, even if not all at the same time or on the same occasion.[61] Many of these scholars also believe that the words were originally spoken by Jesus in Aramaic. If this is the case, as already indicated, then the words that we have in Matthew's Gospel (and presumably also any other parallel passages in Luke and even Mark) are both translated and conveyed in a graphic channel, even though they reflect an oral medium. However, if they were originally delivered in Greek—I believe that a case can be made for this hypothesis on the basis of the complex multilingualism of Palestine and the nature of Jesus's teaching, especially in this context—then the words are possibly original, even though still accessed through written form (graphic channel) and not transcripts of spoken language in the linguistic sense.[62] In any case, these words are

---

[59] I accept the reconstruction of the development of koine Greek by Geoffrey Horrocks, *Greek: A History of the Language and Its Speakers* (London: Longman, 1997), 32–127, esp. 33–7.
[60] See Halliday, "Spoken and Written Modes," 327–8, where his samples are 84, 76, and 57 words.
[61] By my count, Mt. 5:3-48 is 800 words, Mt. 6:1-34 is 650 words, and Mt. 7:1-27 is 486 words, for a total of 1,936 words.
[62] See Stanley E. Porter, "The Role of Greek Language Criteria in Historical Jesus Research," in *Handbook for the Study of the Historical Jesus*. I. *How to Study the Historical Jesus*, ed. Tom Holmén and Stanley E. Porter (Leiden: Brill, 2010), 361–404, esp. 393–404; cf. Porter, "The Use of Greek in First-Century Palestine: A Diachronic and Synchronic Examination," *JGRChJ* 12 (2016): 203–28. See also Hughson T. Ong, *The Multilingual Jesus and the Sociolinguistic World of the New Testament*, LBS 12 (Leiden: Brill, 2015).

recognized as originating in spoken language (spoken medium), even if they are conveyed through written form (graphic channel). Three chapters should be sufficient to formulate some generalizations regarding spoken language, if such formulations are to be secured through the language of the New Testament. The results of my examination are displayed in Tables 6.1–6.4.[63]

TABLE 6.1 Lexical density (Mt. 5–7)

Lexical Density	Mt. 5:3-48	Mt. 6:1-34	Mt. 7:1-27
Non-Embedded Clauses	146	112	84
Content Words	338	327	296
Grammatical Words	458	326	193
Content Words per Non-Embedded Clause	2.3	2.9	3.5

TABLE 6.2 Total lexical density (Mt. 5–7)

Lexical Density	Mt. 5:3-48/Mt. 6:1-34/Mt. 7:1-27 (Mt. 5–7)
Non-Embedded Clauses	342
Content Words	961
Grammatical Words	977
Content Words per Non-Embedded Clause	2.8

TABLE 6.3 Grammatical intricacy (Mt. 5–7)

Grammatical Intricacy	Mt. 5:3-48	Mt. 6:1-34	Mt. 7:1-27
Non-Embedded Clauses	146	112	84
Total Clauses	184	145	106
Clause Complexes	59	58	35
Ranking Clauses per Clause Complex	2.5	1.9	2.4

TABLE 6.4 Total grammatical intricacy (Mt. 5–7)

Grammatical Intricacy	Mt. 5:3-48/Mt. 6:1-34/Mt. 7:1-27 (Mt. 5–7)
Non-Embedded Clauses	342
Total Clauses	435
Clause Complexes	152
Ranking Clauses per Clause Complex	2.25

[63] All the data are based on hand searches and so subject to the possibility (and even likelihood) of error. I do not believe that such errors, if any, greatly affect the results. I have used the OpenText.org clausal displays as the basis of my data gathering, with clause complexes determined by the punctuation boundaries indicated by the *UBSGNT3revised*. Any decision regarding punctuation is subject to criticism, but the *UBSGNT3revised* uses a punctuation system that may have more similarities to modern punctuation and, because of this, provide a stronger basis for comparison with data gathered from English.

In summary, the number of content words per non-embedded clause, for what the information is worth, is slightly higher than what Halliday describes for English. Since Halliday does not provide figures for ranking clauses per complex, we will use these figures for comparison with the other passages.

Acts 12 and 18

I have chosen two chapters from the book of Acts as instances of written language, Acts 12 and 18.[64] I realize that there are, even within the two chapters that I have chosen, purported spoken words of characters. However, there are no sustained speeches, as there are in some other chapters within Acts. The narrative, even if it possibly draws upon spoken language, is represented as being a narrative account in written language form by the author (written medium, graphic channel). I have chosen two chapters from the book to serve to characterize its language, one from the first half and one from the second (see Tables 6.5–6.8).

TABLE 6.5 Lexical density (Acts 12 and Acts 18)

Lexical Density	Acts 12	Acts 18
Non-Embedded Clauses	72	63
Content Words	201	266
Grammatical Words	283	242
Content Words per Non-Embedded Clause	2.8	4.2

TABLE 6.6 Total lexical density (Acts 12 and Acts 18)

Lexical Density	Acts 12/18
Non-Embedded Clauses	135
Content Words	467
Grammatical Words	525
Content Words per Non-Embedded Clause	3.5

TABLE 6.7 Grammatical intricacy (Acts 12 and Acts 18)

Grammatical Intricacy	Acts 12	Acts 18
Non-Embedded Clauses	72	63
Total Clauses	117	112
Clause Complexes	33	30
Ranking Clauses per Clause Complex	2.2	2.1

---

[64]The length of Acts 12 is 492 words and Acts 18 is 509 words, for a total of 1,001 words.

TABLE 6.8 Total grammatical intricacy (Acts 12 and Acts 18)

Grammatical Intricacy	Acts 12/18
Non-Embedded Clauses	135
Total Clauses	229
Clause Complexes	63
Ranking Clauses per Clause Complex	2.1

In the aggregate, the results for the two chapters of Acts are higher in content words per non-embedded clause and lower in clauses per clause complex than the three chapters of the sermon on the mount. However, if these two chapters represent written language (written medium, graphic channel), their results of 3.5 content words per non-embedded clause fall within Halliday's initial estimation of the lexical words in written language, even if they do not reach his limit of 6. The number of ranking clauses per clause complex is very similar to what is found in the three chapters of Matthew (5–7), although the grammatical intricacy is slightly higher for the Matthean material over the Acts material, which is what Halliday's estimation anticipated even if the difference is not very great and arguably not of statistical significance.

Romans 2 and 1 Corinthians 4

I have chosen these two chapters from Romans (Rom. 2) and 1 Corinthians (1 Cor. 4) to represent language that occupies a medial point along a continuum of spoken and written language (spoken medium, graphic channel).[65] Letters in the ancient world—and the Pauline letters in particular—were often dictated to scribes, and so in some sense represent both spoken and written language.[66] By that, I mean that they may have originally been delivered through the spoken medium; however, they were immediately transcribed and preserved in written language form (graphic channel). The process of writing had the effect of taking the spoken language and representing it in not just transcribed spoken form but a type of written language form. I have chosen these two chapters, Romans 2 and 1 Corinthians 4, to attempt to see if we can quantify what the result of the writing process was upon Paul's spoken language in these letters (see Tables 6.9–6.12).

TABLE 6.9 Lexical density (Rom. 2 and 1 Cor. 4)

Lexical Density	Rom. 2	1 Cor. 4
Non-Embedded Clauses	52	67
Content Words	210	154
Grammatical Words	243	191
Content Words per Non-Embedded Clause	4.0	2.3

---

[65] The length of Romans 2 is 448 words and of 1 Corinthians 4 is 344 words, for a total of 792 words.
[66] Scholars often make much of the orality of the Pauline letters and their being meant for reading. On this, see Stanley E. Porter and Bryan R. Dyer, "Oral Texts? A Reassessment of the Oral and Rhetorical Nature of Paul's Letters in Light of Recent Studies," *JETS* 55 (2012): 323–42, esp. 325.

TABLE 6.10 Total lexical density (Rom. 2 and 1 Cor. 4)

Lexical Density	Rom. 2/1 Cor. 4
Non-Embedded Clauses	342
Content Words	961
Grammatical Words	977
Content Words per Non-Embedded Clause	2.8

TABLE 6.11 Grammatical intricacy (Rom. 2 and 1 Cor. 4)

Grammatical Intricacy	Rom. 2	1 Cor. 4
Non-Embedded Clauses	52	67
Total Clauses	82	79
Clause Complexes	26	29
Ranking Clauses per Clause Complex	2.0	2.3

TABLE 6.12 Total grammatical intricacy (Rom. 2 and 1 Cor. 4)

Grammatical Intricacy	Rom. 2/1 Cor. 4
Non-Embedded Clauses	119
Total Clauses	161
Clause Complexes	55
Ranking Clauses per Clause Complex	2.2

Romans 2 has the highest occurrence of content words per non-embedded clause of any selection that I have tested in this chapter. Even though this number does not reach the 6 that Halliday finally postulated, it is the highest of my three sample sets, and certainly falls within Halliday's range of 3 to 6 words for written language. However, 1 Corinthians 4 has a figure that is closer to spoken language, and in fact lower than most of the other samples even in Matthew 5–7 (the exception being Mt. 5). The aggregate of Romans 2/1 Corinthians 4 falls somewhere between Matthew 5–7 and Acts 12/18. The number of ranking clauses per clause complex is also the lowest of our set of passages in Romans 2 and the highest in 1 Corinthians 4, but with an aggregate that is very similar to the other two sets of passages.

What Do We Learn from These Three Sets of Passages?

Before we can draw any further implications from the data that we have gathered, we must gather the data together from the three sets of examples. If one were to use the figures provided by these three sets of samples—and I realize that much more work needs to be done regarding such a study to establish any kind of reliability—we get the following results (Tables 6.13 and 6.14):

TABLE 6.13 Lexical density comparison

Lexical Density	Halliday[67]	Mt. 5–7	Acts 12/18	Rom. 2 + 1 Cor. 4	Rom. 2/1 Cor. 4
Spoken	1.5–2 (2)	2.8		2.3	
Written	3–6 (6)		3.5	4.0	3.1

Concerning lexical density, if Halliday's figures transfer to Greek—and in some ways our knowledge of the New Testament passages can serve as a test of his figures—the two sets of passages that we would suppose are written language (written medium)—Acts 12/18 and Romans 2/1 Corinthians 4—do fall within the broad parameters that he indicated. Romans 2 by itself is the most firmly within the written language range (but none approaches Halliday's figure of 6) but combined with 1 Corinthians 4 at 3.1 is between Matthew 5–7 with 2.8 and Acts 12/18 with 3.5 (but still within the written range). The passage that is purportedly closest to spoken language (spoken medium), Matthew 5–7, is closest to Halliday's estimates, but is still higher than he anticipated, at least for English. The question must be raised regarding how one views Romans in relation to spoken language (spoken or written medium), even when aggregated with 1 Corinthians 4. The results indicate a possible incongruence within their medium. I suggest that the results may indicate that, even if Paul's letters were dictated and even if the letters were originally read aloud (spoken medium), the dictation and subsequent reading process do not necessarily constitute an example of spoken language, but the letter remains within the sphere of written language (written medium). This tentatively calls into question theories regarding the orality of early Christianity that use the letters as examples.

TABLE 6.14 Grammatical intricacy comparison

Grammatical Intricacy	Halliday	Mt. 5–7	Acts 12/18	Rom. 2 + 1 Cor. 4	Rom. 2/1 Cor. 4	
Spoken	?	2.25	2.1	2.0	2.3	2.2
Written	?					

The difference in the figures for grammatical intricacy for the three sets of examples is not great. However, Halliday gives us no guidance on his thought regarding levels of grammatical intricacy. 1 Corinthians 4 has the greatest grammatical intricacy, not expected (according to Halliday) for written language (written medium) (although not necessarily indicating a spoken medium), but Romans 2 has the lowest grammatical intricacy, expected for written language (written medium). Acts 12/18, which would constitute a written document (written medium), does have the lowest aggregate level of grammatical intricacy, as one might expect. Perhaps the most we can say here is that the passage that has the most likelihood of being spoken (spoken medium) has the highest level of grammatical intricacy (Mt. 5–7, although only slightly) as one might expect, whereas the passage that most likely reflects written language (written medium) has the

---

[67] For Halliday's figures I indicate both his early range and his later more definitive comparative figures. See previous discussion in this chapter.

lowest level of grammatical intricacy (Acts 12/18), again as one might expect. The letter passages fall between the other two sets but are closer to Matthew 5–7. This is perhaps to be expected, because even if Matthew 5–7 originated with spoken language, it has gone through the process of being transferred into written form (graphic channel) and now has characteristics of written language, perhaps to the point of not being able to be distinguished from written language concerning grammatical intricacy.

IMPLICATIONS FOR ORALITY AND TEXTUALITY IN EARLY CHRISTIANITY

This chapter's findings based upon three sets of examples from the Greek New Testament are entirely preliminary but are nevertheless suggestive for the topic of orality and textuality in early Christianity. I identify three implications for further consideration.

The first implication is that we must be careful to define our terms well and with appropriate criteria for differentiation. As I have already noted, the only textual access we have to early Christianity is through its written documents. In other words, the only means to either the spoken or written medium is through the graphic channel. The process of inscripturation may have had a major effect on what and how much we are able to say about orality in early Christianity. We may well and appropriately recognize that early Christianity began as a spoken language phenomenon—Jesus was primarily a teacher of those who listened to him, those in his closest circle of followers, his disciples, and wider groups that gathered around him. He was known as and functioned as an oral teacher. There is no doubt that what he said and did were transmitted in this form, for at least some length of time. Many if not most of the early leaders of Christianity functioned similarly, even the apostle Paul. If we are to believe the records in the book of Acts, Paul too was at least initially an oral teacher who conveyed his teachings through spoken language (his speeches), with his letters coming later, even if soon after. At this point, Christianity may be said to have used the spoken medium extensively, if not exclusively, in its earliest days, although the written medium soon came to be used as well. Nevertheless, we only have access to both through the graphic channel of the written texts of the New Testament.

Christianity, however, at some point became a written language phenomenon. When it came time to preserve the sayings and events of early Christianity and to pass these on to others, writing was a necessity. The spoken medium was replaced by the written medium. In order to estimate any differences between orality and textuality in early Christianity, we must find suitable and appropriate and measurable ways to estimate the differences between them—but always mediated through direct access only to written sources. Our attempts to differentiate the oral and written media must be done by means of graphic material. This requires further linguistic modeling to determine such differences and means to estimate and calculate their relative positions, tested upon other corpora (but always realizing that the same restrictions apply to any ancient corpus).

The second implication is that we may need to re-interpret how we examine some of the phenomena of early Christianity. The results gathered here, as preliminary as they recognizably are, do point in approximately the correct directions regarding the differences between spoken and written language gathered from other, comparative study (admittedly on English), even if the differences are not as great as we would like or might even have expected. The material from Matthew 5–7 does have an overall lower level of lexical density when compared to the passages in Acts 12/18 and even Romans 2/1 Corinthians 4. This would be expected for an instance of spoken language (spoken medium). The lexical density level is higher than predicted by Halliday, and this is perhaps because even this instance of originally oral communication is transmitted through the graphic channel. The lexical density levels for the passages in Acts 12/18 and Romans 2/1 Corinthians 4 are within the broad range suggested by Halliday for written language, even if neither achieves the absolute figure that he posited. In these two instances, the examination of criteria for spoken and written language seems able to provide a useful means of distinction and differentiation.

Despite stereotypes to the contrary, based upon the limited data gathered so far, however, we are pushed to consider the letters of Paul as instances of the written language phenomenon (written medium). Romans 2 has a higher level of lexical density than either of the other two sets of passages, even if 1 Corinthians 4 is lower. This result runs contrary to the conclusions of those who wish to see Paul's letters as records of oral performance, meant to be performed for and in his churches. The resulting incongruity merits further exploration. If the passages studied are at all representative (and I happen to think that there are some passages that would make the lexical density higher, such as those with more Old Testament citations), then we must say that dictation does not constitute oral language transmission, even if some of its features are retained, but it constitutes an oral means of creating a written text. This conclusion is in keeping with the facts that we know from ancient letter production. Even if Paul dictated his letters, a given text would probably have originally been recorded on a wax tablet for correction before being written in "final" form on papyrus. This process mirrors the kind of revision process that Halliday envisions when he speaks of the need to compare oral transcriptions with drafts of written communication (and the same would have applied to the transcription of Jesus's sermon on the mount).

The matter of grammatical intricacy is not given specific numerical guidance by Halliday, but the results for the sets of New Testament passages are roughly in keeping with what he suggests. Contrary to what we might expect regarding grammatical intricacy, Matthew 5–7 has a higher level of grammatical intricacy more typical of spoken language (spoken medium) than do the other two sets of passages. The difference is not great, but a difference it seems to be. Acts 12/18 overall are lower in grammatical intricacy than the aggregated Romans 2/1 Corinthians 4 (even if Rom. 2 has the overall lowest intricacy level). This evidence is in conformity with Halliday's supposition regarding written language having lower grammatical intricacy than spoken language. However, this also further supports the need to rethink how we view the Pauline epistles as written rather than spoken language. The result for our knowledge of early Christianity is the possibility of needing to rethink the entire letter-producing and transmission process as one that falls within the scope and purview of written language rather than spoken language production.

The third implication concerns questions of canon. There is an assumption in some circles of New Testament studies that oral material is closer to the original source than written material. Oral sources are thought to be more reflective of their originating circumstances, whereas written materials have gone through a regularizing transmission process. The conclusion drawn from this is to value the (early) oral material in some ways more highly than the (later) written material or to view it as more reliable or authentic. This distinction between oral and written may, indeed, be true in some circumstances. What I have found, however, makes me cautious to use such a distinction. The data that

I have gathered seem to indicate that estimations of the differences between spoken and written language indicate a difference in production, but not necessarily a difference in canonical status. We would expect the language of Jesus to reflect spoken language, and the passage examined, Matthew 5–7, does that. We would expect the language of the author of Acts to reflect written language, and it does seem to do so in Acts 12/18, even if not as strongly in relation to the Matthean passage as we would like. However, the examination of Romans 2/1 Corinthians 4 does not strongly indicate a status within either. Its lexical density does seem to conform more to written language, but its mediating position in grammatical intricacy (noting however individual variations between Rom. 2 and 1 Cor. 4) makes categorization difficult, even if it tends toward the written language. Further study may in fact indicate that we must completely rethink the criteria that Halliday developed for English in order to find tests that are more reflective of the linguistic features of ancient Greek.

CONCLUSION

I would not presume to have solved the issue of being able to differentiate between oral and written sources within the New Testament, or to have solved the issue of the implications of such a distinction for discussion of canon. In fact, if anything, I believe that these preliminary inquiries have indicated that far more needs to be done before we can use such tests as in any way indicative of such matters. Perhaps all that is needed is a study of more samples. However, the random samples that were taken do not indicate that we should expect more significant or widely varying results in other portions of the New Testament. Nevertheless, such studies could and probably should be done. For any such test, however, one must always take into account that we are dealing not with transcriptions of spoken language in any instance but always, at best, with spoken language (spoken medium) mediated through written language (graphic channel). There are some indicators that the origins may have been in either spoken or written media, but the results are probably always going to revert to the middle because of their common graphic form. As a result, such findings are no doubt helpful in confirming results already achieved through other means, if they are not able to suggest new conclusions—apart from the need to reconsider how we think of the letter material. There are some relatively strong indications that we must rethink the notion of the letters as capturing oral performance, by seeing them instead—even though dictated and in that sense having spoken origins—as the products of written language (written medium) even if they retain some spoken features.

Conclusion

This volume is admittedly and intentionally not the usual kind of book that readers in New Testament Greek linguistics have come to expect. Most such volumes are either works of grammar full of various intimidating types of examples or, more recently, introductory-level summaries of the supposed state of research. Most such volumes, unfortunately, reprise work done elsewhere and probably in more technical venues, such as journal articles or individual chapters in technical volumes. This volume is not a book of that sort.

This volume, instead, constitutes my attempt to move linguistic study of the Greek New Testament forward by looking both to the past and to the future. In part one, I have attempted to place contemporary discussion of New Testament Greek linguistics within its historical context. This historical context includes its place within contemporary language study. As a result, the two chapters in part one range over a variety of subjects and time periods. These two chapters offer an informed summary of the history of New Testament Greek language study within the context of the broader developments within language scholarship. The historical survey includes the rationalist period, the comparative-historical period, and the modern linguistic period of language study. However, my purpose has not been simply to trace this historical account in a distant and dispassionate way but to show how the paradigms of thought that have dominated the earlier periods are still, unfortunately, to be found within contemporary study of New Testament Greek. I attempted to place many of the works that are used within New Testament Greek study within this historical narrative. Not only that, but I have also attempted to offer a more detailed study of the major schools of linguistic thought that continue to be used in New Testament studies as a suitable platform for more informed discussion of the present and the future of linguistics and New Testament Greek studies.

The field of linguistics—like probably every academic field—is a complex set of intertwined theories and approaches to the study of language. It has not only its past, but a present and, we anticipate, a future. Despite apparent turmoil within modern linguistics, I have attempted to offer a way through this discussion by presenting and assessing the major linguistic schools that have developed out of the variety of contemporary linguistic theories. I have argued that there is a means of categorizing and evaluating these various theories and bringing order out of what could be perceived to be chaos, so that we may examine in a more informed way how we approach the language of the Greek New Testament. I recognize that there is a healthy variety of different theories and resulting schools of thought within linguistics, including within New Testament studies. However, I also believe that some of these models have proven more linguistically productive than others. I have long been an advocate and active practitioner of Systemic Functional Linguistics (SFL), and so I set the ground for the rest of this volume by presenting a concise outline of SFL architecture and some of the results of its application within New Testament Greek study. These applications of SFL to the study of the New Testament have penetrated a wide variety of arenas within New Testament scholarship and hold out promise of further productive linguistic modeling in the future.

In the second part of this volume, I offer some of my own explorations of dimensions of SFL and the Greek New Testament. As I previously mentioned, many works in Greek linguistics are consciously and overtly grammatical. I too have written such volumes. However, in this volume, I have tackled four different areas where I believe that SFL can make a productive contribution to New Testament Greek study in new and unexpected ways. These areas are metaphor theory, rhetoric, cognition, and orality and textuality. I devote a chapter to each one of these topics, presenting some theory and then treating a variety of examples.

There are many who are probably familiar with conceptual metaphor theory and its progeny as one of the major contributions of Cognitive Linguistics to New Testament study. Far fewer are familiar with the contribution of SFL to metaphor theory, which I explore in the third chapter. However, SFL has a sophisticated approach to metaphor that attempts to move beyond some of the philosophical and literary difficulties by positing a linguistic approach. SFL recognizes what it calls both lexical and grammatical metaphor. Lexical metaphor has significant overlap with other theories of metaphor, but the insightful contribution of SFL is grammatical metaphor. Grammatical metaphor is the means by which the meaning of a text is preserved but the wording is changed (as opposed to lexical metaphor where meaning is diversified). There are two major types of grammatical metaphor, interpersonal and ideational (based upon the SFL metafunctions). I have some questions about interpersonal metaphor, although I recognize a place for it in SFL and possibly in New Testament studies and show some of these possibilities. SFL makes its greatest contribution to grammatical metaphor, in which it emphasizes the process of nominalization. I discuss the significance of this transference of meaning, by which a process becomes an entity, and show its productive and expansive capacity. However, I go further and present a case for verbalization, by which an entity becomes a process. Halliday dismisses this notion, but language is full of such occurrences, including the Greek of the New Testament. These two reciprocal forms of metaphorization open new possibilities within Greek linguistics and for the interpretation of the New Testament, some of which I have begun to explore. I encourage others to explore further.

The next chapter discusses the field of rhetoric and linguistics. Rhetorical studies is a well-developed academic field and its range of applications seems to be growing. New Testament studies is not exempt from this growth, as has been evidenced over the last thirty or more years. There have been two major approaches to rhetoric and the New Testament. Some approach the New Testament from the vantage of classical rhetoric and others from the New Rhetoric, concerned with principles of argumentation. It is widely accepted that language may be used for a variety of purposes and one of those is persuasion. As a result, rhetoric has been given an appropriate place within various linguistic theories, including SFL. Some within SFL place rhetoric within the textual metafunction (concerned with the how of a text), but I place it within the interpersonal metafunction (the who of a text). One of the major features of the architecture of SFL is the differentiation of strata of language. A major stratal differentiation is between the levels of semantics and of the lexicogrammar. I believe—and argue in this fourth chapter—that the attitude semantic system, realized in the lexicogrammar by the mood form system, is a productive means of describing the rhetorical function of language. The attitude system is concerned with various speech functions, that is, how the speaker positions himself/herself in relation to the recipients. I believe that by exploring the speech functions within Greek we can engage in a linguistically grounded approach to the rhetoric of a text. I offer some examples to show how rhetoric may be seen as part of the SFL description of language.

In the fifth chapter, I address the question of SFL and cognition. At several places within this volume, I discuss Cognitive Linguistics. I offer a brief accounting of its history and relationship with other linguistic theories in Chapters One and Two, placing it as a development from the formalism of Noam Chomsky while also recognizing some of its functional characteristics. Cognitive Linguistics draws heavily upon concepts derived from the cognitive sciences. In this chapter, I approach the question of cognition from a SFL standpoint. One of the major features of SFL architecture is the use of system networks to represent the language potential. These system networks have been drawn and re-drawn over the last fifty years or more within SFL as a means of capturing the semantic choices within the various meaning systems of language. In that sense, I regard system networks as a representation of cognition. Rather than appealing to some of the abstract notions from Cognitive Linguistics, I draw upon these system networks to represent what a language user does in acts of communication. Since I introduced the attitudinal system network in the previous chapter, I return to that system here in this chapter (I could have used others). The system is a complex one, with a variety of semantic choices represented and various realization statements as the product. This complex of choices presents a means of representing how a user makes admittedly un-conscious semantic choices within the system network and thereby represents human language cognition within a SFL framework. I explore some of the ways that these choices may be represented within texts and the cognitive possibilities understood from them.

The final chapter, Chapter Six, is concerned with orality and textuality. New Testament studies has long been concerned with questions about the oral origins of the texts of the New Testament and how and when they were transformed into written texts. There are entire theories that are dependent upon such a distinction, often utilizing diachronic arguments in their formulation. Modern linguistics has, for the most part, also emphasized spoken over written texts, although for different reasons and in different ways. One of the few linguists to develop a sustained theory, not just about spoken texts but about their relationship with written texts, is Michael Halliday. In this chapter, I note some of the usual ways that orality and textuality are discussed, and then turn to SFL for a sustained and, I believe, clearer approach to their relationship. Halliday has formulated theories regarding the lexical density and grammatical intricacy of language, with the first more prominent in written texts and the latter in spoken texts. Based upon this distinction and relationship, and using Halliday's numerical estimates as a guide, I examine three sets of passages in the New Testament to determine the degree of their spoken and written characteristics. I recognize that, even though these New Testament texts may have been either spoken or written (spoken or written medium), they are conveyed to us through a graphic channel that affects our ability to analyze them. Nevertheless, I attempt to provide some preliminary findings in that regard. I pose that the Pauline letters present the greatest challenge to the distinction between spoken and written texts.

All the chapters in this volume—including the two historical chapters that define modern linguistics and trace its history—are designed to be preliminary, tentative, and suggestive. As opposed to the tendency found in some circles to make narrow claims for particular or specific features of language, I have taken up some larger questions that reach beyond these narrow confines to grasp some larger interpretive issues within New Testament studies. I have suggested that SFL has the potential to address some of these questions in new and suggestive ways, and I have attempted to point in some useful directions in this endeavor. I leave it to others to explore some of these avenues much more fully and productively.

BIBLIOGRAPHY

Adams, Edward. *Constructing the World: A Study in Paul's Cosmological Language*. Edinburgh: T&T Clark, 2000.

Akamatsu, Tsutomu. *The Theory of Neutralization and the Archiphoneme in Functional Phonology*. Amsterdam: John Benjamins, 1988.

Albuquerque, Roque N. *Presupposition and [E]motion: The Upgraded Function and the Semantics of the Participle in the New Testament*. New York: Peter Lang, 2020.

Allan, Kathryn. *Metaphor and Metonymy: A Diachronic Approach*. Publications of the Philological Society 42. Malden, MA: Wiley-Blackwell, 2008.

Allan, Keith. *The Western Classical Tradition in Linguistics*. 2nd ed. London: Equinox, 2010.

Andreski, Stanislav, ed. *Herbert Spencer: Structure, Function and Evolution*. London: Michael Joseph, 1971.

Andrews, Edna. *Markedness Theory: The Union of Asymmetry and Semiosis in Language*. Durham, NC: Duke University Press, 1990.

Apel, Karl-Otto. *Analytic Philosophy of Language and the Geisteswissenschaften*. Foundations of Language Supplementary Series 4. Dordrecht: Reidel, 1967.

Ayer, Alfred Jules. *Language, Truth and Logic*. 2nd ed. Repr., New York: Dover, 1952 (1936).

Ayer, Alfred Jules, ed. *Logical Positivism*. New York: Free Press, 1959.

Bakhtin, M. M. *The Dialogic Imagination: Four Essays*. Edited by Michael Holquist. Translated by Caryl Emerson and Michael Holquist. Austin: University of Texas Press, 1981.

Bakker, Egbert J. "How Oral Is Oral Composition?" Pages 292–47 in *Signs of Orality: The Oral Tradition and Its Influence in the Greek and Roman World*. Edited by Anne E. Mackay. Leiden: Brill, 1999.

Bal, Mieke. *Narratology: Introduction to the Theory of Narrative*. 3rd ed. Toronto: University of Toronto Press, 2009.

Banks, David. *The Birth of the Academic Article: Le Journal des Sçavans and the Philosophical Transactions 1665–1700*. Sheffield: Equinox, 2017.

Banks, David. *A Systemic Functional Grammar of English: A Simple Introduction*. London: Routledge, 2019.

Bann, S., and J. E. Bowlt, eds. *Russian Formalism: A Collection of Articles and Texts in Translation*. Edinburgh: Scottish Academic Press, 1973.

Barfield, Owen. *Poetic Diction: A Study in Meaning*. New York: McGraw-Hill, 1964 (1938).

Barr, James. *The Semantics of Biblical Language*. Oxford: Oxford University Press, 1961.

Barthes, Roland. *Image—Music—Text*. Translated by S. Heath. New York: Hill and Wang, 1977.

Barthes, Roland. "The Old Rhetoric: An Aide-mémoire." Pages 11–94 in Roland Barthes, *The Semiotic Challenge*. Translated by Richard Howard. Oxford: Blackwell, 1988.

Barthes, Roland. *The Pleasure of the Text*. Translated by Richard Miller. New York: Hill and Wang, 1975.

Barthes, Roland. *The Semiotic Challenge*. Translated by Richard Howard. Oxford: Blackwell, 1988.

Bateman, John A. "The Place of Systemic Functional Linguistics as a Linguistic Theory in the Twenty-First Century." Pages 11–26 in *The Routledge Handbook of Systemic Functional Linguistics*. Edited by Tom Bartlett and Gerard O'Grady. London: Routledge, 2017.

Battistella, Edwin L. *Markedness: The Evaluative Superstructure of Language*. Albany: State University of New York Press, 1990.

Baum, Armin. *Der mündliche Faktor und seine Bedeutung für die synoptische Frage: Analogien aus der antiken Literatur, der Experimentalpsychologie, der Oral Poetry-Forschung und dem rabbinischen Traditionswesen*. Tübingen: Francke, 2008.

Bazell, Charles E. *Linguistic Form*. Istanbul: Istanbul Press, 1953.

Beaugrande, Robert de. *Linguistic Theory: The Discourse of Fundamental Works*. London: Longman, 1991.

Beaugrande, Robert de, and Wolfgang Dressler. *Introduction to Text Linguistics*. London: Longman, 1981.

Bebbington, D. W. *Patterns in History: A Christian View*. Downers Grove, IL: InterVarsity Press, 1979.

Beekman, John, John Callow, and Michael Kopesec. *The Semantic Structure of Written Communication*. 5th ed. Dallas: Summer Institute of Linguistics, 1981.

Bell, Allan. "The Early Greek-Language Tradition behind the Gospels." Pages 229–42 in *Holding Forth the Word of Life: Essays in Honor of Tim Meadowcroft*. Edited by John de Jong and Csilla Saysell. Eugene, OR: Wipf & Stock, 2020.

Berger, Peter L. *Invitation to Sociology: A Humanistic Perspective*. Garden City, NY: Doubleday, 1963.

Berger, Peter L., and Thomas Luckmann. *The Social Construction of Reality: A Treatise in the Sociology of Knowledge*. New York: Doubleday, 1966.

Berry, Margaret. *Introduction to Systemic Linguistics*. 2 vols. London: Batsford, 1975–77.

Berry, Margaret. "Systemic Linguistics and Discourse Analysis: A Multi-Layered Approach to Exchange Structure." Pages 120–45 in *Studies in Discourse Analysis*. Edited by Malcolm Coulthard and Martin Montgomery. London: Routledge & Kegan Paul, 1981.

Betz, Hans Dieter. *Galatians: A Commentary on Paul's Letter to the Churches in Galatia*. Hermeneia. Philadelphia: Fortress, 1979.

Bhat, D. N. S. *The Prominence of Tense, Aspect and Mood*. Amsterdam: John Benjamins, 1999.

Biber, Douglas. *Variation across Speech and Writing*. Cambridge: Cambridge University Press, 1988.

Bičan, Aleš. "Phoneme in Functional and Structural Phonology." *Linguistica Online* (2005): 1–14.

Binnick, Robert I., ed. *The Oxford Handbook of Tense and Aspect*. Oxford: Oxford University Press, 2012.

Black, David Alan. *It's Still Greek to Me: An Easy-to-Understand Guide to Intermediate Greek*. Grand Rapids: Baker, 1998.

Black, David Alan. *Linguistics for Students of New Testament Greek: A Survey of Basic Concepts and Applications*. Grand Rapids: Baker, 1988. 2nd ed., 2000.

Black, Max. *Meaning and Metaphor: Studies in Language and Philosophy*. Ithaca, NY: Cornell University Press, 1962.

Black, Stephanie L. *Sentence Conjunctions in the Gospel of Matthew: καί, δέ, τότε, γάρ, οὖν and Asyndeton in Narrative Discourse*. JSNTSup 216. SNTG 9. London: Sheffield Academic, 2002.

Blass, Friedrich. *Grammatik des Neutestamentlichen Griechisch*. Göttingen: Vandenhoeck & Ruprecht, 1896.

Blass, Friedrich, and Albert Debrunner. *A Greek Grammar of the New Testament and Other Early Christian Literature*. Translated by Robert W. Funk. Chicago: University of Chicago Press, 1961.

Bloom, Paul, Mary A. Peterson, Lynn Nadel, and Merrill F. Garrett, eds. *Language and Space*. Cambridge, MA: MIT Press, 1996.

Bloomfield, Leonard. *Language*. New York: Holt, Rinehart & Winston, 1933.

Bloomfield, Leonard. "Meaning." *MDU* 53 (1943): 101–6. Repr. pages 400–5 in *A Leonard Bloomfield Anthology*. Edited by Charles F. Hockett. Bloomington: Indiana University Press, 1970.

Blount, Brian K. *Cultural Interpretation: Reorienting New Testament Criticism*. Minneapolis: Augsburg Fortress, 1995.

Boas, Franz. "Introduction." Pages 1:1–83 in *Handbook of American Indian Languages*. 3 vols. Washington, DC: American Print Office, 1911–38.

Boas, Franz. *Race, Language, and Culture*. Chicago: University of Chicago Press, 1940.

Booth, Wayne C. *The Rhetoric of Fiction*. Chicago: University of Chicago Press, 1961. 2nd ed., 1983.

Bopp, Franz. *A Comparative Grammar of the Sanscrit, Zend, Greek, Latin, Lithuanian, Gothic, German, and Sclavonic Languages*. Edited by H. H. Wilson. Translated by Lieutenant Eastwick. 3 parts in 2 vols. London: James Madden, 1845–50. Repr., Hildesheim: Georg Olms, 1985.

Bopp, Franz. *Über das Conjugationssystem der Sanskritsprache in Vergleichung mit jenem der griechischen, lateinischen, persischen und germanischen Sprache*. Edited by R. J. Windischmann. Frankfurt am Main: Andreäischen, 1816. Repr., London: Routledge/Thoemmes, 1995.

Botha, Pieter J. J. "The Gospel of Mark, Orality Studies and Performance Criticism." *Religion and Theology* 25 (2018): 350–93.

Botha, Rudolf P. *Challenging Chomsky: The Generative Garden Game*. Oxford: Blackwell, 1989.

Brook-Rose, Christine. *A Grammar of Metaphor*. London: Secker and Warburg, 1958.

Brooks, Cleanth, and Robert Penn Warren. *Modern Rhetoric*. New York: Harcourt Brace Jovanovich, 1949.

Brooks, James A., and Carlton L. Winbery. *Syntax of New Testament Greek*. Washington, DC: University Press of America, 1979. Repub., 1988.

Brugmann, Karl. *Griechische Grammatik*. Munich: Beck, 1885. 4th ed. Edited by Albert Thumb, 1913.

Brugmann, Karl. *Kurze Vergleichende Grammatik der Indogermanische Sprachen*. 3 vols. Strassburg: Trübner, 1903.

Brugmann, Karl, and Berthold Delbrück. *Grundriss der vergleichenden Grammatik der Indogermanischen Sprachen*. 5 vols. Strassburg: Trübner, 1886–1900.

Bühler, Karl. "Das Strukturmodell der Sprache." *TCLP* 6 (1936): 3–12. Repr. pages 220–8 in Karl Bühler, *Schriften zur Sprachtheorie*. Edited by Achim Eschbach. Tübingen: Mohr Siebeck, 2012.

Bühler, Karl. *Schriften zur Sprachtheorie*. Edited by Achim Eschbach. Tübingen: Mohr Siebeck, 2012.

Bühler, Karl. *Theory of Language: The Representational Function of Language*. Translated by Donald Fraser Goodwin. Amsterdam: John Benjamins, 1990. ET of *Sprachtheorie: Die Darstellungfunktion der Sprache*. Jena: Gustav Fischer, 1934. Repr., 1982.

Burke, Kenneth. *Grammar of Motives*. Berkeley: University of California Press, 1945.

Burke, Kenneth. *Language as Symbolic Action: Essays on Life, Literature, and Method*. Berkeley: University of California Press, 1966.

Burke, Kenneth. *Rhetoric of Motives*. Berkeley: University of California Press, 1950.

Buss, Martin J. *The Changing Shape of Form Criticism: A Relational Approach*. Sheffield: Sheffield Phoenix, 2010.

Butler, Christopher S. *Structure and Function: A Guide to Three Major Structural-Functional Theories*. 2 vols. Amsterdam: John Benjamins, 2003.

Buttmann, Alexander. *A Grammar of the New Testament Greek*. Translated by J. H. Thayer. Andover: Warren F. Draper, 1880.

Campbell, Constantine R. *Advances in the Study of Greek: New Insights for Reading the New Testament*. Grand Rapids: Zondervan, 2015.

Campbell, Constantine R. *Verbal Aspect, the Indicative Mood, and Narrative: Soundings in the Greek of the New Testament*. SBG 13. New York: Peter Lang, 2007.

Caragounis, Chrys C. *The Development of Greek and the New Testament: Morphology, Syntax, Phonology, and Textual Transmission*. WUNT 167. Tübingen: Mohr Siebeck, 2004.

Caragounis, Chrys C., ed. *Greek: A Language in Evolution. Essays in Honour of Antonios N. Jannaris*. Hildesheim: Georg Olms, 2010.

Carson, D. A. *Exegetical Fallacies*. Grand Rapids: Baker, 1984. 2nd ed., 1996.

Casson, Sandra H. *Textual Signposts in the Argument of Romans: A Relevance-Theory Approach*. Atlanta: SBL Press, 2019.

Chamberlain, William Douglas. *An Exegetical Grammar of the Greek New Testament*. New York: Macmillan, 1941. Repr., Grand Rapids: Baker, 1994.

Chang, Kai-Hsuan. *The Impact of Bodily Experience on Paul's Resurrection Theology*. LNTS 655. London: T&T Clark, 2022.

Chapman, Siobhan. *Language and Empiricism: After the Vienna Circle*. Basingstoke: Palgrave Macmillan, 2008.

Chatman, Seymour. *Story and Discourse: Narrative Structure in Fiction and Film*. Ithaca, NY: Cornell University Press, 1978.

Chomsky, Noam. *Aspects of the Theory of Syntax*. Cambridge, MA: MIT Press, 1965.

Chomsky, Noam. *Language and Mind*. New York: Harcourt, Brace & World, 1968. Enlarged ed., 1972.

Chomsky, Noam. *Lectures on Government and Binding*. Dordrecht: Foris, 1981.

Chomsky, Noam. "Linguistic Theory" (1965). Repr. pages 152–9 in *Noam Chomsky: Selected Readings on Transformational Theory*. Edited by J. P. B. Allen and Paul van Buren. Oxford: Oxford University Press, 1971.

Chomsky, Noam. *The Minimalist Program*. Cambridge: MA: MIT Press, 1995.

Chomsky, Noam. *Syntactic Structures*. JLSMi 4. The Hague: Mouton, 1957.

Chomsky, Noam. *Topics in the Theory of Generative Grammar*. The Hague: Mouton, 1971.

Cirafesi, Wally V. "ἔχειν πίστιν in Hellenisic Greek and its Contribution to the πίστις Χριστοῦ Debate." *BAGL* 1 (2012): 5–38.

Cirafesi, Wally V. *Verbal Aspect in Synoptic Parallels: On the Method and Meaning of Divergent Tense-Form Usage in the Synoptic Passion Narratives*. LBS 7. Leiden: Brill, 2013.

Clarke, M. L. *Rhetoric at Rome: A Historical Survey*. Revised by D. H. Berry. London: Routledge, 1996.

Classen, Carl Joachim. *Rhetorical Criticism of the New Testament*. WUNT 128. Tübingen: Mohr Siebeck, 2000.

Coleridge, Samuel Taylor. *Biographia Literaria*. Edited by Nigel Leask. London: Dent, 1997.

Collinge, N. E. *The Laws of Indo-European*. Amsterdam: John Benjamins, 1985.

Comrie, Bernard. *Aspect*. CTL. Cambridge: Cambridge University Press, 1976.
Condillac, Étienne Bonnot de. *Essai sur l'origine des connaissances humaines*. Oeuvres de Condillac. Edited by Georges Le Roy. 3 vols. Paris: Presses Universitaires de France, 1947.
Copleston, Frederick. *A History of Philosophy*. Vol. 8 part 1. Garden City, NY: Image, 1966.
Corbett, Edward P. J. *Classical Rhetoric for the Modern Student*. 3rd ed. New York: Oxford University Press, 1990 (1965).
Corbett, Edward P. J. *Rhetorical Analyses of Literary Works*. New York: Oxford University Press, 1969.
Costley, Angela. *Creation and Christ: An Exploration of the Topic of Creation in the Epistle to the Hebrews*. WUNT 2/527. Tübingen: Mohr Siebeck, 2020.
Cotterell, Peter, and Max Turner. *Linguistics and Biblical Interpretation*. Downers Grove, IL: InterVarsity Press, 1989.
Cowie, Fiona. *What's Within? Nativism Reconsidered*. Oxford: Oxford University Press, 1999.
Cranfield, C. E. B. *The Gospel according to St Mark*. CGTC. Cambridge: Cambridge University Press, 1959.
Crellin, Robert. *The Syntax and Semantics of the Perfect Active in Literary Koine Greek*. New York: Wiley Blackwell, 2016.
Croft, William. *Radical Construction Grammar: Syntactic Theory in Typological Perspective*. Oxford: Oxford University Press, 2001.
Croft, William, and D. Alan Cruse. *Cognitive Linguistics*. CTL. Cambridge: Cambridge University Press, 2004.
Crystal, David. *What Is Linguistics?* 3rd ed. London: Edward Arnold, 1974.
Culler, Jonathan. *Saussure*. London: Fontana, 1976.
Curtius, Georg. *Die Bildung der Tempora und Modi im Griechischen und Lateinischen sprachvergleichend dargestellt*. Berlin: Wilhelm Besser, 1846. ET *The Greek Verb: Its Structure and Development*. Translated by A. S. Wilkins and E. B. England. London: John Murray, 1880.
Curtius, Georg. *Erläuterungen zum meiner griechischen Schulgrammatik*. Prague: Tempsky, 1863. ET *Elucidations of the Student's Greek Grammar*. 2nd ed. Translated by E. Abbott. London: John Murray, 1875.
Curtius, Georg. *Griechische Schulgrammatik*. Prague: F. Tempsky, 1852.
Dana, H. E., and Julius R. Mantey. *A Manual Grammar of the Greek New Testament*. New York: Macmillan, 1927.
Danove, Paul L. *A Case Frame Grammar and Lexicon for the Book of Revelation*. LNTS 666. London: T&T Clark, 2022.
Danove, Paul L. *The End of Mark's Story: A Methodological Study*. BINS 3. Leiden: Brill, 1993.
Danove, Paul L. *Grammatical and Exegetical Study of New Testament Verbs of Transference: A Case Frame Guide to Interpretation and Translation*. LNTS 329. SNTG 13. London: T&T Clark, 2009.
Danove, Paul L. *Linguistics and Exegesis in the Gospel of Mark: Applications of a Case Frame Analysis and Lexicon*. JSNTSup 218. SNTG 10. Sheffield: Sheffield Academic, 2002.
Danove, Paul L. *New Testament Verbs of Communication: A Case Frame and Exegetical Study*. LNTS 520. London: Bloomsbury, 2015.
Danove, Paul L. *The Rhetoric of Characterization of God, Jesus, and Jesus' Disciples in the Gospel of Mark*. JSNTSup 290. New York: T&T Clark, 2005.
Danove, Paul L. *Theology of the Gospel of Mark: A Semantic, Narrative, and Rhetorical Study of the Characterization of God*. London: Bloomsbury, 2019.

Davidson, Donald. "The Logical Form of Action Sentences" (1967). Repr. pages 105–22 in Donald Davidson, *Essays on Action and Events*. Oxford: Clarendon, 1980.

Davis, William Hersey. *Beginner's Grammar of the Greek New Testament*. New York: Doran, 1923.

Dawson, Zachary K. "Language as Negotiation: Toward a Systemic Functional Model for Ideological Criticism with Application to James 2:1-13." Pages 362–90 in *Modeling Biblical Language: Selected Papers from the McMaster Divinity College Linguistics Circle*. Edited by Stanley E. Porter, Gregory P. Fewster, and Christopher D. Land. LBS 13. Leiden: Brill, 2016.

Dawson, Zachary K. *The Message of the Jerusalem Council in the Acts of the Apostles: A Linguistic Stylistic Analysis*. LBS 22. Leiden: Brill, 2022.

Dawson, Zachary K. "The Rules of 'Engagement': Assessing the Function of the Diatribe in James 2:14-26 Using Critical Discourse Analysis." Pages 155–95 in *The Epistle of James: Linguistic Exegesis of an Early Christian Letter*. Edited by James D. Dvorak and Zachary K. Dawson. LENT 1. Eugene, OR: Pickwick, 2019.

de Man, Paul. *Allegories of Reading: Figural Language in Rousseau, Nietzsche, Rilke, and Proust*. New Haven: Yale University Press, 1979.

de Man, Paul. "Semiology and Rhetoric." *Diacritics* 3.3 (1973): 27–33. Repr. pages 3–19 in *Allegories of Reading: Figural Language in Rousseau*, Nietzsche, *Rilke, and Proust*. New Haven: Yale University Press, 1979.

Decker, Rodney J. *Reading Koine Greek: An Introduction and Integrated Workbook*. Grand Rapids: Baker, 2014.

Deignan, Alice. "The Cognitive View of Metaphor: Conceptual Metaphor Theory." Pages 44–56 in *Metaphor Analysis: Research Practice in Applied Linguistics, Social Sciences and the Humanities*. Edited by Lynne Cameron and Robert Maslen. Sheffield: Equinox, 2010.

Deissmann, G. Adolf. *Bible Studies*. Translated by Alexander Grieve. 2nd ed. Edinburgh: T&T Clark, 1903.

Deissmann, G. Adolf. *Light from the Ancient East*. Translated by L. R. M. Strachan. London: Hodder and Stoughton, 1910.

Derico, T. M. *Oral Tradition and Synoptic Verbal Agreement: Evaluating the Empirical Evidence for Literary Dependence*. Eugene, OR: Pickwick, 2016.

Derrida, Jacques. *Dissemination*. Translated by Barbara Johnson. London: Continuum, 2004.

Derrida, Jacques. "'Genèsse et structure' et la phénoménologie." In *Genèse et structure*. Edited by Maurice de Gandillac, Lucien Goldmann, and Jean Piaget. The Hague: Mouton, 1964. ET pages 154–68 in *Writing and Difference*. Translated by Alan Bass. Chicago: University of Chicago Press, 1978.

Derrida, Jacques. *Speech and Phenomena, and Other Essays on Husserl's Theory of Signs*. Translated by David B. Allison. Evanston, IL: Northwestern University Press, 1973. ET of *La Voix et la phénomène: Introduction au problème du signe dans la phénoménologie de Husserl*. Paris: PUF, 1967.

Derrida, Jacques. "Structure, Sign, and Play in the Discourse of the Human Sciences." Pages 247–65 in *The Structuralist Controversy: The Languages of Criticism and the Sciences of Man*. Edited by Richard Macksey and Eugenio Donato. Baltimore: Johns Hopkins University Press, 1972. Repr. pages 278–93 in Jacques Derrida, *Writing and Difference*. Translated by Alan Bass. Chicago: University of Chicago Press, 1978. ET of *L'écriture et la différence*. Paris: Seuil, 1967.

Devrim, Devo Y. "Grammatical Metaphor: What Do We Mean? What Exactly Are We Researching?" *Functional Linguistics* 2.3 (2015): 1–15.

Dik, Simon C. *The Theory of Functional Grammar*. 2 vols. Edited by Kees Hengeveld. Berlin: Mouton de Gruyter, 1997.

Dixon, Peter. *Rhetoric*. Critical Idiom. London: Methuen, 1971.

Dooley, Robert E., and Stephen H. Levinsohn. *Analyzing Discourse: A Manual of Basic Concepts*. Dallas: SIL International, 2001.

Downs, David J. *The Offering of the Gentiles: Paul's Collection for Jerusalem in Its Chronological, Cultural, and Cultic Contexts*. Tübingen: Mohr Siebeck, 2008. Repr., Grand Rapids: Eerdmans, 2016.

Droste, Flip, and John E. Joseph, eds. *Linguistic Theory and Grammatical Description*. Amsterdam: John Benjamins, 1991.

du Toit, Andrie. "Exploring Textual Structure: Discourse Analysis." Pages 217–65 in *Focusing on the Message: New Testament Hermeneutics, Exegesis and Methods*. Edited by Andrie du Toit. Pretoria: Protea, 2009.

Duden. *Die Grammatik*. Mannheim: DudenVerlag, 2009.

Dvorak, James D. "Ask and Ye Shall Position the Readers: James's Use of Questions to (re-)Align His Readers." Pages 196–245 in *The Epistle of James: Linguistic Exegesis of an Early Christian Letter*. Edited by James D. Dvorak and Zachary K. Dawson. LENT 1. Eugene, OR: Pickwick, 2019.

Dvorak, James D. "'Evidence That Commands a Verdict': Determining the Semantics of Imperatives in the New Testament." *BAGL* 7 (2018): 201–23.

Dvorak, James D. *The Interpersonal Metafunction in 1 Corinthians 1–4: The Tenor of Toughness*. LBS 19. Leiden: Brill, 2021.

Dvorak, James D. "'Prodding with Prosody': Persuasion and Social Influence through the Lens of Appraisal Theory." *BAGL* 4 (2015): 85–120.

Dvorak, James D. "To Incline Another's Heart: The Role of Attitude in Reader Positioning." Pages 599–624 in *The Language and Literature of the New Testament: Essays in Honor of Stanley E. Porter's 60th Birthday*. Edited by Lois K. Fuller Dow, Craig A. Evans, and Andrew W. Pitts. BINS 150. Leiden: Brill, 2017.

Dyer, Bryan R. *Suffering in the Face of Death: The Epistle to the Hebrews and Its Context of Situation*. LNTS 568. London: Bloomsbury, 2017.

Eagleton, Terry. *Literary Theory: An Introduction*. Oxford: Blackwell, 1983.

Easley, Kendall H. *User-Friendly Greek: A Common Sense Approach to the Greek New Testament*. Nashville: B&H, 1994.

Eemeren, Frans H. van. "Rhetoric and Argumentation." Pages 661–71 in *The Oxford Handbook of Rhetorical Studies*. Edited by Michael J. MacDonald. Oxford: Oxford University Press, 2017.

Elder, Nicholas A. *The Media Matrix of Early Jewish and Christian Narrative*. LNTS 612. London: T&T Clark, 2019.

Eliot, T. S. "'Rhetoric' and Poetic Drama" (1919). Repr. pages 37–42 in T. S. Eliot, *Selected Essays*. 3rd ed. London: Faber and Faber, 1941.

Elledge, Roderick. *Use of the Third Person for Self-Reference by Jesus and Yahweh: A Study of Illeism in the Bible and Ancient Near Eastern Texts and Its Implications for Christology*. LNTS 575. London: Bloomsbury T&T Clark, 2017.

Empson, William. *Seven Types of Ambiguity*. London: Hogarth, 1984 (1930).

Evans, Craig A. *Mark 8: 27–16:20*. WBC 34B. Nashville: Nelson, 2001.

Evans, Vyvyan, and Melanie Green. *Cognitive Linguistics: An Introduction*. Edinburgh: University of Edinburgh Press, 2006.

Eve, Eric. *Behind the Gospels: Understanding the Oral Tradition*. London: SPCK, 2013.

Fairclough, Norman. *Analysing Discourse: Textual Analysis for Social Research*. London: Routledge, 2003.
Fairclough, Norman. *Critical Discourse Analysis: The Critical Study of Language*. 2nd ed. London: Longman, 2010.
Fairclough, Norman. *Discourse and Social Change*. Cambridge: Polity, 1992.
Fairclough, Norman. *Language and Power*. 3rd ed. Abingdon: Routledge, 2015.
Fanning, Buist. *Verbal Aspect in New Testament Greek*. Oxford: Oxford University Press, 1990.
Fanning, Buist, Constantine R. Campbell, and Stanley E. Porter. *The Perfect Storm: Critical Discussion of the Semantics of the Greek Perfect Tense under Aspect Theory*. Edited by D. A. Carson. SBG 21. New York: Peter Lang, 2021.
Fantin, Joseph D. *The Greek Imperative Mood in the New Testament: A Cognitive and Communicative Approach*. SBG 12. New York: Peter Lang, 2010.
Fantin, Joseph D. *The Lord of the Entire World: Lord Jesus, a Challenge to Lord Caesar?* NTM 31. Sheffield: Sheffield Phoenix, 2011.
Fauconnier, Gilles. *Mappings in Thought and Language*. Cambridge: Cambridge University Press, 1997.
Fauconnier, Gilles, and Mark Turner. *The Way We Think: Conceptual Blending and the Mind's Hidden Complexities*. New York: Basic, 2002.
Fawcett, Robin P. *Cognitive Linguistics and Social Interaction: Towards an Integrated Model of a Systemic Functional Grammar and the Other Components of a Communicating Mind*. Heidelberg: Julius Groos; Exeter: Exeter University, 1980.
Fawcett, Robin P. *Invitation to Systemic Functional Linguistics through the Cardiff Grammar: An Extension and Simplification of Halliday's Systemic Functional Grammar*. 3rd ed. London: Equinox, 2008.
Fewster, Gregory P. *Creation Language in Romans 8: A Study in Monosemy*. LBS 8. Leiden: Brill, 2013.
Fewster, Gregory P. "Metaphor Analysis with Some Help from Corpus Linguistics: Contextualizing 'Root' Metaphors in Ephesians and Colossians." Pages 339–61 in *Modeling Biblical Language: Selected Papers from the McMaster Divinity College Linguistics Circle*. Edited by Stanley E. Porter, Gregory P. Fewster, and Christopher D. Land. LBS 13. Leiden: Brill, 2016.
Fillmore, Charles J. "The Case for Case." Pages 1–88 in *Universals in Linguistic Theory*. Edited by Emmon Bach and Robert T. Harms. New York: Holt, Rinehart & Winston, 1968.
Fillmore, Charles J. "The Case for Case Reopened." Pages 59–82 in *Syntax and Semantics*. VIII. *Grammatical Relations*. Edited by Peter Cole and Jerrold M. Sadock. New York: Academic Press, 1977.
Fillmore, Charles J., and Paul Kay. *Construction Grammar*. Stanford, CA: CSLI, 1999.
Finnegan, Ruth. *Literacy and Orality*. Oxford: Blackwell, 1988.
Finnegan, Ruth. *Oral Poetry: Its Nature, Significance and Social Context*. Cambridge: Cambridge University Press, 1977.
Firbas, Jan. *Functional Sentence Perspective in Written and Spoken Communication*. Cambridge: Cambridge University Press, 1992.
Firth, J. R. *Papers in Linguistics 1934–1951*. London: Oxford University Press, 1957.
Firth, J. R. *Selected Papers of J. R. Firth 1952–59*. Edited by F. R. Palmer. London: Longmans, 1968.
Firth, J. R. "A Synopsis of Linguistic Theory, 1930–1955." Pages 1–32 in *Studies in Linguistic Analysis*. Oxford: Blackwell, 1957.

Fletcher, Bryan W. Y. "Voice in the Greek of the New Testament." PhD diss., McMaster Divinity College, 2020.

Fodor, Jerry. "Doing without What's Within: Fiona Cowie's *What's Within? Nativism Reconsidered*." *Mind* 110 (437; 2001): 99–148.

Foley, John Miles. *The Theory of Oral Composition: History and Methodology*. Bloomington: Indiana University Press, 1988.

Fontaine, Lise, Tom Bartlett, and Gerard O'Grady, eds. *Systemic Functional Linguistics: Exploring Choice*. Cambridge: Cambridge University Press, 2013.

Foss, Sonja K. *Rhetorical Criticism: Exploration and Practice*. Longwood, CO: Waveland, 1989. 3rd ed., 2004.

Foss, Sonja K., Karen A. Foss, and Robert Trapp. *Contemporary Perspectives on Rhetoric*. 3rd ed. Long Grove, IL: Waveland, 2002.

Foucault, Michel. *The Archaeology of Knowledge and the Discourse on Language*. Translated by A. M. Sheridan Smith. New York: Pantheon, 1972 (1969).

Foucault, Michel. *Language, Counter-Memory, Practice: Selected Essays and Interviews*. Edited by D. F. Bouchard. Translated by D. F. Bouchard and S. Simon. Ithaca, NY: Cornell University Press, 1977.

France, R. T. *The Gospel of Mark*. NIGTC. Grand Rapids: Eerdmans, 2002.

Fries, Peter H. "Systemic Functional Linguistics: A Close Relative of French Functional Linguistics?" *La Linguistique* 37.2 (2001): 89–100.

Fromkin, Victoria et al. *An Introduction to Language: Third Canadian Edition*. Toronto: Nelson/Thomson, 2006.

Fuller, Daniel. "Hermeneutics." Unpublished manuscript, 1969. 5th ed., 1978.

Funk, Robert W. *A Beginning-Intermediate Grammar of Hellenistic Greek*. 3rd ed. Repr., Sonoma, CA: Polebridge, 2013 (1973).

Galen, F. W. *Historic Structures: The Prague School Project, 1928–1948*. Austin: University of Texas Press, 1985.

Gardiner, Alan. *The Theory of Speech and Language*. Oxford: Clarendon, 1932. 2nd ed., 1951.

Garvin, Paul L., ed. and trans. *A Prague School Reader on Esthetics, Literary Structure, and Style*. Washington, DC: Georgetown University Press, 1964.

Gee, James Paul. "Orality and Literacy: From *The Savage Mind* to *Ways with Words*." *TESOL Quarterly* 20 (1986): 719–46.

Geeraerts, Dirk. *Theories of Lexical Semantics*. Oxford: Oxford University Press, 2010.

Genette, Gérard. "La rhétorique restreinte." Pages 21–40 in *Figures III*. Paris: Éditions du Seuil, 1972. ET pages 103–24 in Gérard Genette, *Figures of Literary Discourse*. Translated by Alan Sheridan. Oxford: Blackwell, 1982.

Ghadessy, Mohsen, ed. *Register Analysis: Theory and Practice*. London: Pinter, 1993.

Giacobbe, Mark S. Review of David L. Mathewson and Elodie Ballantine Emig, *Intermediate Greek Grammar* ... *WTJ* 80.2 (2018): 376–79.

Giannakis, Georgios K. "Can a Historical Greek Grammar Be Written?—An Appraisal of A. N. Jannaris' Work." Pages 296–313 in *Greek: A Language in Evolution. Essays in Honour of Antonios N. Jannaris*. Edited by Chrys C. Caragounis. Hildesheim: Georg Olms, 2010.

Gibson, Richard J., and Constantine R. Campbell. *Reading Biblical Greek: A Grammar for Students*. Grand Rapids: Zondervan, 2017.

Giles, Peter. *A Short Manual of Comparative Philology*. 2nd ed. London: Macmillan, 1901.

Givón, Talmy. *Syntax: A Functional-Typological Introduction*. 2 vols. Amsterdam: John Benjamins, 1984–90.

Givón, Talmy. *Topic Continuity in Discourse*. Philadelphia: John Benjamins, 1983.

Gleason, H. A., Jr. *An Introduction to Descriptive Linguistics*. Rev. ed. New York: Holt, Rinehart & Winston, 1961.
Gleitman, Lila R., and Mark Liberman, eds. *An Invitation to Cognitive Science: Language*. 2nd ed. Cambridge, MA: MIT Press, 1995.
Godel, Robert, ed. *A Geneva School Reader in Linguistics*. Bloomington: Indiana University Press, 1969.
Goetchius, Eugene Van Ness. *The Language of the New Testament*. New York: Scribner, 1965.
Goldberg, Adele E. *Constructions: A Construction Grammar Approach to Argument Structure*. Chicago: University of Chicago Press, 1995.
Gotteri, Nigel J. C. "Towards a Comparison of Systemic Linguistics and Tagmemics: An Interim Report and Bibliography." *Journal of the Midland Association for Linguistic Studies* NS 7 (1982): 31–42.
Gotteri, Nigel J. C. "When Is a System Network Not a System Network? And Is That a Fair Question? Fragments from a Continuing Discussion." *Occasional Papers in Systemic Linguistics* 1 (1987): 5–14.
Gotteri, Nigel J. C., and Stanley E. Porter. "Ambiguity, Vagueness and the Working Systemic Linguist." *SWPLL* 2 (1985): 105–18.
Gould, Ezra P. *A Critical and Exegetical Commentary on the Gospel according to St. Mark*. ICC. Edinburgh: T&T Clark, 1901.
Green, Joel B., and Bonnie Howe, eds. *Cognitive Linguistic Explorations in Biblical Studies*. Berlin: de Gruyter, 2014.
Green, Thomas Sheldon. *A Treatise on the Grammar of the New Testament Dialect; Embracing Observations on the Literal Interpretation of Numerous Passages*. London: Bagster, 1842.
Greenberg, Joseph. *Language Universals*. The Hague: Mouton, 1966.
Greimas, A.-J. *Structural Semantics: An Attempt at a Method*. Translated by Daniel McDowell, Ronald Schleifer, and Alan Velie. Lincoln: University of Nebraska Press, 1983. ET of *Sémantique structural: Recherche de méthode*. Paris: Larousse, 1966.
Grice, H. Paul. "Logic and Conversation." Pages 41–58 in *Syntax and Semantics, Volume 3, Speech Acts*. Edited by Peter Cole and Jerry L. Morgan. New York: Academic Press, 1975. Repr. pages 22–40 in Paul Grice, *Studies in the Way of Words*. Cambridge, MA: Harvard University Press, 1989.
Grice, H. Paul. "Meaning." *The Philosophical Review* 66 (1957): 377–88. Repr. pages 213–23 in Paul Grice, *Studies in the Way of Words*. Cambridge, MA: Harvard University Press, 1989.
Grimm, Jacob. *Deutsche Grammatik*. Göttingen: Dieterichschen Buchhandlung, 1819–37.
Gumperz, John J., and Stephen C. Levinson, eds. *Rethinking Linguistic Relativity*. Cambridge: Cambridge University Press, 1996.
Gundry, Robert H. *Mark: A Commentary on His Apology for the Cross*. Grand Rapids: Eerdmans, 1993.
Gupta, Nijay K. *Worship That Makes Sense to Paul: A New Approach to the Theology and Ethics of Paul's Cultic Metaphors*. BZNW 175. Berlin: de Gruyter, 2010.
Gutt, Ernst-August. *Relevance Theory: A Guide to Successful Communication in Translation*. Dallas: SIL and UBS, 1992.
Gutt, Ernst-August. *Translation and Relevance: Cognition and Context*. Repr., Manchester: St. Jerome, 2010.
Hale, Kenneth. "Walpiri and the Grammar of Non-Configurational Languages." *Natural Language and Linguistic Theory* 1 (1983): 5–47.
Halliday, M. A. K. "Anti-Languages." *AA* 78 (1976): 570–84.

Halliday, M. A. K. "A Brief Sketch of Systemic Grammar." Pages 3–6 in *Halliday: System and Function in Language*. Edited by Gunther R. Kress. Oxford: Oxford University Press, 1976.

Halliday, M. A. K. "Differences between Spoken and Written Language: Some Implications for Literacy Teaching" (1979). Repr. pages 63–80 in M. A. K. Halliday, *Language and Education*. Edited by Jonathan J. Webster. CWMH 9. London: Continuum, 2007.

Halliday, M. A. K. *Explorations in the Functions of Language*. London: Edward Arnold, 1973.

Halliday, M. A. K. "Grammar, Society and the Noun." London: H. K. Lewis for University College London, 1967. Repr. pages 50–73 in M. A. K. Halliday, *On Language and Linguistics*. Edited by Jonathan J. Webster. CWMH 3. London: Continuum, 2003.

Halliday, M. A. K. "Grammatical Metaphor in English and Chinese" (1984). Repr. pages 325–33 in M. A. K. Halliday, *Studies in Chinese Language*. Edited by Jonathan J. Webster. CWMH 8. London: Continuum, 2006.

Halliday, M. A. K. *Halliday: System and Function in Language*. Edited by G. R. Kress. Oxford: Oxford University Press, 1976.

Halliday, M. A. K. *Halliday's Introduction to Functional Grammar* (IFG4). Revised by Christian M. I. M. Matthiessen. 4th ed. London: Routledge, 2014.

Halliday, M. A. K. "Introduction: On the 'Architecture' of Human Language." Pages 1–29 in M. A. K. Halliday, *On Language and Linguistics*. Edited by Jonathan J. Webster. CWMH 3. London: Continuum, 2003.

Halliday, M. A. K. *An Introduction to Functional Grammar* (IFG1). London: Edward Arnold, 1985.

Halliday, M. A. K. "Language and Social Man" (1974). Repr. pages 67–130 in M. A. K. Halliday, *Language and Society*. Edited by Jonathan J. Webster. CWMH 10. London: Continuum, 2007.

Halliday, M. A. K. *Language as Social Semiotic: The Social Interpretation of Language and Meaning*. London: Edward Arnold, 1978.

Halliday, M. A. K. "Language Structure and Language Function." Pages 140–65 in *New Horizons in Linguistics*. Edited by John Lyons. Harmondsworth: Penguin, 1970.

Halliday, M. A. K. "On the Language of Physical Science." Pages 162–78 in *Registers of Written English: Situational Factors and Linguistic Features*. Edited by Mohsen Ghadessy. London: Pinter, 1988. Repr. pages 140–58 in M. A. K. Halliday, *The Language of Science*. Edited by Jonathan J. Webster. CWMH 5. London: Continuum, 2004.

Halliday, M. A. K. *Spoken and Written Language*. 2nd ed. Oxford: Oxford University Press, 1989.

Halliday, M. A. K. "Spoken and Written Modes of Meaning" (1987). Repr. pages 323–51 in M. A. K. Halliday, *On Grammar*. Edited by Jonathan J. Webster. CWMH 1. London: Continuum, 2002.

Halliday, M. A. K. "The Spoken Language Corpus: A Foundation for Grammatical Theory" (2002). Repr. pages 157–89 in M. A. K. Halliday, *Computational and Quantitative Studies*. Edited by Jonathan J. Webster. CWMH 6. London: Continuum, 2005.

Halliday, M. A. K. "Things and Relations: Regrammaticising Experience as Technical Knowledge." Pages 185–235 in *Reading Science: Critical and Functional Perspectives on Discourse of Science*. Edited by J. R. Martin and Robert Veel. London: Routledge, 1998. Repr. pages 49–101 in M. A. K. Halliday, *The Language of Science*. Edited by Jonathan J. Webster. CWMH 5. London: Continuum, 2004.

Halliday, M. A. K., and Christian M. I. M. Matthiessen. *Construing Experience through Meaning: A Language-Based Approach to Cognition*. London: Continuum, 1999.

Halliday, M. A. K., and J. R. Martin. *Writing Science: Literacy and Discursive Power*. London: Falmer Press, 1993.
Halliday, M. A. K., and John J. Webster. *Text Linguistics: The How and Why of Meaning*. Sheffield: Equinox, 2014.
Halliday, M. A. K., and Ruqaiya Hasan. *Cohesion in English*. London: Longman, 1976.
Halliday, M. A. K., and Ruqaiya Hasan. *Language, Context, and Text: Aspects of Language in a Social-Semiotic Perspective*. 2nd ed. Oxford: Oxford University Press, 1989.
Hampden-Turner, Charles. *Maps of the Mind: Charts and Concepts of the Mind and Its Labyrinths*. New York: Macmillan, 1981.
Hampson, Norman. *The Enlightenment*. Harmondsworth: Penguin, 1968.
Harris, Dana M. "The Study of the Greek Language." Pages 120–36 in *The State of New Testament Studies: A Survey of Recent Research*. Edited by Scot McKnight and Nijay K. Gupta. Grand Rapids: Baker, 2019.
Harris, James. *Hermes, or, a Philosophical Inquiry concerning Universal Grammar*. London, 1765.
Harris, Murray J. *Prepositions and Theology in the Greek New Testament*. Grand Rapids: Zondervan, 2012.
Harris, Murray J. *The Second Epistle to the Corinthians*. NIGTC. Grand Rapids: Eerdmans, 2005.
Harris, Randy Allen. *The Linguistics Wars*. Oxford: Oxford University Press, 1993.
Harris, Zellig S. *String Analysis of Sentence Structure*. Papers on Formal Linguistics 1. The Hague: Mouton, 1962.
Hart, Roderick P. *Modern Rhetorical Criticism*. New York: HarperCollins, 1990.
Hasan, Ruqaiya. "The Grammarian's Dream: Lexis as Most Delicate Grammar." Pages 184–211 in *New Developments in Systemic Linguistics, Volume 1: Theory and Description*. Edited by M. A. K. Halliday and Robin P. Fawcett. London: Pinter, 1987.
Hasselbrook, David S. *Studies in New Testament Lexicography: Advancing toward a Full Diachronic Approach with the Greek Language*. WUNT 2/303. Tübingen: Mohr Siebeck, 2011.
Hatzidakis, G. N. *Einleitung in die Neugriechische Grammatik*. Leipzig: Breitkopf & Härtel, 1892. Repr., Hildesheim: Georg Olms, 1977.
Hauser, Gerard A. *Introduction to Rhetorical Theory*. Prospect Heights, IL: Waveland, 1986. 2nd ed., 2002.
Havelock, Eric A. *Preface to Plato*. Cambridge, MA: Belknap Press, 1963.
Havránek, Bohuslav. "The Functional Differentiation of the Standard Language." Pages 3–16 in *A Prague School Reader in Linguistics*. Edited by Josef Vachek. Bloomington: Indiana University Press, 1964.
Hawkes, Terence. *Metaphor*. Critical Idiom. London: Methuen, 1972.
Hawthorne, Gerald F. *Philippians*. Revised by Ralph P. Martin. WBC 43. Rev. ed. Nashville: Nelson, 2004.
Heim, Erin M. *Adoption in Galatians and Romans: Contemporary Metaphor Theories and the Pauline Huiothesia Metaphors*. BINS 153. Leiden: Brill, 2017.
Herder, Johann Gottfried. *Essay on the Origin of Language*. Pages 85–166 in *On the Origin of Language*. Translated by John H. Moran and Alexander Gode. Chicago: University of Chicago Press, 1966.
Hester, James D., and J. David Hester, eds. *Rhetorics in the New Millennium: Promise and Fulfillment*. London: T&T Clark, 2010.

Heyvaert, Liesbet. "Nominalization as Grammatical Metaphor: On the Need for a Radically Systemic and Metafunctional Approach." Pages 65–99 in *Grammatical Metaphor: Views from Systemic Functional Linguistics*. Edited by Anne-Marie Simon-Vandenbergen, Miriam Taverniers, and Louise Ravelli. Amsterdam: John Benjamins, 2003.

Hjelmslev, Louis. *Le cátegorie des cas: Étude de grammaire générale*. 2 parts. Aarhus: Universitetsforlaget, 1935–7.

Hjelmslev, Louis. *Essais linguistiques*. Paris: Minuit, 1971 (1959).

Hjelmslev, Louis. *Principes de grammaire générale*. Copenhagen: Andr. Fred. Høst & Son, 1928.

Hjelmslev, Louis. *Prolegomena to a Theory of Language*. Rev. ed. Translated by Francis J. Whitfield. Madison: University of Wisconsin Press, 1961 (1943).

Hjelmslev, Louis. *Résumé of a Theory of Language*. Edited and translated by Francis J. Whitfield. Madison: University of Wisconsin Press, 1975 (manuscript 1943–4).

Hockett, Charles F. *A Course in Modern Linguistics*. New York: Macmillan, 1958.

Hockett, Charles F., ed. *A Leonard Bloomfield Anthology*. Bloomington: Indiana University Press, 1970.

Hockett, Charles F. *The State of the Art*. JLSMi 78. The Hague: Mouton, 1968.

Hoffmann, Ernst G., and Heinrich von Siebenthal. *Griechische Grammatik zum Neuen Testament*. Basel: Immanuel-Verlag, 1985.

Hoffmann, Otto. *Die Griechischen Dialekte in ihrem historischen Zusammenhange*. 3 vols. Göttingen: Vandenhoeck & Ruprecht, 1891–8.

Hofmannsthal, Hugo von. *The Lord Chandos Letter and Other Writings*. Translated by Joel Rotenberg. New York: New York Review Books, 2005.

Hoijer, Harry, ed. *Language in Culture: Conference on the Interrelations of Language and Other Aspects of Culture*. Chicago: University of Chicago Press, 1954.

Holloway, Paul. *Philippians*. Hermeneia. Minneapolis: Fortress, 2017.

Holt, Jens. *Études d'aspect*. Acta Jutlandica Aarskrift for Aarhus Universitet 15.2. Copenhagen: Universitetsforlaget I Aarhus, 1943.

Honour, Hugh. *Romanticism*. Harmondsworth: Penguin, 1979.

Hopper, Paul, and Elizabeth Closs Traugott. *Grammaticalization*. CTL. Cambridge: Cambridge University Press, 1993.

Horner, Winnifred Bryan, ed. *The Present State of Scholarship in Historical and Contemporary Rhetoric*. Rev. ed. Columbia: University of Missouri Press, 1990.

Horrocks, Geoffrey. *Greek: A History of the Language and Its Speakers*. London: Longman, 1997.

Horsley, Richard A., Jonathan A. Draper, and John Miles Foley, eds. *Performing the Gospel: Orality, Memory, and Mark*. Minneapolis: Fortress, 2011.

Howe, Bonnie. *Because You Bear This Name: Conceptual Metaphor and the Moral Meaning of 1 Peter*. BINS 81. Leiden: Brill, 2008.

Hubbeling, H. G. *Spinoza's Methodology*. Assen: Van Gorcum, 1967.

Hudson, Richard. "Some Issues on Which Linguists Can Agree." *JL* 17 (1981): 333–43.

Humboldt, Wilhelm von. *Über die Verschiedenheit des menschlichen Sprachbaues und ihren Einfluss auf die geistige Entwickelung des Menschengeschlechts*. Berlin: Königlichen Akademie der Wissenschaften, 1836. ET *On Language: On the Diversity of Human Language Construction and Its Influence on the Mental Development of the Human Species*. Edited by Michael Losonsky. Translated by Peter Heath. Cambridge: Cambridge University Press, 1999.

Husserl, Edmund. *Logische Untersuchungen*. Halle: M. Niemeyer, 1900–1. 2nd ed., 1913. ET *Logical Investigations*. Translated by John N. Findlay. New York: Humanities, 1970.

Iverson, Kelly R. "Orality and the Gospels: A Survey of Recent Research." *CBR* 8 (2009): 71–106.
Ivić, Milka. *Trends in Linguistics*. Translated by Muriel Heppell. JLSMi 42. The Hague: Mouton, 1965.
Jakobson, Roman. "Closing Statement: Linguistics and Poetics." Pages 350–77 in *Style in Language*. Edited by Thomas A. Sebeok. Cambridge: MA: MIT Press, 1960.
Jakobson, Roman. *On Language*. Edited by Linda R. Waugh and Monique Monville-Burston. Cambridge, MA: Harvard University Press, 1990.
Jakobson, Roman. "Signe zero." Pages 143–52 in *Mélanges de linguistique et de philology offerts à J. van Ginneken à l'occasion du soixantième anniversaire de sa naissance (21 avril 1937)*. Paris: Klincksieck, 1937. Repr. pages 212–19 in Roman Jakobson, *Selected Writings II: Word and Language*. The Hague: Mouton, 1971.
Jakobson, Roman. "Two Aspects of Language and Two Types of Aphasic Disturbances." Pages 55–82 in Roman Jakobson and Morris Halle, *Fundamentals of Language*. JLSMi 1. The Hague: Mouton, 1956.
Jankowsky, Kurt R. *The Neogrammarians*. JLSMi 116. The Hague: Mouton, 1972.
Jannaris, A. N. *A Historical Greek Grammar Chiefly of the Attic Dialect*. London: Macmillan, 1897.
Jeal, Roy A. *Exploring Philemon: Freedom, Brotherhood, and Partnership in the New Society*. Rhetoric of Religious Antiquity 2. Atlanta: SBL Press, 2015.
Jespersen, Otto. *Essentials of English Grammar*. London: George Allen & Unwin, 1933.
Jespersen, Otto. *Language: Its Nature, Development, and Origin*. London: George Allen & Unwin, 1922.
Jespersen, Otto. *The Philosophy of Grammar*. London: George Allen & Unwin, 1924.
Jiménez, Oscar. *Metaphors in the Narrative of Ephesians 2:11-22: Motion towards Maximal Proximity and Higher Status*. LBS 20. Leiden: Brill, 2022.
Johnson, David E., and Paul M. Postal. *Arc Pair Grammar*. Princeton: Princeton University Press, 1980.
Johnson, Mark. *Moral Imagination: Implications of Cognitive Science for Ethics*. Chicago: University of Chicago Press, 1993.
Johnson, Marta K., ed. and trans. *Recycling the Prague Linguistic Circle*. Ann Arbor, MI: Karoma, 1978.
Johnson, Paul. *The Birth of the Modern: World Society 1815–1830*. New York: HarperCollins, 1991.
Jones, W. T. *The Twentieth Century to Wittgenstein and Sartre*. Vol. 5 of *A History of Western Philosophy*. 2nd ed. New York: Harcourt, Brace, Jovanovich, 1975.
Jones, William. *Discourses: Delivered at the Asiatick Society 1785–1792*. Repr., London: Routledge/Thoemmes, 1993.
Joseph, John E., and Talbot J. Taylor, eds. *Ideologies of Language*. London: Routledge, 1990.
Katz, Jerrold J., and Jerry A. Fodor. "The Structure of a Semantic Theory." *Language* 9 (1963): 170–210.
Kelber, Werner H. "In the Beginning Were the Words: The Apotheosis and Narrative Displacement of the Logos." Repr. pages 75–101 in Werner H. Kelber, *Imprints, Voiceprints, and Footprints of Memory: Collected Essays of Werner H. Kelber*. Atlanta: Society of Biblical Literature, 2013.
Kelber, Werner H. "The Works of Memory: Christian Origins as MnemoHistory—A Response." Pages 221–48 in *Memory, Tradition, and Text: Uses of the Past in Early Christianity*. Edited by Alan Kirk and Tom Thatcher. SemeiaSt 52. Leiden: Brill, 2005.

Kennedy, George A. *The Art of Persuasion in Greece*. Princeton: Princeton University Press, 1963.
Kennedy, George A. "Historical Survey of Rhetoric." Pages 3–41 in *Handbook of Classical Rhetoric in the Hellenistic Period, 330 B.C.–A.D. 400*. Edited by Stanley E. Porter. Leiden: Brill, 1997.
Kennedy, George A. *New Testament Interpretation through Rhetorical Criticism*. Chapel Hill: University of North Carolina Press, 1984.
Kern, Philip H. *Rhetoric and Galatians: Assessing an Approach to Paul's Epistle*. SNTSMS 101. Cambridge: Cambridge University Press, 1998.
Kim, Ji Hoe. "A Hallidayan Approach to Orality and Textuality and Some Implications for Synoptic Gospel Studies." *BAGL* 8 (2019): 111–39.
Kinneavy, James L. *A Theory of Discourse: The Aims of Discourse*. New York: Norton, 1971.
Kirk, G. S. *The Songs of Homer*. Cambridge: Cambridge University Press, 1962.
Kittay, Eva Feder. *Metaphor: Its Cognitive Force and Linguistic Structure*. Oxford: Clarendon, 1987.
Klutz, Todd. *The Exorcism Stories in Luke–Acts: A Sociostylistic Reading*. SNTSMS 129. Cambridge: Cambridge University Press, 2004.
Köhler, Wolfgang. *Gestalt Psychology: An Introduction to New Concepts in Modern Psychology*. New York: Liveright, 1947.
Köstenberger, Andreas J., Benjamin L. Merkle, and Robert L. Plummer. *Going Deeper with New Testament Greek: An Intermediate Study of the Grammar and Syntax of the New Testament*. Nashville: B&H, 2016.
Kövecses, Zoltán. *Metaphor: A Practical Introduction*. Oxford: Oxford University Press, 2002.
Kretschmer, Paul. *Einleitung in die Geschichte der Griechischen Sprache*. Göttingen: Vandenhoeck & Ruprecht, 1896.
Kristeva, Julia. *Language—The Unknown: An Initiation into Linguistics*. Translated by Anne M. Menke. New York: Columbia University Press, 1989.
Kristeva, Julia. *Revolution in Poetic Language*. Translated by M. Waller. New York: Columbia University Press, 1984.
Kristeva, Julia. *Σημειωτικὴ: Recherches pour une sémanalyse*. Paris: Seuil, 1969.
Krumbacher, Karl. *Das Problem des neugriechischen Schriftsprache*. Munich: G. Frank'schen, 1902.
Kuhn, Thomas S. *The Structure of Scientific Revolutions*. Chicago: University of Chicago Press, 1962.
Kurschner, Alan E. *A Linguistic Approach to Revelation 19:11–20:6 and the Millennium Binding of Satan*. LBS 23. Leiden: Brill, 2022.
Kwong, Ivan Shin Chun. *The Word Order of the Gospel of Luke: Its Foregrounded Messages*. LNTS 298. London: T&T Clark, 2006.
Lakoff, George. "The Invariance Hypothesis: Is Abstract Reason Based on Image-Schemas?" *Cognitive Linguistics* 1.1 (1990): 39–74.
Lakoff, George. "On Generative Semantics." Pages 232–96 in *Semantics: An Interdisciplinary Reader in Philosophy, Linguistics and Psychology*. Edited by Danny D. Steinberg and Leon A. Jakobovits. Cambridge: Cambridge University Press, 1971.
Lakoff, George. *Women, Fire, and Dangerous Things: What Categories Reveal about the Mind*. Chicago: University of Chicago Press, 1987.
Lakoff, George, and Mark Johnson. *Metaphors We Live By*. Chicago: University of Chicago Press, 1980.

Lakoff, George, and Mark Johnson. *Philosophy in the Flesh: The Embodied Mind and Its Challenge to Western Thought*. New York: Basic, 1999.
Lakoff, George, and Mark Turner. *More than Cool Reason: A Field Guide to Poetic Metaphor*. Chicago: University of Chicago Press, 1989.
Lamb, David A. *Text, Context and the Johannine Community: A Sociolinguistic Analysis of the Johannine Writings*. LNTS 477. London: Bloomsbury, 2014.
Lamb, Sydney. *Outline of Stratificational Grammar*. Washington, DC: Georgetown University Press, 1966.
Lamb, Sydney. *Pathways of the Brain: The Neurocognitive Basis of Language*. Amsterdam: John Benjamins, 1999.
Lambrecht, Jan. *Second Corinthians*. SP 8. Collegeville, MN: Liturgical, 1999.
Land, Christopher D. *The Integrity of 2 Corinthians and Paul's Aggravating Absence*. NTM 36. Sheffield: Sheffield Phoenix, 2015.
Langacker, Ronald N. *Cognitive Grammar: A Basic Introduction*. Oxford: Oxford University Press, 2008.
Langacker, Ronald W. *Foundations of Cognitive Grammar, Volume 1: Theoretical Prerequisites*. Stanford, CA: Stanford University Press, 1987.
Langacker, Ronald W. *Foundations of Cognitive Grammar*. 2 vols. Stanford, CA: Stanford University Press, 1987–91.
Langendoen, D. Terence. *The London School of Linguistics: A Study of the Linguistic Theories of B. Malinowski and J. R. Firth*. Cambridge, MA: MIT Press, 1968.
Lanier, Gregory R. *Old Testament Conceptual Metaphors and the Christology of Luke's Gospel*. LNTS 591. London: Bloomsbury, 2018.
LaSor, William Sanford. *Handbook of New Testament Greek: An Inductive Approach Based on the Greek Text of Acts*. 2 vols. Grand Rapids: Eerdmans, 1973.
Lausberg, Heinrich. *Handbook of Literary Rhetoric: A Foundation for Literary Study*. Edited by David E. Orton and R. Dean Anderson. Translated by Mathew T. Bliss, Annemiek Jansen, and David E. Orton. Leiden: Brill, 1998 (1960).
Leckie-Tarry, Helen. *Language and Context: A Functional Linguistic Theory of Register*. Edited by David Birch. London: Pinter, 1995.
Lee, Jae Hyun. *Paul's Gospel in Romans: A Discourse Analysis of Rom 1:16–8:39*. LBS 3. Leiden: Brill, 2010.
Lee, Penny. *The Whorf Theory Complex: A Critical Reconstruction*. Amsterdam: John Benjamins, 1996.
Leech, Geoffrey, and Jenny Thomas. "Language, Meaning and Context: Pragmatics." Pages 173–206 in *An Encyclopaedia of Language*. Edited by N. E. Collinge. London: Routledge, 1990.
Lehman, David. *Signs of the Times: Deconstruction and the Fall of Paul de Man*. New York: Poseidon, 1992.
Lehmann, Winfred P., ed. *Reader in Nineteenth-Century Historical Indo-European Linguistics*. Bloomington: Indiana University Press, 1967.
Lemon, Lee T., and Marion J. Reis, eds. and trans. *Russian Formalist Criticism: Four Essays*. Lincoln: University of Nebraska Press, 1965.
Leroy, Maurice. *The Main Trends in Modern Linguistics*. Translated by Glanville Price. Oxford: Blackwell, 1967.
Lévi-Strauss, Claude. *The Elementary Structures of Kinship*. Translated by James Bell, John von Sturmer, and Rodney Needham. Boston: Beacon, 1969.

Lévi-Strauss, Claude. *Mythologiques*. Translated by John and Doreen Weightman. 4 vols. New York: Harper & Row, 1969–81 (orig. 1964–71).
Lévi-Strauss, Claude. *Race and History*. Paris: Unesco Publications, 1958.
Lévi-Strauss, Claude. *The Raw and the Cooked*. Translated by John and Doreen Weightman. New York: Harper and Row, 1969.
Lévi-Strauss, Claude. *The Savage Mind*. Chicago: University of Chicago Press, 1966.
Lévi-Strauss, Claude. *Tristes tropiques*. Translated by John Russell. London: Hutchinson, 1961.
Levinsohn, Stephen H. *Discourse Features of New Testament Greek: A Coursebook on the Information Structure of New Testament Greek*. 2nd ed. Dallas: SIL International, 2000.
Levinson, Stephen C. *Pragmatics*. CTL. Cambridge: Cambridge University Press, 1983.
Libby, James A. "The Pauline Canon Sung in a Linguistic Key: Visualizing New Testament Text Proximity by Linguistic Structure, System, and Strata." *BAGL* 5 (2016): 122–201.
Liebenberg, Jacobus. *The Language of the Kingdom and Jesus: Parable, Aphorism, and Metaphor in the Sayings Material Common to the Synoptic Tradition and the Gospel of Thomas*. BZNW 102. Berlin: de Gruyter, 2001.
Lifschitz, Avi. *Language and Enlightenment: The Berlin Debates of the Eighteenth Century*. Oxford Historical Monographs. Oxford: Oxford University Press, 2012.
Lin, Jo-Wang. "Tenselessness." Pages 668–95 in *The Oxford Handbook of Tense and Aspect*. Edited by Robert I. Binnick. Oxford: Oxford University Press, 2012.
Linnemann, Eta. *Is There a Synoptic Problem? Rethinking the Literary Dependence of the First Three Gospels*. Translated by Robert W. Yarbrough. Grand Rapids: Baker, 1992.
Liu, Chiaen. *Register Variation in the New Testament Petrine Texts*. LBS 21. Leiden: Brill, 2022.
Long, Frederick J. Κοινὴ Γραμματική *Koine Greek Grammar: A Beginning-Intermediate Exegetical and Pragmatic Handbook*. Wilmore, KY: Glossa House, 2015.
Longacre, Robert E. *The Grammar of Discourse*. 2nd ed. New York: Plenum, 1996.
Longenecker, Richard N. *Galatians*. WBC 41. Dallas: Word, 1990.
Lord, Albert B. *Epic Singers and Oral Tradition*. Ithaca, NY: Cornell University Press, 1991.
Lord, Albert B. *The Singer of Tales*. New York: Atheneum, 1960.
Louw, J. P. *Semantics of New Testament Greek*. Philadelphia: Fortress; Chico, CA: Scholars Press, 1982.
Louw, Johannes P., and Eugene A. Nida. *Greek–English Lexicon of the New Testament Based on Semantic Domains*. 2 vols. New York: United Bible Societies, 1988.
Lucy, John A. *Grammatical Categories and Cognition: A Case Study of the Linguistic Relativity Hypothesis*. Cambridge: Cambridge University Press, 1992.
Lucy, John A. *Language Diversity and Thought: A Reformulation of the Linguistic Relativity Hypothesis*. Cambridge: Cambridge University Press, 1992.
Luporni, Antonella. "Grammatical Metaphor through the Lens of Software? Examining 'Crisis' in a Corpus of Articles from *The Financial Times*." Pages 260–75 in *Systemic Functional Linguistics in the Digital Age*. Edited by Sheena Gardner and Siân Alsop. Sheffield: Equinox, 2016.
Lyons, John. *Introduction to Theoretical Linguistics*. Cambridge: Cambridge University Press, 1968.
Lyons, John. *Structural Semantics: An Analysis of Part of the Vocabulary of Plato*. Oxford: Blackwell, 1963.
MacCormac, Earl R. *A Cognitive Theory of Metaphor*. Cambridge, MA: MIT Press, 1985.
MacDonald, Michael J., ed. *The Oxford Handbook of Rhetorical Studies*. Oxford: Oxford University Press, 2017.

Malinowski, Bronisław. "The Problem of Meaning in Primitive Languages." Pages 296–336 in C. K. Ogden and I. A. Richards, *The Meaning of Meaning: A Study of the Influence of Language upon Thought and of the Science of Symbolism*. 3rd ed. rev. New York: Harcourt, Brace, 1930 (1923).

Mann, William C., and Sandra A. Thompson. "Rhetorical Structure Theory: A Theory of Text Organization." *ISI Reprint Series* (June 1987): 1–82.

Mann, William C., and Sandra A. Thompson. "Rhetorical Structure Theory: Toward a Functional Theory of Text Organization." *Text* 8.3 (1988): 243–81.

Mann, William C., Christian M. I. M. Matthiessen, and Sandra A. Thompson. "Rhetorical Structure Theory and Text Analysis." Pages 39–79 in *Discourse Description: Diverse Linguistic Analyses of a Fund-Raising Text*. Edited by William C. Mann and Sandra A. Thompson. Amsterdam: John Benjamins, 1992.

Marchese, Maria Pia, ed. *Ferdinand de Saussure, Phonétique: Il manoscritto di Harvard Houghton Library bMS Fr 266 (8)*. Florence: Unipress, 1995.

Marcus, Joel. *Mark*. 2 vols. AYB 27, 27A. New York: Doubleday; New Haven: Yale University Press, 1999–2009.

Martín-Asensio, Gustavo. "Hallidayan Functional Grammar as Heir to New Testament Rhetorical Criticism." Pages 84–107 in *The Rhetorical Interpretation of Scripture: Essays from the 1996 Malibu Conference*. Edited by Stanley E. Porter and Dennis L. Stamps. JSNTSup 180. Sheffield: Sheffield Academic, 1999.

Martín-Asensio, Gustavo. *Transitivity-Based Foregrounding in the Acts of the Apostles: A Functional-Grammatical Approach to the Lukan Perspective*. JSNTSup 202. SNTG 8. Sheffield: Sheffield Academic, 2000.

Martin, J. R. *English Text: System and Structure*. Amsterdam: John Benjamins, 1992.

Martin, J. R., and David Rose. *Working with Discourse: Meaning beyond the Clause*. 2nd ed. London: Continuum, 2007.

Martin, J. R., and P. R. R. White. *The Language of Evaluation: Appraisal in English*. London: Palgrave Macmillan, 2005.

Martin, J. R., and Y. J. Doran, eds. *Systemic Functional Linguistics*. 5 vols. London: Routledge, 2015.

Martin, Troy W., ed. *Genealogies of New Testament Rhetorical Criticism*. Minneapolis: Fortress, 2014.

Martinet, André. *Elements of General Linguistics*. Translated by Elisabeth Palmer. London: Faber and Faber, 1964. ET of *Elements de Linguistique Générale*. Paris: Armand Colin, 1960.

Martinet, André. *A Functional View of Language*. Oxford: Clarendon, 1962.

Matejka, Ladislav. "Jakobson's Response to Saussure's Cours." *Cahiers de l'ILSL* 9 (1997): 169–76.

Mateos, Juan. *El Aspecto Verbal en el Nuevo Testamento*. Estudios de Nuevo Testamento 1. Madrid: Ediciones Cristiandad, 1977.

Mathesius, Vilém. "On the Potentiality of the Phenomena of Language." Pages 1–32 in *A Prague School Reader in Linguistics*. Edited by Josef Vachek. Bloomington: Indiana University Press, 1964.

Mathewson, David L. *Voice and Mood: A Linguistic Approach*. Essentials of Biblical Greek Grammar. Grand Rapids: Baker, 2021.

Mathewson, David L., and Elodie Ballantine Emig. *Intermediate Greek Grammar: Syntax for Students of the New Testament*. Grand Rapids: Baker, 2016.

Matthews, P. H. *Grammatical Theory in the United States from Bloomfield to Chomsky*. CSL 67. Cambridge: Cambridge University Press, 1993.

Matthews, Robert J. "Concerning a 'Linguistic Theory' of Metaphor." *Foundations of Language* 7 (1971): 413–25.

Matthiessen, Christian M. I. M. "Interpreting the Textual Metafunction." Pages 37–81 in *Advances in Systemic Linguistics: Recent Theory and Practice*. Edited by Martin Davies and Louise Ravelli. London: Pinter, 1992.

McDonald, Edward. *Grammar West to East: The Investigation of Linguistic Meaning in European and Chinese Traditions*. Singapore: Springer Nature, 2020.

McNeel, Jennifer. *Paul as Infant and Nursing Mother: Metaphor, Rhetoric, and Identity in 1 Thessalonians 2:5-8*. Atlanta: SBL Press, 2014.

Meillet, Antoine. *Introduction à l'étude comparative des langues indo-européennes*. Paris: Hachette, 1903.

Merkle, Benjamin L., and Robert L. Plummer. *Greek for Life: Strategies for Learning, Retaining, and Reviving New Testament Greek*. Grand Rapids: Baker, 2017.

Mey, Jacob L. *Pragmatics: An Introduction*. 2nd ed. Oxford: Blackwell, 2001.

Michaelis, Laura A. "Construction Grammar and the Syntax-Semantics Interface." Pages 421–35 in *The Bloomsbury Companion to Syntax*. Edited by Silvia Luraghi and Claudia Parodi. London: Bloomsbury, 2015.

Morales, Nelson R. *Poor and Rich in James: A Relevance Theory Approach to James's Use of the Old Testament*. University Park, PA: Eisenbrauns, 2018.

Moravcsik, Edith A., and Jessica R. Wirth, eds. *Syntax and Semantics: Current Approaches to Syntax*. New York: Academic Press, 1980.

Morrow, Jeffrey L. *Three Skeptics and the Bible: La Peyrère, Hobbes, Spinoza, and the Reception of Modern Biblical Criticism*. Eugene, OR: Pickwick, 2016.

Moule, C. F. D. *An Idiom Book of New Testament Greek*. Cambridge: Cambridge University Press, 1953. 2nd ed., 1959.

Moulton, James Hope. *Prolegomena*. Vol. 1 of *A Grammar of New Testament Greek* by James Hope Moulton. Edinburgh: T&T Clark, 1906. 2nd ed., 1906. 3rd ed., 1908.

Moulton, James Hope, and Wilbert Francis Howard. *Accidence and Word-Formation*. Vol. 2 of *A Grammar of New Testament Greek* by James Hope Moulton. Edinburgh: T&T Clark, 1919–29.

Mounce, William. *Morphology of Biblical Greek*. Grand Rapids: Zondervan, 1994.

Mouton, Nicolaas T. Oosthuizen. "Metaphor, Empiricism and Truth: A Fresh Look at Seventeenth-Century Theories of Figurative Language." Pages 23–49 in *Tropical Truth(s): The Epistemology of Metaphor and Other Tropes*. Edited by Armin Burkhardt and Brigitte Nerlich. Berlin: de Gruyter, 2010.

Muilenburg, James. "Form Criticism and Beyond." *JBL* 88 (1969): 1–18.

Mukarovsky, Jan. "Standard Language and Poetic Language." Pages 17–30 in *A Prague School Reader on Esthetics, Literary Structure, and Style*. Edited by Paul L. Garvin. Washington, DC: Georgetown University Press, 1964.

Mukarovsky, Jan. *The Word and Verbal Art*. Edited and translated by John Burbank and Peter Steiner. New Haven: Yale University Press, 1977.

Müller, Max. *Three Lectures on the Science of Language*. Chicago: Open Court, 1891.

Murphy, James J. *Rhetoric in the Middle Ages: A History of Rhetorical Theory from St. Augustine to the Renaissance*. Berkeley: University of California Press, 1974.

Napoli, Donna Jo. *Syntax: Theory and Problems*. New York: Oxford University Press, 1993.

Nuyts, Jan, and Eric Pederson, eds. *Language and Conceptualization*. Cambridge: Cambridge University Press, 1997.

Nylund, Jan H. "The Prague School of Linguistics and Its Influence on New Testament Language Studies." Pages 155–221 in *The Language of the New Testament: Context, History, and Development*. Edited by Stanley E. Porter and Andrew W. Pitts. ECHC 3. LBS 6. Leiden: Brill, 2013.

O'Brien, Peter. *Philippians*. NIGTC. Grand Rapids: Eerdmans, 1991.

O'Donnell, Matthew Brook. *Corpus Linguistics and the Greek of the New Testament*. NTM 6. Sheffield: Sheffield Phoenix, 2005.

O'Grady, Gerard, Tom Bartlett, and Lise Fontaine, eds. *Choice in Language: Applications in Text Analysis*. Sheffield: Equinox, 2013.

Ochs, Elinor. "Planned and Unplanned Discourse." Pages 51–80 in *Discourse and Syntax*. Edited by Talmy Givón. New York: Academic Press, 1979.

Omanson, Robert L. *A Textual Guide to the Greek New Testament*. Stuttgart: Deutsche Bibelgesellschaft, 2006.

Ong, Hughson T. *The Multilingual Jesus and the Sociolinguistic World of the New Testament*. LBS 12. Leiden: Brill, 2015.

Ong, Hughson T. *Sociolinguistic Analysis of the New Testament: Theories and Applications*. BINS 196. Leiden: Brill, 2021.

Ong, Walter J. *Interfaces of the Word: Studies in the Evolution of Consciousness and Culture*. Ithaca, NY: Cornell University Press, 1977.

Ong, Walter J. *Orality and Literacy: The Technologizing of the Word*. London: Routledge, 1982.

Outram, Dorinda. *The Enlightenment*. Cambridge: Cambridge University Press, 1995.

Palmer, Micheal W. "How Do We Know a Phrase Is a Phrase? A Plea for Procedural Clarity in the Application of Linguistics to Biblical Greek." Pages 152–86 in *Biblical Greek Language and Linguistics: Open Questions in Current Research*. Edited by Stanley E. Porter and D. A. Carson. JSNTSup 80. Sheffield: JSOT Press, 1993.

Palmer, Micheal W. *Levels of Constituent Structure in New Testament Greek*. SBG 6. New York: Peter Lang, 1995.

Pang, Francis. *Revisiting Aspect and Aktionsart: A Corpus Approach to Koine Greek Event Typology*. LBS 14. Leiden: Brill, 2016.

Park, Yoon Man. *Mark's Memory Resources and the Controversy Stories (Mark 2:1–3:6): An Application of the Frame Theory of Cognitive Science to the Markan Oral-Aural Narrative*. LBS 2. Leiden: Brill, 2010.

Pasor, Georg. *Grammatica graeca sacra Novi Testamenti Domini nostri Jesu Christi*. 1655.

Pattemore, Stephen. *The People of God in the Apocalypse: Discourse, Structure and Exegesis*. SNTSMS 128. Cambridge: Cambridge University Press, 2004.

Pattemore, Stephen. *Souls under the Altar: Relevance Theory and the Discourse Structure of Revelation*. New York: UBS, 2003.

Paul, Hermann. *Principles of the History of Language*. Translated by H. A. Strong. London: Longmans, Green, 1888.

Pavel, Thomas G. *The Spell of Language: Poststructuralism and Speculation*. Translated by Linda Jordan and Thomas G. Pavel. Chicago: University of Chicago Press, 1989.

Peabody, Berkley. *The Winged Word: A Study in the Technique of Ancient Greek Oral Composition as Seen Principally through Hesiod's Works and Days*. Albany: State University of New York Press, 1975.

Perelman, Chaim, and Lucie Olbrechts-Tyteca. *The New Rhetoric: A Treatise on Argumentation*. Translated by John Wilkinson and Purcell Weaver. Notre Dame, IN: University of Notre Dame Press, 1969 (1958).

Peters, Ronald D. *The Greek Article: A Functional Grammar of ὁ-items in the Greek New Testament with Special Emphasis on the Greek Article*. LBS 9. Leiden: Brill, 2014.

Pierce, Marc. Review of Seuren, *Saussure … Linguist List* 40–4335, November 14, 2019 (online).

Pike, Kenneth L. *Language in Relation to a Unified Theory of the Structure of Human Behavior*. 2nd ed. The Hague: Mouton, 1967.

Pinker, Steven. *The Language Instinct: How the Mind Creates Language*. New York: William Morrow, 1994.

Poloma, Margaret M. *Contemporary Sociological Theory*. New York: Macmillan, 1979.

Porter, Roy, and Mikuláš Teich, eds. *Romanticism in National Context*. Cambridge: Cambridge University Press, 1988.

Porter, Stanley E. "The Adjectival Attributive Genitive in the New Testament: A Grammatical Study." *TJ* NS 4 (1983): 3–17.

Porter, Stanley E. *The Apostle Paul: His Life, Thought, and Letters*. Grand Rapids: Eerdmans, 2016.

Porter, Stanley E. "Applied Rhetoric and Stylistics in Ancient Greece." Pages 284–307 in *Rhetorik und Stilistic/Rhetoric and Stylistics: Ein internationales Handbuch historischer und systematischer Forschung/An International Handbook of Historical and Systematic Research*. Edited by Ulla Fix, Andreas Gardt, and Joachim Knape. Handbücher zur Sprach- und Kommunikationswissenschaft/Handbooks of Linguistics and Communication Science 31.1. Berlin: de Gruyter, 2008.

Porter, Stanley E. "The Argument of Romans 5: Can a Rhetorical Question Make a Difference?" *JBL* 110 (1991): 655–77. Repr. and revised pages 213–38 in Stanley E. Porter, *Studies in the Greek New Testament: Theory and Practice*. SBG 6. New York: Peter Lang, 1996.

Porter, Stanley E. "Aspect and Imperatives Once More." *BAGL* 7 (2018): 141–72.

Porter, Stanley E. "The Case for Case Revisited." *Jian Dao* 6 (1996): 13–28.

Porter, Stanley E. *Constantine Tischendorf: The Life and Work of a 19th Century Bible Hunter*. London: Bloomsbury, 2015.

Porter, Stanley E. *The Criteria for Authenticity in Historical-Jesus Research: Previous Discussion and New Proposals*. JSNTSup 191. Sheffield: Sheffield Academic, 2000.

Porter, Stanley E. "The Dative Case in Some Examples of Greek Grammatical Discussion." *FN* 34 (2021): 17–37.

Porter, Stanley E. "Dialect and Register in the Greek of the New Testament: Theory." Pages 190–208 in *Rethinking Contexts, Rereading Texts: Contributions from the Social Sciences to Biblical Interpretation*. Edited by M. Daniel Carroll R. JSOTSup 299. Sheffield: Sheffield Academic, 2000.

Porter, Stanley E., ed. *Diglossia and Other Topics in New Testament Linguistics*. JSNTSup 193. SNTG 6. Sheffield: Sheffield Academic, 2000.

Porter, Stanley E. "The Functional Distribution of Koine Greek in First-Century Palestine." Pages 53–78 in *Diglossia and Other Topics in New Testament Linguistics*. Edited by Stanley E. Porter. JSNTSup 193. SNTG 6. Sheffield: Sheffield Academic, 2000.

Porter, Stanley E. "Greek Grammar and Syntax." Pages 76–103 in *The Face of New Testament Studies: A Survey of Recent Research*. Edited by Scot McKnight and Grant R. Osborne. Grand Rapids: Baker, 2004.

Porter, Stanley E. *Hermeneutics, Linguistics, and the Bible: The Importance of Context*. T&T Clark Library of New Testament Greek 3. London: T&T Clark, forthcoming.

Porter, Stanley E. *Idioms of the Greek New Testament*. Sheffield: Sheffield Academic, 1992. 2nd ed., 1994.

Porter, Stanley E. "James Hope Moulton and Koine Greek: An Introduction to Moulton's *Prolegomena*." Pages vii–xlv in James Hope Moulton, *Prolegomena*. Vol. 1 of *A Grammar of New Testament Greek*. 3rd ed. Edinburgh: T&T Clark, 1908. Repr., London: Bloomsbury, 2019.

Porter, Stanley E. "James Hope Moulton and Wilbert Francis Howard and Greek Phonology and Morphology: An Introduction to Moulton and Howard's *Accidence and Word-Formation*." Pages ix–lxxii in James Hope Moulton and Wilbert Francis Howard, *Accidence and Word-Formation*. Vol. 2 of *A Grammar of New Testament Greek* by James Hope Moulton. Edinburgh: T&T Clark, 1919–29. Repr., London: Bloomsbury, 2019.

Porter, Stanley E. "Jesus and Resurrection." Pages 323–54 in *Jesus in Continuum*. Edited by Tom Holmén. WUNT 289. Tübingen: Mohr Siebeck, 2012.

Porter, Stanley E. *Καταλλάσσω in Ancient Greek Literature, with Reference to the Pauline Writings*. Estudios de Filología Neotestamentaria 5. Cordoba: Ediciones El Almendro, 1994.

Porter, Stanley E. *The Letter to the Romans: A Linguistic and Literary Commentary*. NTM 37. Sheffield: Sheffield Phoenix, 2015.

Porter, Stanley E. "Lexical Semantics and New Testament Greek: A Review Article of Some Major Works." *FN* 32 (2019): 113–55.

Porter, Stanley E. *Linguistic Analysis of the Greek New Testament: Studies in Tools, Methods, and Practice*. Grand Rapids: Baker, 2015.

Porter, Stanley E. "Linguistic Theory in Greek and Hebrew Language Study." In *Putting the Pieces Together: Formalizing Units and Relations in the Biblical Languages*. Edited by Stanley E. Porter, Christopher D. Land, and Francis G. H. Pang. MNTS. Eugene, OR: Pickwick, forthcoming.

Porter, Stanley E. "Linguistics and Rhetorical Criticism." Pages 63–92 in *Linguistics and the New Testament: Critical Junctures*. Edited by Stanley E. Porter and D. A. Carson. JSNTSup 168. SNTG 5. Sheffield: Sheffield Academic, 1999.

Porter, Stanley E. *New Testament Theology and the Greek Language: A Linguistic Reconceptualization*. Cambridge: Cambridge University Press, 2022.

Porter, Stanley E. "Nigel Turner and Greek Syntax: An Introduction to Moulton's Third Volume, *Syntax*." Pages ix–l in Nigel Turner, *Syntax*. Vol. 3 of *A Grammar of New Testament Greek* by James Hope Moulton. Edinburgh: T&T Clark, 1963. Repr., London: Bloomsbury, 2019.

Porter, Stanley E. "Nigel Turner and Greek Style: An Introduction to Moulton's Fourth Volume, *Style*." Pages vii–xliv in Nigel Turner, *Style*. Vol. 4 of *A Grammar of New Testament Greek* by James Hope Moulton. Edinburgh: T&T Clark, 1976. Repr., London: Bloomsbury, 2019.

Porter, Stanley E. *The Pastoral Epistles: A Commentary on the Greek Text*. Grand Rapids: Baker, forthcoming.

Porter, Stanley E. "Paul of Tarsus and His Letters." Pages 533–86 in *Handbook of Classical Rhetoric in the Hellenistic Period, 330 B.C.–A.D. 400*. Edited by Stanley E. Porter. Leiden: Brill, 1997.

Porter, Stanley E. "Register in the Greek of the New Testament: Application with Reference to Mark's Gospel." Pages 208–29 in *Rethinking Contexts, Rereading Texts: Contributions from the Social Sciences to Biblical Interpretation*. Edited by M. Daniel Carroll R. JSOTSup 299. Sheffield: Sheffield Academic, 2000.

Porter, Stanley E. "Revisiting the Greek Verb: An Extended Critique." *FN* 31 (2018): 3–16.

Porter, Stanley E. "Rhetoric and New Testament Studies." Pages 649–59 in *The Oxford Handbook of Rhetorical Studies*. Edited by Michael J. MacDonald. Oxford: Oxford University Press, 2017.

Porter, Stanley E. "The Role of Greek Language Criteria in Historical Jesus Research." Pages 361–404 in *Handbook for the Study of the Historical Jesus*. I. *How to Study the Historical Jesus*. Edited by Tom Holmén and Stanley E. Porter. Leiden: Brill, 2010.

Porter, Stanley E. *Sacred Tradition in the New Testament: Tracing Old Testament Themes in the Gospels and Epistles*. Grand Rapids: Baker, 2016.

Porter, Stanley E. "So What Have We Learned in the Last Thirty Years of Greek Linguistic Study?" Pages 9–38 in *Getting into the Text: New Testament Essays in Honor of David Alan Black*. Edited by David L. Aiken and Thomas W. Hudgins. Eugene, OR: Pickwick, 2017.

Porter, Stanley E. "Studying Ancient Languages from a Modern Linguistic Perspective: Essential Terms and Terminology." *FN* 2 (1989): 147–72.

Porter, Stanley E. "Systemic Functional Linguistics and the Greek Language: The Need for Further Modeling." Pages 9–47 in *Modeling Biblical Language: Selected Papers from the McMaster Divinity College Linguistics Circle*. Edited by Stanley E. Porter, Gregory P. Fewster, and Christopher D. Land. LBS 13. Leiden: Brill, 2016.

Porter, Stanley E. "Thucydides 1.22.1 and Speeches in Acts: Is There a Thucydidean View?" *NovT* 32 (1990): 121–42. Repr. pages 173–93 in Stanley E. Porter, *Studies in the Greek New Testament: Theory and Practice*. SBG 6. New York: Peter Lang, 1996.

Porter, Stanley E. "The Use of Greek in First-Century Palestine: A Diachronic and Synchronic Examination." *JGRChJ* 12 (2016): 203–28.

Porter, Stanley E. *Verbal Aspect in the Greek of the New Testament, with Reference to Tense and Mood*. SBG 1. New York: Peter Lang, 1989.

Porter, Stanley E. "William Fiddian Moulton and Greek Grammar: An Introduction to Moulton's Translation of Winer's Grammar." Pages xi–xl in Georg Benedikt Winer, *A Treatise on the Grammar of New Testament Greek*. Translated by William Fiddian Moulton. 3rd ed. Edinburgh: T&T Clark, 1882. Repr., London: Bloomsbury, 2019.

Porter, Stanley E., and Andrew W. Pitts. "New Testament Greek Language and Linguistics in Recent Research." *CBR* 6.2 (2008): 214–55.

Porter, Stanley E., and Bryan R. Dyer. "Oral Texts? A Reassessment of the Oral and Rhetorical Nature of Paul's Letters in Light of Recent Studies." *JETS* 55 (2012): 323–42.

Porter, Stanley E., and D. A. Carson, eds. *Biblical Greek Language and Linguistics: Open Questions in Current Research*. JSNTSup 80. Sheffield: Sheffield Academic, 1993.

Porter, Stanley E., and Jason C. Robinson. *Hermeneutics: An Introduction to Interpretive Theory*. Grand Rapids: Eerdmans, 2011.

Porter, Stanley E., and Jeffrey T. Reed. "Greek Grammar since BDF: A Retrospective and Prospective Analysis." *FN* 4 (1991): 143–64.

Porter, Stanley E., and Matthew Brook O'Donnell. *Discourse Analysis and the Greek New Testament: Text-Generating Resources*. T&T Clark Library of New Testament Greek 2. London: T&T Clark, 2023.

Porter, Stanley E., and Matthew Brook O'Donnell. "The Greek Verbal Network Viewed from a Probabilistic Standpoint: An Exercise in Hallidayan Linguistics." *FN* 14 (2001): 3–41.

Porter, Stanley E., Jeffrey T. Reed, and Matthew Brook O'Donnell. *Fundamentals of New Testament Greek*. Grand Rapids: Eerdmans, 2010.

Powers, B. Ward. *Learn to Read the Greek New Testament: An Approach to New Testament Greek Based upon Linguistic Principles*. Adelaide: SPCK Australia, 1979. 5th ed., 1995.

Propp, Vladimir. *Morphology of the Folktale*. Translated by Laurence Scott. 2nd ed. Austin: University of Texas Press, 1968.
Radermacher, Ludwig. *Neutestamentliche Grammatik*. HNT 1. Tübingen: Mohr Siebeck, 1911. 2nd ed., 1925.
Ravelli, Louise Jane. "Grammatical Metaphor: An Initial Analysis." Pages 133–47 in *Pragmatics, Discourse and Text*. Edited by Erich H. Steiner and Robert Veltman. Norwood, NJ: Ablex, 1988.
Ravelli, Louise Jane. *Metaphor, Mode and Complexity: An Exploration of Co-Varying Patterns*. Nottingham: Nottingham Trent University, 1999.
Ravelli, Louise Jane. "Renewal of Connection: Integrating Theory and Practice in Understanding of Grammatical Metaphor." Pages 37–64 in *Grammatical Metaphor: Views from Systemic Functional Linguistics*. Edited by Anne-Marie Simon-Vandenbergen, Miriam Taverniers, and Louise Ravelli. Amsterdam: John Benjamins, 2003.
Reed, Jeffrey T. *A Discourse Analysis of Philippians: Method and Rhetoric in the Debate over Literary Integrity*. JSNTSup 136. Sheffield: Sheffield Academic, 1997.
Reed, Jeffrey T. "Using Ancient Rhetorical Categories to Interpret Paul's Letters: A Question of Genre." Pages 292–324 in *Rhetoric and the New Testament: Essays from the 1992 Heidelberg Conference*. Edited by Stanley E. Porter and Thomas H. Olbricht. JSNTSup 90. Sheffield: Sheffield Academic, 1993.
Regier, Terry. *The Human Semantic Potential: Spatial Language and Constrained Connectionism*. Cambridge, MA: MIT Press, 1996.
Reicke, Bo. *The Roots of the Synoptic Gospels*. Philadelphia: Fortress, 1986.
Rhoads, David M. "Performance Criticism: An Emerging Methodology in Second Testament Studies." *BTB* 36 (2006): 118–33 (part 1) and 164–84 (part 2).
Richards, I. A. *Coleridge on Imagination*. 3rd ed. London: Routledge & Kegan Paul, 1962.
Richards, I. A. *The Philosophy of Rhetoric*. London: Oxford University Press, 1936.
Richards, Jennifer. *Rhetoric*. New Critical Idiom. London: Routledge, 2008.
Rico, Christophe. *Speaking Ancient Greek as a Living Language*. 2 vols. Jerusalem: Polis Institute Press, 2015.
Ricoeur, Paul. *The Rule of Metaphor: Multi-Disciplinary Studies of the Creation of Meaning in Language*. Translated by Robert Czerny with Kathleen McLaughlin and John Costello. Toronto: University of Toronto Press, 1975.
Riesner, Rainer. *Jesus als Lehrer: Eine Untersuchung zum Ursprung der Evangelien-Überlieferung*. WUNT 2/7. Tübingen: Mohr Siebeck, 1988.
Ritchie, L. David, and Min Zhu. "'Nixon Stonewalled the Investigation': Potential Contributions of Grammatical Metaphor to Conceptual Metaphor Theory and Analysis." *Metaphor and Symbol* 30.2 (2015): 118–36.
Ritzer, George. *Contemporary Sociological Theory*. 3rd ed. New York: McGraw-Hill, 1992.
Robbins, Vernon K. *The Tapestry of Early Christian Discourse: Rhetoric, Society and Ideology*. London: Routledge, 1996.
Robbins, Vernon K., Robert H. von Thaden Jr., and Bart B. Bruehler, eds. *Foundations for Sociorhetorical Exploration: A Rhetoric of Religious Antiquity Reader*. Rhetoric of Religious Antiquity 4. Atlanta: SBL Press, 2016.
Robertson, A. T. *A Grammar of the Greek New Testament in the Light of Historical Research*. Nashville: Broadman, 1914. 4th ed., 1934.
Robertson, A. T. *A Short Grammar of the Greek New Testament*. New York: Hodder and Stoughton, 1908. 10th ed., with W. Hersey Davis, 1933.

Robertson, J. G. *A History of German Literature*. Edited by Dorothy Reich. 6th ed. Edinburgh: William Blackwood, 1970.
Robey, David, ed. *Structuralism: An Introduction*. Oxford: Clarendon, 1973.
Robins, R. H. *A Short History of Linguistics*. 3rd ed. London: Longman, 1990.
Robinson, Thomas A. *Mastering New Testament Greek: Essential Tools for Students*. Peabody, MA: Hendrickson, 2007.
Robinson, William E. W. *Metaphor, Morality, and the Spirit in Romans 8:1-17*. Atlanta: SBL Press, 2016.
Rodríguez, Rafael. *Oral Tradition and the New Testament: A Guide for the Perplexed*. London: T&T Clark, 2013.
Rodríguez, Rafael. *Structuring Early Christian Memory: Jesus in Tradition, Performance, and Text*. London: T&T Clark, 2010.
Ross, William A., and Steven E. Runge, eds. *Postclassical Greek Prepositions and Conceptual Metaphor: Cognitive Semantic Analysis and Biblical Interpretation*. Berlin: de Gruyter, 2022.
Rousseau, Jean-Jacques. *Essay on the Origin of Languages*. Pages 1–74 in *On the Origin of Language*. Translated by John H. Moran and Alexander Gode. Chicago: University of Chicago Press, 1966.
Ruipérez, M. Sanchez. *Estructura del Sistema de Aspectos y Tiempos del Verbo Griego Antiguo: Análisis Funcional Sincrónico*. Theses et Studia Philologica Salmanticensia 7. Salamanca: Colegio Trilingue de la Universidad, 1954.
Runge, Steven E. *Discourse Grammar of the Greek New Testament: A Practical Introduction for Teaching and Exegesis*. Peabody, MA: Hendrickson, 2010.
Runge, Steven E., and Christopher J. Fresch, eds. *The Greek Verb Revisited: A Fresh Approach for Biblical Exegesis*. Bellingham, WA: Lexham, 2016.
Sacks, Sheldon, ed. *On Metaphor*. Chicago: University of Chicago Press, 1979.
Sampson, Geoffrey. *Empirical Linguistics*. London: Continuum, 2001.
Sampson, Geoffrey. *The Form of Language*. London: Weidenfeld and Nicolson, 1975.
Sampson, Geoffrey. *The "Language Instinct" Debate*. Rev. ed. London: Continuum, 2005 (1997).
Sampson, Geoffrey. *Liberty and Language*. Oxford: Oxford University Press, 1979.
Sampson, Geoffrey. *The Linguistics Delusion*. Sheffield: Equinox, 2017.
Sampson, Geoffrey. *Making Sense*. Oxford: Oxford University Press, 1980.
Sampson, Geoffrey. *Schools of Linguistics*. Stanford, CA: Stanford University Press, 1980.
Sapir, Edward. *Language: An Introduction to the Study of Speech*. New York: Harcourt, Brace, 1921.
Sapir, Edward. *Selected Writings in Language, Culture, and Personality*. Edited by David G. Mandelbaum. Berkeley: University of California Press, 1949.
Sapir, Edward. "The Status of Linguistics as a Science." Pages 160–6 in *Selected Writings in Language, Culture, and Personality*. Edited by David G. Mandelbaum. Berkeley: University of California Press, 1949.
Saussure, Ferdinand de. *Course in General Linguistics*. Edited by Charles Bally and Albert Sechehaye, with Albert Riedlinger. Translated by Wade Baskin. New York: Philosophical Library, 1959. ET of *Cours de linguistique générale*. Edited by Charles Bally and Albert Sechehaye, with Albert Riedlinger. Paris: Payot et Rivages, 1995 (1916).
Saussure, Ferdinand de. *Mémoire sur le système primitif des voyelles dans les langues indo-européennes*. Leipzig: Teubner, 1879. ET of excerpt in "Mémoire on the Primitive System of Vowels in the Indo-European Languages." Pages 217–24 in *A Reader in Nineteenth-Century*

Historical Indo-European Linguistics. Edited and translated by Winfred P. Lehmann. Bloomington: Indiana University Press, 1967.
Saussure, Ferdinand de. *Writings in General Linguistics*. Oxford: Oxford University Press, 2006.
Schlegel, Friedrich. *Ueber die Sprache und Weisheit der Indier: Ein Beitrag zur Begründung der Alterthumstunde*. Heidelberg: Mohr und Zimmer, 1808. Repr., London: Routledge/Thoemmes, 1995.
Schleicher, August. *Compendium der vergleichenden Grammatik der indogermanischen Sprachen; kurzer Abriss einer Laut- und Formenlehre der indogermanischen Ursprache*. Weimar: Hermann Böhlau, 1861. 4th ed., 1876.
Schmidt, Daryl Dean. *Hellenistic Greek Grammar and Noam Chomsky*. SBLDS 62. Chico, CA: Scholars Press, 1981.
Schnabel, Eckhard J. *Mark*. TNTC. Downers Grove, IL: IVP, 2017.
Schreiner, Thomas R. *Interpreting the Pauline Epistles*. Grand Rapids: Baker, 1990.
Schweizer, Eduard. *Grammatik der Pergamenischen Inschriften*. Berlin: Weidmannsche, 1898.
Seuren, Pieter A. M. *From Whorf to Montague: Explorations in the Theory of Language*. Oxford: Oxford University Press, 2013.
Seuren, Pieter A. M. *Saussure and Sechehaye: Myth and Genius. A Study in the History of Linguistics and the Foundations of Language*. Leiden: Brill, 2018.
Seuren, Pieter A. M. *Western Linguistics: An Historical Introduction*. Oxford: Blackwell, 1998.
Shiell, William D. *Reading Acts: The Lector and the Early Christian Audience*. Leiden: Brill, 2004.
Shiner, Whitney. *Proclaiming the Gospel: First-Century Performance of Mark*. Harrisburg, PA: Trinity Press International, 2003.
Siebenthal, Heinrich von. *Ancient Greek Grammar for the Study of the New Testament*. Oxford: Peter Lang, 2019.
Siebenthal, Heinrich von. *Griechische Grammatik zum Neuen Testament*. Giessen: Brunnen; Basel: Immanuel-Verlag, 2011.
Siewierska, Anna. *Person*. CTL. Cambridge: Cambridge University Press, 2004.
Silva, Moisés. *Biblical Words and Their Meaning: An Introduction to Lexical Semantics*. Grand Rapids: Zondervan, 1983.
Silva, Moisés. *God, Language, and Scripture: Reading the Bible in the Light of General Linguistics*. Grand Rapids: Zondervan, 1990.
Sim, Margaret G. *Marking Thought and Talk in New Testament Greek: New Light from Linguistics on the Particles ἵνα and ὅτι*. Eugene, OR: Pickwick, 2010.
Sim, Margaret G. *A Relevant Way to Read: A New Approach to Exegesis and Communication*. Eugene, OR: Pickwick, 2016.
Simon-Vandenbergen, Anne-Marie. "Lexical Metaphor and Interpersonal Meaning." Pages 326–31 in *Grammatical Metaphor: Views from Systemic Functional Linguistics*. Edited by Anne-Marie Simon-Vandenbergen, Miriam Taverniers, and Louise Ravelli. Amsterdam: John Benjamins, 2003.
Simon-Vandenbergen, Anne-Marie, Miriam Taverniers, and Louise Ravelli, eds. *Grammatical Metaphor: Views from Systemic Functional Linguistics*. Amsterdam: John Benjamins, 2003.
Soskice, Janet Martin. *Metaphor and Religious Language*. Oxford: Clarendon, 1985.
Sperber, Dan, and Deirdre Wilson. *Relevance: Communication and Cognition*. 2nd ed. Oxford: Blackwell, 1995 (1991).
Spinoza, Baruch. *Theological-Political Treatise*. 2nd ed. Translated by Samuel Shirley. Indianapolis: Hackett, 2001.

Spradley, James P., ed. *Culture and Cognition: Rules, Maps, and Plans.* San Francisco: Chandler, 1972.
Stack, Judith V. *Metaphor and the Portrayal of the Cause(s) of Sin and Evil in the Gospel of Matthew.* BINS 182. Leiden: Brill, 2020.
Stanley, Christopher D. *Arguing with Scripture: The Rhetoric of Quotations in the Letters of Paul.* New York: T&T Clark International, 2004.
Stein, Robert H. *Mark.* BECNT. Grand Rapids: Baker, 2008.
Steiner, Peter, ed. *The Prague School: Selected Writings, 1929–1946.* Austin: University of Texas Press, 1982.
Stovell, Beth M. *Mapping Metaphorical Discourse in the Fourth Gospel: John's Eternal King.* LBS 5. Leiden: Brill, 2012.
Stump, Gregory. *Inflectional Morphology: A Theory of Paradigm Structure.* Cambridge: Cambridge University Press, 2001.
Sturtevant, E. H. *Studies in Greek Noun Formation.* 4 vols. Chicago: University of Chicago Press, 1910–13.
Talmy, Leonard. *Toward a Cognitive Semantics.* 2 vols. Cambridge, MA: MIT Press, 2000.
Tannen, Deborah. "The Myth of Orality and Literacy." Pages 37–50 in *Linguistics and Literacy: Topics in Language and Linguistics.* Edited by W. Frawley. Boston: Springer, 1982.
Tannen, Deborah. "Oral and Literate Strategies in Spoken and Written Narratives." *Language* 58 (1982): 1–21.
Tannen, Deborah, ed. *Spoken and Written Language: Exploring Orality and Literacy.* Advances in Discourse Processes 9. Norwood, NJ: Ablex, 1982.
Tappenden, Frederick S. *Resurrection in Paul: Cognition, Metaphor, and Transformation.* Atlanta: SBL Press, 2016.
Tasker, R. V. G. *The Greek New Testament: Being the Text Translated in The New English Bible 1961.* Oxford: Oxford University Press; Cambridge: Cambridge University Press, 1964.
Taverniers, Miriam. "Grammatical Metaphor and Lexical Metaphor: Different Perspectives on Semantic Variation." *Neophilologus* 90 (2006): 321–32.
Taylor, Charles. *The Language Animal: The Full Shape of the Human Language Capacity.* Cambridge, MA: Harvard University Press, 2016.
Taylor, John R. *Linguistic Categorization: Prototypes in Linguistic Theory.* 2nd ed. Oxford: Clarendon, 1995 (1989).
ten Hacken, Pius. *Chomskyan Linguistics and Its Competitors.* Sheffield: Equinox, 2007.
"Thèses présentées au Premier Congrès des philologues slaves." Pages 33–58 in *A Prague School Reader in Linguistics.* Edited by Josef Vachek. Bloomington: Indiana University Press, 1964.
Thiselton, Anthony C. *The First Epistle to the Corinthians.* NIGTC. Grand Rapids: Eerdmans, 2000.
Thomas, Rosalind. *Literacy and Orality in Ancient Greece.* Cambridge: Cambridge University Press, 1992.
Thompson, Geoff. *Introducing Functional Grammar.* 2nd ed. London: Hodder Education, 2004.
Thompson, Jeremy, and Wendy Widder. "Major Approaches to Linguistics." Pages 87–134 in *Linguistics and Biblical Exegesis.* Edited by Douglas Mangum and Josh Westbury. Bellingham, WA: Lexham, 2017.
Thomson, Christopher J. "What Is Aspect? Contrasting Definitions in General Linguistics and New Testament Studies." Pages 13–80 in *The Greek Verb Revisited: A Fresh Approach for Biblical Exegesis.* Edited by Steven E. Runge and Christopher J. Fresch. Bellingham, WA: Lexham, 2016.

Thornhill, A. Chadwick. *Greek for Everyone: Introductory Greek for Bible Study and Application*. Grand Rapids: Baker, 2016.

Thrall, Margaret E. *A Critical and Exegetical Commentary on the Second Epistle to the Corinthians*. 2 vols. ICC. Edinburgh: T&T Clark, 1994–2000.

Thumb, Albert. *Die griechische Sprache im Zeitalter des Hellenismus: Beiträge zur Geschichte und Beurteilung der κοινή*. Strassburg: Trübner, 1901.

Thumb, Albert. "On the Value of Modern Greek for the Study of Ancient Greek." *CQ* 8 (1914): 181–205.

Thurén, Lauri. *Argument and Theology in 1 Peter: The Origins of Christian Paraenesis*. JSNTSup 114. Sheffield: Sheffield Academic, 1995.

Tooke, John Horne. *ΕΠΕΑ ΠΤΕΡΟΕΝΤΑ, or the Diversions of Purley*. 2 vols. Edited by Richard Taylor. London: Thomas Tegg, 1829. Repr., London: Routledge/Thoemmes, 1993.

Traugott, Elizabeth Closs, and Bernd Heine, eds. *Approaches to Grammaticalization*. 2 vols. Typological Studies in Language 19. Amsterdam: John Benjamins, 1991.

Trible, Phyllis. *Rhetorical Criticism: Context, Method, and the Book of Jonah*. GBS. Minneapolis: Fortress, 1994.

Trubetzkoy, Nikolai S. *Introduction to the Principles of Phonological Descriptions*. Edited by H. Bluhme. Translated by L. A. Murray. The Hague: Martinus Nijhoff, 1968. ET of *Anleitung zu phonologischen Beschreibungen*. Brno: Cercle linguistique de Prague, 1935.

Trubetzkoy, Nikolai S. *Principles of Phonology*. Translated by Christiane A. M. Baltaxe. Berkeley: University of California Press, 1969. ET of *Grundzüge der Phonologie*. Prague: Travaux du Cercle linguistique de Prague, 1939.

Trubetzkoy, Nikolai S. "A Theory of Phonological Oppositions." Pages 14–21 in *N. S. Trubetzkoy: Studies in General Linguistics and Language Structure*. Edited by Anatoly Liberman. Translated by Marvin Taylor and Anatoly Liberman. Durham, NC: Duke University Press, 2001. ET of "Essai d'une théorie des oppositions phonologiques." *JP* 33 (1936): 5–18.

Trubetzkoy, Nikolai S. "Zur allgemeinen Theorie phonologischer Vokalsysteme." *TCLP* 1 (1929): 36–67. Repr. pages 108–42 in *A Prague School Reader in Linguistics*. Edited by Josef Vachek. Bloomington: Indiana University Press, 1964.

Turbayne, Colin Murray. *The Myth of Metaphor*. Rev. ed. Columbia: University of South Carolina Press, 1970.

Turner, Mark. *The Literary Mind: The Origins of Thought and Language*. New York: Oxford University Press, 1996.

Turner, Nigel. *Style*. Vol. 4 of *A Grammar of New Testament Greek* by James Hope Moulton. Edinburgh: T&T Clark, 1976.

Turner, Nigel. *Syntax*. Vol. 3 of *A Grammar of New Testament Greek* by James Hope Moulton. Edinburgh: T&T Clark, 1963.

Ullmann, Stephen. *The Principles of Semantics*. 2nd ed. Oxford: Blackwell, 1957.

Vachek, Josef. *The Linguistic School of Prague*. Bloomington: Indiana University Press, 1966.

Vachek, Josef, ed. *A Prague School Reader in Linguistics*. Bloomington: Indiana University Press, 1964.

Vaina, Lucia, and Jaakko Hintikka, eds. *Cognitive Constraints on Communication: Representations and Processes*. Dordrecht: Reidel, 1984.

van Dijk, Teun A. "Introduction: Discourse as a New Cross-Discipline." Pages 1–10 in *Handbook of Discourse Analysis*. I. *Disciplines of Discourse*. Edited by Teun A. van Dijk. London: Academic Press, 1985.

Van Neste, Ray. *Cohesion and Structure in the Pastoral Epistles*. JSNTSup 280. London: T&T Clark, 2004.
Van Valin, Robert D., Jr., and Randy J. LaPolla. *Syntax: Structure, Meaning and Function*. CTL. Cambridge: Cambridge University Press, 1997.
van Wolde, Ellen. *Reframing Biblical Studies: When Language and Text Meet Culture, Cognition, and Context*. Winona Lake, IN: Eisenbrauns, 2009.
Vaughan, Curtis, and Virtus E. Gideon. *A Greek Grammar of the New Testament: A Workbook Approach to Intermediate Grammar*. Nashville: Broadman, 1979.
Vickers, Brian. *In Defense of Rhetoric*. Oxford: Clarendon, 1988.
Von Thaden, Robert H., Jr. *Sex, Christ, and Embodied Cognition: Paul's Wisdom for Corinth*. Atlanta: SBL Press, 2017.
Wackernagel, Jacob. *Lectures on Syntax*. Edited by David Langslow. Oxford: Oxford University Press, 2009.
Wallace, Daniel B. *Greek Grammar beyond the Basics: An Exegetical Syntax of the New Testament*. Grand Rapids: Zondervan, 1995.
Wallace, Ruth A., and Alison Wolf. *Contemporary Sociological Theory: Expanding the Classical Tradition*. 5th ed. Upper Saddle River, NJ: Prentice Hall, 1999.
Wansbrough, Henry, ed. *Jesus and the Oral Gospel Tradition*. JSNTSup 64. Sheffield: Sheffield Academic, 1992.
Watson, Duane F. *Invention, Arrangement and Style: Rhetorical Criticism of Jude and Second Peter*. Atlanta: Scholars Press, 1988.
Watson, Janet, ed. *Speaking Volumes: Orality and Literacy in the Greek and Roman World*. MnS 218. Leiden: Brill, 2001.
Watt, Jonathan M. *Code-Switching in Luke and Acts*. Berkeley Insights in Linguistics and Semiotics 31. New York: Peter Lang, 1997.
Way, Eileen Cornell. *Knowledge Representation and Metaphor*. Studies in Cognitive Systems. Dordrecht: Kluwer, 1991.
Weiser, Irwin. "Linguistics." Pages 390–1 in *Encyclopedia of Rhetoric and Composition: Communication from Ancient Times to the Information Age*. Edited by Theresa Enos. London: Routledge, 1996.
Welch, Kathleen E. *The Contemporary Reception of Classical Rhetoric: Appropriations of Ancient Discourse*. Hillsdale, NJ: Lawrence Erlbaum, 1990.
Wellek, René. "The Literary Theory and Aesthetics of the Prague School." Pages 275–303 in René Wellek, *Discriminations: Further Concepts of Criticism*. New Haven: Yale University Press, 1970.
Wellek, René. "Vilém Mathesius (1882–1945): Founder of the Prague Linguistic Circle." Pages 1–5 in *Sound, Sign and Meaning: Quinquagenary of the Prague Linguistic Circle*. Edited by Ladislav Matejka. Ann Arbor, MI: Department of Slavic Languages and Literature University of Michigan, 1976.
Westcott, Brooke Foss. *An Introduction to the Study of the Gospels*. 7th ed. London: Macmillan, 1888 (1851).
Westfall, Cynthia Long. *A Discourse Analysis of the Letter to the Hebrews: The Relationship between Form and Meaning*. LNTS 297. London: T&T Clark, 2005.
Wheelwright, Philip. *The Burning Fountain: A Study in the Language of Symbolism*. Rev. ed. Repr., Gloucester, MA: Peter Smith, 1982 (1968).
Wheelwright, Philip. *Metaphor and Reality*. Bloomington: Indiana University Press, 1962.
White, Eugene E. *The Context of Human Discourse: A Configurational Criticism of Rhetoric*. Columbia: University of South Carolina Press, 1992.

Whitney, William Dwight. *The Life and Growth of Language*. London: Kegan Paul, Trench, Trübner, 1875. Repr., London: Routledge/Thoemmes, 1994.

Whorf, Benjamin Lee. "An American Indian Model of the Universe." Pages 73–82 in *Language, Thought and Reality: Selected Writings of Benjamin Lee Whorf*. Edited by John B. Carroll, Stephen C. Levinson, and Penny Lee. 2nd ed. Cambridge, MA: MIT Press, 2012.

Whorf, Benjamin Lee. *Language, Thought, and Reality: Selected Writings of Benjamin Lee Whorf*. Edited by John B. Carroll, Stephen C. Levinson, and Penny Lee. 2nd ed. Cambridge, MA: MIT Press, 2012.

Wierzbicka, Anna. *Understanding Cultures through Their Key Words: English, Russian, Polish, German, Japanese*. New York: Oxford University Press, 1997.

Wierzbicka, Anna. *What Did Jesus Mean? Explaining the Sermon on the Mount and the Parables in Simple and Universal Human Concepts*. Oxford: Oxford University Press, 2001.

Wilson, Deirdre. "Metarepresentation in Linguistic Communication." Pages 411–48 in *Metarepresentations: A Multidisciplinary Perspective*. Edited by Deirdre Wilson. Oxford: Oxford University Press, 2000.

Wilson, Deirdre, and Dan Sperber. "Relevance Theory." Pages 607–32 in *The Handbook of Pragmatics*. Edited by Laurence R. Horn and Gregory Ward. Malden, MA: Blackwell, 2006.

Wimsatt, W. K., Jr. "Rhetoric and Poems: Alexander Pope." Pages 169–85 in W. K. Wimsatt Jr., *The Verbal Icon: Studies in the Meaning of Poetry*. New York: Noonday, 1958.

Wimsatt, W. K., Jr. *The Verbal Icon: Studies in the Meaning of Poetry*. New York: Noonday, 1958.

Winer, G. B. *Grammatik des neutestamentlichen Sprachidioms*. Leipzig: Vogel, 1822. 2nd ed., 1828. 3rd ed., 1830. 4th ed., 1836. 5th ed., 1844. 6th ed., 1855. 7th ed. Edited by Gottlieb Lünemann, 1868. 8th ed. Edited by Paul Schmiedel. Göttingen: Vandenhoeck & Ruprecht, 1894–8.

Winer, G. B. *A Treatise on the Grammar of New Testament Greek, Regarded as a Sure Basis for New Testament Exegesis*. Translated by W. F. Moulton. 3rd ed. Edinburgh: T&T Clark, 1882.

Winner, Thomas G. "Jan Mukarovsky: The Beginnings of Structural and Semiotic Aesthetics." Pages 433–55 in *Sound, Sign and Meaning: Quinquagenary of the Prague Linguistic Circle*. Edited by Ladislav Matejka. Ann Arbor, MI: Department of Slavic Languages and Literature University of Michigan, 1976.

Winters, Clifford T. *Argument Is War: Relevance-Theoretic Comprehension of the Conceptual Metaphor of War in the Apocalypse*. LBS 18. Leiden: Brill, 2020.

Wire, Antoinette C. *The Case for Mark Composed in Performance*. Eugene, OR: Cascade, 2011.

Wishart, Ryder A. "Friedrich Blass and A. T. Robertson: Comprehensive and Comparative Greek Grammars from the Modern Vantage Point." Pages 89–109 in *Pillars in the History of Biblical Interpretation, Volume 3: Further Essays on Prevailing Methods*. Edited by Stanley E. Porter and Zachary K. Dawson. MBSS 6. Eugene, OR: Pickwick, 2021.

Witherington, Ben, III. *New Testament Rhetoric: An Introductory Guide to the Art of Persuasion in and of the New Testament*. Eugene, OR: Cascade, 2009.

Wittgenstein, Ludwig. *Philosophical Investigations*. Translated by G. E. M. Anscombe. 2nd ed. Oxford: Blackwell, 1958.

Wong, Simon S. M. *A Classification of Semantic Case-Relations in the Pauline Epistles*. SBG 9. New York: Peter Lang, 1997.

Wong, Simon S. M. "What Case Is This Case? An Application of Semantic Case in Biblical Exegesis." *Jian Dao* 1 (1994): 49–73.

Wonneberger, Reinhard. "Der Beitrag der generativen Syntax zur Exegese: Ein Beispiel (2.Kor 5,2f) und neun Thesen." *Bijdragen* 36 (1975): 312–17.
Wonneberger, Reinhard. "Generative Stylistics: An Algorithmic Approach to Stylistic and Source Data Retrieval Problems Based on Generative Syntax." Pages 389–99 in *Bedeutung, Sprechakte und Texte: Akten des 13. Linguistischen Kolloquiums*, 2. Edited by Willy Vandeweghe and Marc Van de Velde. Tübingen: Niemeyer, 1979.
Wonneberger, Reinhard. "Greek Syntax: A New Approach." *LLC* 2.2 (1986): 71–9.
Wonneberger, Reinhard. *Syntax und Exegese: Eine generative Theorie der griechischen Syntax und ihr Beitrag zur Auslegung des Neuen Testaments, dargestellt an 2. Corinther 5.2 und Römer 3.21–26*. BBET 13. New York: Peter Lang, 1979.
Wordsworth, William, and Samuel Taylor Coleridge. *Lyrical Ballads*. 1798. Edited by R. L. Brett and A. R. Jones. 2nd ed. Repr., London: Routledge, 1991.
Wright, Joseph. *Comparative Grammar of the Greek Language*. London: Oxford University Press, 1912.
Xuan, Winfred Wenhui, and Shukun Chen. "A Synthesis of Research on Grammatical Metaphor: Meta-Data and Content Analysis." *WORD* 65.4 (2019): 213–33.
Yoon, David I. *A Discourse Analysis of Galatians and the New Perspective on Paul*. LBS 17. Leiden: Brill, 2019.
Yoon, Hye-Joon. *The Rhetoric of Tenses in Adam Smith's The Wealth of Nations*. Leiden: Brill, 2018.
Young, Richard A. *Intermediate New Testament Greek: A Linguistic and Exegetical Approach*. Nashville: Broadman & Holman, 1994.
Zerwick, Maximilian. *Biblical Greek Illustrated by Examples*. Translated by Joseph Smith. Rome: Pontifical Biblical Institute, 1963 (1944).
Zumthor, P. *Essai de poétique médiévale*. Paris: Seuil, 1972.
Zumthor, P. *Oral Poetry: An Introduction*. Translated by K. Murphy-Judy. Theory and History of Literature 70. Minneapolis: University of Minnesota Press, 1990.

MODERN AUTHORS INDEX

Adam, A. K. M. 24
Adams, Edward 71
Aiken, David L. 25
Akamatsu, Tsutomu 44
Albuquerque, Roque 72
Allan, Kathryn 85–86
Allan, Keith 19, 38
Allen, J. P. B. 55
Alsop, Siân 89
Anderson, R. Dean 115
Andreski, Stanislav 26
Andrews, Edna 44
Apel, Karl-Otto 37
Ayer, Alfred Jules 37

Bakhtin, Mikhail M. 47
Bakker, Egbert J. 166
Bal, Mieke 46
Bally, Charles 1, 39, 43, 113, 158
Banks, David 18, 52
Bann, S. 39
Barfield, Owen 84
Barr, James 48–49
Barthes, Roland 47, 114
Bartlett, Tom 18, 43
Bateman, John A. 18
Battistella, Edwin L. 44
Baum, Armin 159
Bazell, Charles E. 43, 68, 142
Beaugrande, Robert de 38, 45, 50, 52, 69, 117
Bebbington, D. W. 20
Beekman, John 54
Beetham, Frank 24
Bell, Allan 169
Berger, Peter L. 70, 98
Berry, D. H. 112
Berry, Margaret 70, 119–20
Betts, Gavin 24
Betz, Hans Dieter 116–17
Bhat, D. N. S. 11
Biber, Douglas 161, 165
Bičan, Aleš 44
Binnick, Robert I. 10, 12

Birch, David 121, 163
Black, David Alan 24, 49–50, 67
Black, Max 83
Black, Stephanie L. 71
Blass, Friedrich 3, 25, 29–31, 33–34
Bloom, Paul 61
Bloomfield, Leonard 14, 16, 48, 54, 67
Blount, Brian K. 71
Bluhme, H. 40
Boas, Franz 14, 41, 67
Booth, Wayne C. 115
Bopp, Franz 27–28, 32
Botha, Pieter J. J. 159
Botha, Rudolf P. 55
Bouchard, D. F. 47
Bowlt, J. E. 39
Brett, R. L. 20
Brook-Rose, Christine 89
Brooks, Cleanth 115
Brooks, James A. 33
Bruehler, Bart B. 117
Brugmann, Karl 10, 27–29, 32, 38, 45, 48
Bühler, Karl 43–44, 48, 69
Burke, Kenneth 113–14
Burkhardt, Armin 83
Buss, Martin J. 39, 43, 120
Butler, Christopher S. 70, 74
Buttmann, Alexander 24

Callow, John 54
Cameron, Lynne 61, 86
Campbell, Constantine R. 11, 15, 50
Caragounis, Chrys C. 34
Carroll, John B. 41, 85, 114
Carroll R., M. Daniel 120
Carson, D. A. 11, 49–50, 54, 117
Cartledge, Samuel 24
Casson, Sandra H. 65
Chamberlain, William Douglas 33
Chang, Kai-Hsuan 62
Chapman, Siobhan 37
Chatman, Seymour 46
Chen, Shukun 88

Chomsky, Noam 3, 14–16, 18, 28, 42–43, 45, 47, 52–60, 63
Cirafesi, Wally V. 72, 95
Clarke, M. L. 112
Classen, Carl Joachim 116
Cole, Peter 57, 63
Coleridge, Samuel Taylor 20, 83
Collinge, N. E. 27, 38, 64
Colwell, Ernest Cadman 24
Comrie, Bernard 11
Condillac, Étienne Bonnot de 20–21
Copleston, Frederick 26
Corbett, Edward P. J. 115
Costley, Angela 72
Cotterell, Peter 49
Coulthard, Malcolm 119
Countryman, William 24
Cowie, Fiona 55
Cranfield, C. E. B. 153
Crellin, Robert 53–55
Croft, William 16, 56, 59, 86–87, 92, 138–39
Cruse, Alan 16, 59, 86–87, 92, 138–39
Crystal, David 19
Culler, Jonathan 38, 42
Curtius, Georg 10, 29, 32

Dana, H. E. 33
Daneš, Frantisek 40
Danove, Paul L. 3, 57–58
Davidson, Donald 55
Davies, Martin 118
Davis, W. Hersey 32
Dawson, Zachary K. 29, 72–73, 119–20, 130
de Man, Paul 114–15
Debrunner, Albert 3, 50, 32–34
Decker, Rodney J. 50
Deignan, Alice 61–62, 86–87
Deissmann, G. Adolf 30–33
Delbrück, Berthold 28, 32, 48
Derico, T. M. 159
Derrida, Jacques 46, 114
Devrim, Devo Y. 88, 96
Dik, Simon 17
Dixon, Peter 115
Dobson, John 24
Donato, Eugenio 46
Dooley, Robert A. 66
Doran, Y. J. 121
Dow, Lois K. Fuller 119
Downs, David 61
Draper, Jonathan A. 159
Dressler, Wolfgang 117

Droste, Flip G. 17
Dvorak, James D. 72–73, 119, 123, 130–31
Dyer, Bryan R. 72, 173

Eagleton, Terry 115
Easley, Kendall 49
Eemeren, Frans H. van 114
Efird, James 24
Elder, Nicholas A. 161–62
Eliot, T. S. 115
Elledge, Roderick 128
Emig, Elodie Ballantine 50–51
Empson, William 84
Enos, Theresa 119
Eschbach, Achim 44
Evans, Craig A. 119, 153
Evans, Vyvyan 59–60, 62, 86–87, 92, 138–41, 144
Eve, Eric 158–59

Fairclough, Norman 47
Fanning, Buist 11
Fantin, Joseph D. 65
Fauconnier, Gilles 61, 86–87
Fawcett, Robin P. 69, 90, 142
Fewster, Gregory P. 72, 95, 99, 119, 121, 141
Fick, August 29
Fillmore, Charles J. 56–57
Finnegan, Ruth 158–59
Firbas, Jan 40
Firth, J. R. 15, 43, 46, 48, 69, 121
Fix, Ulla 112
Fletcher, Bryan W. Y. 127
Fodor, Jerry A. 53, 56
Foley, John Miles 157, 159
Fontaine, Lise 43
Foss, Karen A. 114
Foss, Sonja K. 114–15
Foucault, Michel 47, 115
Found, James 24
France, R. T. 153
Frawley, W. 166
Fresch, Christopher J. 11, 68
Fries, Peter H. 42
Fromkin, Victoria 161–62
Fuller, Daniel 118
Funk, Robert W. 34, 50, 54

Galen, F. W. 39, 45
Gandillac, Maurice de 46
Gardiner, Alan 43

Gardner, Sheena 89
Gardt, Andreas 112
Garvin, Paul L. 40, 84
Gee, James Paul 160
Geeraerts, Dirk 53, 60
Genette, Gérard 114
Ghadessy, Mohsen 88, 121, 163
Giannakis, Georgios K. 34
Gibson, Richard J. 50
Gideon, Virtus E. 33
Giles, Peter 32
Givón, Talmy 67, 161
Gleason, Henry A., Jr. 49, 54
Gleitman, Lila R. 138
Gode, Alexander 20
Godel, Robert 39
Goetchius, Eugene Van Ness 49–50
Goldberg, Adele E. 56
Goldmann, Lucien 46
Gooder, Paula 24
Goodrick, Edward W. 24
Gotteri, Nigel J. C. 71, 142
Gould, Ezra P. 153
Green, Joel B. 62
Green, Melanie 59–60, 62, 86–87, 92, 138–41, 144
Green, Thomas Sheldon 24
Greenberg, Joseph H. 44, 48
Greimas, A.-J. 46
Grice, H. Paul 63–64
Grimm, Jacob 27
Gumperz, John J. 42
Gundry, Robert H. 153
Gupta, Nijay K. 15, 61
Gutt, Ernest-August 64

Hacken, Pius ten 17, 53
Hale, Kenneth 73
Halle, Morris 85, 114
Halliday, Michael A. K. 3, 15–17, 43, 45–47, 68–73, 88–92, 94–102, 105, 107, 114, 118–19, 121, 127, 137, 140–42, 144, 147, 149, 162–70, 173–75, 181
Hampden-Turner, Charles 140
Hampson, Norman 19
Harper, William Rainey 24
Harris, Dana M. 15
Harris, James 21
Harris, Murray J. 34, 155
Harris, Randy Allen 53
Harris, Zellig S. 45, 47, 52
Hart, Roderick P. 115

Hasan, Ruqaiya 47, 69, 71, 90, 118–19, 121, 163, 166–68
Hasselbrook, David S. 34
Hatzidakis, Georgios N. 34
Hauser, Gerard A. 115
Havelock, Eric A. 158
Havránek, Bohuslav 44
Hawkes, Terence 82–85, 89, 113
Hawthorne, Gerald F. 146
Heim, Erin M. 62
Heine, Bernd 103
Hengeveld, Kees 17
Herder, Johann Gottfried 20
Hester, J. David 116
Hester, James D. 116
Hewett, James 24
Heyvaert, Liesbet 88, 102
Hintikka, Jaakko 138
Hjelmslev, Louis 11, 14, 43, 45
Hockett, Charles F. 14, 45, 49, 55
Hoffmann, Ernst G. 33, 51
Hoffmann, Otto 32
Hofmannsthal, Hugo von 38
Hoijer, Harry 41, 48
Holloway, Paul 146
Holmén, Tom 94, 170
Holt, Jens 11
Hopper, Paul H. 103
Horn, Laurence R. 64
Horner, Winifred Bryan 110
Horrocks, Geoffrey 170
Horsley, Richard A. 159
Howard, Wilbert Francis 31
Howe, Bonnie 61
Hubbeling, H. G. 20
Hudgins, Thomas W. 25
Hudson, D. F. 24
Hudson, Richard 13
Humboldt, Wilhelm von 20, 27–28, 40, 43, 45, 48
Hunter, Ian 46
Husserl, Edmund 37, 46

Iverson, Kelly R. 159
Ivić, Milka 19, 38

Jakobovits, Leon A. 53
Jakobson, Roman 11, 39–40, 44, 52, 85, 114
Jankowsky, Kurt R. 28
Jannaris, A. N. 32, 34
Jay, Eric 24
Jeal, Roy R. 117

Jespersen, Otto 43, 48, 101
Jiménez, Oscar 62
Johnson, David E. 118
Johnson, Mark 60, 81, 86, 91, 139
Johnson, Marta K. 40, 43
Jones, A. R. 20
Jones, William T. 21, 32, 37
Joseph, John E. 17

Katz, Jerrold J. 53
Kay, Paul 57–58
Kelber, Werner H. 162
Kennedy, George A. 112, 116–17
Kern, Philip H. 116
Kevern, Peter 24
Kim, Ji Hoe 168
Kinneavy, James L. 115
Kirk, Alan 162
Kirk, G. S. 158
Kittay, Eva Feder 86
Klutz, Todd 71
Knape, Joachim 112
Köhler, Wolfgang 138
Kopesec, Michael 54
Köstenberger, Andreas J. 24–26, 51
Kövecses, Zoltán 61, 86
Kress, Gunther R. 142
Kretschmer, Paul 32
Kristeva, Julia 19–20, 27, 37–38, 47
Krumbacher, Karl 32
Kuhn, Thomas S. 36
Kurschner, Alan E. 72
Kwong, Ivan Shin Chun 71–73

Lakoff, George 53, 56–58, 60–61, 81, 86, 91, 139
Lamb, David 72
Lamb, Sydney 14, 65
Land, Christopher D. 18, 53, 72, 95, 99, 119, 121, 141, 154
Langacker, Ronald W. 17, 56, 58–59, 63, 138
Langendoen, D. Terence 69
Lanier, Gregory R. 62
LaPolla, Randy J. 15–17, 52–53, 58, 74, 137
LaSor, William Sanford 33
Lausberg, Heinrich 115
Leask, Nigel 83
Leckie-Tarry, Helen 121
Lee, Jae Hyun 72
Lee, Penny 41, 85, 114
Leech, Geoffrey 64
Lehman, David 46

Lehmann, Winfred P. 27, 38
Lemon, Lee T. 39
Le Roy, Georges 20
Leroy, Maurice 19, 38
Levinsohn, Stephen H. 66–69, 75
Levinson, Stephen C. 41, 85, 114, 127
Lévi-Strauss, Claude 40, 46, 158
Libby, James A. 166
Liberman, Anatoly 44
Liberman, Mark 138
Liebenberg, Jacobus 61
Lifschitz, Avi 19
Lin, Jo-Wang 12
Linnemann, Eta 159
Liu, Chiaen 72
Locke, John 20
Long, Frederick J. 50
Longacre, Robert E. 48, 66, 72
Longenecker, Richard N. 116
Lord, Albert B. 158
Losonsky, Michael 28, 40
Louw, Johannes P. 49, 53–54, 92, 118, 131, 147
Luckmann, Thomas 70, 98
Lucy, John A. 41
Luporni, Antonella 89
Luraghi, Silvia 56
Lyons, John 45, 68

MacCormac, Earl R. 83, 86
MacDonald, Michael J. 110, 114, 116
Machen, J. Gresham 24
Mackay, Anne E. 166
Macksey, Richard 46
Malinowski, Bronisław 46, 69
Mandelbaum, David G. 41, 85, 114
Mangum, Douglas 15
Mann, William C. 118
Mantey, Julius R. 33
Marchese, Maria Pia 38
Marcus, Joel 153
Martin, J. R. 69, 88, 95–96, 119, 121, 131
Martin, R. A. 24
Martin, Ralph P. 146
Martin, Troy W. 117
Martín-Asensio, Gustavo 71, 73, 118
Martinet, André 46
Maslen, Robert 61, 86
Matejka, Ladislav 39–40, 43
Mateos, Juan 11
Mathesius, Vilém 39–40, 43, 45
Mathewson, David L. 50–51, 72, 122, 127

Matthews, P. H. 38, 53, 57
Matthews, Robert J. 86
Matthiessen, Christian M. I. M. 17, 69, 88–92, 94, 96, 118, 137, 140, 147, 169
McDonald, Edward 39
McKnight, Scot 15
McLean, B. H. 24
McNeel, Jennifer 61
Meillet, Antoine 32, 48
Merkle, Benjamin L. 24–25, 67
Mey, Jacob L. 64
Michaelis, Laura A. 56
Montgomery, Martin 119
Monville-Burston, Monique 40
Morales, Nelson R. 65
Moran, John H. 20
Moravcsik, Edith A. 17
Morgan, Jerry L. 63
Morrow, Jeffrey L. 20
Moule, C. F. D. 33
Moulton, James Hope 3, 22, 29–33
Mounce, William 24–25
Mouton, Nicolaas T. Oosthuizen 83
Muilenburg, James 116
Mukarovsky, Jan 39, 44, 84
Müller, Max 32
Murphy, James J. 83, 112

Napoli, Donna Jo 126
Nerlich, Brigitte 83
Nida, Eugene A. 48–49, 92, 131, 147
Nuyts, Jan 138
Nylund, Jan H. 40

O'Brien, Peter 146
O'Donnell, Matthew Brook 14, 49, 71, 84, 119, 121–22, 127, 143, 163, 168
O'Grady, Gerard 18, 43
Ochs, Elinor 161
Ogden, C. K. 46, 113
Olbrechts-Tyteca, Lucie 113–14
Olbricht, Thomas H. 116
Omanson, Roger L. 153, 155
Ong, Hughson T. 73, 170
Ong, Walter 157
Orton, David E. 115
Osborne, Grant R. 15
Outram, Dorinda 19

Palmer, F. R. 46
Palmer, Micheal W. 53–54
Pang, Francis G. H. 10, 53

Park, Yoon Man 60
Parodi, Claudia 56
Pasor, Georg 22
Pattemore, Stephen 65
Paul, Hermann 32
Pavel, Thomas G. 47
Peabody, Berkley 158
Pederson, Eric 138
Perelman, Chaim 113–14
Peters, Ronald 72
Piaget, Jean 46
Pierce, Marc 38
Pike, Kenneth L. 14, 50, 66
Pinker, Steven 52, 56
Pitts, Andrew W. 14–15, 40, 119
Plummer, Robert L. 24–25
Poloma, Margaret M. 98
Porter, Stanley E. 10–11, 13–15, 18–19, 22, 25, 29–31, 34, 37–38, 40–42, 49–51, 53–54, 57, 68, 71, 73, 84, 92, 94–95, 99–100, 103, 112, 116–23, 125, 127–29, 134, 141–44, 146, 153–56, 163, 165, 168, 170, 173
Postal, Paul M. 118
Powers, B. Ward 49–50
Propp, Vladimir 158

Radermacher, Ludwig 33
Rask, Rasmus 27
Ravelli, Louise Jane 88–89, 96, 101, 118
Reed, Jeffrey T. 29, 49, 71, 73, 116, 146
Regier, Terry 61
Rehkopf, Friedrich 30
Reich, Dorothy 27
Reich, Peter 14
Reicke, Bo 159
Reis, Marion J. 39
Rhoads, David M. 159
Richards, I. A. 46, 83–84, 113–14
Richards, Jennifer 112–15
Rico, Christophe 50
Ricoeur, Paul 82–83, 85
Riedlinger, Albert 1, 39, 113, 158
Riesner, Rainer 159
Ritchie, L. David 88, 102
Ritzer, George 98
Robbins, Vernon K. 117–18
Robertson, A. T. 3, 29, 31–33
Robertson, J. G. 27
Robey, David 42
Robins, R. H. 19–21, 26–28, 38, 43
Robinson, Jason C. 37–38, 42, 86

Robinson, Thomas A. 33
Robinson, William E. W. 61–62, 82
Rodríguez, Rafael 159
Rose, David 119–20
Ross, William A. 62
Rousseau, Jean-Jacques 20
Ruipérez, M. Sanchez 11
Runge, Steven E. 11, 62, 66–69, 75

Sadock, Jerrold M. 57
Sampson, Geoffrey 13–15, 19, 38, 42, 48–49, 52, 55–56, 63, 67, 69
Sapir, Edward 41, 48, 85, 114
Saussure, Ferdinand de 1–3, 14, 26–27, 29, 38–39, 42–43, 47–48, 51, 53, 63, 70, 113, 158
Schlegel, Friedrich 26–27
Schleicher, August 27–28
Schmidt, Daryl Dean 11, 53–54
Schnabel, Eckhard J. 153
Schoch, Reto 24
Schreiner, Thomas R. 118
Schweizer, Eduard 32
Sebeok, Thomas A. 85
Sechehaye, Albert 1, 39, 113, 158
Seuren, Pieter A. M. 19, 38, 41, 57
Shiell, William D. 159
Shiner, Whitney 159
Siebenthal, Heinrich von 33, 51
Sievers, Eduard 27
Silva, Moisés 11, 49–50
Sim, Margaret G. 64–65
Simon-Vandenbergen, Anne-Marie 88–89
Soskice, Janet Martin 84
Sperber, Daniel 64–65
Spinoza, Baruch 20
Spradley, James P. 138
Stack, Judith V. 62
Stamps, Dennis L. 116, 118
Stanley, Christopher D. 116
Stein, Robert H. 151, 153
Steinberg, Danny D. 53
Steiner, Erich H. 88
Steiner, Peter 40
Story, Cullen 24
Story, Lyle 24
Stovell, Beth M. 61–62, 72–73, 82, 86, 88, 140
Stump, Gregory 25
Sturtevant, E. H. 32
Summers, Ray 24
Swetnam, James 24

Tabachowitz, David 30
Talmy, Leonard 15
Tannen, Deborah 161, 166
Tappenden, Frederick S. 61
Tasker, R. V. G. 124
Taverniers, Miriam 88–89
Taylor, Charles 41
Taylor, John R. 59, 140
Taylor, Richard 21
Taylor, Talbot J. 17
Thatcher, Tom 162
Thiselton, Anthony C. 104
Thomas, Jenny 64
Thomas, Rosalind 157
Thompson, Geoff 88, 95, 121, 126, 131
Thompson, Jeremy 15
Thompson, Sandra A. 118
Thornhill, A. Chadwick 50
Thrall, Margert E. 154–55
Thumb, Albert 30, 32, 34
Thurén, Lauri 116
Toit, Andrie du 118
Tooke, John Horne 21
Trapp, Robert 114
Traugott, Elizabeth Closs 103
Trible, Phyllis 116
Trubetzkoy, Nikolai S. 40, 44
Tune, Ernest 24
Turbayne, Colin Murray 81
Turner, Mark 61, 86–87
Turner, Max 49
Turner, Nigel 31

Ullmann, Stephen 48

Vachek, Josef 39, 40, 44–45
Vaina, Lucia 138
van Buren, Paul 55
van Dijk, Teun A. 117
Van Neste, Ray 71
Van Valin, Robert D., Jr. 15–17, 52–53, 58, 74, 137
van Wolde, Ellen 139
Vandeweghe, Willy 54
Vaughan, Curtis 33
Veel, Robert 88
Velde, Marc Van de 54
Veltman, Robert 88
Verner, Karl 27
Vickers, Brian 115
Von Thaden, Robert H., Jr. 62, 117

Wackernagel, Jacob 32
Wallace, Daniel B. 24–26, 51
Wallace, Ruth A. 70
Wansbrough, Henry 159
Ward, Gregory 64
Warren, Robert Penn 115
Watson, Duane F. 116
Watson, Janet 158
Watt, Jonathan M. 73
Waugh, Linda R. 40
Way, Eileen Cornell 81
Webster, Jonathan J. 43, 73, 88, 114, 162
Weidner, Revere Franklin 24
Weiser, Irwin 119
Welch, Kathleen E. 115
Wellek, René 39–40
Wenham, John 24
Westbury, Josh 15
Westcott, Brooke Foss 159
Westfall, Cynthia Long 71, 73
Wheelwright, Philip 84
White, Eugene E. 116
White, P. R. R. 119, 131
Whitney, William Dwight 32–33
Whittaker, Molly 24
Whorf, Benjamin Lee 41, 48, 85, 114
Widder, Wendy 15
Wierzbicka, Anna 60

Wilson, Deirdre 64–65
Wilson, H. H. 27
Wimsatt, W. K., Jr. 115
Winbery, Carlton L. 33
Winer, Georg Benedikt 3, 21–23, 31–32
Winner, Thomas G. 39
Winters, Clifford T. 62
Wire, Antoinette C. 159
Wirth, Jessica R. 17
Wishart, Ryder A. 29, 31
Witherington, Ben, III 116
Wittgenstein, Ludwig 62
Wolf, Alison 70
Wong, Simon S. M. 57
Wonneberger, Reinhard 53–54
Wordsworth, William 20
Wright, Joseph 32

Xuan, Winfred Wenhui 88

Yoon, David I. 72–73, 121
Yoon, Hye-Joon 21
Young, Richard A. 50

Zacharias, H. Daniel 24
Zerwick, Maximilian 33
Zhu, Min 88, 102
Zumthor, P. 162

ANCIENT SOURCES INDEX

Old Testament

Psalms
68:18   107
110:1   129

Daniel
7:13   128–29

New Testament

Matthew
2:10   133
2:16   133
5–7   170–71, 173–78
5:3-48   171
5:3–7:27   170
5:11   128
5:18   133
6:1-34   170–71
7:1-27   170–71
10:32   128
12:2   134
15:7   132
15:22   132
16:13   128
18:33   135
23:16   134
23:23   135
24:45   132

Mark
1:40   126
1:40-41   126
1:40-44   126
1:41   126
4:41   132
6:56   133
8:27   128
14:32-42   150
14:37   151
14:37-38   150
14:41   150, 152–53
14:61   129
14:62   128–29

Luke
6:22   128
7:39   134
11:53   134
12:8   128
12:12   134
20:13   133
23:10   133

John
1:51   133
4   92, 94
4:7   92
4:9   92
4:10   92
4:14   93
11   92, 94
11:23   94
11:24   94
11:25   94
21   125
21:15–17   125

Acts
2:29   134
12   172–78
12:18   133
18   172–78
18:28   133
20:12   133
20:38   133
25:10   132
27:21   135
28:4   133

Romans
1:1   129
2   173–75, 177
3:22–4:25   124
5   124

5:1	124	1:19-20	107
5:1-2	123	1:21	107
5:7	133	1:23	107–8
5:9-11	101	2:4	108
6	100	3:19	107
6:1	124	4:4	106
6:11	100	4:8	107
6:13	100	4:29	108
6:15	124	4:32	108
6:22	100	5:1	108
7:7	98	5:2	108
7:7-25	98	6:18	108
7:8	98		
7:9	98	Philippians	
7:10	98	1:17	132
7:14	98–99	2:19-30	148–49
7:15	99	3:1	146–48
8	62, 72	3:1-2	145–46, 148–50
12:1	100	3:1-11	145, 149
		3:2	146–48
1 Corinthians		3:3	148
1–4	130	3:3-11	149
1:1	129	3:4	149
1:10	124	3:4-6	148
1:12	124		
1:13	124–25	Colossians	
4	173–75, 177–78	1:9	106
4:8	135	1:10	106
4:21	124	1:11	106
5:1	132	1:29	106–7
5:18	103	2:9	106
5:18-20	103	2:9-10	107
5:19	103	2:9-11	106
5:20	104	2:10	106
6:12	104	2:11	105–6
15:6	134	2:19	105
15:32	132	3:15	106
16:6	134		
		1 Timothy	
2 Corinthians		1:2	129
1–9	154		
10–13	154	2 Timothy	
10:7	154–55	1:2	129
11:1	135		
		Titus	
Galatians		1:4	129
4:17	132		
		Philemon	
Ephesians		1-2	130
1:3	107		
1:3-23	107	James	
1:6	107	3:10	135
1:7	107		

Revelation
16:21	134
19:11–20:6	72

Other Ancient Writings

Aristotle
Poetics
21–5	82

Rhetoric
1.3	111
3	82

Cicero
De Oratore
3.35.155	82

Quintilian
Rhetoric ad Herennium
4	82

Didache
7.3	93

www.ingramcontent.com/pod-product-compliance
Lightning Source LLC
Chambersburg PA
CBHW051521230426
43668CB00012B/1695